Samuel Langhorne Clemens (November 30, 1835 - April 21, 1910), known by his pen name Mark Twain, was an American writer, humorist, entrepreneur, publisher, and lecturer. He was lauded as the "greatest humorist this country has produced", and William Faulkner called him "the father of American literature". His novels include The Adventures of Tom Sawyer (1876) and its sequel, the Adventures of Huckleberry Finn (1884), the latter often called "The Great American Novel".

Twain was raised in Hannibal, Missouri, which later provided the setting for Tom Sawyer and Huckleberry Finn. He served an apprenticeship with a printer and then worked as a typesetter, contributing articles to the newspaper of his older brother Orion Clemens. He later became a riverboat pilot on the Mississippi River before heading west to join Orion in Nevada. (Source: Wikipedia)

Literary works:

The Gilded Age: A Tale of Today (1873)
The Prince and the Pauper (1881)
A Connecticut Yankee in
King Arthur's Court (1889)
The American Claimant (1892)
Pudd'nhead Wilson (1894)
Personal Recollections of Joan of Arc (1896)
A Horse's Tale (1907)
The Mysterious Stranger (1916, posthumous)
The Adventures of Tom Sawyer (1876)
Adventures of Huckleberry Finn (1884)
Tom Sawyer Abroad (1894)
Tom Sawyer, Detective (1896)
"Eve's Diary" (1906)

MARK TWAIN'S LETTERS

VOLUME 4.5 & 6

MARK TWAIN

PRINCE CLASSICS

PRINCE CLASSICS

This is a work of fiction. Names, characters, places, and incidents either are the product of the author's imagination or are used fictitiously. Any resemblance to actual persons, living or dead, events, or locales is entirely coincidental.

First Printing: 2020

ISBN 978-93-5385-550-5 (paperback)

ISBN 978-93-5385-551-2 (Hardcover)

Published by Prince Classics

www.princeclassics.com

Contents

MARK TWAIN'S LETTERS
VOLUME 4,5 & 6

MARK TWAIN'S LETTERS—1853-1866

VOLUME 4

XXVI. LETTERS, 1886-87. JANE CLEMENS'S ROMANCE. UNMAILED LETTERS, ETC.

*When Clemens had been platforming with Cable and returned to Hartford for his Christmas vacation, the Warner and Clemens families had joined in preparing for him a surprise performance of The Prince and the Pauper. The Clemens household was always given to theatricals, and it was about this time that scenery and a stage were prepared—mainly by the sculptor Gerhardt—for these home performances, after which productions of The Prince and the Pauper were given with considerable regularity to audiences consisting of parents and invited friends. The subject is a fascinating one, but it has been dwelt upon elsewhere.—[In Mark Twain: A on***n, chaps. cliii and clx.]—We get a glimpse of one of these occasions as well as of Mark Twain's financial progress in the next brief*

To W. D. Howells; in Boston:

Jan. 3, '86.

MY DEAR HOWELLS,—The date set for the Prince and Pauper play is ten days hence—Jan. 13. I hope you and Pilla can take a train that arrives here during the day; the one that leaves Boston toward the end of the afternoon would be a trifle late; the performance would have already begun when you reached the house.

I'm out of the woods. On the last day of the year I had paid out $182,000 on the Grant book and it was totally free from debt.

Yrs ever

MARK.

Mark Twain's mother was a woman of sturdy character and with a keen sense of humor and tender sympathies. Her husband, John Marshall Clemens, had been a man of high moral character, honored by all who knew him, respected and apparently loved by his wife. No one would ever have supposed that during all her years of marriage, and almost to her death, she carried a secret romance that would only be told at last in the weary disappointment of old age. It is a curious story, and it came to light in this curious way:

To W. D. Howells, in Boston:

HARTFORD, May 19, '86.

MY DEAR HOWELLS,—..... Here's a secret. A most curious and pathetic romance, which has just come to light. Read these things, but don't mention them. Last fall, my old mother—then 82—took a notion to attend a convention of old settlers of the Mississippi Valley in an Iowa town. My brother's wife was astonished; and represented to her the hardships and fatigues of such a trip, and said my mother might possibly not even survive them; and said there could be no possible interest for her in such a meeting and such a crowd. But my mother insisted, and persisted; and finally gained her point. They started; and all the way my mother was young again with excitement, interest, eagerness, anticipation. They reached the town and the hotel. My mother strode with the same eagerness in her eye and her step, to the counter, and said:

"Is Dr. Barrett of St. Louis, here?"

"No. He was here, but he returned to St. Louis this morning."

"Will he come again?"

"No."

My mother turned away, the fire all gone from her, and said, "Let us go home."

They went straight back to Keokuk. My mother sat silent and thinking for many days—a thing which had never happened before. Then one day she said:

"I will tell you a secret. When I was eighteen, a young medical student named Barrett lived in Columbia (Ky.) eighteen miles away; and he used to ride over to see me. This continued for some time. I loved him with my whole heart, and I knew that he felt the same toward me, though no words had been spoken. He was too bashful to speak—he could not do it. Everybody supposed we were engaged—took it for granted we were—but we were not. By and by there was to be a party in a neighboring town, and he wrote my uncle telling him his feelings, and asking him to drive me over in his buggy and let him (Barrett) drive me back, so that he might have that opportunity to propose. My uncle should have done as he was asked, without explaining anything to me; but instead, he read me the letter; and then, of course, I could not go—and did not. He (Barrett) left the country presently, and I, to stop the clacking tongues, and to show him that I did not care, married, in a pet. In all these sixty-four years I have not seen him since. I saw in a paper that he was going to attend that Old Settlers' Convention. Only three hours before we reached that hotel, he had been standing there!"

Since then, her memory is wholly faded out and gone; and now she writes letters to the school-mates who had been dead forty years, and wonders why they neglect her and do not answer.

Think of her carrying that pathetic burden in her old heart sixty-four years, and no human being ever suspecting it!

Yrs ever,

MARK.

We do not get the idea from this letter that those two long ago sweethearts quarreled, but Mark Twain once spoke of their having done so, and there may have been a disagreement, assuming that there was a subsequent meeting. It does not matter, now. In speaking of it, Mark Twain once said: "It is as pathetic a romance as any that has crossed the field of my personal experience in a long lifetime."—[When Mark Twain: A Biography was written this letter had not come to light, and the matter was stated there in accordance with Mark Twain's latest memory of it.]

Howells wrote: "After all, how poor and hackneyed all the inventions are compared with the simple and stately facts. Who could have imagined such a heart-break as that? Yet it went along with the fulfillment of everyday duty and made no more noise than a grave under foot. I doubt if fiction will ever get the knack of such things."

Jane Clemens now lived with her son Orion and his wife, in Keokuk, where she was more contented than elsewhere. In these later days her memory had become erratic, her realization of events about her uncertain, but there were times when she was quite her former self, remembering clearly and talking with her old-time gaiety of spirit. Mark Twain frequently sent her playful letters to amuse her, letters full of such boyish gaiety as had amused her long years before. The one that follows is a fair example. It was written after a visit which Clemens and his family had paid to Keokuk.

To Jane Clemens, in Keokuk:

ELMIRA, Aug. 7, '86.

DEAR MA,—I heard that Molly and Orion and Pamela had been sick, but I see by your letter that they are much better now, or nearly well. When we visited you a month ago, it seemed to us that your Keokuk weather was pretty hot; Jean and Clara sat up in bed at Mrs. McElroy's and cried about it, and so did I; but I judge by your letter that it has cooled down, now, so that a person is comparatively comfortable, with his skin off. Well it did need cooling; I remember that I burnt a hole in my shirt, there, with some ice cream that fell on it; and Miss Jenkins told me they never used a stove, but cooked their meals on a marble-topped table in the drawing-room, just with the natural heat. If anybody else had told me, I would not have believed it. I was told by the Bishop of Keokuk that he did not allow crying at funerals, because it scalded the furniture. If Miss Jenkins had told me that, I would have believed it. This reminds me that you speak of Dr. Jenkins and his family as if they were strangers to me. Indeed they are not. Don't you suppose I remember gratefully how tender the doctor was with Jean when she hurt her arm, and how quickly he got the pain out of the hurt, whereas I supposed it was going to last at least an hour? No, I don't forget some things as easily as

I do others.

Yes, it was pretty hot weather. Now here, when a person is going to die, he is always in a sweat about where he is going to; but in Keokuk of course they don't care, because they are fixed for everything. It has set me reflecting, it has taught me a lesson. By and by, when my health fails, I am going to put all my affairs in order, and bid good-bye to my friends here, and kill all the people I don't like, and go out to Keokuk and prepare for death.

They are all well in this family, and we all send love.

Affly Your Son

SAM.

The ways of city officials and corporations are often past understanding, and Mark Twain sometimes found it necessary to write picturesque letters of protest. The following to a Hartford lighting company is a fair example of these documents.

To a gas and electric-lighting company, in Hartford:

GENTLEMEN,—There are but two places in our whole street where lights could be of any value, by any accident, and you have measured and appointed your intervals so ingeniously as to leave each of those places in the centre of a couple of hundred yards of solid darkness. When I noticed that you were setting one of your lights in such a way that I could almost see how to get into my gate at night, I suspected that it was a piece of carelessness on the part of the workmen, and would be corrected as soon as you should go around inspecting and find it out. My judgment was right; it is always right, when you axe concerned. For fifteen years, in spite of my prayers and tears, you persistently kept a gas lamp exactly half way between my gates, so that I couldn't find either of them after dark; and then furnished such execrable gas that I had to hang a danger signal on the lamp post to keep teams from running into it, nights. Now I suppose your present idea is, to leave us a little more in the dark.

Don't mind us—out our way; we possess but one vote apiece, and no rights which you are in any way bound to respect. Please take your electric light and go to—but never mind, it is not for me to suggest; you will probably find the way; and any way you can reasonably count on divine assistance if you lose your bearings.

S. L. CLEMENS.

[Etext Editor's Note: Twain wrote another note to Hartford Gas and Electric, which he may not have mailed and which Paine does not include in these volumes:

"Gentleman:—Someday you are going to move me almost to the point of irritation with your God-damned chuckle headed fashion of turning off your God-damned gas without giving notice to your God-damned parishioners—and you did it again last night—" D.W.]

Frequently Clemens did not send letters of this sort after they were written. Sometimes he realized the uselessness of such protest, sometimes the mere writing of them had furnished the necessary relief, and he put, the letter away, or into the wastebasket, and wrote something more temperate, or nothing at all. A few such letters here follow.

Clemens was all the time receiving application from people who wished him to recommend one article or another; books, plays, tobacco, and what not. They were generally persistent people, unable to accept a polite or kindly denial. Once he set down some remarks on this particular phase of correspondence. He wrote:

I

No doubt Mr. Edison has been offered a large interest in many and many an electrical project, for the use of his name to float it withal. And no doubt all men who have achieved for their names, in any line of activity whatever, a sure market value, have been familiar with this sort of solicitation. Reputation is a hall-mark: it can remove doubt from pure silver, and it can also make the plated article pass for pure.

And so, people without a hall-mark of their own are always trying to get the loan of somebody else's.

As a rule, that kind of a person sees only one side of the case. He sees that his invention or his painting or his book is—apparently—a trifle better than you yourself can do, therefore why shouldn't you be willing to put your hall-mark on it? You will be giving the purchaser his full money's worth; so who is hurt, and where is the harm? Besides, are you not helping a struggling fellow-craftsman, and is it not your duty to do that?

That side is plenty clear enough to him, but he can't and won't see the other side, to-wit: that you are a rascal if you put your hall-mark upon a thing which you did not produce yourself, howsoever good it may be. How simple that is; and yet there are not two applicants in a hundred who can, be made to see it.

When one receives an application of this sort, his first emotion is an indignant sense of insult; his first deed is the penning of a sharp answer. He blames nobody but that other person. That person is a very base being; he must be; he would degrade himself for money, otherwise it would not occur to him that you would do such a thing. But all the same, that application has done its work, and taken you down in your own estimation. You recognize that everybody hasn't as high an opinion of you as you have of yourself; and in spite of you there ensues an interval during which you are not, in your own estimation as fine a bird as you were before.

However, being old and experienced, you do not mail your sharp letter, but leave it lying a day. That saves you. For by that time you have begun to reflect that you are a person who deals in exaggerations—and exaggerations are lies. You meant yours to be playful, and thought you made them unmistakably so. But you couldn't make them playfulnesses to a man who has no sense of the playful and can see nothing but the serious side of things. You rattle on quite playfully, and with measureless extravagance, about how you wept at the tomb of Adam; and all in good time you find to your astonishment that no end of people took you at your word and believed you. And presently they find out that you were not in earnest. They have been deceived; therefore, (as they argue—and there is a sort of argument in it,) you are a deceiver. If you will deceive in one way, why shouldn't you in another? So they apply for the use of your trade-mark. You are amazed and affronted. You retort that you are not that kind of person. Then they are amazed and affronted; and wonder "since when?"

By this time you have got your bearings. You realize that perhaps there is a little blame on both sides. You are in the right frame, now. So you write a letter void of offense, declining. You mail this one; you pigeon-hole the other.

That is, being old and experienced, you do, but early in your career, you don't: you mail the first one.

II

An enthusiast who had a new system of musical notation, wrote to me and suggested that a magazine article from me, contrasting the absurdities of the old system with the simplicities of his new one, would be sure to make a "rousing hit." He shouted and shouted over the marvels wrought by his system, and quoted the handsome compliments which had been paid it by famous musical people; but he forgot to tell me what his notation was like, or what its simplicities consisted in. So I could not have written the article if I had wanted to—which I didn't; because I hate strangers with axes to grind. I wrote him a courteous note explaining how busy I was—I always explain how busy I am—and casually drooped this remark:

"I judge the X-X notation to be a rational mode of representing music, in place of the prevailing fashion, which was the invention of an idiot."

Next mail he asked permission to print that meaningless remark. I answered, no—courteously, but still, no; explaining that I could not afford to be placed in the attitude of trying to influence people with a mere worthless guess. What a scorcher I got, next mail! Such irony! such sarcasm, such caustic praise of my superhonorable loyalty to the public! And withal, such compassion for my stupidity, too, in not being able to understand my own language. I cannot remember the words of this letter broadside, but there was about a page used up in turning this idea round and round and exposing it in different lights.

Unmailed Answer:

DEAR SIR,—What is the trouble with you? If it is your viscera, you cannot have them taken out and reorganized a moment too soon. I mean, if they are inside. But if you are composed of them, that is another matter. Is it your brain? But it could not be your brain. Possibly it is your skull: you want to look out for that. Some people, when they get an idea, it pries the structure apart. Your system of notation has got in there, and couldn't find room, without a doubt that is what the trouble is. Your skull was not made to put ideas in, it was made to throw potatoes at.

Yours Truly.

Mailed Answer:

DEAR SIR,—Come, come—take a walk; you disturb the children.

Yours Truly.

There was a day, now happily nearly over, when certain newspapers made a practice of inviting men distinguished in any walk of life to give their time and effort without charge to express themselves on some subject of the day, or perhaps they were asked to send their favorite passages in prose or verse, with the reasons why. Such symposiums were "features" that cost the newspapers only the writing of a number of letters, stationery, and postage. To one such invitation Mark Twain wrote two replies. They follow herewith:

Unmailed Answer:

DEAR SIR,—I have received your proposition—which you have

imitated from a pauper London periodical which had previously imitated the idea of this sort of mendicancy from seventh-rate American journalism, where it originated as a variation of the inexpensive "interview."

Why do you buy Associated Press dispatches? To make your paper the more salable, you answer. But why don't you try to beg them? Why do you discriminate? I can sell my stuff; why should I give it to you? Why don't you ask me for a shirt? What is the difference between asking me for the worth of a shirt and asking me for the shirt itself? Perhaps you didn't know you were begging. I would not use that argument—it makes the user a fool. The passage of poetry—or prose, if you will—which has taken deepest root in my thought, and which I oftenest return to and dwell upon with keenest no matter what, is this: That the proper place for journalists who solicit literary charity is on the street corner with their hats in their hands.

Mailed Answer:

DEAR SIR,—Your favor of recent date is received, but I am obliged by press of work to decline.

The manager of a traveling theatrical company wrote that he had taken the liberty of dramatizing Tom Sawyer, and would like also the use of the author's name—the idea being to convey to the public that it was a Mark Twain play. In return for this slight favor the manager sent an invitation for Mark Twain to come and see the play—to be present on the opening night, as it were, at his (the manager's) expense. He added that if the play should be a go in the cities there might be some "arrangement" of profits. Apparently these inducements did not appeal to Mark Twain. The long unmailed reply is the more interesting, but probably the briefer one that follows it was quite as effective.

Unmailed Answer:

HARTFORD, Sept. 8, '87.

DEAR SIR,—And so it has got around to you, at last; and you also have "taken the liberty." You are No. 1365. When 1364 sweeter and better people, including the author, have "tried" to dramatize Tom Sawyer and did not arrive, what sort of show do you suppose you stand? That is a book, dear sir, which cannot be dramatized. One might as well try to dramatize any other hymn. Tom Sawyer is simply a hymn, put into prose form to give it a worldly air.

Why the pale doubt that flitteth dim and nebulous athwart the forecastle of your third sentence? Have no fears. Your piece will be a Go. It will go out the back door on the first night. They've all done it—the 1364. So will 1365. Not one of us ever thought of the simple device of half-soling himself with a stove-lid. Ah, what suffering a little hindsight would have saved us. Treasure this hint.

How kind of you to invite me to the funeral. Go to; I have attended a thousand of them. I have seen Tom Sawyer's remains in all the different kinds of dramatic shrouds there are. You cannot start anything fresh. Are you serious when you propose to pay my expence—if that is the Susquehannian way of spelling it? And can you be aware that I charge a hundred dollars a mile when I travel for pleasure? Do you realize that it is 432 miles to Susquehanna? Would it be handy for you to send me the $43,200 first, so I could be counting it as I come along; because railroading is pretty dreary to a sensitive nature when there's nothing sordid to buck at for Zeitvertreib.

Now as I understand it, dear and magnanimous 1365, you are going to recreate Tom Sawyer dramatically, and then do me the compliment to put me in the bills as father of this shady offspring. Sir, do you know that this kind of a compliment has destroyed people before now? Listen.

Twenty-four years ago, I was strangely handsome. The remains of it are still visible through the rifts of time. I was so handsome that human activities ceased as if spellbound when I came in view, and even inanimate things stopped to look—like locomotives, and district messenger boys and so-on. In San Francisco, in the rainy season I was often mistaken for fair weather. Upon one occasion I was traveling in the Sonora region, and stopped for an hour's nooning, to rest my horse and myself. All the town came out to look. The tribes of Indians gathered to look. A Piute squaw named her baby for me,—a voluntary compliment which pleased me greatly. Other attentions were paid me. Last of all arrived the president and faculty of Sonora University and offered me the post of Professor of Moral Culture and the Dogmatic Humanities; which I accepted gratefully, and entered at once upon my duties. But my name had pleased the Indians, and in the deadly kindness of their hearts they went on naming their babies after me. I tried to stop it, but the Indians could not understand why I should object to so manifest a compliment. The thing grew and grew and spread and spread and became exceedingly embarrassing. The University stood it a couple of years; but then for the sake of the college they felt obliged to call a halt, although I had the sympathy of the whole faculty. The president himself said to me, "I am as sorry as I can be for you, and would still hold out if there were any hope ahead; but you see how it is: there are a hundred and thirty-two of them already, and fourteen precincts to hear from. The circumstance has brought your name into most wide and unfortunate renown. It causes much comment—I believe that that is not an over-statement. Some of this comment is palliative, but some of it—by patrons at a distance, who only know the statistics without the explanation,—is offensive, and in some cases even violent. Nine students have been called home. The trustees of the college have been growing more and more uneasy all these last months—steadily along with the implacable increase in your census—and I will not conceal from you that more than once they have touched upon the expediency of a change in the Professorship of Moral Culture. The coarsely sarcastic editorial in yesterday's Alta, headed Give the Moral Acrobat a Rest—has brought things to a crisis, and I am charged with the unpleasant duty of receiving your resignation."

I know you only mean me a kindness, dear 1365, but it is a most deadly mistake. Please do not name your Injun for me. Truly Yours.

Mailed Answer:

NEW YORK, Sept. 8. 1887.

DEAR SIR,—Necessarily I cannot assent to so strange a proposition. And I think it but fair to warn you that if you put the piece on the stage, you must take the legal consequences.

Yours respectfully,

S. L. CLEMENS.

Before the days of international copyright no American author's books were pirated more freely by Canadian publishers than those of Mark Twain. It was always a sore point with him that these books, cheaply printed, found their way into the United States, and were sold in competition with his better editions. The law on the subject seemed to be rather hazy, and its various interpretations exasperating. In the next unmailed letter Mark Twain relieves himself to a misguided official. The letter is worth reading today, if for no other reason, to show the absurdity of copyright conditions which prevailed at that time.

Unmailed Letter to H. C. Christiancy, on book Piracy:

HARTFORD, Dec. 18, '87.

H. C. CHRISTIANCY, ESQ.

DEAR SIR,—As I understand it, the position of the U. S. Government is this: If a person be captured on the border with counterfeit bonds in his hands—bonds of the N. Y. Central Railway, for instance—the procedure in his case shall be as follows:

1. If the N. Y. C. have not previously filed in the several police offices

along the border, proof of ownership of the originals of the bonds, the government officials must collect a duty on the counterfeits, and then let them go ahead and circulate in this country.

2. But if there is proof already on file, then the N. Y. C. may pay the duty and take the counterfeits.

But in no case will the United States consent to go without its share of the swag. It is delicious. The biggest and proudest government on earth turned sneak-thief; collecting pennies on stolen property, and pocketing them with a greasy and libidinous leer; going into partnership with foreign thieves to rob its own children; and when the child escapes the foreigner, descending to the abysmal baseness of hanging on and robbing the infant all alone by itself! Dear sir, this is not any more respectable than for a father to collect toll on the forced prostitution of his own daughter; in fact it is the same thing. Upon these terms, what is a U. S. custom house but a "fence?" That is all it is: a legalized trader in stolen goods.

And this nasty law, this filthy law, this unspeakable law calls itself a "regulation for the protection of owners of copyright!" Can sarcasm go further than that? In what way does it protect them? Inspiration itself could not furnish a rational answer to that question. Whom does it protect, then? Nobody, as far as I can see, but the foreign thief—sometimes—and his fellow-footpad the U. S. government, all the time. What could the Central Company do with the counterfeit bonds after it had bought them of the star spangled banner Master-thief? Sell them at a dollar apiece and fetch down the market for the genuine hundred-dollar bond? What could I do with that 20-cent copy of "Roughing It" which the United States has collared on the border and is waiting to release to me for cash in case I am willing to come down to its moral level and help rob myself? Sell it at ten or fifteen cents—duty added—and destroy the market for the original $3,50 book? Who ever did invent that law? I would like to know the name of that immortal jackass.

Dear sir, I appreciate your courtesy in stretching your authority in the desire to do me a kindness, and I sincerely thank you for it. But I have no use for that book; and if I were even starving for it I would not pay duty on in either to get it or suppress it. No doubt there are ways in which I might consent to go into partnership with thieves and fences, but this is not one of them. This one revolts the remains of my self-respect; turns my stomach. I think I could companion with a highwayman who carried a shot-gun and took many risks; yes, I think I should like that if I were younger; but to go in with a big rich government that robs paupers, and the widows and orphans of paupers and takes no risk—why the thought just gags me.

Oh, no, I shall never pay any duties on pirated books of mine. I am much too respectable for that—yet awhile. But here—one thing that grovels me is this: as far as I can discover—while freely granting that the U. S. copyright laws are far and away the most idiotic that exist anywhere on the face of the earth—they don't authorize the government to admit pirated books into this country, toll or no toll. And so I think that that regulation is the invention of one of those people—as a rule, early stricken of God, intellectually—the departmental interpreters of the laws, in Washington. They can always be depended on to take any reasonably good law and interpret the common sense all out of it. They can be depended on, every time, to defeat a good law, and make it inoperative—yes, and utterly grotesque, too, mere matter for laughter and derision. Take some of the decisions of the Post-office Department, for instance—though I do not mean to suggest that that asylum is any worse than the others for the breeding and nourishing of incredible lunatics—I merely instance it because it happens to be the first to come into my mind. Take that case of a few years ago where the P. M. General suddenly issued an edict requiring you to add the name of the State after Boston, New York, Chicago, &c, in your superscriptions, on pain of having your letter stopped and forwarded to the dead-letter office; yes, and I believe he required the county, too. He made one little concession in favor of New York: you could say "New York City," and stop there; but if you left off the "city," you must add "N. Y." to your "New York." Why, it threw the business of the whole country into chaos and brought commerce almost to a stand-still. Now think of that! When that man goes to—to—well, wherever he is going to—we shan't want the microscopic details of his address. I guess we can find him.

Well, as I was saying, I believe that this whole paltry and ridiculous swindle is a pure creation of one of those cabbages that used to be at the head of one of those Retreats down there—Departments, you know—and that you will find it so, if you will look into it. And moreover—but land, I reckon we are both tired by this time.

Truly Yours,

MARK TWAIN.

XXVII. MISCELLANEOUS LETTERS OF 1887. LITERARY ARTICLES. PEACEFUL DAYS AT THE FARM. FAVORITE READING. APOLOGY TO MRS. CLEVELAND, ETC.

We have seen in the preceding chapter how unknown aspirants in one field or another were always seeking to benefit by Mark Twain's reputation. Once he remarked, "The symbol of the human race ought to be an ax; every human being has one concealed about him somewhere." He declared when a stranger called on him, or wrote to him, in nine cases out of ten he could distinguish the gleam of the ax almost immediately. The following letter is closely related to those of the foregoing chapter, only that this one was mailed—not once, but many times, in some form adapted to the specific applicant. It does not matter to whom it was originally written, the name would not be recognized.

To Mrs. T. Concerning unearned credentials, etc.

HARTFORD, 1887.

MY DEAR MADAM,—It is an idea which many people have had, but it is of no value. I have seen it tried out many and many a time. I have seen a lady lecturer urged and urged upon the public in a lavishly complimentary document signed by Longfellow, Whittier, Holmes and some others of supreme celebrity, but—there was nothing in her and she failed. If there had been any great merit in her she never would have needed those men's help and (at her rather mature age,) would never have consented to ask for it.

There is an unwritten law about human successes, and your sister must bow to that law, she must submit to its requirements. In brief this law is:

1. *No occupation without an apprenticeship.*

2. *No pay to the apprentice.*

This law stands right in the way of the subaltern who wants to be a General before he has smelt powder; and it stands (and should stand) in everybody's way who applies for pay or position before he has served his apprenticeship and proved himself. Your sister's course is perfectly plain. Let her enclose this letter to Maj. J. B. Pond, and offer to lecture a year for $10 a week and her expenses, the contract to be annullable by him at any time, after a month's notice, but not annullable by her at all. The second year, he to have her services, if he wants them, at a trifle under the best price offered her by anybody else.

She can learn her trade in those two years, and then be entitled to remuneration—but she can not learn it in any less time than that, unless she is a human miracle.

Try it, and do not be afraid. It is the fair and right thing. If she wins, she will win squarely and righteously, and never have to blush.

Truly yours,

S. L. CLEMENS.

Howells wrote, in February, offering to get a publisher to take the Library of Humor off Mark Twain's hands. Howells had been paid twenty-six hundred dollars for the work on it, and his conscience hurt him when he reflected that the book might never be used. In this letter he also refers to one of the disastrous inventions in which Clemens had invested—a method of casting brass dies for stamping book-covers and wall-paper. Howells's purpose was to introduce something of the matter into his next story. Mark Twain's reply gives us a light on this particular invention.

HARTFORD, Feb. 15, '87.

DEAR HOWELLS,—I was in New York five days ago, and Webster mentioned the Library, and proposed to publish it a year or a year and half hence. I have written him your proposition to-day. (The Library is part of the property of the C. L. W. & Co. firm.)

I don't remember what that technical phrase was, but I think you will find it in any Cyclopedia under the head of "Brass." The thing I best remember is, that the self-styled "inventor" had a very ingenious way of keeping me from seeing him apply his invention: the first appointment was spoiled by his burning down the man's shop in which it was to be done, the night before; the second was spoiled by his burning down his own shop the night before. He unquestionably did both of these things. He really had no invention; the whole project was a blackmailing swindle, and cost me several thousand dollars.

The slip you sent me from the May "Study" has delighted Mrs. Clemens and me to the marrow. To think that thing might be possible to many; but to be brave enough to say it is possible to you only, I certainly believe. The longer I live the clearer I perceive how unmatchable, how unapproachable, a compliment one pays when he says of a man "he has the courage (to utter) his convictions." Haven't you had reviewers talk Alps to you, and then print potato hills?

I haven't as good an opinion of my work as you hold of it, but I've always done what I could to secure and enlarge my good opinion of it. I've always said to myself, "Everybody reads it and that's something—it surely isn't pernicious, or the most acceptable people would get pretty tired of it." And when a critic said by implication that it wasn't high and fine, through the remark "High and fine literature is wine" I retorted (confidentially, to myself,) "yes, high and fine literature is wine, and mine is only water; but everybody likes water."

You didn't tell me to return that proof-slip, so I have pasted it into my private scrap-book. None will see it there. With a thousand thanks.

Ys Ever

MARK.

Our next letter is an unmailed answer, but it does not belong with the others, having been withheld for reasons of quite a different sort. Jeanette Gilder, then of the Critic, was one of Mark Twain's valued friends. In the comment which he made, when it was shown to him twenty-two years later, he tells us why he thinks this letter was not sent. The name, "Rest-and-be-Thankful," was the official title given to the summer place at Elmira, but it was more often known as "Quarry."

To Jeannette Gilder (not mailed):

HARTFORD, May 14, '87.

MY DEAR MISS GILDER,—We shall spend the summer at the same old place-the remote farm called "Rest-and-be-Thankful," on top of the hills three miles from Elmira, N. Y. Your other question is harder to answer. It is my habit to keep four or five books in process of erection all the time, and every summer add a few courses of bricks to two or three of them; but I cannot forecast which of the two or three it is going to be. It takes seven years to complete a book by this method, but still it is a good method: gives the public a rest. I have been accused of "rushing into print" prematurely, moved thereto by greediness for money; but in truth I have never done that. Do you care for trifles of information? (Well, then, "Tom Sawyer" and "The Prince and the Pauper" were each on the stocks two or three years, and "Old Times on the Mississippi" eight.) One of my unfinished books has been on the stocks sixteen years; another seventeen. This latter book could have been finished in a day, at any time during the past five years. But as in the first of these two narratives all the action takes place in Noah's ark, and as in the other the action takes place in heaven, there seemed to be no hurry, and so I have not hurried. Tales of stirring adventure in those localities do not need to be rushed to publication lest they get stale by waiting. In twenty-one years, with all my time at my free disposal I have written and completed only eleven books, whereas with half the labor that a journalist does I could have written sixty in that time. I do not greatly mind being accused of a proclivity for rushing into print, but at the same time I don't believe that the charge is really well founded. Suppose I did write eleven books, have you nothing to be grateful for? Go to—-remember the forty-nine which I didn't write.

Truly Yours

S. L. CLEMENS.

Notes (added twenty-two years later):

Stormfield, April 30, 1909. It seems the letter was not sent. I probably feared she might print it, and I couldn't find a way to say so without running a risk of hurting her. No one would hurt Jeannette Gilder purposely, and no one would want to run the risk of doing it unintentionally. She is my neighbor, six miles away, now, and I must ask her about this ancient letter.

I note with pride and pleasure that I told no untruths in my unsent answer. I still have the habit of keeping unfinished books lying around years and years, waiting. I have four or five novels on hand at present in a half-finished condition, and it is more than three years since I have looked at any of them. I have no intention of finishing them. I could complete all of them in less than a year, if the impulse should come powerfully upon me: Long, long ago money-necessity furnished that impulse once, ("Following the Equator"), but mere desire for money has never furnished it, so far as I remember. Not even money-necessity was able to overcome me on a couple of occasions when perhaps I ought to have allowed it to succeed. While I was a bankrupt and in debt two offers were made me for weekly literary contributions to continue during a year, and they would have made a debtless man of me, but I declined them, with my wife's full approval, for I had known of no instance where a man had pumped himself out once a week and failed to run "emptyings" before the year was finished.

As to that "Noah's Ark" book, I began it in Edinburgh in 1873;—[This is not quite correct. The "Noah's Ark" book was begun in Buffalo in 1870.] I don't know where the manuscript is now. It was a Diary, which professed to be the work of Shem, but wasn't. I began it again several months ago, but only for recreation; I hadn't any intention of carrying it to a finish—or even to the end of the first chapter, in fact.

As to the book whose action "takes place in Heaven." That was a small thing, ("Captain Stormfield's Visit to Heaven.") It lay in my pigeon-holes 40 years, then I took it out and printed it in Harper's Monthly last year.

S. L. C.

In the next letter we get a pretty and peaceful picture of "Rest-and-be-Thankful." These were Mark Twain's balmy days. The financial drain of the type-machine was heavy but not yet exhausting, and the prospect of vast returns from it seemed to grow brighter each day. His publishing business, though less profitable, was still prosperous, his family life was ideal. How gratefully, then, he could enter into the peace of that "perfect day."

To Mrs. Orion Clemens, in Keokuk, Ia.:

ON THE HILL NEAR ELMIRA, July 10, '87.

DEAR MOLLIE,—This is a superb Sunday for weather—very cloudy, and the thermometer as low as 65. The city in the valley is purple with shade, as seen from up here at the study. The Cranes are reading and loafing in the canvas-curtained summer-house 50 yards away on a higher (the highest) point; the cats are loafing over at "Ellerslie" which is the children's estate and dwellinghouse in their own private grounds (by deed from Susie Crane) a hundred yards from the study, amongst the clover and young oaks and willows. Livy is down at the house, but I shall now go and bring her up to the Cranes to help us occupy the lounges and hammocks—whence a great panorama of distant hill and valley and city is seeable. The children have gone on a lark through the neighboring hills and woods. It is a perfect day indeed.

With love to you all.

SAM.

Two days after this letter was written we get a hint of what was the beginning of business trouble—that is to say, of the failing health of Charles L. Webster. Webster was ambitious, nervous, and not robust. He had overworked and was paying the penalty. His trouble was neurasthenia, and he was presently obliged to retire altogether from the business. The "Sam and Mary" mentioned were Samuel Moffet and his wife.

To Mrs. Pamela Moffett, in Fredonia, N. Y.

ELMIRA, July 12, '87

MY DEAR SISTER,—I had no idea that Charley's case was so serious. I knew it was bad, and persistent, but I was not aware of the full size of the matter.

I have just been writing to a friend in Hartford' who treated what I imagine was a similar case surgically last fall, and produced a permanent cure. If this is a like case, Charley must go to him.

If relief fails there, he must take the required rest, whether the business can stand it or not.

It is most pleasant to hear such prosperous accounts of Sam and Mary, I do not see how Sam could well be more advantageously fixed. He can grow up with that paper, and achieve a successful life.

It is not all holiday here with Susie and Clara this time. They have to put in some little time every day on their studies. Jean thinks she is studying too, but I don't know what it is unless it is the horses; she spends the day under their heels in the stables—and that is but a continuation of her Hartford system of culture.

With love from us all to you all.

Affectionately

SAM.

Mark Twain had a few books that he read regularly every year or two.

Among these were 'Pepys's Diary', Suetonius's 'Lives of the Twelve Caesars', and Thomas Carlyle's 'French Revolution'. He had a passion for history, biography, and personal memoirs of any sort. In his early life he had cared very little for poetry, but along in the middle eighties he somehow acquired a taste for Browning and became absorbed in it. A Browning club assembled as often as once a week at the Clemens home in Hartford to listen to his readings of the master. He was an impressive reader, and he carefully prepared himself for these occasions, indicating by graduated underscorings, the exact values he wished to give to words and phrases. Those were memorable gatherings, and they must have continued through at least two winters. It is one of the puzzling phases of Mark Twain's character that, notwithstanding his passion for direct and lucid expression, he should have found pleasure in the poems of Robert Browning.

To W. D. Howells, in Boston:

ELMIRA, Aug. 22, '87.

MY DEAR HOWELLS,—How stunning are the changes which age makes in a man while he sleeps. When I finished Carlyle's French Revolution in 1871, I was a Girondin; every time I have read it since, I have read it differently being influenced and changed, little by little, by life and environment (and Taine and St. Simon): and now I lay the book down once more, and recognize that I am a Sansculotte!—And not a pale, characterless Sansculotte, but a Marat. Carlyle teaches no such gospel so the change is in me—in my vision of the evidences.

People pretend that the Bible means the same to them at 50 that it did at all former milestones in their journey. I wonder how they can lie so. It comes of practice, no doubt. They would not say that of Dickens's or Scott's books. Nothing remains the same. When a man goes back to look at the house of his childhood, it has always shrunk: there is no instance of such a house being as big as the picture in memory and imagination call for. Shrunk how? Why, to its correct dimensions: the house hasn't altered; this is the first time it has been in focus.

Well, that's loss. To have house and Bible shrink so, under the disillusioning corrected angle, is loss-for a moment. But there are compensations. You tilt the tube skyward and bring planets and comets and corona flames a hundred and fifty thousand miles high into the field. Which I see you have done, and found Tolstoi. I haven't got him in focus yet, but I've got Browning....

Ys Ever

MARK.

Mention has been made already of Mark Twain's tendency to absentmindedness. He was always forgetting engagements, or getting them wrong. Once he hurried to an afternoon party, and finding the mistress of the house alone, sat down and talked to her comfortably for an hour or two, not remembering his errand at all. It was only when he reached home that he learned that the party had taken place the week before. It was always dangerous for him to make engagements, and he never seemed to profit by sorrowful experience. We, however, may profit now by one of his amusing apologies.

To Mrs. Grover Cleveland, in Washington:

HARTFORD, Nov. 6, 1887.

MY DEAR MADAM,—I do not know how it is in the White House, but in this house of ours whenever the minor half of the administration tries to run itself without the help of the major half it gets aground. Last night when I was offered the opportunity to assist you in the throwing open the Warner brothers superb benefaction in Bridgeport to those fortunate women, I naturally appreciated the honor done me, and promptly seized my chance. I had an engagement, but the circumstances washed it out of my mind. If I had only laid the matter before the major half of the administration on the spot, there would have been no blunder; but I never thought of that. So when I did lay it before her, later, I realized once more that it will not do for the literary fraction of a combination to try to manage affairs which properly belong in the office of the business bulk of it. I suppose the President often acts just like that: goes and makes an impossible promise, and you never find it out until it is next to impossible to break it up and set things straight again. Well, that is just our way, exactly-one half of the administration always busy getting the family into trouble, and the other half busy getting it out again. And so we do seem to be all pretty much alike, after all. The fact is, I had forgotten that we were to have a dinner party on that Bridgeport date—I thought it was the next day: which is a good deal of an improvement for me, because I am more used to being behind a day or two than ahead. But that is just the difference between one end of this kind of an administration and the other end of it, as you have noticed, yourself—the other end does not forget these things. Just so with a funeral; if it is the man's funeral, he is most always there, of course—but that is no credit to him, he wouldn't be there if you depended on him to remember about it; whereas, if on the other hand—but I seem to have got off from my line of argument somehow; never mind about the funeral. Of course I am not meaning to say anything against funerals—that is, as occasions—mere occasions—for as diversions I don't think they amount to much But as I was saying—if you are not busy I will look back and see what it was I was saying.

I don't seem to find the place; but anyway she was as sorry as ever anybody could be that I could not go to Bridgeport, but there was no help for it. And I, I have been not only sorry but very sincerely ashamed of having made an engagement to go without first making sure that I could keep it, and I do not know how to apologize enough for my heedless breach of good manners.

With the sincerest respect,

S. L. CLEMENS.

Samuel Clemens was one of the very few authors to copyright a book in England before the enactment of the international copyright law.

As early as 1872 he copyrighted 'Roughing It' in England, and piratical publishers there respected his rights. Finally, in 1887, the inland revenue office assessed him with income tax, which he very willingly paid, instructing his London publishers, Chatto & Windus, to pay on the full amount he had received from them. But when the receipt for his taxes came it was nearly a yard square with due postage of considerable amount. Then he wrote:

To Mr. Chatto, of Chatto & Windus, in London:

HARTFORD, Dec. 5, '87.

MY DEAR CHATTO,—Look here, I don't mind paying the tax, but don't you let the Inland Revenue Office send me any more receipts for it, for the postage is something perfectly demoralizing. If they feel obliged to print a receipt on a horse-blanket, why don't they hire a ship and send it over at their own expense?

Wasn't it good that they caught me out with an old book instead of a new one? The tax on a new book would bankrupt a body. It was my purpose to go to England next May and stay the rest of the year, but I've found that tax office out just in time. My new book would issue in March, and they would tax the sale in both countries. Come, we must get up a compromise somehow. You go and work in on the good side of those revenue people and get them to take the profits and give me the tax. Then I will come over and we will divide the swag and have a good time.

I wish you to thank Mr. Christmas for me; but we won't resist. The country that allows me copyright has a right to tax me.

Sincerely Yours

S. L. CLEMENS.

Another English tax assessment came that year, based on the report that it was understood that he was going to become an English resident, and had leased Buckenham Hall, Norwich, for a year. Clemens wrote his publishers: "I will explain that all that about Buckenham Hall was an English newspaper's mistake. I was not in England, and if I had been I wouldn't have been at Buckenham Hall, anyway, but at Buckingham Palace, or I would have endeavored to find out the reason why." Clemens made literature out of this tax experience. He wrote an open letter to Her Majesty Queen Victoria. Such a letter has no place in this collection. It was published in the "Drawer" of Harper's Magazine, December, 1887, and is now included in the uniform edition of his works under the title of, "A Petition to the Queen of England."

From the following letter, written at the end of the year, we gather that the type-setter costs were beginning to make a difference in the Clemens economies.

To Mrs. Moffett, in Fredonia:

HARTFORD, Dec. 18, '87.

DEAR PAMELA,—will you take this $15 and buy some candy or some other trifle for yourself and Sam and his wife to remember that we remember you, by?

If we weren't a little crowded this year by the typesetter, I'd send a check large enough to buy a family Bible or some other useful thing like that.

However we go on and on, but the type-setter goes on forever—at $3,000 a month; which is much more satisfactory than was the case the first seventeen months, when the bill only averaged $2,000, and promised to take a thousand years. We'll be through, now, in 3 or 4 months, I reckon, and then the strain will let up and we can breathe freely once more, whether success ensues or failure.

Even with a type-setter on hand we ought not to be in the least scrimped—but it would take a long letter to explain why and who is to blame.

All the family send love to all of you and best Christmas wishes for your prosperity.

Affectionately,

SAM.

XXVIII. LETTERS,1888. A YALE DEGREE. WORK ON "THE YANKEE." ON INTERVIEWING, ETC.

Mark Twain received his first college degree when he was made Master of Arts by Yale, in June, 1888. Editor of the Courant, Charles H. Clarke, was selected to notify him of his new title. Clarke was an old friend to whom Clemens could write familiarly.

To Charles H. Clarke, in Hartford:

ELMIRA, July 2, '88.

MY DEAR CHARLES,—Thanks for your thanks, and for your initiation intentions. I shall be ready for you. I feel mighty proud of that degree; in fact, I could squeeze the truth a little closer and say vain of it. And why shouldn't I be?—I am the only literary animal of my particular subspecies who has ever been given a degree by any College in any age of the world, as far as I know.

Sincerely Yours

S. L. Clemens M. A.

Reply: Charles H. Clarke to S. L Clemens:

MY DEAR FRIEND, You are "the only literary animal of your particular subspecies" in existence and you've no cause for humility in the fact. Yale has done herself at least as much credit as she has done you, and "Don't you forget it."

C. H. C.

With the exception of his brief return to the river in 1882. Mark Twain had been twenty-seven years away from pilots and piloting.

Nevertheless, he always kept a tender place in his heart for the old times and for old river comrades. Major "Jack" Downing had been a Mississippi pilot of early days, but had long since retired from the river to a comfortable life ashore, in an Ohio town. Clemens had not heard from him for years when a letter came which invited the following answer.

To Major "Jack" Downing, in Middleport Ohio:

ELMIRA, N. Y.[no month] 1888.

DEAR MAJOR,—And has it come to this that the dead rise up and speak? For I supposed that you were dead, it has been so long since I heard your name.

And how young you've grown! I was a mere boy when I knew you on the river, where you had been piloting for 35 years, and now you are only a year and a half older than I am! I mean to go to Hot Springs myself and get 30 or 40 years knocked off my age. It's manifestly the place that Ponce de Leon was striking for, but the poor fellow lost the trail.

Possibly I may see you, for I shall be in St. Louis a day or two in November. I propose to go down the river and "note the changes" once more before I make the long crossing, and perhaps you can come there. Will you? I want to see all the boys that are left alive.

And so Grant Marsh, too, is flourishing yet? A mighty good fellow, and smart too. When we were taking that wood flat down to the Chambers, which was aground, I soon saw that I was a perfect lubber at piloting such a thing. I saw that I could never hit the Chambers with it, so I resigned in Marsh's favor, and he accomplished the task to my admiration. We should all have gone to the mischief if I had remained in authority. I always had good judgement, more judgement than talent, in fact.

No; the nom de plume did not originate in that way. Capt. Sellers used the signature, "Mark Twain," himself, when he used to write up the antiquities in the way of river reminiscences for the New Orleans Picayune. He hated me for burlesquing them in an article in the True Delta; so four years later when he died, I robbed the corpse—that is I confiscated the nom de plume. I have published this vital fact 3,000 times now. But no matter, it is good practice; it is about the only fact that I can tell the same way every time. Very glad, indeed, to hear from you Major, and shall be gladder still to see you in November.

Truly yours,

S. L. CLEMENS.

He did not make the journey down the river planned for that year. He had always hoped to make another steamboat trip with Bixby, but one thing and another interfered and he did not go again.

Authors were always sending their books to Mark Twain to read, and no busy man was ever more kindly disposed toward such offerings, more generously considerate of the senders. Louis Pendleton was a young unknown writer in 1888, but Clemens took time to read his story carefully, and to write to him about it a letter that cost precious time, thought, and effort. It must have rejoiced the young man's heart to receive a letter like that, from one whom all young authors held supreme.

To Louis Pendleton, in Georgia:

ELMIRA, N. Y., Aug. 4, '88.

MY DEAR SIR,—I found your letter an hour ago among some others which had lain forgotten a couple of weeks, and I at once stole time enough to read Ariadne. Stole is the right word, for the summer "Vacation" is the only chance I get for work; so, no minute subtracted from work is borrowed, it is stolen. But this time I do not repent. As a rule, people don't send me books which I can thank them for, and so I say nothing—which looks uncourteous. But I thank you. Ariadne is a beautiful and satisfying story; and true, too—which is the best part of a story; or indeed of any other thing. Even liars have to admit that, if they are intelligent liars; I mean in their private [the word conscientious written but erased] intervals. (I struck that word out because a man's private thought can never be a lie; what he thinks, is to him the truth, always; what he speaks—but these be platitudes.)

If you want me to pick some flaws—very well—but I do it unwillingly. I notice one thing—which one may notice also in my books, and in all books whether written by man or God: trifling carelessness of statement or Expression. If I think that you meant that she took the lizard from the water which she had drawn from the well, it is evidence—it is almost proof—that your words were not as clear as they should have been. True, it is only a trifling thing; but so is mist on a mirror. I would have hung the pail on Ariadne's arm. You did not deceive me when you said that she carried it under her arm, for I knew she didn't; still it was not your right to mar my enjoyment of the graceful picture. If the pail had been a portfolio, I wouldn't be making these remarks. The engraver of a fine picture revises, and revises, and revises—and then revises, and revises, and revises; and then repeats. And always the charm of that picture grows, under his hand. It was good enough before—told its story, and was beautiful. True: and a lovely girl is lovely, with freckles; but she isn't at her level best with them.

This is not hypercriticism; you have had training enough to know that.

So much concerning exactness of statement. In that other not-small matter—selection of the exact single word—you are hard to catch. Still, I should hold that Mrs. Walker considered that there was no occasion for concealment; that "motive" implied a deeper mental search than she expended on the matter; that it doesn't reflect the attitude of her mind with precision. Is this hypercriticism? I shan't dispute it. I only say, that if Mrs. Walker didn't go so far as to have a motive, I had to suggest that when a word is so near the right one that a body can't quite tell whether it is or isn't, it's good politics to strike it out and go for the Thesaurus. That's all. Motive may stand; but you have allowed a snake to scream, and I will not concede that that was the best word.

I do not apologize for saying these things, for they are not said in the speck-hunting spirit, but in the spirit of want-to-help-if-I-can. They would be useful to me if said to me once a month, they may be useful to you, said once.

I save the other stories for my real vacation—which is nine months long, to my sorrow. I thank you again.

Truly Yours

S. L. CLEMENS.

In the next letter we get a sidelight on the type-setting machine, the Frankenstein monster that was draining their substance and holding out false hopes of relief and golden return. The program here outlined was one that would continue for several years yet, with the end always in sight, but never quite attained.

To Orion Clemens, in Keokuk, Ia.:

Oct. 3, '88.

Private.

Saturday 29th, by a closely calculated estimate, there were 85 days' work to do on the machine.

We can use 4 men, but not constantly. If they could work constantly it would complete the machine in 21 days, of course. They will all be on hand and under wages, and each will get in all the work there is opportunity for, but by how much they can reduce the 85 days toward the 21 days, nobody can tell.

To-day I pay Pratt & Whitney $10,000. This squares back indebtedness and everything to date. They began about May or April or March 1886—along there somewhere, and have always kept from a dozen to two dozen master-hands on the machine.

That outgo is done; 4 men for a month or two will close up that leak and caulk it. Work on the patents is also kind of drawing toward a conclusion.

Love to you both. All well here.

And give our love to Ma if she can get the idea.

SAM.

Mark Twain that year was working pretty steadily on 'The Yankee at King Arthur's Court', a book which he had begun two years before. He had published nothing since the Huck Finn story, and his company was badly in need of a new book by an author of distinction. Also it was highly desirable to earn money for himself; wherefore he set to work to finish the Yankee story. He had worked pretty steadily that summer in his Elmira study, but on his return to Hartford found a good deal of confusion in the house, so went over to Twichell's, where carpenter work was in progress. He seems to have worked there successfully, though what improvement of conditions he found in that numerous, lively household, over those at home it would be difficult to say.

To Theodore W. Crane, at Quarry Farm, Elmira, N. Y.

Friday, Oct.,5, '88.

DEAR THEO,—I am here in Twichell's house at work, with the noise of the children and an army of carpenters to help. Of course they don't help, but neither do they hinder. It's like a boiler-factory for racket, and in nailing a wooden ceiling onto the room under me the hammering tickles my feet amazingly sometimes, and jars my table a good deal; but I never am conscious of the racket at all, and I move my feet into position of relief without knowing when I do it. I began here Monday morning, and have done eighty pages since. I was so tired last night that I thought I would lie abed and rest, to-day; but I couldn't resist. I mean to try to knock off tomorrow, but it's doubtful if I do. I want to finish the day the machine finishes, and a week ago the closest calculations for that indicated Oct. 22—but experience teaches me that their calculations will miss fire, as usual.

The other day the children were projecting a purchase, Livy and I to furnish the money—a dollar and a half. Jean discouraged the idea. She said: "We haven't got any money. Children, if you would think, you would remember the machine isn't done."

It's billiards to-night. I wish you were here.

With love to you both

S. L. C.

P. S. I got it all wrong. It wasn't the children, it was Marie. She wanted a box of blacking, for the children's shoes. Jean reproved her—and said:

"Why, Marie, you mustn't ask for things now. The machine isn't done."

S. L. C.

The letter that follows is to another of his old pilot friends, one who was also a schoolmate, Will Bowen, of Hannibal. There is today no means of knowing the occasion upon which this letter was written, but it does not matter; it is the letter itself that is of chief value.

To Will Bowen, in Hannibal, Mo.:

HARTFORD, Nov 4, '88.

DEAR WILL,—I received your letter yesterday evening, just as I was starting out of town to attend a wedding, and so my mind was privately busy, all the evening, in the midst of the maelstrom of chat and chaff and laughter, with the sort of reflections which create themselves, examine themselves, and continue themselves, unaffected by surroundings—unaffected, that is understood, by the surroundings, but not uninfluenced by them. Here was the near presence of the two supreme events of life: marriage, which is the beginning of life, and death which is the end of it. I found myself seeking chances to shirk into corners where I might think, undisturbed; and the most I got out of my thought, was this: both marriage and death ought to be welcome: the one promises happiness, doubtless the other assures it. A long procession of people filed through my mind—people whom you and I knew so many years ago—so many centuries ago, it seems like-and these ancient dead marched to the soft marriage music of a band concealed in some remote room of the house; and the contented music and the dreaming shades seemed in right accord with each other, and fitting. Nobody else knew that a procession of the dead was passing though this noisy swarm of the living, but there it was, and to me there was nothing uncanny about it; Rio, they were welcome faces to me. I would have liked to bring up every creature we knew in those days—even the dumb animals—it would be bathing in the fabled Fountain of Youth.

We all feel your deep trouble with you; and we would hope, if we might, but your words deny us that privilege. To die one's self is a thing that must be easy, and of light consequence, but to lose a part of one's self—well, we know how deep that pang goes, we who have suffered that disaster, received that wound which cannot heal.

Sincerely your friend

S. L. CLEMENS.

His next is of quite a different nature. Evidently the typesetting conditions had alarmed Orion, and he was undertaking some economies with a view of retrenchment. Orion was always reducing economy to science. Once, at an earlier date, he recorded that he had figured his personal living expenses down to sixty cents a week, but inasmuch as he was then, by his own confession, unable to earn the sixty cents, this particular economy was wasted. Orion was a trial, certainly, and the explosion that follows was not without excuse. Furthermore, it was not as bad as it sounds. Mark Twain's rages always had an element of humor in them, a fact which no one more than Orion himself would appreciate. He preserved this letter, quietly noting on the envelope, "Letter from Sam, about ma's nurse."

Letter to Orion Clemens, in Keokuk, Iowa:

NOV. 29, '88.

Jesus Christ!—It is perilous to write such a man. You can go crazy on less material than anybody that ever lived. What in hell has produced all these maniacal imaginings? You told me you had hired an attendant for ma. Now hire one instantly, and stop this nonsense of wearing Mollie and yourself out trying to do that nursing yourselves. Hire the attendant, and tell me her cost so that I can instruct Webster & Co. to add it every month to what they already send. Don't fool away any more time about this. And don't write me any more damned rot about "storms," and inability to pay trivial sums of money and—and—hell and damnation! You see I've read only the first page of your letter; I wouldn't read the rest for a million dollars.

Yr

SAM.

P. S. Don't imagine that I have lost my temper, because I swear. I swear all day, but I do not lose my temper. And don't imagine that I am on my way to the poorhouse, for I am not; or that I am uneasy, for I am not; or that I am uncomfortable or unhappy—for I never am. I don't know what it is to be unhappy or uneasy; and I am not going to try to learn how, at this late day.

SAM.

Few men were ever interviewed oftener than Mark Twain, yet he never welcomed interviewers and was seldom satisfied with them. "What I say in an interview loses it character in print," he often remarked, "all its life and personality. The reporter realizes this himself, and tries to improve upon me, but he doesn't help matters any."

Edward W. Bok, before he became editor of the Ladies Home Journal, was conducting a weekly syndicate column under the title of "Bok's Literary Leaves." It usually consisted of news and gossip of writers, comment, etc., literary odds and ends, and occasional interviews with distinguished authors. He went up to Hartford one day to interview Mark Twain. The result seemed satisfactory to Bok, but wishing to be certain that it would be satisfactory to Clemens, he sent him a copy for approval. The interview was not returned; in the place of it came a letter-not altogether disappointing, as the reader may believe.

To Edward W. Bok, in New York:

MY DEAR MR. BOK,—No, no. It is like most interviews, pure twaddle and valueless.

For several quite plain and simple reasons, an "interview" must, as a rule, be an absurdity, and chiefly for this reason—It is an attempt to use a boat on land or a wagon on water, to speak figuratively. Spoken speech is one thing, written speech is quite another. Print is the proper vehicle for the latter, but it isn't for the former. The moment "talk" is put into print you recognize that it is not what it was when you heard it; you perceive that an immense something has disappeared from it. That is its soul. You have nothing but a dead carcass left on your hands. Color, play of feature, the varying modulations of the voice, the laugh, the smile, the informing inflections, everything that gave that body warmth, grace, friendliness and charm and commended it to your affections—or, at least, to your tolerance—is gone and nothing is left but a pallid, stiff and repulsive cadaver.

Such is "talk" almost invariably, as you see it lying in state in an "interview". The interviewer seldom tries to tell one how a thing was said; he merely puts in the naked remark and stops there. When one writes for print his methods are very different. He follows forms which have but little resemblance to conversation, but they make the reader understand what the writer is trying to convey. And when the writer is making a story and finds it necessary to report some of the talk of his characters observe how cautiously and anxiously he goes at that risky and difficult thing. "If he had dared to say that thing in my presence," said Alfred, "taking a mock heroic attitude, and casting an arch glance upon the company, blood would have flowed."

"If he had dared to say that thing in my presence," said Hawkwood, with that in his eye which caused more than one heart in that guilty assemblage to quake, "blood would have flowed."

"If he had dared to say that thing in my presence," said the paltry blusterer, with valor on his tongue and pallor on his lips, "blood would have flowed."

So painfully aware is the novelist that naked talk in print conveys no meaning that he loads, and often overloads, almost every utterance of his characters with explanations and interpretations. It is a loud confession that print is a poor vehicle for "talk"; it is a recognition that uninterpreted talk in print would result in confusion to the reader, not instruction.

Now, in your interview, you have certainly been most accurate; you have set down the sentences I uttered as I said them. But you have not a word of explanation; what my manner was at several points is not indicated. Therefore, no reader can possibly know where I was in earnest and where I was joking; or whether I was joking altogether or in earnest altogether. Such a report of a conversation has no value. It can convey many meanings to the reader, but never the right one. To add interpretations which would convey the right meaning is a something which would require—what? An art so high and fine and difficult that no possessor of it would ever be allowed to waste it on interviews.

No; spare the reader, and spare me; leave the whole interview out; it is rubbish. I wouldn't talk in my sleep if I couldn't talk better than that.

If you wish to print anything print this letter; it may have some value, for it may explain to a reader here and there why it is that in interviews, as a rule, men seem to talk like anybody but themselves.

Very sincerely yours,

MARK TWAIN.

XXIX. LETTERS, 1889. THE MACHINE. DEATH OF MR. CRANE. CONCLUSION OF THE YANKEE.

In January, 1889, Clemens believed, after his long seven years of waiting, fruition had come in the matter of the type machine. Paige, the inventor, seemed at last to have given it its finishing touches. The mechanical marvel that had cost so much time, mental stress, and a fortune in money, stood complete, responsive to the human will and touch—the latest, and one of the greatest, wonders of the world. To George Standring, a London printer and publisher, Clemens wrote: "The machine is finished!" and added, "This is by far the most marvelous invention ever contrived by man. And it is not a thing of rags and patches; it is made of massive steel, and will last a century."

In his fever of enthusiasm on that day when he had actually seen it in operation, he wrote a number of exuberant letters. They were more or less duplicates, but as the one to his brother is of fuller detail and more intimate than the others, it has been selected for preservation here.

To Orion Clemens, in Keokuk:

HARTFORD, Jan. 5, '89.

DEAR ORION,—At 12.20 this afternoon a line of movable types was spaced and justified by machinery, for the first time in the history of the world! And I was there to see. It was done automatically—instantly—perfectly. This is indeed the first line of movable types that ever was perfectly spaced and perfectly justified on this earth.

This was the last function that remained to be tested—and so by long odds the most amazing and extraordinary invention ever born of the brain of man stands completed and perfect. Livy is down stairs celebrating.

But it's a cunning devil, is that machine!—and knows more than any man that ever lived. You shall see. We made the test in this way. We set up a lot of random letters in a stick—three-fourths of a line; then filled out the line with quads representing 14 spaces, each space to be 35/1000 of an inch thick. Then we threw aside the quads and put the letters into the machine and formed them into 15 two-letter words, leaving the words separated by two-inch vacancies. Then we started up the machine slowly, by hand, and fastened our eyes on the space-selecting pins. The first pin-block projected its third pin as the first word came traveling along the race-way; second block did the same; but the third block projected its second pin!

"Oh, hell! stop the machine—something wrong—it's going to set a 30/1000 space!"

General consternation. "A foreign substance has got into the spacing plates." This from the head mathematician.

"Yes, that is the trouble," assented the foreman.

Paige examined. "No—look in, and you can see that there's nothing of the kind." Further examination. "Now I know what it is—what it must be: one of those plates projects and binds. It's too bad—the first test is a failure." A pause. "Well, boys, no use to cry. Get to work—take the machine down.—No—Hold on! don't touch a thing! Go right ahead! We are fools, the machine isn't. The machine knows what it's about. There is a speck of dirt on one of those types, and the machine is putting in a thinner space to allow for it!"

That was just it. The machine went right ahead, spaced the line, justified it to a hair, and shoved it into the galley complete and perfect! We took it out and examined it with a glass. You could not tell by your eye that the third space was thinner than the others, but the glass and the calipers showed the difference. Paige had always said that the machine would measure invisible particles of dirt and allow for them, but even he had forgotten that vast fact for the moment.

All the witnesses made written record of the immense historical birth—the first justification of a line of movable type by machinery—and also set down the hour and the minute. Nobody had drank anything, and yet everybody seemed drunk. Well-dizzy, stupefied, stunned.

All the other wonderful inventions of the human brain sink pretty nearly into commonplace contrasted with this awful mechanical miracle. Telephones, telegraphs, locomotives, cotton gins, sewing machines, Babbage calculators, jacquard looms, perfecting presses, Arkwright's frames—all mere toys, simplicities! The Paige Compositor marches alone and far in the lead of human inventions.

In two or three weeks we shall work the stiffness out of her joints and have her performing as smoothly and softly as human muscles, and then we shall speak out the big secret and let the world come and gaze.

Return me this letter when you have read it.

SAM.

Judge of the elation which such a letter would produce in Keokuk! Yet it was no greater than that which existed in Hartford—for a time.

Then further delays. Before the machine got "the stiffness out of her joints" that "cunning devil" manifested a tendency to break the types, and Paige, who was never happier than when he was pulling things to pieces and making improvements, had the type-setter apart again and the day of complete triumph was postponed.

There was sadness at the Elmira farm that spring. Theodore Crane, who had long been in poor health, seemed to grow daily worse. In February he had paid a visit to Hartford and saw the machine in operation, but by the end of May his condition was very serious. Remembering his keen sense of humor, Clemens reported to him cheering and amusing incidents.

To Mrs. Theodore Crane. in Elmira, N. Y.:

HARTFORD, May 28, '89.

Susie dear, I want you to tell this to Theodore. You know how absent-minded Twichell is, and how desolate his face is when he is in that frame. At such times, he passes the word with a friend on the street and is not aware of the meeting at all. Twice in a week, our Clara had this latter experience with him within the past month. But the second instance was too much for her, and she woke him up, in his tracks, with a reproach. She said:

"Uncle Joe, why do you always look as if you were just going down into the grave, when you meet a person on the street?"—and then went on to reveal to him the funereal spectacle which he presented on such occasions. Well, she has met Twichell three times since then, and would swim the Connecticut to avoid meeting him the fourth. As soon as he sights her, no matter how public the place nor how far off she is, he makes a bound into the air, heaves arms and legs into all sorts of frantic gestures of delight, and so comes prancing, skipping and pirouetting for her like a drunken Indian entering heaven.

With a full invoice of love from us all to you and Theodore.

S. L. C.

The reference in the next to the "closing sentence" in a letter written by Howells to Clemens about this time, refers to a heart-broken utterance of the former concerning his daughter Winnie, who had died some time before. She had been a gentle talented girl, but never of robust health. Her death had followed a long period of gradual decline.

To W. D. Howells, in Boston:

HARTFORD, Judy 13, '89.

DEAR HOWELLS,—I came on from Elmira a day or two ago, where I left a house of mourning. Mr. Crane died, after ten months of pain and two whole days of dying, at the farm on the hill, the 3rd inst: A man who had always hoped for a swift death. Mrs. Crane and Mrs. Clemens and the children were in a gloom which brought back to me the days of nineteen years ago, when Mr. Langdon died. It is heart-breaking to see Mrs. Crane. Many a time, in the past ten days, the sight of her has reminded me, with a pang, of the desolation which uttered itself in the closing sentence of your last letter to me. I do see that there is an argument against suicide: the grief of the worshipers left behind; the awful famine in their hearts, these are too costly terms for the release.

I shall be here ten days yet, and all alone: nobody in the house but the servants. Can't Mrs. Howells spare you to me? Can't you come and stay with me? The house is cool and pleasant; your work will not be interrupted; we will keep to ourselves and let the rest of the world do the same; you can have your choice of three bedrooms, and you will find the Children's schoolroom (which was built for my study,) the perfection of a retired and silent den for work. There isn't a fly or a mosquito on the estate. Come—say you will.

With kindest regards to Mrs. Howells, and Pilla and John,

Yours Ever

MARK.

Howells was more hopeful. He wrote: "I read something in a strange book, The Physical Theory of Another Life, that consoles a little; namely, we see and feel the power of Deity in such fullness that we ought to infer the infinite justice and Goodness which we do not see or feel." And a few days later, he wrote: "I would rather see and talk with you than any other man in the world outside my own blood."

A Connecticut Yankee at King Arthur's Court was brought to an end that year and given to the artist and printer. Dan Beard was selected for the drawings, and was given a free hand, as the next letter shows.

To Fred J. Hall, Manager Charles L. Webster & Co.:

[Charles L. Webster, owing to poor health, had by this time retired from the firm.]

ELMIRA, July 20, '89.

DEAR MR. HALL,—Upon reflection—thus: tell Beard to obey his own inspiration, and when he sees a picture in his mind put that picture on paper, be it humorous or be it serious. I want his genius to be wholly unhampered, I shan't have fears as to the result. They will be better pictures than if I mixed in and tried to give him points on his own trade.

Send this note and he'll understand.

Yr

S. L. C.

Clemens had made a good choice in selecting Beard for the illustrations. He was well qualified for the work, and being of a socialistic turn of mind put his whole soul into it. When the drawings were completed, Clemens wrote: "Hold me under permanent obligations. What luck it was to find you! There are hundreds of artists that could illustrate any other book of mine, but there was only one who could illustrate this one. Yes, it was a fortunate hour that I went netting for lightning bugs and caught a meteor. Live forever!"

Clemens, of course, was anxious for Howells to read The Yankee, and Mrs. Clemens particularly so. Her eyes were giving her trouble that summer, so that she could not read the MS. for herself, and she had grave doubts as to some of its chapters. It may be said here that the book to-day might have been better if Mrs. Clemens had been able to read it. Howells was a peerless critic, but the revolutionary subject-matter of the book so delighted him that he was perhaps somewhat blinded to its literary defects. However, this is premature. Howells did not at once see the story. He had promised to come to Hartford, but wrote that trivial matters had made his visit impossible. From the next letter we get the situation at this time. The "Mr. Church" mentioned was Frederick S. Church, the well-known artist.

To W. D. Howells, in Boston:

ELMIRA, July 24, '89.

DEAR HOWELLS,—I, too, was as sorry as I could be; yes, and desperately disappointed. I even did a heroic thing: shipped my book off to New York lest I should forget hospitality and embitter your visit with it. Not that I think you wouldn't like to read it, for I think you would; but not on a holiday that's not the time. I see how you were situated—another familiarity of Providence and wholly wanton intrusion—and of course we could not help ourselves. Well, just think of it: a while ago, while Providence's attention was absorbed in disordering some time-tables so as to break up a trip of mine to Mr. Church's on the Hudson, that Johnstown dam got loose. I swear I was afraid to pray, for fear I should laugh. Well, I'm not going to despair; we'll manage a meet yet.

I expect to go to Hartford again in August and maybe remain till I have to come back here and fetch the family. And, along there in August, some time, you let on that you are going to Mexico, and I will let on that I am going to Spitzbergen, and then under cover of this clever stratagem we will glide from the trains at Worcester and have a time. I have noticed that Providence is indifferent about Mexico and Spitzbergen.

Ys Ever

MARK.

Possibly Mark Twain was not particularly anxious that Howells should see his MS., fearing that he might lay a ruthless hand on some of his more violent fulminations and wild fancies. However this may be, further postponement was soon at an end. Mrs. Clemens's eyes troubled her and would not permit her to read, so she requested that the Yankee be passed upon by soberminded critics, such as Howells and Edmund Clarence Stedman. Howells wrote that even if he hadn't wanted to read the book for its own sake, or for the author's sake, he would still want to do it for Mrs. Clemens's. Whereupon the proofs were started in his direction.

To W. D. Howells, in Boston:

ELMIRA, Aug. 24, '89.

DEAR HOWELLS,—If you should be moved to speak of my book in the Study, I shall be glad and proud—and the sooner it gets in, the better for the book; though I don't suppose you can get it in earlier than the November number—why, no, you can't get it in till a month later than that. Well, anyway I don't think I'll send out any other press copy—except perhaps to Stedman. I'm not writing for those parties who miscall themselves critics, and I don't care to have them paw the book at all. It's my swan-song, my retirement from literature permanently, and I wish to pass to the cemetery unclodded.

I judge that the proofs have begun to reach you about this time, as I had some (though not revises,) this morning. I'm sure I'm going to be charmed with Beard's pictures. Observe his nice take-off of Middle-Age art-dinner-table scene.

Ys sincerely

MARK.

Howells's approval of the Yankee came almost in the form of exultant shouts, one after reading each batch of proof. First he wrote: "It's charming, original, wonderful! good in fancy and sound to the core in morals." And again, "It's a mighty great book, and it makes my heart burn with wrath. It seems God did not forget to put a soul into you. He shuts most literary men off with a brain, merely." Then, a few days later: "The book is glorious—simply noble; what masses of virgin truth never touched in print before!" and, finally, "Last night I read your last chapter. As Stedman says of the whole book, it's titanic."

To W. D. Howells, in Boston:

HARTFORD, Sept. 22, '89.

DEAR HOWELLS,—It is immensely good of you to grind through that stuff for me; but it gives peace to Mrs. Clemens's soul; and I am as grateful to you as a body can be. I am glad you approve of what I say about the French Revolution. Few people will. It is odd that even to this day Americans still observe that immortal benefaction through English and other monarchical eyes, and have no shred of an opinion about it that they didn't get at second-hand.

Next to the 4th of July and its results, it was the noblest and the holiest thing and the most precious that ever happened in this earth. And its gracious work is not done yet—not anywhere in the remote neighborhood of it.

Don't trouble to send me all the proofs; send me the pages with your corrections on them, and waste-basket the rest. We issue the book Dec. 10; consequently a notice that appears Dec. 20 will be just in good time.

I am waiting to see your Study set a fashion in criticism. When that happens—as please God it must—consider that if you lived three centuries you couldn't do a more valuable work for this country, or a humaner.

As a rule a critic's dissent merely enrages, and so does no good; but by the new art which you use, your dissent must be as welcome as your approval, and as valuable. I do not know what the secret of it is, unless it is your attitude—man courteously reasoning with man and brother, in place of the worn and wearisome critical attitude of all this long time—superior being lecturing a boy.

Well, my book is written—let it go. But if it were only to write over again there wouldn't be so many things left out. They burn in me; and they keep multiplying and multiplying; but now they can't ever be said. And besides, they would require a library—and a pen warmed up in hell.

Ys Ever

MARK.

The type-setting machine began to loom large in the background. Clemens believed it perfected by this time. Paige had got it together again and it was running steadily—or approximately so —setting type at a marvelous speed and with perfect accuracy. In time an expert operator would be able to set as high as eight thousand ems per hour, or about ten times as much as a good compositor could set and distribute by hand. Those who saw it were convinced—most of them—that the type-setting problem was solved by this great mechanical miracle. If there were any who doubted, it was because of its marvelously minute accuracy which the others only admired. Such accuracy, it was sometimes whispered, required absolutely perfect adjustment, and what would happen when the great inventor—"the poet in steel," as Clemens once called him—was no longer at hand to supervise and to correct the slightest variation. But no such breath of doubt came to Mark Twain; he believed the machine as reliable as a constellation.

But now there was need of capital to manufacture and market the wonder. Clemens, casting about in his mind, remembered Senator Jones, of Nevada, a man of great wealth, and his old friend, Joe Goodman, of Nevada, in whom Jones had unlimited confidence. He wrote to Goodman, and in this letter we get a pretty full exposition of the whole matter as it stood in the fall of 1889. We note in this communication that Clemens says that he has been at the machine three years and seven months, but this was only the period during which he had spent the regular monthly sum of three thousand dollars. His interest in the invention had begun as far back as 1880.

To Joseph T. Goodman, in Nevada:

Private. HARTFORD, Oct. 7, '89.

DEAR JOE,—I had a letter from Aleck Badlam day before yesterday, and in answering him I mentioned a matter which I asked him to consider a secret except to you and John McComb,—[This is Col. McComb, of the

Alta-California, who had sent Mark Twain on the Quaker City excursion]—as I am not ready yet to get into the newspapers.

I have come near writing you about this matter several times, but it wasn't ripe, and I waited. It is ripe, now. It is a type-setting machine which I undertook to build for the inventor (for a consideration). I have been at it three years and seven months without losing a day, at a cost of $3,000 a month, and in so private a way that Hartford has known nothing about it. Indeed only a dozen men have known of the matter. I have reported progress from time to time to the proprietors of the N. Y. Sun, Herald, Times, World, Harper Brothers and John F. Trow; also to the proprietors of the Boston Herald and the Boston Globe. Three years ago I asked all these people to squelch their frantic desire to load up their offices with the Mergenthaler (N. Y. Tribune) machine, and wait for mine and then choose between the two. They have waited—with no very gaudy patience—but still they have waited; and I could prove to them to-day that they have not lost anything by it. But I reserve the proof for the present—except in the case of the N. Y. Herald; I sent an invitation there the other day—a courtesy due a paper which ordered $240,000 worth of our machines long ago when it was still in a crude condition. The Herald has ordered its foreman to come up here next Thursday; but that is the only invitation which will go out for some time yet.

The machine was finished several weeks ago, and has been running ever since in the machine shop. It is a magnificent creature of steel, all of Pratt & Whitney's super-best workmanship, and as nicely adjusted and as accurate as a watch. In construction it is as elaborate and complex as that machine which it ranks next to, by every right—Man—and in performance it is as simple and sure.

Anybody can set type on it who can read—and can do it after only 15 minutes' instruction. The operator does not need to leave his seat at the keyboard; for the reason that he is not required to do anything but strike the keys and set type—merely one function; the spacing, justifying, emptying into the galley, and distributing of dead matter is all done by the machine without anybody's help—four functions.

The ease with which a cub can learn is surprising. Day before yesterday I saw our newest cub set, perfectly space and perfectly justify 2,150 ems of solid nonpareil in an hour and distribute the like amount in the same hour—and six hours previously he had never seen the machine or its keyboard. It was a good hour's work for 3-year veterans on the other type-setting machines to do. We have 3 cubs. The dean of the trio is a school youth of 18. Yesterday morning he had been an apprentice on the machine 16 working days (8-hour days); and we speeded him to see what he could do in an hour. In the hour he set 5,900 ems solid nonpareil, and the machine perfectly spaced and justified it, and of course distributed the like amount in the same hour. Considering that a good fair compositor sets 700 and distributes 700 in the one hour, this boy did the work of about 8 x a compositors in that hour. This fact sends all other type-setting machines a thousand miles to the rear, and the best of them will never be heard of again after we publicly exhibit in New York.

We shall put on 3 more cubs. We have one school boy and two compositors, now,—and we think of putting on a type writer, a stenographer, and perhaps a shoemaker, to show that no special gifts or training are required with this machine. We shall train these beginners two or three months—or until some one of them gets up to 7,000 an hour—then we will show up in New York and run the machine 24 hours a day 7 days in the week, for several months—to prove that this is a machine which will never get out of order or cause delay, and can stand anything an anvil can stand. You know there is no other typesetting machine that can run two hours on a stretch without causing trouble and delay with its incurable caprices.

We own the whole field—every inch of it—and nothing can dislodge us.

Now then, above is my preachment, and here follows the reason and purpose of it. I want you to run over here, roost over the machine a week and satisfy yourself, and then go to John P. Jones or to whom you please, and sell me a hundred thousand dollars' worth of this property and take ten per cent in cash or the "property" for your trouble—the latter, if you are wise, because the price I ask is a long way short of the value.

What I call "property" is this. A small part of my ownership consists of a royalty of $500 on every machine marketed under the American patents. My selling-terms are, a permanent royalty of one dollar on every American-marketed machine for a thousand dollars cash to me in hand paid. We shan't market any fewer than 5,000 machines in 15 years—a return of fifteen thousand dollars for one thousand. A royalty is better than stock, in one way—it must be paid, every six months, rain or shine; it is a debt, and must be paid before dividends are declared. By and by, when we become a stock company I shall buy these royalties back for stock if I can get them for anything like reasonable terms.

I have never borrowed a penny to use on the machine, and never sold a penny's worth of the property until the machine was entirely finished and proven by the severest tests to be what she started out to be—perfect, permanent, and occupying the position, as regards all kindred machines, which the City of Paris occupies as regards the canvas-backs of the mercantile marine.

It is my purpose to sell two hundred dollars of my royalties at the above price during the next two months and keep the other $300.

Mrs. Clemens begs Mrs. Goodman to come with you, and asks pardon for not writing the message herself—which would be a pathetically-welcome spectacle to me; for I have been her amanuensis for 8 months, now, since her eyes failed her. Yours as always

MARK.

While this letter with its amazing contents is on its way to astonish Joe Goodman, we will consider one of quite a different, but equally characteristic sort. We may assume that Mark Twain's sister Pamela had been visiting him in Hartford and was now making a visit in Keokuk.

To Mrs. Moffett, in Keokuk:

HARTFORD, Oct 9, '89.

DEAR PAMELA,—An hour after you left I was suddenly struck with a realizing sense of the utter chuckle-headedness of that notion of mine: to send your trunk after you. Land! it was idiotic. None but a lunatic would, separate himself from his baggage.

Well, I am soulfully glad the baggage fetcher saved me from consummating my insane inspiration. I met him on the street in the afternoon and paid him again. I shall pay him several times more, as opportunity offers.

I declined the invitation to banquet with the visiting South American Congress, in a polite note explaining that I had to go to New York today. I conveyed the note privately to Patrick; he got the envelope soiled, and asked Livy to put on a clean one. That is why I am going to the banquet; also why I have disinvited the boys I thought I was going to punch billiards with, upstairs to-night.

Patrick is one of the injudiciousest people I ever struck. And I am the other.

Your Brother

SAM.

The Yankee was now ready for publication, and advance sheets were already in the reviewers' hands. Just at this moment the Brazilian monarchy crumbled, and Clemens was moved to write Sylvester Baxter, of the Boston Herald, a letter which is of special interest in its prophecy of the new day, the dawn of which was even nearer than he suspected.

DEAR MR. BAXTER, Another throne has gone down, and I swim in oceans of satisfaction. I wish I might live fifty years longer; I believe I should see the thrones of Europe selling at auction for old iron. I believe I should really see the end of what is surely the grotesquest of all the swindles ever invented by man-monarchy. It is enough to make a graven image laugh, to see apparently rational people, away down here in this wholesome and merciless slaughter-day for shams, still mouthing empty reverence for those moss-backed frauds and scoundrelisms, hereditary kingship and so-called "nobility." It is enough to make the monarchs and nobles themselves laugh—and in private they do; there can be no question about that. I think there is only one funnier thing, and that is the spectacle of these bastard Americans—these Hamersleys and Huntingtons and such—offering cash, encumbered by themselves, for rotten carcases and stolen titles. When our great brethren the disenslaved Brazilians frame their Declaration of Independence, I hope they will insert this missing link: "We hold these truths to be self-evident: that all monarchs are usurpers, and descendants of usurpers; for the reason that no throne was ever set up in this world by the will, freely exercised, of the only body possessing the legitimate right to set it up—the numerical mass of the nation."

You already have the advance sheets of my forthcoming book in your hands. If you will turn to about the five hundredth page, you will find a state paper of my Connecticut Yankee in which he announces the dissolution of King Arthur's monarchy and proclaims the English Republic. Compare it with the state paper which announces the downfall of the Brazilian monarchy and proclaims the Republic of the United States of Brazil, and stand by to defend the Yankee from plagiarism. There is merely a resemblance of ideas, nothing more. The Yankee's proclamation was already in print a week ago. This is merely one of those odd coincidences which are always turning up. Come, protect the Yank from that cheapest and easiest of all charges—plagiarism. Otherwise, you see, he will have to protect himself by charging approximate and indefinite plagiarism upon the official servants of our majestic twin down yonder, and then there might be war, or some similar annoyance.

Have you noticed the rumor that the Portuguese throne is unsteady, and that the Portuguese slaves are getting restive? Also, that the head slave-driver of Europe, Alexander III, has so reduced his usual monthly order for chains that the Russian foundries are running on only half time now? Also that other rumor that English nobility acquired an added stench the other day—and had to ship it to India and the continent because there wasn't any more room for it at home? Things are working. By and by there is going to be an emigration, may be. Of course we shall make no preparation; we never do. In a few years from now we shall have nothing but played-out kings and dukes on the police, and driving the horse-cars, and whitewashing fences, and in fact overcrowding all the avenues of unskilled labor; and then we shall wish, when it is too late, that we had taken common and reasonable precautions and drowned them at Castle Garden.

There followed at this time a number of letters to Goodman, but as there is much of a sameness in them, we need not print them all. Clemens, in fact, kept the mails warm with letters bulging with schemes for capitalization, and promising vast wealth to all concerned. When the letters did not go fast enough he sent telegrams. In one of the letters Goodman is promised "five hundred thousand dollars out of the profits before we get anything ourselves." One thing we gather from these letters is that Paige has taken the machine apart again, never satisfied with its perfection, or perhaps getting a hint that certain of its perfections were not permanent. A letter at the end of November seems worth preserving here.

To Joseph T. Goodman, in California:

HARTFORD, Nov. 29, '89.

DEAR JOE, Things are getting into better and more flexible shape every day. Papers are now being drawn which will greatly simplify the raising of capital; I shall be in supreme command; it will not be necessary for the capitalist to arrive at terms with anybody but me. I don't want to dicker with anybody but Jones. I know him; that is to say, I want to dicker with you, and through you with Jones. Try to see if you can't be here by the 15th of January.

The machine was as perfect as a watch when we took her apart the other day; but when she goes together again the 15th of January we expect her to be perfecter than a watch.

Joe, I want you to sell some royalties to the boys out there, if you can, for I want to be financially strong when we go to New York. You know the machine, and you appreciate its future enormous career better than any man I know. At the lowest conceivable estimate (2,000 machines a year,) we shall sell 34,000 in the life of the patent—17 years.

All the family send love to you—and they mean it, or they wouldn't say it.

Yours ever

MARK.

The Yankee had come from the press, and Howells had praised it in the "Editor's Study" in Harper's Magazine. He had given it his highest commendation, and it seems that his opinion of it did not change with time. "Of all fanciful schemes of fiction it pleases me most," he in one place declared, and again referred to it as "a greatly imagined and symmetrically developed tale."

In more than one letter to Goodman, Clemens had urged him to come East without delay. "Take the train, Joe, and come along," he wrote early in December. And we judge from the following that Joe had decided to come.

To W. D. Howells, in Boston:

HARTFORD, Dec. 23, '89.

DEAR HOWELLS,—The magazine came last night, and the Study notice is just great. The satisfaction it affords us could not be more prodigious if the book deserved every word of it; and maybe it does; I hope it does, though of course I can't realize it and believe it. But I am your grateful servant, anyway and always.

I am going to read to the Cadets at West Point Jan. 11. I go from here to New York the 9th, and up to the Point the 11th. Can't you go with me? It's great fun. I'm going to read the passages in the "Yankee" in which the Yankee's West Point cadets figure—and shall covertly work in a lecture on aristocracy to those boys. I am to be the guest of the Superintendent, but if you will go I will shake him and we will go to the hotel. He is a splendid fellow, and I know him well enough to take that liberty.

And won't you give me a day or two's visit toward the end of January? For two reasons: the machine will be at work again by that time, and we want to hear the rest of the dream-story; Mrs. Clemens keeps speaking about it and hankering for it. And we can have Joe Goodman on hand again by that time, and I want you to get to know him thoroughly. It's well worth it. I am going to run up and stay over night with you as soon as I can get a chance.

We are in the full rush of the holidays now, and an awful rush it is, too. You ought to have been here the other day, to make that day perfect and complete. All alone I managed to inflict agonies on Mrs. Clemens, whereas I was expecting nothing but praises. I made a party call the day after the party—and called the lady down from breakfast to receive it. I then left there and called on a new bride, who received me in her dressing-gown; and as things went pretty well, I stayed to luncheon. The error here was, that the appointed reception-hour was 3 in the afternoon, and not at the bride's house but at her aunt's in another part of the town. However, as I meant well, none of these disasters distressed me.

Yrs ever

MARK.

The Yankee did not find a very hearty welcome in England. English readers did not fancy any burlesque of their Arthurian tales, or American strictures on their institutions. Mark Twain's publishers had feared this, and asked that the story be especially edited for the English edition. Clemens, however, would not listen to any suggestions of the sort.

To Messrs. Chatto & Windus, in London, Eng.:

GENTLEMEN,—Concerning The Yankee, I have already revised the story twice; and it has been read critically by W. D. Howells and Edmund Clarence Stedman, and my wife has caused me to strike out several passages that have been brought to her attention, and to soften others. Furthermore, I have read chapters of the book in public where Englishmen were present and have profited by their suggestions.

Now, mind you, I have taken all this pains because I wanted to say a Yankee mechanic's say against monarchy and its several natural props, and yet make a book which you would be willing to print exactly as it comes to you, without altering a word.

We are spoken of (by Englishmen) as a thin-skinned people. It is you who are thin-skinned. An Englishman may write with the most brutal frankness about any man or institution among us and we republish him without dreaming of altering a line or a word. But England cannot stand that kind of a book written about herself. It is England that is thin-skinned. It causeth me to smile when I read the modifications of my language which have been made in my English editions to fit them for the sensitive English palate.

Now, as I say, I have taken laborious pains to so trim this book of offense that you might not lack the nerve to print it just as it stands. I am going to get the proofs to you just as early as I can. I want you to read it carefully. If you can publish it without altering a single word, go ahead. Otherwise, please hand it to J. R. Osgood in time for him to have it published at my expense.

This is important, for the reason that the book was not written for America; it was written for England. So many Englishmen have done their sincerest best to teach us something for our betterment that it seems to me high time that some of us should substantially recognize the good intent by trying to pry up the English nation to a little higher level of manhood in turn.

Very truly yours,

S. L. CLEMENS.

The English nation, at least a considerable portion of it, did not wish to be "pried up to a higher level of manhood" by a Connecticut Yankee. The papers pretty generally denounced the book as coarse; in fact, a vulgar travesty. Some of the critics concluded that England, after all, had made a mistake in admiring Mark Twain. Clemens stood this for a time and then seems to have decided that something should be done. One of the foremost of English critics was his friend and admirer; he would state the case to him fully and invite his assistance.

To Andrew Lang, in London:

[First page missing.]

1889

They vote but do not print. The head tells you pretty promptly whether the food is satisfactory or not; and everybody hears, and thinks the whole man has spoken. It is a delusion. Only his taste and his smell have been heard from—important, both, in a way, but these do not build up the man; and preserve his life and fortify it.

The little child is permitted to label its drawings "This is a cow this is a horse," and so on. This protects the child. It saves it from the sorrow and wrong of hearing its cows and its horses criticized as kangaroos and work benches. A man who is white-washing a fence is doing a useful thing, so also is the man who is adorning a rich man's house with costly frescoes; and all of us are sane enough to judge these performances by standards proper to each. Now, then, to be fair, an author ought to be allowed to put upon his book an explanatory line: "This is written for the Head;" "This is written for the Belly and the Members." And the critic ought to hold himself in honor bound to put away from him his ancient habit of judging all books by one standard, and thenceforth follow a fairer course.

The critic assumes, every time, that if a book doesn't meet the cultivated-class standard, it isn't valuable. Let us apply his law all around: for if it is sound in the case of novels, narratives, pictures, and such things, it is certainly sound and applicable to all the steps which lead up to culture and make culture possible. It condemns the spelling book, for a spelling book is of no use to a person of culture; it condemns all school books and all schools which lie between the child's primer and Greek, and between the infant school and the university; it condemns all the rounds of art which lie between the cheap terra cotta groups and the Venus de Medici, and between the chromo and the Transfiguration; it requires Whitcomb Riley to sing no more till he can sing like Shakespeare, and it forbids all amateur music and will grant its sanction to nothing below the "classic."

Is this an extravagant statement? No, it is a mere statement of fact. It is the fact itself that is extravagant and grotesque. And what is the result? This—and it is sufficiently curious: the critic has actually imposed upon the world the superstition that a painting by Raphael is more valuable to the civilizations of the earth than is a chromo; and the august opera than the hurdy-gurdy and the villagers' singing society; and Homer than the little everybody's-poet whose rhymes are in all mouths today and will be in nobody's mouth next generation; and the Latin classics than Kipling's far-reaching bugle-note; and Jonathan Edwards than the Salvation Army; and the Venus de Medici than the plaster-cast peddler; the superstition, in a word, that the vast and awful comet that trails its cold lustre through the remote abysses of space once a century and interests and instructs a cultivated handful of astronomers is worth more to the world than the sun which warms and cheers all the nations every day and makes the crops to grow.

If a critic should start a religion it would not have any object but to convert angels: and they wouldn't need it. The thin top crust of humanity—the cultivated—are worth pacifying, worth pleasing, worth coddling, worth nourishing and preserving with dainties and delicacies, it is true; but to be caterer to that little faction is no very dignified or valuable occupation, it seems to me; it is merely feeding the over-fed, and there must be small satisfaction in that. It is not that little minority who are already saved that are best worth trying to uplift, I should think, but the mighty mass of the uncultivated who are underneath. That mass will never see the Old Masters—that sight is for the few; but the chromo maker can lift them all one step upward toward appreciation of art; they cannot have the opera, but the hurdy-gurdy and the singing class lift them a little way toward that far light; they will never know Homer, but the passing rhymester of their day leaves them higher than he found them; they may never even hear of the Latin classics, but they will strike step with Kipling's drum-beat, and they will march; for all Jonathan Edwards's help they would die in their slums, but the Salvation Army will beguile some of them up to pure air and a cleaner life; they know no sculpture, the Venus is not even a name to them, but they are a grade higher in the scale of civilization by the ministrations of the plaster-cast than they were before it took its place upon then mantel and made it beautiful to their unexacting eyes.

Indeed I have been misjudged, from the very first. I have never tried in even one single instance, to help cultivate the cultivated classes. I was not equipped for it, either by native gifts or training. And I never had any ambition in that direction, but always hunted for bigger game—the masses. I have seldom deliberately tried to instruct them, but have done my best to entertain them. To simply amuse them would have satisfied my dearest ambition at any time; for they could get instruction elsewhere, and I had two chances to help to the teacher's one: for amusement is a good preparation for study and a good healer of fatigue after it. My audience is dumb, it has no voice in print, and so I cannot know whether I have won its approbation or only got its censure.

Yes, you see, I have always catered for the Belly and the Members, but have been served like the others—criticized from the culture-standard—to my sorrow and pain; because, honestly, I never cared what became of the cultured classes; they could go to the theatre and the opera—they had no use for me and the melodeon.

And now at last I arrive at my object and tender my petition, making supplication to this effect: that the critics adopt a rule recognizing the Belly and the Members, and formulate a standard whereby work done for them shall be judged. Help me, Mr. Lang; no voice can reach further than yours in a case of this kind, or carry greater weight of authority.

Lang's reply was an article in the Illustrated London News on "The Art of Mark Twain." Lang had no admiration to express for the Yankee, which he confessed he had not cared to read, but he glorified Huck Finn to the highest. "I can never forget, nor be ungrateful for the exquisite pleasure with which I read Huckleberry Finn for the first time, years ago," he wrote; "I read it again last night, deserting Kenilworth for Huck. I never laid it down till I had finished it."

Lang closed his article by referring to the story of Huck as the "great American novel which had escaped the eyes of those who watched to see this new planet swim into their ken."

XXX. LETTERS, 1890, CHIEFLY TO JOS. T. GOODMAN. THE GREAT MACHINE ENTERPRISE

Dr. John Brown's son, whom Mark Twain and his wife had known in 1873 as "Jock," sent copies of Dr. John Brown and His Sister Isabella, by E. T. McLaren. It was a gift appreciated in the Clemens home.

To Mr. John Brown, in Edinburgh, Scotland:

HARTFORD, Feby 11, 1890.

DEAR MR. BROWN,—Both copies came, and we are reading and re-reading the one, and lending the other, to old time adorers of "Rab and his Friends." It is an exquisite book; the perfection of literary workmanship. It says in every line, "Don't look at me, look at him"—and one tries to be good and obey; but the charm of the painter is so strong that one can't keep his entire attention on the developing portrait, but must steal side-glimpses of the artist, and try to divine the trick of her felicitous brush. In this book the doctor lives and moves just as he was. He was the most extensive slave-holder of his time, and the kindest; and yet he died without setting one of his bondmen free. We all send our very, very kindest regards.

Sincerely yours

S. L. CLEMENS.

If Mark Twain had been less interested in the type-setting machine he might possibly have found a profit that winter in the old Sellers play, which he had written with Howells seven years before. The play had eventually been produced at the Lyceum Theatre in New York, with A. P. Burbank in the leading role, and Clemens and Howells as financial backers. But it was a losing investment, nor did it pay any better when Clemens finally sent Burbank with it on the road. Now, however, James A. Herne, a well-known actor and playwright, became interested in the idea, after a discussion of the matter with Howells, and there seemed a probability that with changes made under Herne's advisement the play might be made sensible and successful.

But Mark Twain's greater interest was now all in the type-machine, and certainly he had no money to put into any other venture. His next letter to Goodman is illuminating—the urgency of his need for funds opposed to that conscientiousness which was one of the most positive forces of Mark Twain's body spiritual. The Mr. Arnot of this letter was an Elmira capitalist.

To Jos. T. Goodman, in California:

HARTFORD, March 31, '90.

DEAR JOE,—If you were here, I should say, "Get you to Washington and beg Senator Jones to take the chances and put up about ten or "—no, I wouldn't. The money would burn a hole in my pocket and get away from me if the furnisher of it were proceeding upon merely your judgment and mine and without other evidence. It is too much of a responsibility.

But I am in as close a place to-day as ever I was; $3,000 due for the last month's machine-expenses, and the purse empty. I notified Mr. Arnot a month ago that I should want $5,000 to-day, and his check arrived last night; but I sent it back to him, because when he bought of me on the 9th of December I said that I would not draw upon him for 3 months, and that before that date Senator Jones would have examined the machine and approved, or done the other thing. If Jones should arrive here a week or ten days from now (as he expects to do,) and should not approve, and shouldn't buy any royalties, my deal with Arnot would not be symmetrically square, and then how could I refund? The surest way was to return his check.

I have talked with the madam, and here is the result. I will go down to the factory and notify Paige that I will scrape together $6,000 to meet the March and April expenses, and will retire on the 30th of April and return the assignment to him if in the meantime I have not found financial relief.

It is very rough; for the machine does at last seem perfect, and just a bird to go! I think she's going to be good for 8,000 ems an hour in the hands of a good ordinary man after a solid year's practice. I may be in error, but I most solidly believe it.

There's an improved Mergenthaler in New York; Paige and Davis and I watched it two whole afternoons.

With the love of us all,

MARK.

Arnot wrote Clemens urging him to accept the check for five thousand dollars in this moment of need. Clemens was probably as sorely tempted to compromise with his conscience as he had ever been in his life, but his resolution field firm.

To M. H. Arnot, in Elmira, N. Y.:

MR. M. H. ARNOT

DEAR SIR,—No—no, I could not think of taking it, with you unsatisfied; and you ought not to be satisfied until you have made personal examination of the machine and had a consensus of testimony of disinterested people, besides. My own perfect knowledge of what is required of such a machine, and my perfect knowledge of the fact that this is the only machine that can meet that requirement, make it difficult for me to realize that a doubt is possible to less well-posted men; and so I would have taken your money without thinking, and thus would have done a great wrong to you and a great one to myself. And now that I go back over the ground, I remember that where I said I could get along 3 months without drawing on you, that delay contemplated a visit from you to the machine in the interval, and your satisfaction with its character and prospects. I had forgotten all that. But I remember it now; and the fact that it was not "so nominated in the bond" does not alter the case or justify me in making my call so prematurely. I do not know that you regarded all that as a part of the bargain—for you were thoroughly and magnanimously unexacting—but I so regarded it, notwithstanding I have so easily managed to forget all about it.

You so gratified me, and did me so much honor in bonding yourself to me in a large sum, upon no evidence but my word and with no protection but my honor, that my pride in that is much stronger than my desire to reap a money advantage from it.

With the sincerest appreciation I am Truly yours

S L. CLEMENS.

P. S. I have written a good many words and yet I seem to have failed to say the main thing in exact enough language—which is, that the transaction between us is not complete and binding until you shall have convinced yourself that the machine's character and prospects are satisfactory.

I ought to explain that the grippe delayed us some weeks, and that we have since been waiting for Mr. Jones. When he was ready, we were not; and now we have been ready more than a month, while he has been kept in Washington by the Silver bill. He said the other day that to venture out of the Capitol for a day at this time could easily chance to hurt him if the bill came up for action, meantime, although it couldn't hurt the bill, which would pass anyway. Mrs. Jones said she would send me two or three days' notice, right after the passage of the bill, and that they would follow as soon as I should return word that their coming would not inconvenience us. I suppose I ought to go to New York without waiting for Mr. Jones, but it would not be wise to go there without money.

The bill is still pending.

The Mergenthaler machine, like the Paige, was also at this time in the middle stages of experimental development. It was a slower machine, but it was simpler, less expensive, occupied less room. There was not so much about it to get out of order; it was not so delicate, not so human. These were immense advantages.

But no one at this time could say with certainty which typesetter would reap the harvest of millions. It was only sure that at least one of them would, and the Mergenthaler people were willing to trade stock for stock with the Paige company in order to insure financial success for both, whichever won. Clemens, with a faith that never faltered, declined this offer, a decision that was to cost him millions.

Winter and spring had gone and summer had come, but still there had been no financial conclusion with Jones, Mackay, and the other rich Californians who were to put up the necessary million for the machine's manufacture. Goodman was spending a large part of his time traveling back and forth between California and Washington, trying to keep business going at both ends. Paige spent most of his time working out improvements for the type-setter, delicate attachments which complicated its construction more and more.

To Joe T. Goodman, in Washington:

HARTFORD, June 22, '90.

DEAR JOE,—I have been sitting by the machine 2 hours, this afternoon, and my admiration of it towers higher than ever. There is no sort of mistake about it, it is the Big Bonanza. In the 2 hours, the time lost by type-breakage was 3 minutes.

This machine is totally without a rival. Rivalry with it is impossible. Last Friday, Fred Whitmore (it was the 28th day of his apprenticeship on the machine) stacked up 49,700 ems of solid nonpareil in 8 hours, and the type-breaking delay was only 6 minutes for the day.

I claim yet, as I have always claimed, that the machine's market (abroad and here together,) is today worth $150,000,000 without saying anything about the doubling and trebling of this sum that will follow within the life of the patents. Now here is a queer fact: I am one of the wealthiest grandees in America—one of the Vanderbilt gang, in fact—and yet if you asked me to lend you a couple of dollars I should have to ask you to take my note instead.

It makes me cheerful to sit by the machine: come up with Mrs. Goodman and refresh yourself with a draught of the same.

Ys ever

MARK.

The machine was still breaking the types now and then, and no doubt Paige was itching to take it to pieces, and only restrained by force from doing so. He was never thoroughly happy unless he was taking the machine apart or setting it up again. Finally, he was allowed to go at it—a disasterous permission, for it was just then that Jones decided to steal a day or two from the Silver Bill and watch the type-setter in operation. Paige already had it in parts when this word came from Goodman, and Jones's visit had to be called off.

His enthusiasm would seem to have weakened from that day. In July, Goodman wrote that both Mackay and Jones had become somewhat diffident in the matter of huge capitalization. He thought it partly due, at least, to "the fatal delays that have sicklied over the bloom of original enthusiasm." Clemens himself went down to Washington and perhaps warmed Jones with his eloquence; at least, Jones seemed to have agreed to make some effort in the matter a qualified promise, the careful word of a wary politician and capitalist. How many Washington trips were made is not certain, but certainly more than one. Jones would seem to have suggested forms of contracts, but if he came to the point of signing any there is no evidence of it to-day.

Any one who has read Mark Twain's, "A Connecticut Yankee in King Arthur's Court," has a pretty good idea of his opinion of kings in general, and tyrants in particular. Rule by "divine right," however liberal, was distasteful to him; where it meant oppression it stirred him to violence. In his article, "The Czar's Soliloquy," he gave himself loose rein concerning atrocities charged to the master of Russia, and in a letter which he wrote during the summer of 1890, he offered a hint as to remedies. The letter was written by editorial request, but was never mailed. Perhaps it seemed too openly revolutionary at the moment.

Yet scarcely more than a quarter of a century was needed to make it "timely." Clemens and his family were spending some weeks in the Catskills when it was written.

An unpublished letter on the Czar.

ONTEORA, 1890.

TO THE EDITOR OF FREE RUSSIA,—I thank you for the compliment of your invitation to say something, but when I ponder the bottom paragraph on your first page, and then study your statement on your third page, of the objects of the several Russian liberation-parties, I do not quite know how to proceed. Let me quote here the paragraph referred to:

"But men's hearts are so made that the sight of one voluntary victim for a noble idea stirs them more deeply than the sight of a crowd submitting to a dire fate they cannot escape. Besides, foreigners could not see so clearly as the Russians how much the Government was responsible for the grinding poverty of the masses; nor could they very well realize the moral wretchedness imposed by that Government upon the whole of educated Russia. But the atrocities committed upon the defenceless prisoners are there in all their baseness, concrete and palpable, admitting of no excuse, no doubt or hesitation, crying out to the heart of humanity against Russian tyranny. And the Tzar's Government, stupidly confident in its apparently unassailable position, instead of taking warning from the first rebukes, seems to mock this humanitarian age by the aggravation of brutalities. Not satisfied with slowly killing its prisoners, and with burying the flower of our young generation in the Siberian desserts, the Government of Alexander III. resolved to break their spirit by deliberately submitting them to a regime of unheard-of brutality and degradation."

When one reads that paragraph in the glare of George Kennan's revelations, and considers how much it means; considers that all earthly figures fail to typify the Czar's government, and that one must descend into hell to find its counterpart, one turns hopefully to your statement of the objects of the several liberation-parties—and is disappointed. Apparently none of them can bear to think of losing the present hell entirely, they merely want the temperature cooled down a little.

I now perceive why all men are the deadly and uncompromising enemies of the rattlesnake: it is merely because the rattlesnake has not speech. Monarchy has speech, and by it has been able to persuade men that it differs somehow from the rattlesnake, has something valuable about it somewhere, something worth preserving, something even good and high and fine, when properly "modified," something entitling it to protection from the club of the first comer who catches it out of its hole. It seems a most strange delusion and not reconcilable with our superstition that man is a reasoning being. If a house is afire, we reason confidently that it is the first comer's plain duty to put the fire out in any way he can—drown it with water, blow it up with dynamite, use any and all means to stop the spread of the fire and save the rest of the city. What is the Czar of Russia but a house afire in the midst of a city of eighty millions of inhabitants? Yet instead of extinguishing him, together with his nest and system, the liberation-parties are all anxious to merely cool him down a little and keep him.

It seems to me that this is illogical—idiotic, in fact. Suppose you had this granite-hearted, bloody-jawed maniac of Russia loose in your house, chasing the helpless women and little children—your own. What would you do with him, supposing you had a shotgun? Well, he is loose in your house-Russia. And with your shotgun in your hand, you stand trying to think up ways to "modify" him.

Do these liberation-parties think that they can succeed in a project which has been attempted a million times in the history of the world and has never in one single instance been successful—the "modification" of a despotism by other means than bloodshed? They seem to think they can. My privilege to write these sanguinary sentences in soft security was bought for me by rivers of blood poured upon many fields, in many lands, but I possess not one single little paltry right or privilege that come to me as a result of petition, persuasion, agitation for reform, or any kindred method of procedure. When we consider that not even the most responsible English monarch ever yielded back a stolen public right until it was wrenched from them by bloody violence, is it rational to suppose that gentler methods can win privileges in Russia?

Of course I know that the properest way to demolish the Russian throne would be by revolution. But it is not possible to get up a revolution there; so the only thing left to do, apparently, is to keep the throne vacant by dynamite until a day when candidates shall decline with thanks. Then organize the Republic. And on the whole this method has some large advantages; for whereas a revolution destroys some lives which cannot well be spared, the dynamite way doesn't. Consider this: the conspirators against the Czar's life are caught in every rank of life, from the low to the high. And consider: if so many take an active part, where the peril is so dire, is this not evidence that the sympathizers who keep still and do not show their hands, are countless for multitudes? Can you break the hearts of thousands of families with the awful Siberian exodus every year for generations and not eventually cover all Russia from limit to limit with bereaved fathers and mothers and brothers and sisters who secretly hate the perpetrator of this prodigious crime and hunger and thirst for his life? Do you not believe that if your wife or your child or your father was exiled to the mines of Siberia for some trivial utterances wrung from a smarting spirit by the Czar's intolerable tyranny, and you got a chance to kill him and did not do it, that you would always be ashamed to be in your own society the rest of your life? Suppose that that refined and lovely Russian lady who was lately stripped bare before a brutal soldiery and whipped to death by the Czar's hand in the person of the Czar's creature had been your wife, or your daughter or your sister, and to-day the Czar should pass within reach of your hand, how would you feel—and what would you do? Consider, that all over vast Russia, from boundary to boundary, a myriad of eyes filled with tears when that piteous news came, and through those tears that myriad of eyes saw, not that poor lady, but lost darlings of their own whose fate her fate brought back with new access of grief out of a black and bitter past never to be forgotten or forgiven.

If I am a Swinburnian—and clear to the marrow I am—I hold human nature in sufficient honor to believe there are eighty million mute Russians that are of the same stripe, and only one Russian family that isn't.

MARK TWAIN.

Type-setter matters were going badly. Clemens still had faith in Jones, and he had lost no grain of faith in the machine. The money situation, however, was troublesome. With an expensive establishment, and work of one sort or another still to be done on the machine, his income would not reach. Perhaps Goodman had already given up hope, for he does not seem to have returned from California after the next letter was written—a colorless letter —in which we feel a note of resignation. The last few lines are sufficient.

To Joe T. Goodman, in California:

DEAR JOE,—...... I wish you could get a day off and make those two or three Californians buy those privileges, for I'm going to need money before long.

I don't know where the Senator is; but out on the Coast I reckon.

I guess we've got a perfect machine at last. We never break a type, now, and the new device for enabling the operator to touch the last letters and justify the line simultaneously works, to a charm.

With love to you both,

MARK

The year closed gloomily enough. The type-setter seemed to be perfected, but capital for its manufacture was not forthcoming. The publishing business of Charles L. Webster & Co. was returning little or no profit. Clemens's mother had died in Keokuk at the end of October, and his wife's mother, in Elmira a month later. Mark Twain, writing a short business letter to his publishing manager, Fred J. Ball, closed it: "Merry Xmas to you!—and I wish to God I could have one myself before I die."

XXXI. LETTERS, 1891, TO HOWELLS, MRS. CLEMENS AND OTHERS. RETURN TO LITERATURE. AMERICAN CLAIMANT. LEAVING HARTFORD. EUROPE. DOWN THE RHINE.

Clemens was still not without hope in the machine, at the beginning of the new year (1891) but it was a hope no longer active, and it presently became a moribund. Jones, on about the middle of February, backed out altogether, laying the blame chiefly on Mackay and the others, who, he said, had decided not to invest. Jones "let his victim down easy" with friendly words, but it was the end, for the present, at least, of machine financiering.

It was also the end of Mark Twain's capital. His publishing business was not good. It was already in debt and needing more money. There was just one thing for him to do and he did it at once, not stopping to cry over spilt milk, but with good courage and the old enthusiasm that never failed him, he returned to the trade of authorship. He dug out half-finished articles and stories, finished them and sold them, and within a week after the Jones collapse he was at work on a novel based an the old Sellers idea, which eight years before he and Howells had worked into a play. The brief letter in which he reported this news to Howells bears no marks of depression, though the writer of it was in his fifty-sixth year; he was by no means well, and his financial prospects were anything but golden.

To W. D. Howells, in Boston:

HARTFORD, Feb. 24, '91

DEAR HOWELLS,—Mrs. Clemens has been sick abed for near two weeks, but is up and around the room now, and gaining. I don't know whether she has written Mrs. Howells or not—I only know she was going to—and will yet, if she hasn't. We are promising ourselves a whole world of pleasure in the visit, and you mustn't dream of disappointing us.

Does this item stir an interest in you? Began a novel four days ago, and this moment finished chapter four. Title of the book:

"Colonel Mulberry Sellers.

American Claimant

Of the

Great Earldom of Rossmore'

in the

Peerage of Great Britain."

Ys Ever

MARK.

Probably Mark Twain did not return to literary work reluctantly. He had always enjoyed writing and felt now that he was equipped better than ever for authorship, at least so far as material was concerned. There exists a fragmentary copy of a letter to some unknown correspondent, in which he recites his qualifications. It bears evidence of having been written just at this time and is of unusual interest at this point.

Fragment of Letter to ———, 1891:

.... I confine myself to life with which I am familiar when pretending to portray life. But I confined myself to the boy-life out on the Mississippi because that had a peculiar charm for me, and not because I was not familiar with other phases of life. I was a soldier two weeks once in the beginning of the war, and was hunted like a rat the whole time. Familiar? My splendid Kipling himself hasn't a more burnt-in, hard-baked, and unforgetable familiarity with that death-on-the-pale-horse-with-hell-following-after, which is a raw soldier's first fortnight in the field—and which, without any doubt, is the most tremendous fortnight and the vividest he is ever going to see.

Yes, and I have shoveled silver tailings in a quartz-mill a couple of weeks, and acquired the last possibilities of culture in that direction. And I've done "pocket-mining" during three months in the one little patch of ground in the whole globe where Nature conceals gold in pockets—or did before we robbed all of those pockets and exhausted, obliterated, annihilated the most curious freak Nature ever indulged in. There are not thirty men left alive who, being told there was a pocket hidden on the broad slope of a mountain, would know how to go and find it, or have even the faintest idea of how to set about it; but I am one of the possible 20 or 30 who possess the secret, and I could go and put my hand on that hidden treasure with a most deadly precision.

And I've been a prospector, and know pay rock from poor when I find it—just with a touch of the tongue. And I've been a silver miner and know how to dig and shovel and drill and put in a blast. And so I know the mines and the miners interiorly as well as Bret Harte knows them exteriorly.

And I was a newspaper reporter four years in cities, and so saw the inside of many things; and was reporter in a legislature two sessions and the same in Congress one session, and thus learned to know personally three sample bodies of the smallest minds and the selfishest souls and the cowardliest hearts that God makes.

And I was some years a Mississippi pilot, and familiarly knew all the different kinds of steam-boatmen—a race apart, and not like other folk.

And I was for some years a traveling "jour" printer, and wandered from city to city—and so I know that sect familiarly.

And I was a lecturer on the public platform a number of seasons and was a responder to toasts at all the different kinds of banquets—and so I know a great many secrets about audiences—secrets not to be got out of books, but only acquirable by experience.

And I watched over one dear project of mine for years, spent a fortune on it, and failed to make it go—and the history of that would make a large book in which a million men would see themselves as in a mirror; and they would testify and say, Verily, this is not imagination; this fellow has been there—and after would cast dust upon their heads, cursing and blaspheming.

And I am a publisher, and did pay to one author's widow (General Grant's) the largest copyright checks this world has seen—aggregating more than L80,000 in the first year.

And I have been an author for 20 years and an ass for 55.

Now then; as the most valuable capital or culture or education usable in the building of novels is personal experience I ought to be well equipped for that trade.

I surely have the equipment, a wide culture, and all of it real, none of it artificial, for I don't know anything about books.

[No signature.]

Clemens for several years had been bothered by rheumatism in his shoulder. The return now to the steady use of the pen aggravated his trouble, and at times he was nearly disabled. The phonograph for commercial dictation had been tried experimentally, and Mark Twain was always ready for any innovation.

To W. D. Howells, in Boston:

HARTFORD, Feb. 28, '91.

DEAR HOWELLS,—Won't you drop-in at the Boylston Building (New England Phonograph Co) and talk into a phonograph in an ordinary conversation-voice and see if another person (who didn't hear you do it) can take the words from the thing without difficulty and repeat them to you. If the experiment is satisfactory (also make somebody put in a message which you don't hear, and see if afterward you can get it out without difficulty) won't you then ask them on what terms they will rent me a phonograph for 3 months and furnish me cylinders enough to carry 75,000 words. 175 cylinders, ain't it?

I don't want to erase any of them. My right arm is nearly disabled by rheumatism, but I am bound to write this book (and sell 100,000 copies of it—no, I mean a million—next fall) I feel sure I can dictate the book into a phonograph if I don't have to yell. I write 2,000 words a day; I think I can dictate twice as many.

But mind, if this is going to be too much trouble to you—go ahead and do it, all the same.

Ys ever

MARK.

Howells, always willing to help, visited the phonograph place, and a few days later reported results. He wrote: "I talked your letter into a fonograf in my usual tone at my usual gait of speech. Then the fonograf man talked his answer in at his wonted swing and swell. Then we took the cylinder to a type-writer in the next room, and she put the hooks into her ears and wrote the whole out. I send you the result. There is a mistake of one word. I think that if you have the cheek to dictate the story into the fonograf, all the rest is perfectly easy. It wouldn't fatigue me to talk for an hour as I did."

Clemens did not find the phonograph entirely satisfactory, at least not for a time, and he appears never to have used it steadily. His early experience with it, however, seems interesting.

To W. D. Howells, in Boston:

HARTFORD, Apl. 4, '91.

DEAR HOWELLS,—I'm ashamed. It happened in this way. I was proposing to acknowledge the receipt of the play and the little book per phonograph, so that you could see that the instrument is good enough for mere letter-writing; then I meant to add the fact that you can't write literature with it, because it hasn't any ideas and it hasn't any gift for elaboration, or smartness of talk, or vigor of action, or felicity of expression, but is just matter-of-fact, compressive, unornamental, and as grave and unsmiling as the devil.

I filled four dozen cylinders in two sittings, then found I could have said about as much with the pen and said it a deal better. Then I resigned.

I believe it could teach one to dictate literature to a phonographer—and some time I will experiment in that line.

The little book is charmingly written, and it interested me. But it flies too high for me. Its concretest things are filmy abstractions to me, and when I lay my grip on one of them and open my hand, I feel as embarrassed as I use to feel when I thought I had caught a fly. I'm going to try to mail it back to you to-day—I mean I am going to charge my memory. Charging my memory is one of my chief industries....

With our loves and our kindest regards distributed among you according to the proprieties.

Yrs ever

MARK.

P. S.—I'm sending that ancient "Mental Telegraphy" article to Harper's—with a modest postscript. Probably read it to you years ago.

S. L. C.

The "little book" mentioned in this letter was by Swedenborg, an author in whom the Boston literary set was always deeply interested. "Mental Telegraphy" appeared in Harper's Magazine, and is now included in the Uniform Edition of Mark Twain's books. It was written in 1878.

Joe Goodman had long since returned to California, it being clear that nothing could be gained by remaining in Washington. On receipt of the news of the type-setter's collapse he sent a consoling word. Perhaps he thought Clemens would rage over the unhappy circumstance, and possibly hold him in some measure to blame. But it was generally the smaller annoyances of life that made Mark Twain rage; the larger catastrophes were likely to stir only his philosophy.

The Library of American Literature, mentioned in the following letter, was a work in many volumes, edited by Edmund Clarence Stedman and Ellen Mackay Hutchinson.

To Joe T. Goodman:

April [?] 1891.

DEAR JOE, Well, it's all right, anyway. Diplomacy couldn't have saved it—diplomacy of mine—at that late day. I hadn't any diplomacy in stock, anyway. In order to meet Jones's requirements I had to surrender the old contract (a contract which made me boss of the situation and gave me the whip-hand of Paige) and allow the new one to be drafted and put in its place. I was running an immense risk, but it was justified by Jones's promises—promises made to me not merely once but every time I tallied with him. When February arrived, I saw signs which were mighty plain reading. Signs which meant that Paige was hoping and praying that Jones would go back on me—which would leave Paige boss, and me robbed and out in the cold. His prayers were answered, and I am out in the cold. If I ever get back my nine-twentieths interest, it will be by law-suit—which will be instituted in the indefinite future, when the time comes.

I am at work again—on a book. Not with a great deal of spirit, but with enough—yes, plenty. And I am pushing my publishing house. It has turned the corner after cleaning $50,000 a year for three consecutive years, and piling every cent of it into one book—Library of American Literature—and from next January onward it will resume dividends. But I've got to earn $50,000 for it between now and then—which I will do if I keep my health. This additional capital is needed for that same book, because its prosperity is growing so great and exacting.

It is dreadful to think of you in ill health—I can't realize it; you are always to me the same that you were in those days when matchless health, and glowing spirits and delight in life were commonplaces with us. Lord save us all from old age and broken health and a hope-tree that has lost the faculty of putting out blossoms.

With love to you both from us all.

MARK.

Mark Twain's residence in Hartford was drawing rapidly to a close. Mrs. Clemens was poorly, and his own health was uncertain. They believed that some of the European baths would help them.

Furthermore, Mark Twain could no longer afford the luxury of his Hartford home. In Europe life could be simpler and vastly cheaper. He was offered a thousand dollars apiece for six European letters, by the McClure syndicate and W. M. Laffan, of the Sun. This would at least give him a start on the other side. The family began immediately their sad arrangements for departure.

To Fred J. Hall (manager Chas. L. Webster & Co.), N. Y.:

HARTFORD, Apl. 14, '91.

DEAR MR. HALL,—Privately—keep it to yourself—as you, are already aware, we are going to Europe in June, for an indefinite stay. We shall sell the horses and shut up the house. We wish to provide a place for our coachman, who has been with us a 21 years, and is sober, active, diligent, and unusually bright and capable. You spoke of hiring a colored man as engineer and helper in the packing room. Patrick would soon learn that trade and be very valuable. We will cease to need him by the middle or end of June. Have you made irrevocable arrangements with the colored man, or would you prefer to have Patrick, if he thinks he would like to try?

I have not said anything to him about it yet.

Yours

S. L. C.

It was to be a complete breaking up of their beautiful establishment. Patrick McAleer, George the butler, and others of their household help had been like members of the family. We may guess at the heartbreak of it all, even though the letters remain cheerful.

Howells, strangely enough, seems to have been about the last one to be told of their European plans; in fact, he first got wind of it from the papers, and wrote for information. Likely enough Clemens had not until then had the courage to confess.

To W. D. Howells, in Boston:

HARTFORD, May 20, '91.

DEAR HOWELLS,—For her health's sake Mrs. Clemens must try baths somewhere, and this it is that has determined us to go to Europe. The water required seems to be provided at a little obscure and little-visited nook up in the hills back of the Rhine somewhere and you get to it by Rhine traffic-boat and country stage-coach. Come, get "sick or sorry enough" and join us. We shall be a little while at that bath, and the rest of the summer at Annecy (this confidential to you) in Haute Savoie, 22 miles from Geneva. Spend the winters in Berlin. I don't know how long we shall be in Europe—I have a vote, but I don't cast it. I'm going to do whatever the others desire, with leave to change their mind, without prejudice, whenever they want to. Travel has no longer, any charm for me. I have seen all the foreign countries I want to see except heaven and hell, and I have only a vague curiosity as concerns one of those.

I found I couldn't use the play—I had departed too far from its lines when I came to look at it. I thought I might get a great deal of dialogue out of it, but I got only 15 loosely written pages—they saved me half a days work. It was the cursing phonograph. There was abundance of good dialogue, but it couldn't befitted into the new conditions of the story.

Oh, look here—I did to-day what I have several times in past years thought of doing: answered an interviewing proposition from a rich newspaper with the reminder that they had not stated the terms; that my time was all occupied with writing, at good pay, and that as talking was harder work I should not care to venture it unless I knew the pay was going to be proportionately higher. I wish I had thought of this the other day when Charley Stoddard turned a pleasant Englishman loose on me and I couldn't think of any rational excuse.

Ys Ever

MARK.

Clemens had finished his Sellers book and had disposed of the serial rights to the McClure syndicate. The house in Hartford was closed early in June, and on the 6th the family, with one maid, Katie Leary, sailed on the Gascogne. Two weeks later they had begun a residence abroad which was to last for more than nine years.

It was not easy to get to work in Europe. Clemens's arm remained lame, and any effort at writing brought suffering. The Century Magazine proposed another set of letters, but by the end of July he had barely begun on those promised to McClure and Laffan. In August, however, he was able to send three: one from Aix about the baths there, another from Bayreuth concerning the Wagner festival, and a third from Marienbad, in Bohemia, where they rested for a time. He decided that he would arrange for no more European letters when the six were finished, but would gather material for a book. He would take a courier and a kodak and go tramping again in some fashion that would be interesting to do and to write.

The idea finally matured when he reached Switzerland and settled the family at the Hotel Beau Rivage, Ouchy, Lausanne, facing Lake Leman.

He decided to make a floating trip down the Rhone, and he engaged Joseph Very, a courier that had served him on a former European trip, to accompany him. The courier went over to Bourget and bought for five dollars a flat-bottomed boat and engaged its owner as their pilot. It was the morning of September 20, when they began their floating-trip down the beautiful historic river that flows through the loveliest and most romantic region of France. He wrote daily to Mrs. Clemens, and his letters tell the story of that drowsy, happy experience better than the notes made with a view to publication. Clemens had arrived at Lake Bourget on the evening before the morning of their start and slept on the Island of Chatillon, in an old castle of the same name. Lake Bourget connects with the Rhone by a small canal.

Letters and Memoranda to Mrs. Clemens, in Ouchy, Switzerland:

Sept. 20, 1891.

Sunday, 11 a.m.

On the lake Bourget—just started. The castle of Chatillon high overhead showing above the trees. It was a wonderfully still place to sleep in. Beside us there was nobody in it but a woman, a boy and a dog. A Pope was born in the room I slept in. No, he became a Pope later.

The lake is smooth as glass—a brilliant sun is shining.

Our boat is comfortable and shady with its awning.

11.20 We have crossed the lake and are entering the canal. Shall presently be in the Rhone.

Noon. Nearly down to the Rhone. Passing the village of Chanaz.

3.15 p. m. Sunday. We have been in the Rhone 3 hours. It is unimaginably still and reposeful and cool and soft and breezy. No rowing or work of any kind to do—we merely float with the current—we glide noiseless and swift—as fast as a London cab-horse rips along—8 miles an hour—the swiftest current I've ever boated in. We have the entire river to ourselves—nowhere a boat of any kind.

Good bye Sweetheart

S. L. C.

PORT DE GROLEE, Monday, 4.15 p.m.

[Sept. 21, 1891]

Name of the village which we left five minutes ago.

We went ashore at 5 p. m. yesterday, dear heart, and walked a short mile to St. Geuix, a big village, and took quarters at the principal inn; had a good dinner and afterwards along walk out of town on the banks of the Guiers till 7.30.

Went to bed at 8.30 and continued to make notes and read books and newspapers till midnight. Slept until 8, breakfasted in bed, and lay till noon, because there had been a very heavy rain in the night and the day was still dark and lowering. But at noon the sun broke through and in 15 minutes we were tramping toward the river. Got afloat at 1 p. m. but at 2.40 we had to rush suddenly ashore and take refuge in the above village. Just as we got ourselves and traps safely housed in the inn, the rain let go and came down in great style. We lost an hour and a half there, but we are off again, now, with bright sunshine.

I wrote you yesterday my darling, and shall expect to write you every day.

Good-day, and love to all of you.

SAML.

ON THE RHONE BELOW VILLEBOIS,

Tuesday noon.

Good morning, sweetheart. Night caught us yesterday where we had to take quarters in a peasant's house which was occupied by the family and a lot of cows and calves—also several rabbits.—[His word for fleas.]—The latter had a ball, and I was the ball-room; but they were very friendly and didn't bite.

The peasants were mighty kind and hearty, and flew around and did their best to make us comfortable. This morning I breakfasted on the shore in the open air with two sociable dogs and a cat. Clean cloth, napkin and table furniture, white sugar, a vast hunk of excellent butter, good bread, first class coffee with pure milk, fried fish just caught. Wonderful that so much cleanliness should come out of such a phenomenally dirty house.

An hour ago we saw the Falls of the Rhone, a prodigiously rough and dangerous looking place; shipped a little water but came to no harm. It was one of the most beautiful pieces of piloting and boat-management I ever saw. Our admiral knew his business.

We have had to run ashore for shelter every time it has rained heretofore, but Joseph has been putting in his odd time making a water-proof sun-bonnet for the boat, and now we sail along dry although we had many heavy showers this morning.

With a word of love to you all and particularly you,

SAML.

ON THE RHONE, BELOW VIENNA.

I salute you, my darling. Your telegram reached me in Lyons last night and was very pleasant news indeed.

I was up and shaved before 8 this morning, but we got delayed and didn't sail from Lyons till 10.30—an hour and a half lost. And we've lost another hour—two of them, I guess—since, by an error. We came in sight of Vienne at 2 o'clock, several miles ahead, on a hill, and I proposed to walk down there and let the boat go ahead of us. So Joseph and I got out and struck through a willow swamp along a dim path, and by and by came out on the steep bank of a slough or inlet or something, and we followed that bank forever and ever trying to get around the head of that slough. Finally I noticed a twig standing up in the water, and by George it had a distinct and even vigorous quiver to it! I don't know when I have felt so much like a donkey. On an island! I wanted to drown somebody, but I hadn't anybody I could spare. However, after another long tramp we found a lonely native, and he had a scow and soon we were on the mainland—yes, and a blamed sight further from Vienne than we were when we started.

Notes—I make millions of them; and so I get no time to write to you. If you've got a pad there, please send it poste-restante to Avignon. I may not need it but I fear I shall.

I'm straining to reach St. Pierre de Boef, but it's going to be a close fit, I reckon.

AFLOAT, Friday, 3 p.m., '91.

Livy darling, we sailed from St. Pierre de Boef six hours ago, and are now approaching Tournon, where we shall not stop, but go on and make Valence, a City Of 25,000 people. It's too delicious, floating with the swift current under the awning these superb sunshiny days in deep peace and quietness. Some of these curious old historical towns strangely persuade me, but it is so lovely afloat that I don't stop, but view them from the outside and sail on. We get abundance of grapes and peaches for next to nothing.

Joseph is perfect. He is at his very best—and never was better in his life. I guess he gets discouraged and feels disliked and in the way when he is lying around—but here he is perfection, and brim full of useful alacrities and helps and ingenuities.

When I woke up an hour ago and heard the clock strike 4, I said "I seem to have been asleep an immensely long time; I must have gone to bed mighty early; I wonder what time I did go to bed." And I got up and lit a candle and looked at my watch to see.

AFLOAT

2 HOURS BELOW BOURG ST. ANDEOL.

Monday, 11 a.m., Sept. 28.

Livy darling, I didn't write yesterday. We left La Voulte in a driving storm of cold rain—couldn't write in it—and at 1 p. m. when we were not thinking of stopping, we saw a picturesque and mighty ruin on a high hill back of a village, and I was seized with a desire to explore it; so we landed at once and set out with rubbers and umbrella, sending the boat ahead to St. Andeol, and we spent 3 hours clambering about those cloudy heights among those worn and vast and idiotic ruins of a castle built by two crusaders 650 years ago. The work of these asses was full of interest, and we had a good time inspecting, examining and scrutinizing it. All the hills on both sides of the Rhone have peaks and precipices, and each has its gray and wasted pile of mouldy walls and broken towers. The Romans displaced the Gauls, the Visigoths displaced the Romans, the Saracens displaced the Visigoths, the Christians displaced the Saracens, and it was these pious animals who built these strange lairs and cut each other's throats in the name and for the glory of God, and robbed and burned and slew in peace and war; and the pauper and the slave built churches, and the credit of it went to the Bishop who racked the money out of them. These are pathetic shores, and they make one despise the human race.

We came down in an hour by rail, but I couldn't get your telegram till this morning, for it was Sunday and they had shut up the post office to go to the circus. I went, too. It was all one family—parents and 5 children—performing in the open air to 200 of these enchanted villagers, who contributed coppers when called on. It was a most gay and strange and pathetic show. I got up at 7 this morning to see the poor devils cook their poor breakfast and pack up their sordid fineries.

This is a 9 k-m. current and the wind is with us; we shall make Avignon before 4 o'clock. I saw watermelons and pomegranates for sale at St. Andeol.

With a power of love, Sweetheart.

SAML.

HOTEL D'EUROPE, AVIGNON,

Monday, 6 p.m., Sept. 28.

Well, Livy darling, I have been having a perfect feast of letters for an hour, and I thank you and dear Clam with all my heart. It's like hearing from home after a long absence.

It is early to be in bed, but I'm always abed before 9, on this voyage; and up at 7 or a trifle later, every morning. If I ever take such a trip again, I will have myself called at the first tinge of dawn and get to sea as soon after as possible. The early dawn on the water-nothing can be finer, as I know by old Mississippi experience. I did so long for you and Sue yesterday morning—the most superb sunrise!—the most marvelous sunrise! and I saw it all from the very faintest suspicion of the coming dawn all the way through to the final explosion of glory. But it had interest private to itself and not to be found elsewhere in the world; for between me and it, in the far distant-eastward, was a silhouette mountain-range in which I had discovered, the previous afternoon, a most noble face upturned to the sky, and mighty form out stretched, which I had named Napoleon Dreaming of Universal Empire—and now, this prodigious face, soft, rich, blue, spirituelle, asleep, tranquil, reposeful, lay against that giant conflagration of ruddy and golden splendors all rayed like a wheel with the upstreaming and far-reaching lances of the sun. It made one want to cry for delight, it was so supreme in its unimaginable majesty and beauty.

We had a curious experience today. A little after I had sealed and directed my letter to you, in which I said we should make Avignon before 4, we got lost. We ceased to encounter any village or ruin mentioned in our "particularizes" and detailed Guide of the Rhone—went drifting along by the hour in a wholly unknown land and on an uncharted river! Confound it, we stopped talking and did nothing but stand up in the boat and search the horizons with the glass and wonder what in the devil had happened. And at last, away yonder at 5 o'clock when some east towers and fortresses hove in sight we couldn't recognize them for Avignon—yet we knew by the broken bridge that it was Avignon.

Then we saw what the trouble was—at some time or other we had drifted down the wrong side of an island and followed a sluggish branch of the Rhone not frequented in modern times. We lost an hour and a half by it and missed one of the most picturesque and gigantic and history-sodden masses of castellated medieval ruin that Europe can show.

It was dark by the time we had wandered through the town and got the letters and found the hotel—so I went to bed.

We shall leave here at noon tomorrow and float down to Arles, arriving about dark, and there bid good bye to the boat, the river-trip finished. Between Arles and Nimes (and Avignon again,) we shall be till Saturday morning—then rail it through on that day to Ouchy, reaching the hotel at 11 at night if the train isn't late.

Next day (Sunday) if you like, go to Basel, and Monday to Berlin. But I shall be at your disposal, to do exactly as you desire and prefer.

With no end of love to all of you and twice as much to you,

sweetheart,

SAML.

I believe my arm is a trifle better than it was when I started.

The mention in the foregoing letter of the Napoleon effigy is the beginning of what proved to be a rather interesting episode. Mark Twain thought a great deal of his discovery, as he called it—the giant figure of Napoleon outlined by the distant mountain range. In his note-book he entered memoranda telling just where it was to be seen, and added a pencil sketch of the huge profile. But then he characteristically forgot all about it, and when he recalled the incident ten years later, he could not remember the name of the village, Beauchastel, from which the great figure could be seen; also, that he had made a record of the place.

But he was by this time more certain than ever that his discovery was a remarkable one, which, if known, would become one of the great natural wonders, such as Niagara Falls. Theodore Stanton was visiting him at the time, and Clemens urged him, on his return to France, to make an excursion to the Rhone and locate the Lost Napoleon, as he now called it. But Clemens remembered the wonder as being somewhere between Arles and Avignon, instead of about a hundred miles above the last-named town. Stanton naturally failed to find it, and it remained for the writer of these notes, motoring up the Rhone one September day, exactly twenty-two years after the first discovery, to re-locate the vast reclining figure of the first consul of France, "dreaming of Universal Empire." The re-discovery was not difficult—with Mark Twain's memoranda as a guide—and it was worth while. Perhaps the Lost Napoleon is not so important a natural wonder as Mark Twain believed, but it is a striking picture, and on a clear day the calm blue face outlined against the sky will long hold the traveler's attention.

To Clara Clemens, in Ouchy, Switzerland:

AFLOAT, 11.20 a.m., Sept. 29, Tuesday.

DEAR OLD BEN,—The vast stone masses and huge towers of the

ancient papal palace of Avignon are projected above an intervening wooded island a mile up the river behind me—for we are already on our way to Arles. It is a perfectly still morning, with a brilliant sun, and very hot—outside; but I am under cover of the linen hood, and it is cool and shady in here.

Please tell mamma I got her very last letter this morning, and I perceive by it that I do not need to arrive at Ouchy before Saturday midnight. I am glad, because I couldn't do the railroading I am proposing to do during the next two or three days and get there earlier. I could put in the time till Sunday midnight, but shall not venture it without telegraphic instructions from her to Nimes day after tomorrow, Oct. 1, care Hotel Manivet.

The only adventures we have is in drifting into rough seas now and then. They are not dangerous, but they go thro' all the motions of it. Yesterday when we shot the Bridge of the Holy Spirit it was probably in charge of some inexperienced deputy spirit for the day, for we were allowed to go through the wrong arch, which brought us into a tourbillon below which tried to make this old scow stand on its head. Of course I lost my temper and blew it off in a way to be heard above the roar of the tossing waters. I lost it because the admiral had taken that arch in deference to my opinion that it was the best one, while his own judgment told him to take the one nearest the other side of the river. I could have poisoned him I was so mad to think I had hired such a turnip. A boatman in command should obey nobody's orders but his own, and yield to nobody's suggestions.

It was very sweet of you to write me, dear, and I thank you ever so much. With greatest love and kisses,

PAPA.

To Mrs. Clemens, in Ouchy, Switzerland:

ARLES, Sept. 30, noon.

Livy darling, I hain't got no time to write today, because I am sight seeing industriously and imagining my chapter.

Bade good-bye to the river trip and gave away the boat yesterday evening. We had ten great days in her.

We reached here after dark. We were due about 4.30, counting by distance, but we couldn't calculate on such a lifeless current as we found.

I love you, sweetheart.

SAML.

It had been a long time since Clemens had written to his old friend Twichell, but the Rhone trip must have reminded him of those days thirteen years earlier, when, comparatively young men, he and Twichell were tramping through the Black Forest and scaling Gemmi Pass. He sent Twichell a reminder of that happy time.

To Rev. Joseph H. Twichell, in Hartford, Conn:

NIMES, Oct. 1, '91.

DEAR JOE,—I have been ten days floating down the Rhone on a raft, from Lake Bourget, and a most curious and darling kind of a trip it has been. You ought to have been along—I could have made room for you easily—and you would have found that a pedestrian tour in Europe doesn't begin with a raft-voyage for hilarity and mild adventure, and intimate contact with the unvisited native of the back settlements, and extinction from the world and newspapers, and a conscience in a state of coma, and lazy comfort, and solid happiness. In fact there's nothing that's so lovely.

But it's all over. I gave the raft away yesterday at Arles, and am loafing along back by short stages on the rail to Ouchy-Lausanne where the tribe are staying.

Love to you all

MARK.

The Clemenses settled in Berlin for the winter, at 7 Kornerstrasse, and later at the Hotel Royal. There had been no permanent improvement in Mark Twain's arm and he found writing difficult.

Some of the letters promised to Laffan and McClure were still unfinished.

Young Hall, his publishing manager in America, was working hard to keep the business afloat, and being full of the optimism of his years did not fail to make as good a showing as he could. We may believe his letters were very welcome to Clemens and his wife, who found little enough in the general prospect to comfort them.

To Mr. Hall, in New York:

BERLIN, Nov. 27, '91.

DEAR MR. HALL,—That kind of a statement is valuable. It came this morning. This is the first time since the business began that I have had a report that furnished the kind of information I wanted, and was really enlightening and satisfactory. Keep it up. Don't let it fall into desuetude.

Everything looks so fine and handsome with the business, now, that I feel a great let-up from depression. The rewards of your long and patient industry are on their way, and their arrival safe in port, presently, seems assured.

By George, I shall be glad when the ship comes in!

My arm is so much better that I was able to make a speech last night to 250 Americans. But when they threw my portrait on the screen it was a sorrowful reminder, for it was from a negative of 15 years ago, and hadn't a gray hair in it. And now that my arm is better, I have stolen a couple of days and finished up a couple of McClure letters that have been lying a long time.

I shall mail one of them to you next Tuesday—registered. Lookout for it.

I shall register and mail the other one (concerning the "Jungfrau") next Friday look out for it also, and drop me a line to let me know they have arrived.

I shall write the 6th and last letter by and by when I have studied Berlin sufficiently.

Yours in a most cheerful frame of mind, and with my and all the family's Thanksgiving greetings and best wishes,

S. L. CLEMENS.

Postscript by Mrs. Clemens written on Mr. Clemens's letter:

DEAR MR. HALL,—This is my birthday and your letter this morning was a happy addition to the little gifts on the breakfast table. I thought of going out and spending money for something unnecessary after it came, but concluded perhaps I better wait a little longer.

Sincerely yours

O. L. CLEMENS.

"The German Chicago" was the last of the six McClure letters and was finished that winter in Berlin. It is now included in the Uniform Edition of Mark Twain's works, and is one of the best descriptive articles of the German capital ever written. He made no use of the Rhone notes further than to put them together in literary form. They did not seem to him to contain enough substance to warrant publication. A letter to Hall, written toward the end of December, we find rather gloomy in tone, though he is still able to extract comfort and even cheerfulness from one of Mr. Hall's reports.

Memorandum to Fred J. Hall, in New York:

Among the MSS I left with you are a few that have a recent look and are written on rather stiff pale green paper. If you will have those type-writered and keep the originals and send me the copies (one per mail, not two.) I'll see if I can use them.

But tell Howells and other inquirers that my hopes of writing anything are very slender—I seem to be disabled for life.

Drop McClure a line and tell him the same. I can't dare to make an engagement now for even a single letter.

I am glad Howells is on a magazine, but sorry he gave up the Study. I shall have to go on a magazine myself if this L. A. L. continues to hold my nose down to the grind-stone much longer.

I'm going to hold my breath, now, for 30 days—then the annual statement will arrive and I shall know how we feel! Merry Xmas to you from us all.

Sincerely,

S. L. C.

P. S. Just finished the above and finished raging at the eternal German tax-gatherer, and so all the jubilant things which I was going to say about the past year's business got knocked out of me. After writing this present letter I was feeling blue about Huck Finn, but I sat down and overhauled your reports from now back to last April and compared them with the splendid Oct.-Nov. business, and went to bed feeling refreshed and fine, for certainly it has been a handsome year. Now rush me along the Annual Report and let's see how we feel!

S. L. C.

XXXII. LETTERS, 1892, CHIEFLY TO MR. HALL AND MRS. CRANE. IN BERLIN, MENTONE, BAD-NAUHEIM, FLORENCE.

Mark Twain was the notable literary figure in Berlin that winter, the center of every great gathering. He was entertained by the Kaiser, and shown many special attentions by Germans of every rank. His books were as well known in Berlin as in New York, and at court assemblies and embassies he was always a chief center of interest.

He was too popular for his own good; the gaiety of the capital told on him. Finally, one night, after delivering a lecture in a hot room, he contracted a severe cold, driving to a ball at General von Versen's, and a few days later was confined to his bed with pneumonia. It was not a severe attack, but it was long continued. He could write some letters and even work a little, but he was not allowed to leave his bed for many weeks, a condition which he did not find a hardship, for no man ever enjoyed the loose luxury of undress and the comfort of pillows more than Mark Twain. In a memorandum of that time he wrote: "I am having a booming time all to myself."

Meantime, Hall, in America, was sending favorable reports of the publishing business, and this naturally helped to keep up his spirits. He wrote frequently to Hall, of course, but the letters for the most part are purely of a business nature and of little interest to the general reader.

To Fred J. Hall, in New York:

HOTEL ROYAL, BERLIN, Feb. 12.

DEAR MR. HALL,—Daly wants to get the stage rights of the "American Claimant." The foundation from which I wrote the story is a play of the same name which has been in A. P. Burbank's hands 5 or 6 years. That play cost me some money (helping Burbank stage it) but has never brought me any. I have written Burbank (Lotos Club) and asked him to give me back his rights in the old play so that I can treat with Daly and utilize this chance to even myself up. Burbank is a lovely fellow, and if he objects I can't urge him. But you run in at the Lotos and see him; and if he relinquishes his claim, then I would like you to conduct the business with Daly; or have Whitford or some other lawyer do it under your supervision if you prefer.

This morning I seem to have rheumatism in my right foot.

I am ordered south by the doctor and shall expect to be well enough to start by the end of this month.

[No signature.]

It is curious, after Clemens and Howells had tried so hard and so long to place their "Sellers" Play, that now, when the story appeared in book form, Augustin Daly should have thought it worth dramatizing. Daly and Clemens were old friends, and it would seem that Daly could hardly have escaped seeing the play when it was going the rounds. But perhaps there is nothing more mysterious in the world than the ways and wants of theatrical managers. The matter came to nothing, of course, but the fact that Daly should have thought a story built from an old discarded play had a play in it seems interesting.

Clemens and his wife were advised to leave the cold of Berlin as soon as he was able to travel. This was not until the first of March, when, taking their old courier, Joseph Very, they left the children in good hands and journeyed to the south of France.

To Susy Clemens, in Berlin:

MENTONE, Mch 22, '92.

SUSY DEAR,—I have been delighted to note your easy facility with your pen and proud to note also your literary superiorities of one kind and another—clearness of statement, directness, felicity of expression, photographic ability in setting forth an incident—style—good style—no barnacles on it in the way of unnecessary, retarding words (the Shipman scrapes off the barnacles when he wants his racer to go her best gait and straight to the buoy.) You should write a letter every day, long or short—and so ought I, but I don't.

Mamma says, tell Clara yes, she will have to write a note if the fan comes back mended.

We couldn't go to Nice to-day—had to give it up, on various accounts—and this was the last chance. I am sorry for Mamma—I wish she could have gone. She got a heavy fall yesterday evening and was pretty stiff and lame this morning, but is working it off trunk packing.

Joseph is gone to Nice to educate himself in Kodaking—and to get the pictures mounted which Mamma thinks she took here; but I noticed she didn't take the plug out, as a rule. When she did, she took nine pictures on top of each other—composites.

With lots of love.

PAPA.

In the course of their Italian wanderings they reached Florence, where they were so comfortable and well that they decided to engage a villa for the next winter. Through Prof. Willard Fiske, they discovered the Villa Viviani, near Settignano, an old palace beautifully located on the hilltops east of Florence, commanding a wonderful view of the ancient city. Clemens felt that he could work there, and time proved that he was right.

For the summer, however, they returned to Germany, and located at Bad-Nauheim. Clemens presently decided to make a trip to America to give some personal attention to business matters. For one thing, his publishing-house, in spite of prosperity, seemed constantly to be requiring more capital, and then a Chicago company had been persuaded by Paige to undertake the manufacture of the type-setter. It was the beginning of a series of feverish trips which he would make back and forth across the ocean during the next two years.

To Fred J. Hall, in New York:

BAD-NAUHEIM, June 11, '92.

Saturday.

DEAR MR. HALL,—If this arrives before I do, let it inform you that I am leaving Bremen for New York next Tuesday in the "Havel."

If you can meet me when the ship arrives, you can help me to get away from the reporters; and maybe you can take me to your own or some other lodgings where they can't find me.

But if the hour is too early or too late for you, I shall obscure myself somewhere till I can come to the office.

Yours sincerely S. L. C.

Nothing of importance happened in America. The new Paige company had a factory started in Chicago and expected to manufacture fifty machines as a beginning. They claimed to have capital, or to be able to command it, and as the main control had passed from Clemens's hands, he could do no more than look over the ground and hope for the best. As for the business, about all that he could do was to sign certain notes necessary to provide such additional capital as was needed, and agree with Hall that hereafter they would concentrate their efforts and resist further temptation in the way of new enterprise. Then he returned to Bad-Nauheim and settled down to literature. This was the middle of July, and he must have worked pretty steadily, for he presently had a variety of MSS. ready to offer.

To Fred J. Hall, in New York:

Aug. 10, '92.

DEAR MR. HALL,—I have dropped that novel I wrote you about, because I saw a more effective way of using the main episode—to wit: by telling it through the lips of Huck Finn. So I have started Huck Finn and Tom Sawyer (still 15 years old) and their friend the freed slave Jim around the world in a stray balloon, with Huck as narrator, and somewhere after the end of that great voyage he will work in the said episode and then nobody will suspect that a whole book has been written and the globe circumnavigated merely to get that episode in an effective (and at the same time apparently unintentional) way. I have written 12,000 words of this narrative, and find that the humor flows as easily as the adventures and surprises—so I shall go along and make a book of from 50,000 to 100,000 words.

It is a story for boys, of course, and I think will interest any boy between 8 years and 80.

When I was in New York the other day Mrs. Dodge, editor of St. Nicholas, wrote and, offered me $5,000 for (serial right) a story for boys 50,000 words long. I wrote back and declined, for I had other matter in my mind, then.

I conceive that the right way to write a story for boys is to write so that it will not only interest boys but will also strongly interest any man who has ever been a boy. That immensely enlarges the audience.

Now this story doesn't need to be restricted to a Childs magazine—it is proper enough for any magazine, I should think, or for a syndicate. I don't swear it, but I think so.

Proposed title of the story, "New Adventures of Huckleberry Finn."

[No signature.]

The "novel" mentioned in the foregoing was The Extraordinary Twins, a story from which Pudd'nhead Wilson would be evolved later. It was a wildly extravagant farce—just the sort of thing that now and then Mark Twain plunged into with an enthusiasm that had to work itself out and die a natural death, or mellow into something worth while. Tom Sawyer Abroad, as the new Huck story was finally called, was completed and disposed of to St. Nicholas for serial publication.

The Twichells were in Europe that summer, and came to Bad-Nauheim. The next letter records a pleasant incident. The Prince of Wales of that day later became King Edward VII.

To Mr. and Mrs. Orion Clemens, in Keokuk, Iowa.:

Private. BAD-NAUHEIM, Aug. 23, '92.

DEAR ORION AND MOLLIE,—("Private" because no newspaper-man or other gossip must get hold of it)

Livy is getting along pretty well, and the doctor thinks another summer here will cure her.

The Twichell's have been here four days and we have had good times with them. Joe and I ran over to Homburg, the great pleasure resort, Saturday, to dine with some friends, and in the morning I went walking in the promenade and met the British Ambassador to the Court of Berlin, and he introduced me to the Prince of Wales, and I found him a most unusually comfortable and unembarrassing Englishman to talk with—quick to see the obscurest point, and equipped with a laugh which is spontaneous and catching. Am invited by a near friend of his to meet him at dinner day after tomorrow, and there could be a good time, but the brass band will smash the talk and spoil everything.

We are expecting to move to Florence ten or twelve days hence, but if this hot weather continues we shall wait for cooler. I take Clara to Berlin for the winter-music, mainly, with German and French added. Thus far, Jean is our only glib French scholar.

We all send love to you all and to Pamela and Sam's family, and Annie.

SAM

Clemens and family left Bad-Nauheim for Italy by way of Switzerland. In September Mrs. Clemens's sister, Mrs. Crane, who had been with them in Europe during the first year, had now returned to America. Mrs. Clemens had improved at the baths, though she had by no means recovered her health. We get a general report of conditions from the letter which Clemens wrote Mrs. Crane from Lucerne, Switzerland, where the party rested for several days. The "Phelps" mentioned in this letter was William Walter Phelps, United States Minister to Germany. The Phelps and Clemens families had been much associated in Berlin. "Mason" was Frank Mason, Consul General at Frankfort, and in later years at Paris. "Charlie and Ida" were Charles and Mrs. Langdon, of Elmira.

To Mrs. Crane, in Elmira, N. Y.:

LUCERNE, Sept. 18, '92.

DEAR AUNT SUE,—Imagine how I felt to find that you had actually gone off without filling my traveling ink stand which you gave me! I found it out yesterday. Livy advised me to write you about it.

I have been driving this pen hard. I wrote 280 pages on a yarn called "Tom Sawyer Abroad," then took up the "Twins" again, destroyed the last half of the manuscript and re-wrote it in another form, and am going to continue it and finish it in Florence. "Tom Sawyer" seems rather pale to the family after the extravagances of the Twins, but they came to like it after they got used to it.

We remained in Nauheim a little too long. If we had left there four or five days earlier we should have made Florence in 3 days; but by the time we got started Livy had got smitten with what we feared might be erysipelas—greatly swollen neck and face, and unceasing headaches. We lay idle in Frankfort 4 days, doctoring. We started Thursday and made Bale. Hard trip, because it was one of those trains that gets tired every seven minutes and stops to rest three quarters of an hour. It took us 3 1/2 hours to get here, instead of the regulation 2.20. We reached here Friday evening and will leave tomorrow (Tuesday) morning. The rest has made the headaches better. We shall pull through to Milan tomorrow if possible. Next day we shall start at 10 a. m., and try to make Bologna, 5 hours. Next day (Thursday) Florence, D. V. Next year we will walk, for these excursions have got to be made over again. I've got seven trunks, and I undertook to be courier because I meant to express them to Florence direct, but we were a couple of days too late. All continental roads had issued a peremptory order that no baggage should travel a mile except in the company of the owner. (All over Europe people are howling; they are separated from their baggage and can't get it forwarded to them) I have to re-ship my trunks every day. It is very amusing—uncommonly so. There seemed grave doubts about our being able to get these trunks over the Italian frontier, but I've got a very handsome note from the Frankfort Italian

Consul General addressed to all Italian Customs Officers, and we shall get through if anybody does.

The Phelpses came to Frankfort and we had some great times—dinner at his hotel, the Masons, supper at our inn—Livy not in it. She was merely allowed a glimpse, no more. Of course, Phelps said she was merely pretending to be ill; was never looking so well and fine.

The children are all right. They paddle around a little, and drive-so do we all. Lucerne seems to be pretty full of tourists. The Fleulen boat went out crowded yesterday morning.

The Paris Herald has created a public interest by inoculating one of its correspondents with cholera. A man said yesterday he wished to God they would inoculate all of them. Yes, the interest is quite general and strong, and much hope is felt.

Livy says, I have said enough bad things, and better send all our loves to you and Charley and Ida and all the children and shut up. Which I do—and shut up.

S. L. C.

They reached Florence on the 26th, and four days later we find Clemens writing again to Mrs. Crane, detailing everything at length. Little comment on this letter is required; it fully explains itself. Perhaps a word of description from one of his memoranda will not be out of place. Of the villa he wrote: "It is a plain, square building, like a box, and is painted light green and has green window-shutters. It stands in a commanding position on the artificial terrace of liberal dimensions, which is walled around with masonry. From the walls the vineyards and olive groves of the estate slant away toward the valley.... Roses overflow the retaining walls and the battered and mossy stone urn on the gate-post, in pink and yellow cataracts, exactly as they do on the drop-curtains in the theaters. The house is a very fortress for strength."

The Mrs. Ross in this letter was Janet Ross, daughter of Lady Duff Gordon, remembered to-day for her Egyptian letters. The Ross castle was but a little distance away.

To Mrs. Crane, in Elmira:

VILLA VIVIANI, SETTIGNANO, FLORENCE.

Sept. 30, 1892

DEAR SUE,—We have been in the house several days, and certainly it is a beautiful place,—particularly at this moment, when the skies are a deep leaden color, the domes of Florence dim in the drizzling rain, and occasional perpendicular coils of lightning quivering intensely in the black sky about Galileo's Tower. It is a charming panorama, and the most conspicuous towers and domes down in the city look to-day just as they looked when Boccaccio and Dante used to contemplate them from this hillock five and six hundred years ago.

The Mademoiselle is a great help to Livy in the housekeeping, and is a cheery and cheerful presence in the house. The butler is equipped with a little French, and it is this fact that enables the house to go—but it won't go well until the family get some sort of facility with the Italian tongue, for the cook, the woman-of-all-work and the coachman understand only that. It is a stubborn and devilish language to learn, but Jean and the others will master it. Livy's German Nauheim girl is the worst off of anybody, as there is no market for her tongue at all among the help.

With the furniture in and the curtains up the house is very pretty, and not unhomelike. At mid-night last night we heard screams up stairs—Susy had set the lofty window curtains afire with a candle. This sounds kind of frightful, whereas when you come to think of it, a burning curtain or pile of furniture hasn't any element of danger about it in this fortress. There isn't any conceivable way to burn this house down, or enable a conflagration on one floor to climb to the next.

Mrs. Ross laid in our wood, wine and servants for us, and they are excellent. She had the house scoured from Cellar to rook the curtains washed and put up, all beds pulled to pieces, beaten, washed and put together again, and beguiled the Marchese into putting a big porcelain stove in the vast central hall. She is a wonderful woman, and we don't quite see how or when we should have gotten under way without her.

Observe our address above—the post delivers letters daily at the house.

Even with the work and fuss of settling the house Livy has improved—and the best is yet to come. There is going to be absolute seclusion here—a hermit life, in fact. We (the rest of us) shall run over to the Ross's frequently, and they will come here now and then and see Livy—that is all. Mr. Fiske is away—nobody knows where—and the work on his house has been stopped and his servants discharged. Therefore we shall merely go Rossing—as far as society is concerned—shan't circulate in Florence until Livy shall be well enough to take a share in it.

This present house is modern. It is not much more than two centuries old; but parts of it, and also its foundations are of high antiquity. The fine beautiful family portraits—the great carved ones in the large ovals over the doors of the big hall—carry one well back into the past. One of them is dated 1305—he could have known Dante, you see. Another is dated 1343—he could have known Boccaccio and spent his afternoons in Fiesole listening to the Decameron tales. Another is dated 1463—he could have met Columbus.....

Evening. The storm thundered away until night, and the rain came down in floods. For awhile there was a partial break, which furnished about such a sunset as will be exhibited when the Last Day comes and the universe tumbles together in wreck and ruin. I have never seen anything more spectacular and impressive.

One person is satisfied with the villa, anyway. Jean prefers it to all Europe, save Venice. Jean is eager to get at the Italian tongue again, now, and I see that she has forgotten little or nothing of what she learned of it in Rome and Venice last spring.

I am the head French duffer of the family. Most of the talk goes over my head at the table. I catch only words, not phrases. When Italian comes to be substituted I shall be even worse off than I am now, I suppose.

This reminds me that this evening the German girl said to Livy, "Man hat mir gesagt loss Sie una candella verlaught habe"—unconsciously dropping in a couple of Italian words, you see. So she is going to join the polyglots, too, it appears. They say it is good entertainment to hear her and the butler talk together in their respective tongues, piecing out and patching up with the universal sign-language as they go along. Five languages in use in the house (including the sign-language-hardest-worked of them all) and yet with all this opulence of resource we do seem to have an uncommonly tough time making ourselves understood.

What we lack is a cat. If we only had Germania! That was the most satisfactory all-round cat I have seen yet. Totally ungermanic in the raciness of his character and in the sparkle of his mind and the spontaneity of his movements. We shall not look upon his like again....

S. L. C.

Clemens got well settled down to work presently. He found the situation, the climate, the background, entirely suited to literary production, and in a little while he had accomplished more than at any other time since his arrival in Europe. From letters to Mrs. Crane and to Mr. Hall we learn something of his employments and his satisfaction.

To Mrs. Crane, in Elmira:

VILLA VIVIANI

SETTIGNANO, FLORENCE. Oct. 22, '92.

DEAR SUE,—We are getting wonted. The open fires have driven away the cold and the doubt, and now a cheery spirit pervades the place. Livy and the Kings and Mademoiselle having been taking their tea a number of times, lately, on the open terrace with the city and the hills and the sunset for company. I stop work, a few minutes, as a rule, when the sun gets down to the hilltops west of Florence, and join the tea-group to wonder and exclaim. There is always some new miracle in the view, a new and exquisite variation in the show, a variation which occurs every 15 minutes between dawn and night. Once early in the morning, a multitude of white villas not before perceived, revealed themselves on the far hills; then we recognized that all those great hills are snowed thick with them, clear to the summit.

The variety of lovely effects, the infinitude of change, is something not to be believed by any who has not seen it. No view that I am acquainted with in the world is at all comparable to this for delicacy, charm, exquisiteness, dainty coloring, and bewildering rapidity of change. It keeps a person drunk with pleasure all the time. Sometimes Florence ceases to be substantial, and becomes just a faint soft dream, with domes and towers of air, and one is persuaded that he might blow it away with a puff of his breath.

Livy is progressing admirably. This is just the place for her.

[Remainder missing.]

To Fred J. Hall, in New York:

Dec. 12, '92.

DEAR MR. HALL,—November check received.

I have lent the Californian's Story to Arthur Stedman for his Author Club Book, so your suggestion that my new spring-book bear that name arrives too late, as he probably would not want us to use that story in a book of ours until the Author book had had its run. That is for him to decide—and I don't want him hampered at all in his decision. I, for my part, prefer the "$1,000,000 Banknote and Other Stories' by Mark Twain as a title, but above my judgment I prefer yours. I mean this—it is not taffy.

I told Arthur to leave out the former squib or paragraph and use only the Californian's Story. Tell him this is because I am going to use that in the book I am now writing.

I finished "Those Extraordinary Twins" night before last makes 60 or 80,000 words—haven't counted.

The last third of it suits me to a dot. I begin, to-day, to entirely recast and re-write the first two-thirds—new plan, with two minor characters, made very prominent, one major character cropped out, and the Twins subordinated to a minor but not insignificant place.

The minor character will now become the chiefest, and I will name the story after him—"Puddn'head Wilson."

Merry Xmas to you, and great prosperity and felicity!

S. L. CLEMENS.

XXXIII. LETTERS, 1893, TO MR. HALL, MRS. CLEMENS, AND OTHERS. FLORENCE. BUSINESS TROUBLES. "PUDD'NHEAD WILSON." "JOAN OF ARC." AT THE PLAYERS, NEW

YORK.

The reader may have suspected that young Mr. Hall in New York was having his troubles. He was by this time one-third owner in the business of Charles L. Webster & Co., as well as its general manager. The business had been drained of its capital one way and another-partly by the publication of unprofitable books; partly by the earlier demands of the typesetter, but more than all by the manufacturing cost and agents' commissions demanded by L. A. L.; that is to say, the eleven large volumes constituting the Library of American Literature, which Webster had undertaken to place in a million American homes. There was plenty of sale for it—indeed, that was just the trouble; for it was sold on payments—small monthly payments—while the cost of manufacture and the liberal agents' commissions were cash items, and it would require a considerable period before the dribble of collections would swell into a tide large enough to satisfy the steady outflow of expense. A sale of twenty-five sets a day meant prosperity on paper, but unless capital could be raised from some other source to make and market those books through a period of months, perhaps even years, to come, it meant bankruptcy in reality. It was Hall's job, with Clemens to back him, to keep their ship afloat on these steadily ebbing financial waters. It was also Hall's affair to keep Mark Twain cheerful, to look pleasant himself, and to show how they were steadily getting rich because orders were pouring in, though a cloud that resembled bankruptcy loomed always a little higher upon the horizon. If Hall had not been young and an optimist, he would have been frightened out of his boots early in the game. As it was, he made a brave steady fight, kept as cheerful and stiff an upper lip as possible, always hoping that something would happen—some grand sale of his other books, some unexpected inflow from the typesetter interests—anything that would sustain his ship until the L. A. L. tide should turn and float it into safety.

Clemens had faith in Hall and was fond of him. He never found fault with him; he tried to accept his encouraging reports at their face value. He lent the firm every dollar of his literary earnings not absolutely needed for the family's support; he signed new notes; he allowed Mrs. Clemens to put in such remnants of her patrimony as the type-setter had spared.

The situation in 1893 was about as here outlined. The letters to Hall of that year are frequent and carry along the story. To any who had formed the idea that Mark Twain was irascible, exacting, and faultfinding, they will perhaps be a revelation.

To Fred J. Hall, in New York:

FLORENCE, Jan. 1, '93.

DEAR MR. HALL,—Yours of Dec. 19 is to hand, and Mrs. Clemens is deeply distressed, for she thinks I have been blaming you or finding fault with you about something. But most surely that cannot be. I tell her that although I am prone to write hasty and regrettable things to other people, I am not a bit likely to write such things to you. I can't believe I have done anything so ungrateful. If I have, pile coals of fire on my head, for I deserve it!

I wonder if my letter of credit isn't an encumbrance? Do you have to deposit the whole amount it calls for? If that is so, it is an encumbrance, and we must withdraw it and take the money out of soak. I have never made drafts upon it except when compelled, because I thought you deposited nothing against it, and only had to put up money that I drew upon it; that therefore the less I drew the easier it would be for you.

I am dreadfully sorry I didn't know it would be a help to you to let my monthly check pass over a couple of months. I could have stood that by drawing what is left of Mrs. Clemens's letter of credit, and we would have done it cheerfully.

I will write Whitmore to send you the "Century" check for $1,000, and you can collect Mrs. Dodge's $2,000 (Whitmore has power of attorney which I think will enable him to endorse it over to you in my name.) If you need that $3,000 put it in the business and use it, and send Whitmore the Company's note for a year. If you don't need it, turn it over to Mr. Halsey and let him invest it for me.

I've a mighty poor financial head, and I may be all wrong—but tell me if I am wrong in supposing that in lending my own firm money at 6 per cent I pay 4 of it myself and so really get only a per cent? Now don't laugh if that is stupid.

Of course my friend declined to buy a quarter interest in the L. A. L. for $200,000. I judged he would. I hoped he would offer $100,000, but he didn't. If the cholera breaks out in America, a few months hence, we can't borrow or sell; but if it doesn't we must try hard to raise $100,000. I wish we could do it before there is a cholera scare.

I have been in bed two or three days with a cold, but I got up an hour ago, and I believe I am all right again.

How I wish I had appreciated the need of $100,000 when I was in New York last summer! I would have tried my best to raise it. It would make us able to stand 1,000 sets of L. A. L. per month, but not any more, I guess.

You have done magnificently with the business, and we must raise the money somehow, to enable you to reap the reward of all that labor.

Sincerely Yours

S. L. CLEMENS.

"Whitmore," in this letter, was F. G. Whitmore, of Hartford, Mark Twain's financial agent. The money due from Mrs. Dodge was a balance on Tom Sawyer Abroad, which had been accepted by St. Nicholas. Mr. Halsey was a down-town broker.

Clemens, who was growing weary of the constant demands of L. A. L., had conceived the idea that it would be well to dispose of a portion of it for enough cash to finance its manufacture.

We don't know who the friend was to whom he offered a quarter interest for the modest sum of two hundred thousand dollars. But in the next letter we discover designs on a certain very canny Scotchman of Skibo.

To Fred J. Hall, in New York:

FLORENCE, Jan. 28, '92.

DEAR MR. HALL,—I want to throw out a suggestion and see what you think of it. We have a good start, and solid ground under us; we have a valuable reputation; our business organization is practical, sound and well-devised; our publications are of a respect-worthy character and of a money-breeding species. Now then I think that the association with us of some one of great name and with capital would give our business a prodigious impetus—that phrase is not too strong.

As I look at it, it is not money merely that is needed; if that were all, the firm has friends enough who would take an interest in a paying venture; we need some one who has made his life a success not only from a business standpoint, but with that achievement back of him, has been great enough to make his power felt as a thinker and a literary man. It is a pretty usual thing for publishers to have this sort of partners. Now you see what a power Carnegie is, and how far his voice reaches in the several lines I speak of. Do you know him? You do by correspondence or purely business talks about his books—but personally, I mean? so that it would not be an intrusion for you to speak to him about this desire of mine—for I would like you to put it before him, and if you fail to interest him in it, you will probably get at least some valuable suggestions from him. I'll enclose a note of introduction—you needn't use it if you don't need to.

Yours S. L. C.

P. S. Yes, I think I have already acknowledged the Dec. $1,000 and the Jan. $500—and if another $500 was mailed 3 days ago there's no hiatus.

I think I also reminded you that the new letter of credit does not cover the unexpended balance of the old one but falls considerably short of it.

Do your best with Carnegie, and don't wait to consider any of my intermediate suggestions or talks about our raising half of the $200,000 ourselves. I mean, wait for nothing. To make my suggestion available I should have to go over and see Arnot, and I don't want to until I can mention Carnegie's name to him as going in with us.

My book is type-written and ready for print—"Pudd'nhead Wilson-a Tale." (Or, "Those Extraordinary Twins," if preferable.)

It makes 82,500 words—12,000 more than Huck Finn. But I don't know what to do with it. Mrs. Clemens thinks it wouldn't do to go to the Am. Pub. Co. or anywhere outside of our own house; we have no subscription machinery, and a book in the trade is a book thrown away, as far as money-profit goes. I am in a quandary. Give me a lift out of it.

I will mail the book to you and get you to examine it and see if it is good or if it is bad. I think it is good, and I thought the Claimant bad, when I saw it in print; but as for real judgment, I think I am destitute of it.

I am writing a companion to the Prince and Pauper, which is half done and will make 200,000 words; and I have had the idea that if it were gotten up in handsome style, with many illustrations and put at a high enough price maybe the L. A. L. canvassers would take it and run it with that book. Would they? It could be priced anywhere from $4 up to $10, according to how it was gotten up, I suppose.

I don't want it to go into a magazine.

S. L. C.

I am having several short things type-"writered." I will send them to you presently. I like the Century and Harper's, but I don't know that I have any business to object to the Cosmopolitan if they pay as good rates. I suppose a man ought to stick to one magazine, but that may be only superstition. What do you think?

S. L. C.

"The companion to The Prince and the Pauper," mentioned in this letter, was the story of Joan of Arc, perhaps the most finished of Mark Twain's literary productions. His interest in Joan had been

first awakened when, as a printer's apprentice in Hannibal, he had found blowing along the street a stray leaf from some printed story of her life. That fragment of history had pictured Joan in prison, insulted and mistreated by ruffians. It had aroused all the sympathy and indignation in the boy, Sam Clemens; also, it had awakened his interest in history, and, indeed, in all literature.

His love for the character of Joan had grown with the years, until in time he had conceived the idea of writing her story. As far back as the early eighties he had collected material for it, and had begun to make the notes. One thing and another had interfered, and he had found no opportunity for such a story. Now, however, in Florence, in the ancient villa, and in the quiet garden, looking across the vineyards and olive groves to the dream city along the Arno, he felt moved to take up the tale of the shepherd girl of France, the soldier maid, or, as he called her, "The noble child, the most innocent, the most lovely, the most adorable the ages have produced." His surroundings and background would seem to have been perfect, and he must have written with considerable ease to have completed a hundred thousand words in a period of not more than six weeks.

Perhaps Hall did not even go to see Carnegie; at all events nothing seems to have come of the idea. Once, at a later time, Mask Twain himself mentioned the matter to Carnegie, and suggested to him that it was poor financiering to put all of one's eggs into one basket, meaning into iron. But Carnegie answered, "That's a mistake; put all your eggs into one basket and watch that basket."

It was March when Clemens felt that once more his presence was demanded in America. He must see if anything could be realized from the type-setter or L. A. L.

To Fred J. Hall, in New York:

March 13, '93.

DEAR MR. HALL,—I am busy getting ready to sail the 22d, in the Kaiser Wilhelm II.

I send herewith 2 magazine articles.

The Story contains 3,800 to 4,000 words.

The "Diary" contains 3,800 words.

Each would make about 4 pages of the Century.

The Diary is a gem, if I do say it myself that shouldn't.

If the Cosmopolitan wishes to pay $600 for either of them or $1,200 for both, gather in the check, and I will use the money in America instead of breaking into your treasury.

If they don't wish to trade for either, send the articles to the Century, without naming a price, and if their check isn't large enough I will call and abuse them when I come.

I signed and mailed the notes yesterday.

Yours

S. L. C.

Clemens reached New York on the 3d of April and made a trip to Chicago, but accomplished nothing, except to visit the World's Fair and be laid up with a severe cold. The machine situation had not progressed. The financial stringency of 1893 had brought everything to a standstill. The New York bank would advance Webster & Co. no more money. So disturbed were his affairs, so disordered was everything, that sometimes he felt himself as one walking amid unrealities. A fragment of a letter to Mrs. Crane conveys this:

"I dreamed I was born and grew up and was a pilot on the Mississippi and a miner and a journalist in Nevada and a pilgrim in the Quaker City, and had a wife and children and went to live in a villa at Florence—and this dream goes on and on and sometimes seems so real that I almost believe it is real. I wonder if it is? But there is no way to tell, for if one applies tests they would be part of the dream, too, and so would simply aid the deceit. I wish I knew whether it is a dream or real."

He saw Warner, briefly, in America; also Howells, now living in New York, but he had little time for visiting. On May 13th he sailed again for Europe on the Kaiser Wilhelm II. On the night before sailing he sent Howells a good-by word.

To W. D. Howells, in New York City:

MURRAY HILL HOTEL, NEW YORE, May 12, 1893.

Midnight.

DEAR HOWELLS—I am so sorry I missed you.

I am very glad to have that book for sea entertainment, and I thank you ever so much for it.

I've had a little visit with Warner at last; I was getting afraid I wasn't going to have a chance to see him at all. I forgot to tell you how thoroughly I enjoyed your account of the country printing office, and how true it all was and how intimately recognizable in all its details. But Warner was full of delight over it, and that reminded me, and I am glad, for I wanted to speak of it.

You have given me a book; Annie Trumbull has sent me her book; I bought a couple of books; Mr. Hall gave me a choice German book; Laflan gave me two bottles of whisky and a box of cigars—I go to sea nobly equipped.

Good-bye and all good fortune attend you and yours—and upon you all I leave my benediction.

MARK.

Mention has already been made of the Ross home being very near to Viviani, and the association of the Ross and Clemens families. There was a fine vegetable garden on the Ross estate, and it was in the interest of it that the next letter was written to the Secretary of Agriculture.

To Hon. J. Sterling Morton, in Washington, D. C.: Editorial Department Century Magazine, Union Square,

NEW YORK, April 6, 1893.

TO THE HON. J. STERLING MORTON,—Dear Sir: Your petitioner, Mark Twain, a poor farmer of Connecticut—indeed, the poorest one there, in the opinion of many-desires a few choice breeds of seed corn (maize), and in return will zealously support the Administration in all ways honorable and otherwise.

To speak by the card, I want these things to hurry to Italy to an English lady. She is a neighbor of mine outside of Florence, and has a great garden and thinks she could raise corn for her table if she had the right ammunition. I myself feel a warm interest in this enterprise, both on patriotic grounds and because I have a key to that garden, which I got made from a wax impression. It is not very good soil, still I think she can grow enough for one table and I am in a position to select the table. If you are willing to aid and abet a countryman (and Gilder thinks you are,) please find the signature and address of your petitioner below.

Respectfully and truly yours.

MARK TWAIN,

67 Fifth Avenue, New York.

P. S.—A handful of choice (Southern) watermelon seeds would pleasantly add to that lady's employments and give my table a corresponding lift.

His idea of business values had moderated considerably by the time he had returned to Florence. He was not hopeless yet, but he was clearly a good deal disheartened—anxious for freedom.

To Fred J. Hall, in New York:

FLORENCE May 30, '93

DEAR MR. HALL,—You were to cable me if you sold any machine royalties—so I judge you have not succeeded.

This has depressed me. I have been looking over the past year's letters and statements and am depressed still more.

I am terribly tired of business. I am by nature and disposition unfitted for it and I want to get out of it. I am standing on the Mount Morris volcano with help from the machine a long way off—doubtless a long way further off than the Connecticut Co. imagines.

Now here is my idea for getting out.

The firm owes Mrs. Clemens and me—I do not know quite how much, but it is about $170,000 or $175,000, I suppose (I make this guess from the documents here, whose technicalities confuse me horribly.)

The firm owes other sums, but there is stock and cash assets to cover the entire indebtedness and $116,679.20 over. Is that it? In addition we have the L. A. L. plates and copyright, worth more than $130,000—is that correct?

That is to say, we have property worth about $250,000 above indebtedness, I suppose—or, by one of your estimates, $300,000? The greater part of the first debts to me is in notes paying 6 percent. The rest (the old $70,000 or whatever it is) pays no interest.

Now then, will Harper or Appleton, or Putnam give me $200,000 for those debts and my two-thirds interest in the firm? (The firm of course taking the Mount Morris and all such obligations off my hands and leaving me clear of all responsibility.)

I don't want much money. I only want first class notes—$200,000 worth of them at 6 per cent, payable monthly;—yearly notes, renewable annually for 3 years, with $5,000 of the principal payable at the beginning and middle of each year. After that, the notes renewable annually and (perhaps) a larger part of the principal payable semi-annually.

Please advise me and suggest alterations and emendations of the above scheme, for I need that sort of help, being ignorant of business and not able to learn a single detail of it.

Such a deal would make it easy for a big firm to pour in a big cash capital and jump L. A. L. up to enormous prosperity. Then your one-third would be a fortune—and I hope to see that day!

I enclose an authority to use with Whitmore in case you have sold any royalties. But if you can't make this deal don't make any. Wait a little and see if you can't make the deal. Do make the deal if you possibly can. And if any presence shall be necessary in order to complete it I will come over, though I hope it can be done without that.

Get me out of business!

And I will be yours forever gratefully,

S. L. CLEMENS.

My idea is, that I am offering my 2/3 of L. A. L. and the business for thirty or forty thousand dollars. Is that it?

P. S. S. The new firm could retain my books and reduce them to a 10 percent royalty.

S. L. C.

To Rev. Jos. H. Twichell, in Hartford:

VILLA VIVIANI, SETTIGNANO (FLORENCE)

June 9, '93.

DEAR JOE,—The sea voyage set me up and I reached here May 27 in tolerable condition—nothing left but weakness, cough all gone.

Old Sir Henry Layard was here the other day, visiting our neighbor Janet Ross, daughter of Lady Duff Gordon, and since then I have been reading his account of the adventures of his youth in the far East. In a footnote he has something to say about a sailor which I thought might interest you—viz:

"This same quartermaster was celebrated among the English in Mesopotamia for an entry which he made in his log-book-after a perilous storm; 'The windy and watery elements raged. Tears and prayers was had recourse to, but was of no manner of use. So we hauled up the anchor and got round the point.'"

There—it isn't Ned Wakeman; it was before his day.

With love,

MARK.

They closed Villa Viviani in June and near the end of the month arrived in Munich in order that Mrs. Clemens might visit some of the German baths. The next letter is written by her and shows her deep sympathy with Hall in his desperate struggle. There have been few more unselfish and courageous women in history than Mark Twain's wife.

From Mrs. Clemens to Mr. Hall, in New York:

June 27th 1893

MUNICH.

DEAR MR. HALL,—Your letter to Mr. Clemens of June 16th has just reached here; as he has gone to Berlin for Clara I am going to send you just a line in answer to it.

Mr. Clemens did not realize what trouble you would be in when his letter should reach you or he would not have sent it just then. I hope you will not worry any more than you can help. Do not let our interests weigh on you too heavily. We both know you will, as you always have, look in every way to the best interests of all.

I think Mr. Clemens is right in feeling that he should get out of business, that he is not fitted for it; it worries him too much.

But he need be in no haste about it, and of course, it would be the very farthest from his desire to imperil, in the slightest degree, your interests in order to save his own.

I am sure that I voice his wish as well as mine when I say that he would simply like you to bear in mind the fact that he greatly desires to be released from his present anxiety and worry, at a time when it shall not endanger your interest or the safety of the business.

I am more sorry than I can express that this letter of Mr. Clemens' should have reached you when you were struggling under such terrible pressure. I hope now that the weight is not quite so heavy. He would not have written you about the money if he had known that it was an inconvenience for you to send it. He thought the book-keeper whose duty it is to forward it had forgotten.

We can draw on Mr. Langdon for money for a few weeks until things are a little easier with you. As Mr. Clemens wrote you we would say "do not send us any more money at present" if we were not afraid to do so. I will say, however, do not trouble yourself if for a few weeks you are not able to send the usual amount.

Mr. Clemens and I have the greatest possible desire, not to increase in any way your burdens, and sincerely wish we might aid you.

I trust my brother may be able, in his talk with you, to throw some helpful light on the situation.

Hoping you will see a change for the better and begin to reap the fruit of your long and hard labor.

Believe me

Very Cordially yours

OLIVIA L. CLEMENS.

Hall, naturally, did not wish to be left alone with the business. He realized that his credit would suffer, both at the bank and with the public, if his distinguished partner should retire. He wrote, therefore, proposing as an alternate that they dispose of the big subscription set that was swamping them. It was a good plan—if it would work—and we find Clemens entering into it heartily.

To Fred J. Hall, in New York:

MUNICH, July 3, '93.

DEAR MR. HALL,—You make a suggestion which has once or twice flitted dimly through my mind heretofore to wit, sell L. A. L.

I like that better than the other scheme, for it is no doubt feasible, whereas the other is perhaps not.

The firm is in debt, but L. A. L. is free—and not only free but has large money owing to it. A proposition to sell that by itself to a big house could be made without embarrassment we merely confess that we cannot spare capital from the rest of the business to run it on the huge scale necessary to make it an opulent success.

It will be selling a good thing—for somebody; and it will be getting rid of a load which we are clearly not able to carry. Whoever buys will have a noble good opening—a complete equipment, a well organized business, a capable and experienced manager, and enterprise not experimental but under full sail, and immediately able to pay 50 per cent a year on every dollar the publisher shall actually invest in it—I mean in making and selling the books.

I am miserably sorry to be adding bothers and torments to the over-supply which you already have in these hideous times, but I feel so troubled, myself, considering the dreary fact that we are getting deeper and deeper in debt and the L. A. L. getting to be a heavier and heavier burden all the time, that I must bestir myself and seek a way of relief.

It did not occur to me that in selling out I would injure you—for that I am not going to do. But to sell L. A. L. will not injure you it will put you in better shape.

Sincerely Yours

S. L. CLEMENS.

To Fred J. Hall, in New York:

July 8, '92.

DEAR MR. HALL,—I am sincerely glad you are going to sell L. A. L.

I am glad you are shutting off the agents, and I hope the fatal book will be out of our hands before it will be time to put them on again. With nothing but our non-existent capital to work with the book has no value for us, rich a prize as it will be to any competent house that gets it.

I hope you are making an effort to sell before you discharge too many agents, for I suppose the agents are a valuable part of the property.

We have been stopping in Munich for awhile, but we shall make a break for some country resort in a few days now.

Sincerely Yours

S. L. C.

July 8

P. S. No, I suppose I am wrong in suggesting that you wait a moment before discharging your L. A. L. agents—in fact I didn't mean that. I judge your only hope of salvation is in discharging them all at once, since it is their commissions that threaten to swamp us. It is they who have eaten up the $14,000 I left with you in such a brief time, no doubt.

I feel panicky.

I think the sale might be made with better advantage, however, now, than later when the agents have got out of the purchaser's reach.

S. L. C.

P. S. No monthly report for many months.

Those who are old enough to remember the summer of 1893 may recall it as a black financial season. Banks were denying credit, businesses were forced to the wall. It was a poor time to float any costly enterprise. The Chicago company who was trying to build the machines made little progress. The book business everywhere was bad. In a brief note following the foregoing letters Clemens wrote

Hall:

"It is now past the middle of July and no cablegram to say the machine is finished. We are afraid you are having miserable days and worried nights, and we sincerely wish we could relieve you, but it is all black with us and we don't know any helpful thing to say or do."

He inclosed some kind of manuscript proposition for John Brisben Walker, of the Cosmopolitan, with the comment: "It is my ingenious scheme to protect the family against the alms-house for one more year—and after that—well, goodness knows! I have never felt so desperate in my life—and good reason, for I haven't got a penny to my name, and Mrs. Clemens hasn't enough laid up with Langdon to keep us two months."

It was like Mark Twain, in the midst of all this turmoil, to project an entirely new enterprise; his busy mind was always visioning success in unusual undertakings, regardless of immediate conditions and the steps necessary to achievement.

To Fred J. Hall, in New York:

July 26, '93.

DEAR MR. HALL,—..... I hope the machine will be finished this month; but it took me four years and cost me $100,000 to finish the other machine after it was apparently entirely complete and setting type like a house-afire.

I wonder what they call "finished." After it is absolutely perfect it can't go into a printing-office until it has had a month's wear, running night and day, to get the bearings smooth, I judge.

I may be able to run over about mid-October. Then if I find you relieved of L. A. L. we will start a magazine inexpensive, and of an entirely unique sort. Arthur Stedman and his father editors of it. Arthur could do all the work, merely submitting it to his father for approval.

The first number should pay—and all subsequent ones—25 cents a number. Cost of first number (20,000 copies) $2,000. Give most of them away, sell the rest. Advertising and other expenses—cost unknown. Send one to all newspapers—it would get a notice—favorable, too.

But we cannot undertake it until L. A. L, is out of the way. With our hands free and some capital to spare, we could make it hum.

Where is the Shelley article? If you have it on hand, keep it and I will presently tell you what to do with it.

Don't forget to tell me.

Yours Sincerely

S. L. C.

The Shelley article mentioned in this letter was the "Defense of Harriet Sheller," one of the very best of his essays. How he could have written this splendid paper at a time of such distraction passes comprehension. Furthermore, it is clear that he had revised, indeed rewritten, the long story of Pudd'nhead Wilson.

To Fred J. Hall, in New York:

July 30, '93.

DEAR MR. HALL,—This time "Pudd'nhead Wilson" is a success! Even

Mrs. Clemens, the most difficult of critics, confesses it, and without reserves or qualifications. Formerly she would not consent that it be published either before or after my death. I have pulled the twins apart and made two individuals of them; I have sunk them out of sight, they are mere flitting shadows, now, and of no importance; their story has disappeared from the book. Aunt Betsy Hale has vanished wholly, leaving not a trace behind; aunt Patsy Cooper and her daughter Rowena have almost disappeared—they scarcely walk across the stage. The whole story is centered on the murder and the trial; from the first chapter the movement is straight ahead without divergence or side-play to the murder and the trial; everything that is done or said or that happens is a preparation for those events. Therefore, 3 people stand up high, from beginning to end, and only 3—Pudd'nhead, "Tom" Driscoll, and his nigger mother, Roxana; none of the others are important, or get in the way of the story or require the reader's attention. Consequently, the scenes and episodes which were the strength of the book formerly are stronger than ever, now.

When I began this final reconstruction the story contained 81,500 words, now it contains only 58,000. I have knocked out everything that delayed the march of the story—even the description of a Mississippi steamboat. There's no weather in, and no scenery—the story is stripped for flight!

Now, then what is she worth? The amount of matter is but 3,000 words short of the American Claimant, for which the syndicate paid $12,500. There was nothing new in that story, but the finger-prints in this one is virgin ground—absolutely fresh, and mighty curious and interesting to everybody.

I don't want any more syndicating—nothing short of $20,000, anyway, and that I can't get—but won't you see how much the Cosmopolitan will stand?

Do your best for me, for I do not sleep these nights, for visions of the poor-house.

This in spite of the hopeful tone of yours of 11th to Langdon (just received) for in me hope is very nearly expiring. Everything does look so blue, so dismally blue!

By and by I shall take up the Rhone open-boat voyage again, but not now—we are going to be moving around too much. I have torn up some of it, but still have 15,000 words that Mrs. Clemens approves of, and that I like. I may go at it in Paris again next winter, but not unless I know I can write it to suit me.

Otherwise I shall tackle Adam once more, and do him in a kind of a friendly and respectful way that will commend him to the Sunday schools. I've been thinking out his first life-days to-day and framing his childish and ignorant impressions and opinions for him.

Will ship Pudd'nhead in a few days. When you get it cable

Mark Twain

Care Brownship, London

Received.

I mean to ship "Pudd'nhead Wilson" to you-say, tomorrow. It'll furnish me hash for awhile I reckon. I am almost sorry it is finished; it was good entertainment to work at it, and kept my mind away from things.

We leave here in about ten days, but the doctors have changed our plans again. I think we shall be in Bohemia or thereabouts till near the end of September, then go to Paris and take a rest.

Yours Sincerely

S. L. C.

P. S. Mrs. Clemens has come in since, and read your letter and is deeply distressed. She thinks that in some letter of mine I must have reproached you. She says it is wonderful that you have kept the ship afloat in this storm that has seen fleets and fleets go down; that from what she learns of the American business-situation from her home letters you have accomplished a marvel in the circumstances, and that she cannot bear to have a word said to you that shall voice anything but praise and the heartiest appreciation—and not the shadow of a reproach will she allow.

I tell her I didn't reproach you and never thought of such a thing. And I said I would break open my letter and say so.

Mrs. Clemens says I must tell you not to send any money for a month or two—so that you may be afforded what little relief is in our power. All right—I'm willing; (this is honest) but I wish Brer Chatto would send along his little yearly contribution. I dropped him a line about another matter a week ago—asked him to subscribe for the Daily News for me—you see I wanted to remind him in a covert way that it was pay-up time—but doubtless I directed the letter to you or some one else, for I don't hear from him and don't get any Daily News either.

To Fred J. Hall, in New York:

Aug. 6, '93.

DEAR MR. HALL,—I am very sorry—it was thoughtless in me. Let the reports go. Send me once a month two items, and two only:

Cash liabilities—(so much) Cash assets—(so much)

I can perceive the condition of the business at a glance, then, and that will be sufficient.

Here we never see a newspaper, but even if we did I could not come anywhere near appreciating or correctly estimating the tempest you have been buffeting your way through—only the man who is in it can do that—but I have tried not to burden you thoughtlessly or wantonly. I have been wrought and unsettled in mind by apprehensions, and that is a thing that is not helpable when one is in a strange land and sees his resources melt down to a two months' supply and can't see any sure daylight beyond. The bloody machine offered but a doubtful outlook—and will still offer nothing much better for a long time to come; for when Davis's "three weeks" is up there's three months' tinkering to follow I guess. That is unquestionably the boss machine of the world, but is the toughest one on prophets, when it is in an incomplete state, that has ever seen the light. Neither Davis nor any other man can foretell with any considerable approach to certainty when it will be ready to get down to actual work in a printing office.

[No signature.]

Three days after the foregoing letter was written he wrote, briefly: "Great Scott but it's a long year-for you and me! I never knew the almanac to drag so. At least since I was finishing that other machine.

"I watch for your letters hungrily—just as I used to watch for the cablegram saying the machine's finished; but when 'next week certainly' swelled into 'three weeks sure' I recognized the old familiar tune I used to hear so much. Ward don't know what sick-heartedness is—but he is in a way to find out."

Always the quaint form of his humor, no matter how dark the way. We may picture him walking the floor, planning, scheming, and smoking—always smoking—trying to find a way out. It was not the kind of scheming that many men have done under the circumstances; not scheming to avoid payment of debts, but to pay them.

To Fred J. Hall, in New York:

Aug. 14, '93

DEAR MR. HALL,—I am very glad indeed if you and Mr. Langdon are able to see any daylight ahead. To me none is visible. I strongly advise that every penny that comes in shall be applied to paying off debts. I may be in error about this, but it seems to me that we have no other course open. We can pay a part of the debts owing to outsiders—none to the Clemenses. In very prosperous times we might regard our stock and copyrights as assets sufficient, with the money owing to us, to square up and quit even, but I suppose we may not hope for such luck in the present condition of things.

What I am mainly hoping for, is to save my royalties. If they come into danger I hope you will cable me, so that I can come over and try to save them, for if they go I am a beggar.

I would sail to-day if I had anybody to take charge of my family and help them through the difficult journeys commanded by the doctors. I may be able to sail ten days hence; I hope so, and expect so.

We can never resurrect the L. A. L. I would not spend any more money on that book. You spoke, a while back, of trying to start it up again as a preparation to disposing of it, but we are not in shape to venture that, I think. It would require more borrowing, and we must not do that.

Yours Sincerely

S. L. C.

Aug. 16. I have thought, and thought, but I don't seem to arrive in any very definite place. Of course you will not have an instant's safety until the bank debts are paid. There is nothing to be thought of but to hand over every penny as fast as it comes in—and that will be slow enough! Or could you secure them by pledging part of our cash assets and—

I am coming over, just as soon as I can get the family moved and settled.

S. L. C.

Two weeks following this letter he could endure the suspense no longer, and on August 29th sailed once more for America. In New York, Clemens settled down at the Players Club, where he could live cheaply, and undertook some literary work while he was casting about for ways and means to relieve the financial situation. Nothing promising occurred, until one night at the Murray Hill Hotel he was introduced by Dr. Clarence C. Rice to Henry H. Rogers, of the Standard Oil group of financiers. Rogers had a keen sense of humor and had always been a great admirer of Mark Twain's work. It was a mirthful evening, and certainly an eventful one in Mark Twain's life. A day or two later Doctor Rice asked the millionaire to interest himself a little in Clemens's business affairs, which he thought a good deal confused. Just what happened is not remembered now, but from the date of the next letter we realize that a discussion of the matter by Clemens and Rogers must have followed pretty promptly.

To Mrs. Clemens, in Europe:

Oct. 18, '93.

DEAR, DEAR SWEETHEART,—I don't seem to get even half a chance to write you, these last two days, and yet there's lots to say.

Apparently everything is at last settled as to the giveaway of L. A. L., and the papers will be signed and the transfer made to-morrow morning.

Meantime I have got the best and wisest man in the whole Standard Oil group of mufti-millionaires a good deal interested in looking into the type-setter (this is private, don't mention it.) He has been searching into that thing for three weeks, and yesterday he said to me, "I find the machine to be all you represented it—I have here exhaustive reports from my own experts, and I know every detail of its capacity, its immense value, its construction, cost, history, and all about its inventor's character. I know that the New York Co. and the Chicago Co. are both stupid, and that they are unbusinesslike people, destitute of money and in a hopeless boggle."

Then he told me the scheme he had planned, then said: "If I can arrange with these people on this basis—it will take several weeks to find out—I will see to it that they get the money they need. Then the thing will move right along and your royalties will cease to be waste paper. I will post you the minute my scheme fails or succeeds. In the meantime, you stop walking the floor. Go off to the country and try to be gay. You may have to go to walking again, but don't begin till I tell you my scheme has failed." And he added: "Keep me posted always as to where you are—for if I need you and can use you—I want to know where to put my hand on you."

If I should even divulge the fact that the Standard Oil is merely talking remotely about going into the type-setter, it would send my royalties up.

With worlds and worlds of love and kisses to you all,

SAML.

With so great a burden of care shifted to the broad financial shoulders of H. H. Rogers, Mark Twain's spirits went ballooning, soaring toward the stars. He awoke, too, to some of the social gaieties about him, and found pleasure in the things that in the hour of his gloom had seemed mainly mockery. We find him going to a Sunday evening at Howells's, to John Mackay's, and elsewhere.

To Mrs. Clemens, in Paris:

Dec. 2, '93.

LIVY DARLING,—Last night at John Mackay's the dinner consisted of soup, raw oysters, corned beef and cabbage, and something like a custard. I ate without fear or stint, and yet have escaped all suggestion of indigestion. The men present were old gray Pacific-coasters whom I knew when I and they were young and not gray. The talk was of the days when we went gypsying a long time ago—thirty years. Indeed it was a talk of the dead. Mainly that. And of how they looked, and the harum-scarum things they did and said. For there were no cares in that life, no aches and pains, and not time enough in the day (and three-fourths of the night) to work off one's surplus vigor and energy. Of the mid-night highway robbery joke played upon me with revolvers at my head on the windswept and desolate Gold Hill Divide, no witness is left but me, the victim. All the friendly robbers are gone. These old fools last night laughed till they cried over the particulars of that old forgotten crime.

John Mackay has no family here but a pet monkey—a most affectionate and winning little devil. But he makes trouble for the servants, for he is full of curiosity and likes to take everything out of the drawers and examine it minutely; and he puts nothing back. The examinations of yesterday count for nothing to-day—he makes a new examination every day. But he injures nothing.

I went with Laffan to the Racquet Club the other night and played, billiards two hours without starting up any rheumatism. I suppose it was all really taken out of me in Berlin.

Richard Harding Davis spoke yesterday of Clara's impersonations at Mrs. Van Rensselaer's here and said they were a wonderful piece of work.

Livy dear, I do hope you are comfortable, as to quarters and food at the Hotel Brighton. But if you're not don't stay there. Make one more effort—don't give it up. Dear heart, this is from one who loves you—which is Saml.

It was decided that Rogers and Clemens should make a trip to Chicago to investigate personally the type-setter situation there. Clemens reports the details of the excursion to Mrs. Clemens in a long subdivided letter, most of which has no general interest and is here omitted. The trip, as a whole, would seem to have been satisfactory. The personal portions of the long Christmas letter may properly be preserved.

To Mrs. Clemens, in Paris:

THE PLAYERS, Xmas, 1893.

No. 1.

Merry Xmas, my darling, and all my darlings! I arrived from Chicago close upon midnight last night, and wrote and sent down my Christmas cablegram before undressing: "Merry Xmas! Promising progress made in Chicago." It would get to the telegraph office toward 8 this morning and reach you at luncheon.

I was vaguely hoping, all the past week, that my Xmas cablegram would be definite, and make you all jump with jubilation; but the thought always intruded itself, "You are not going out there to negotiate with a man, but with a louse. This makes results uncertain."

I was asleep as Christmas struck upon the clock at mid night, and didn't wake again till two hours ago. It is now half past 10 Xmas morning; I have had my coffee and bread, and shan't get out of bed till it is time to dress for Mrs. Laflan's Christmas dinner this evening—where I shall meet Bram Stoker and must make sure about that photo with Irving's autograph. I will get the picture and he will attend to the rest. In order to remember and not forget—well, I will go there with my dress coat wrong side out; it will cause remark and then I shall remember.

No. 2 and 3.

I tell you it was interesting! The Chicago campaign, I mean. On the way out Mr. Rogers would plan out the campaign while I walked the floor and smoked and assented. Then he would close it up with a snap and drop it and we would totally change the subject and take up the scenery, etc.

(Here follows the long detailed report of the Chicago conference, of interest only to the parties directly concerned.)

No. 4.

We had nice tripe, going and coming. Mr. Rogers had telegraphed the Pennsylvania Railroad for a couple of sections for us in the fast train leaving at 2 p. m. the 22nd. The Vice President telegraphed back that every berth was engaged (which was not true—it goes without saying) but that he was sending his own car for us. It was mighty nice and comfortable. In its parlor it had two sofas, which could become beds at night. It had four comfortably-cushioned cane arm-chairs. It had a very nice bedroom with a wide bed in it; which I said I would take because I believed I was a little wider than Mr. Rogers—which turned out to be true; so I took it. It had a darling back-porch—railed, roofed and roomy; and there we sat, most of the time, and viewed the scenery and talked, for the weather was May weather, and the soft dream-pictures of hill and river and mountain and sky were clear and away beyond anything I have ever seen for exquisiteness and daintiness.

The colored waiter knew his business, and the colored cook was a finished artist. Breakfasts: coffee with real cream; beefsteaks, sausage, bacon, chops, eggs in various ways, potatoes in various—yes, and quite wonderful baked potatoes, and hot as fire. Dinners—all manner of things, including canvas-back duck, apollinaris, claret, champagne, etc.

We sat up chatting till midnight, going and coming; seldom read a line, day or night, though we were well fixed with magazines, etc.; then I finished off with a hot Scotch and we went to bed and slept till 9.30 a.m. I honestly tried to pay my share of hotel bills, fees, etc., but I was not allowed—and I knew the reason why, and respected the motive. I will explain when I see you, and then you will understand.

We were 25 hours going to Chicago; we were there 24 hours; we were 30 hours returning. Brisk work, but all of it enjoyable. We insisted on leaving the car at Philadelphia so that our waiter and cook (to whom Mr. R. gave $10 apiece,) could have their Christmas-eve at home.

Mr. Rogers's carriage was waiting for us in Jersey City and deposited me at the Players. There—that's all. This letter is to make up for the three letterless days. I love you, dear heart, I love you all.

SAML.

XXXIV. LETTERS 1894. A WINTER IN NEW YORK. BUSINESS FAILURE. END OF THE MACHINE.

The beginning of the new year found Mark Twain sailing buoyantly on a tide of optimism. He believed that with H. H. Rogers as his financial pilot he could weather safely any storm or stress. He could divert himself, or rest, or work, and consider his business affairs with interest and amusement, instead of with haggard anxiety. He ran over to Hartford to see an amateur play; to Boston to give a charity reading; to Fair Haven to open the library which Mr. Rogers had established there; he attended gay dinners, receptions, and late studio parties, acquiring the name of the "Belle of New York." In the letters that follow we get the echo of some of these things. The Mrs. Rice mentioned in the next brief letter was the wife of Dr. Clarence C. Rice, who had introduced H. H. Rogers to Mark Twain.

To Mrs. Clemens, in Paris:

Jan. 12, '94

Livy darling, I came down from Hartford yesterday with Kipling, and he and Hutton and I had the small smoking compartment to ourselves and found him at last at his ease, and not shy. He was very pleasant company indeed. He is to be in the city a week, and I wish I could invite him to dinner, but it won't do. I should be interrupted by business, of course. The construction of a contract that will suit Paige's lawyer (not Paige) turns out to be very difficult. He is embarrassed by earlier advice to Paige, and hates to retire from it and stultify himself. The negotiations are being conducted, by means of tedious long telegrams and by talks over the long-distance telephone. We keep the wires loaded.

Dear me, dinner is ready. So Mrs. Rice says.

With worlds of love,

SAML.

Clemens and Oliver Wendell Holmes had met and become friends soon after the publication of Innocents Abroad, in 1869. Now, twenty-five years later, we find a record of what without doubt was their last meeting. It occurred at the home of Mrs. James T. Field.

To Mrs. Clemens, in Paris:

BOSTON, Jan. 25, '94.

Livy darling, I am caught out worse this time than ever before, in the matter of letters. Tuesday morning I was smart enough to finish and mail my long letter to you before breakfast—for I was suspecting that I would not have another spare moment during the day. It turned out just so.

In a thoughtless moment I agreed to come up here and read for the poor. I did not reflect that it would cost me three days. I could not get released. Yesterday I had myself called at 8 and ran out to Mr. Rogers's house at 9, and talked business until half past 10; then caught 11 o'clock train and arrived here at 6; was shaven and dressed by 7 and ready for dinner here in Mrs. Field's charming house.

Dr. Oliver Wendell Holmes never goes out now (he is in his 84th year,) but he came out this time—said he wanted to "have a time" once more with me.

Mrs. Fields said Aldrich begged to come and went away crying because she wouldn't let him. She allowed only her family (Sarah Orne Jewett and sister) to be present, because much company would overtax Dr. Holmes.

Well, he was just delightful! He did as brilliant and beautiful talking (and listening) as ever he did in his life, I guess. Fields and Jewett said he hadn't been in such splendid form in years. He had ordered his carriage for 9.

The coachman sent in for him at 9; but he said, "Oh, nonsense!—leave glories and grandeurs like these? Tell him to go away and come in an hour!"

At 10 he was called for again, and Mrs. Fields, getting uneasy, rose, but he wouldn't go—and so we rattled ahead the same as ever. Twice more Mrs. Fields rose, but he wouldn't go—and he didn't go till half past 10—

an unwarrantable dissipation for him in these days. He was prodigiously complimentary about some of my books, and is having Pudd'nhead read to him. I told him you and I used the Autocrat as a courting book and marked it all through, and that you keep it in the sacred green box with the love letters, and it pleased him.

Good-bye, my dear darling, it is 15 minutes to dinner and I'm not dressed yet. I have a reception to-night and will be out very late at that place and at Irving's Theatre where I have a complimentary box. I wish you were all here.

SAML.

In the next letter we meet James J. Corbett—"Gentleman Jim," as he was sometimes called—the champion pugilist of that day.

The Howells incident so amusingly dramatized will perhaps be more appreciated if the reader remembers that Mark Twain himself had at intervals been a mind-healing enthusiast. Indeed, in spite of his strictures on Mrs. Eddy, his interest in the subject of mind-cure continued to the end of his life.

To Mrs. Clemens, in Paris:

Sunday, 9.30 a. m.

Livy dear, when we got out to the house last night, Mrs. Rogers, who is up and around, now, didn't want to go down stairs to dinner, but Mr. R. persuaded her and we had a very good time indeed. By 8 o'clock we were down again and bought a fifteen-dollar box in the Madison Square Garden (Rogers bought it, not I,) then he went and fetched Dr. Rice while I (went) to the Players and picked up two artists—Reid and Simmons—and thus we filled 5 of the 6 seats. There was a vast multitude of people in the brilliant place. Stanford White came along presently and invited me to go to the

World-Champion's dressing room, which I was very glad to do. Corbett has a fine face and is modest and diffident, besides being the most perfectly and beautifully constructed human animal in the world. I said:

"You have whipped Mitchell, and maybe you will whip Jackson in June—but you are not done, then. You will have to tackle me."

He answered, so gravely that one might easily have thought him in earnest:

"No—I am not going to meet you in the ring. It is not fair or right to require it. You might chance to knock me out, by no merit of your own, but by a purely accidental blow; and then my reputation would be gone and you would have a double one. You have got fame enough and you ought not to want to take mine away from me."

Corbett was for a long time a clerk in the Nevada Bank in San Francisco.

There were lots of little boxing matches, to entertain the crowd: then at last Corbett appeared in the ring and the 8,000 people present went mad with enthusiasm. My two artists went mad about his form. They said they had never seen anything that came reasonably near equaling its perfection except Greek statues, and they didn't surpass it.

Corbett boxed 3 rounds with the middle-weight Australian champion—oh, beautiful to see!—then the show was over and we struggled out through a perfect wash of humanity. When we reached the street I found I had left my arctics in the box. I had to have them, so Simmons said he would go back and get them, and I didn't dissuade him. I couldn't see how he was going to make his way a single yard into that solid oncoming wave of people—yet he must plow through it full 50 yards. He was back with the shoes in 3 minutes!

How do you reckon he accomplished that miracle? By saying:

"Way, gentlemen, please—coming to fetch Mr. Corbett's overshoes."

The word flew from mouth to mouth, the Red Sea divided, and Simmons walked comfortably through and back, dry shod. Simmons (this was revealed to me under seal of secrecy by Reid) is the hero of "Gwen," and he and

Gwen's author were once engaged to marry. This is "fire-escape" Simmons, the inveterate talker, you know: "Exit—in case of Simmons."

I had an engagement at a beautiful dwelling close to the Players for 10.30; I was there by 10.45. Thirty cultivated and very musical ladies and gentlemen present—all of them acquaintances and many of them personal friends of mine. That wonderful Hungarian Band was there (they charge $500 for an evening.) Conversation and Band until midnight; then a bite of supper; then the company was compactly grouped before me and I told about Dr. B. E. Martin and the etchings, and followed it with the Scotch-Irish Christening. My, but the Martin is a darling story! Next, the head tenor from the Opera sang half a dozen great songs that set the company wild, yes, mad with delight, that nobly handsome young Damrosch accompanying on the piano.

Just a little pause—then the Band burst out into an explosion of weird and tremendous dance music, a Hungarian celebrity and his wife took the floor—I followed; I couldn't help it; the others drifted in, one by one, and it was Onteora over again.

By half past 4 I had danced all those people down—and yet was not tired; merely breathless. I was in bed at 5, and asleep in ten minutes. Up at 9 and presently at work on this letter to you. I think I wrote until 2 or half past. Then I walked leisurely out to Mr. Rogers's (it is called 3 miles but it is short of it) arriving at 3.30, but he was out—to return at 5.30—(and a person was in, whom I don't particularly like)—so I didn't stay, but dropped over and chatted with the Howellses until 6.

First, Howells and I had a chat together. I asked about Mrs. H. He said she was fine, still steadily improving, and nearly back to her old best health. I asked (as if I didn't know):

"What do you attribute this strange miracle to?"

"Mind-cure—simply mind-cure."

"Lord, what a conversion! You were a scoffer three months ago."

"I? I wasn't."

"You were. You made elaborate fun of me in this very room."

"I did not, Clemens."

"It's a lie, Howells, you did."

I detailed to him the conversation of that time—with the stately argument furnished by Boyesen in the fact that a patient had actually been killed by a mind-curist; and Howells's own smart remark that when the mind-curist is done with you, you have to call in a "regular" at last because the former can't procure you a burial permit.

At last he gave in—he said he remembered that talk, but had now been a mind-curist so long it was difficult for him to realize that he had ever been anything else.

Mrs. H. came skipping in, presently, the very person, to a dot, that she used to be, so many years ago.

Mrs. H. said: "People may call it what they like, but it is just hypnotism, and that's all it is—hypnotism pure and simple. Mind-cure!—the idea! Why, this woman that cured me hasn't got any mind. She's a good creature, but she's dull and dumb and illiterate and—"

"Now Eleanor!"

"I know what I'm talking about!—don't I go there twice a week? And Mr. Clemens, if you could only see her wooden and satisfied face when she snubs me for forgetting myself and showing by a thoughtless remark that to me weather is still weather, instead of being just an abstraction and a superstition—oh, it's the funniest thing you ever saw! A-n-d-when she tilts up her nose-well, it's—it's—Well it's that kind of a nose that—"

"Now Eleanor!—the woman is not responsible for her nose—" and so-on and so-on. It didn't seem to me that I had any right to be having this feast and you not there.

She convinced me before she got through, that she and William James are right—hypnotism and mind-cure are the same thing; no difference between them. Very well; the very source, the very center of hypnotism is Paris. Dr. Charcot's pupils and disciples are right there and ready to your hand without fetching poor dear old Susy across the stormy sea. Let Mrs. Mackay (to whom I send my best respects), tell you whom to go to to learn all you need to learn and how to proceed. Do, do it, honey. Don't lose a minute.

.... At 11 o'clock last night Mr. Rogers said:

"I am able to feel physical fatigue—and I feel it now. You never show any, either in your eyes or your movements; do you ever feel any?"

I was able to say that I had forgotten what that feeling was like. Don't you remember how almost impossible it was for me to tire myself at the Villa? Well, it is just so in New York. I go to bed unfatigued at 3, I get up fresh and fine six hours later. I believe I have taken only one daylight nap since I have been here.

When the anchor is down, then I shall say:

"Farewell—a long farewell—to business! I will never touch it again!"

I will live in literature, I will wallow in it, revel in it, I will swim in ink! Joan of Arc—but all this is premature; the anchor is not down yet.

To-morrow (Tuesday) I will add a P. S. if I've any to add; but, whether or no, I must mail this to morrow, for the mail steamer goes next day.

5.30 p. m. Great Scott, this is Tuesday! I must rush this letter into the mail instantly.

Tell that sassy Ben I've got her welcome letter, and I'll write her as soon as I get a daylight chance. I've most time at night, but I'd druther write daytimes.

SAML.

The Reid and Simmons mentioned in the foregoing were Robert Reid and Edward Simmons, distinguished painter—the latter a brilliant, fluent, and industrious talker. The title "Fire-escape Simmons," which Clemens gives him, originated when Oliver Herford, whose quaint wit has so long delighted New-Yorkers, one day pinned up by the back door of the Players the notice: "Exit in case of Simmons." Gwen, a popular novel of that day, was written by Blanche Willis Howard.

"Jamie" Dodge, in the next letter, was the son of Mrs. Mary Mapes Dodge, editor of St. Nicholas.

To Clara Clemens, in Paris:

MR. ROGERS'S OFFICE, Feb. 5, '94.

Dear Benny—I was intending to answer your letter to-day, but I am away down town, and will simply whirl together a sentence or two for good-fellowship. I have bought photographs of Coquelin and Jane Hading and will ask them to sign them. I shall meet Coquelin tomorrow night, and if Hading is not present I will send her picture to her by somebody.

I am to breakfast with Madame Nordica in a few days, and meantime I hope to get a good picture of her to sign. She was of the breakfast company yesterday, but the picture of herself which she signed and gave me does not do her majestic beauty justice.

I am too busy to attend to the photo-collecting right, because I have to live up to the name which Jamie Dodge has given me—the "Belle of New York"—and it just keeps me rushing. Yesterday I had engagements to breakfast at noon, dine at 3, and dine again at 7. I got away from the long breakfast at 2 p. m., went and excused myself from the 3 o'clock dinner, then lunched with Mrs. Dodge in 58th street, returned to the Players and dressed, dined out at 9, and was back at Mrs. Dodge's at 10 p. m. where we had magic-lantern views of a superb sort, and a lot of yarns until an hour after midnight, and got to bed at 2 this morning—a good deal of a gain on my recent hours. But I don't get tired; I sleep as sound as a dead person, and always wake up fresh and strong—usually at exactly 9.

I was at breakfast lately where people of seven separate nationalities sat and the seven languages were going all the time. At my side sat a charming gentleman who was a delightful and active talker, and interesting. He talked glibly to those folks in all those seven languages and still had a language to spare! I wanted to kill him, for very envy.

I greet you with love and kisses.

PAPA.

To Mrs. Clemens, in Paris:

Feb.—.

Livy dear, last night I played billiards with Mr. Rogers until 11, then went to Robert Reid's studio and had a most delightful time until 4 this morning. No ladies were invited this time. Among the people present were—

Coquelin;

Richard Harding Davis;

Harrison, the great out-door painter;

Wm. H. Chase, the artist;

Bettini, inventor of the new phonograph.

Nikola Tesla, the world-wide illustrious electrician; see article about him in Jan. or Feb. Century.

John Drew, actor;

James Barnes, a marvelous mimic; my, you should see him!

Smedley the artist;

Zorn the artist;

Zogbaum the artist;

Reinhart the artist;

Metcalf the artist;

Ancona, head tenor at the Opera;

Oh, a great lot of others. Everybody there had done something and was in his way famous.

Somebody welcomed Coquelin in a nice little French speech; John Drew did the like for me in English, and then the fun began. Coquelin did some excellent French monologues—one of them an ungrammatical Englishman telling a colorless historiette in French. It nearly killed the fifteen or twenty people who understood it.

I told a yarn, Ancona sang half a dozen songs, Barnes did his darling imitations, Harding Davis sang the hanging of Danny Deever, which was of course good, but he followed it with that most fascinating (for what reason I don't know) of all Kipling's poems, "On the Road to Mandalay," sang it tenderly, and it searched me deeper and charmed me more than the Deever.

Young Gerrit Smith played some ravishing dance music and we all danced about an hour. There couldn't be a pleasanter night than that one was. Some of those people complained of fatigue but I don't seem to know what the sense of fatigue is.

Coquelin talks quite good English now. He said:

"I have a brother who has the fine mind—ah, a charming and delicate fancy, and he knows your writings so well, and loves them—and that is the same with me. It will stir him so when I write and tell him I have seen you!"

Wasn't that nice? We talked a good deal together. He is as winning as his own face. But he wouldn't sign that photograph for Clara. "That? No! She shall have a better one. I will send it to you."

He is much driven, and will forget it, but Reid has promised to get the picture for me, and I will try and keep him reminded.

Oh, dear, my time is all used up and your letters are not answered.

Mama, dear, I don't go everywhere—I decline most things. But there are plenty that I can't well get out of.

I will remember what you say and not make my yarning too common.

I am so glad Susy has gone on that trip and that you are trying the electric. May you both prosper. For you are mighty dear to me and in my thoughts always.

SAML.

The affairs of the Webster Publishing Company were by this time getting into a very serious condition indeed. The effects of the panic of the year before could not be overcome. Creditors were pressing their claims and profits were negligible. In the following letter we get a Mark Twain estimate of the great financier who so cheerfully was willing to undertake the solving of Mark Twain's financial problems.

To Mrs. Clemens, in Paris:

THE PLAYERS, Feb. 15, '94. 11.30 p. m.

Livy darling, Yesterday I talked all my various matters over with Mr. Rogers and we decided that it would be safe for me to leave here the 7th of March, in the New York. So his private secretary, Miss Harrison, wrote and ordered a berth for me and then I lost no time in cabling you that I should reach Southampton March 14, and Paris the 15th. Land, but it made my pulses leap, to think I was going to see you again!... One thing at a time. I never fully laid Webster's disastrous condition before Mr. Rogers until tonight after billiards. I did hate to burden his good heart and over-worked head with it, but he took hold with avidity and said it was no burden to work for his friends, but a pleasure. We discussed it from various standpoints, and found it a sufficiently difficult problem to solve; but he thinks that after he has slept upon it and thought it over he will know what to suggest.

You must not think I am ever rude with Mr. Rogers, I am not. He is not common clay, but fine—fine and delicate—and that sort do not call out the coarsenesses that are in my sort. I am never afraid of wounding him; I do not need to watch myself in that matter. The sight of him is peace.

He wants to go to Japan—it is his dream; wants to go with me—which means, the two families—and hear no more about business for awhile, and have a rest. And he needs it. But it is like all the dreams of all busy men—fated to remain dreams.

You perceive that he is a pleasant text for me. It is easy to write about him. When I arrived in September, lord how black the prospect was—how desperate, how incurably desperate! Webster and Co. had to have a small sum of money or go under at once. I flew to Hartford—to my friends—but they were not moved, not strongly interested, and I was ashamed that I went. It was from Mr. Rogers, a stranger, that I got the money and was by it saved. And then—while still a stranger—he set himself the task of saving my financial life without putting upon me (in his native delicacy) any sense that I was the recipient of a charity, a benevolence—and he has accomplished that task; accomplished it at a cost of three months of wearing and difficult labor. He gave that time to me—time which could not be bought by any man at a hundred thousand dollars a month—no, nor for three times the money.

Well, in the midst of that great fight, that long and admirable fight, George Warner came to me and said:

"There is a splendid chance open to you. I know a man—a prominent man—who has written a book that will go like wildfire; a book that arraigns the Standard Oil fiends, and gives them unmitigated hell, individual by individual. It is the very book for you to publish; there is a fortune in it, and I can put you in communication with the author."

I wanted to say:

"The only man I care for in the world; the only man I would give a damn for; the only man who is lavishing his sweat and blood to save me and mine from starvation and shame, is a Standard Oil fiend. If you know me, you know whether I want the book or not."

But I didn't say that. I said I didn't want any book; I wanted to get out of the publishing business and out of all business, and was here for that purpose and would accomplish it if I could.

But there's enough. I shall be asleep by 3, and I don't need much sleep, because I am never drowsy or tired these days. Dear, dear Susy my strength reproaches me when I think of her and you, my darling.

SAML.

But even so able a man as Henry Rogers could not accomplish the impossible. The affairs of the Webster Company were hopeless, the business was not worth saving. By Mr. Rogers's advice an assignment was made April, 18, 1894. After its early spectacular success less than ten years had brought the business to failure. The publication of the Grant memoirs had been its only great achievement.

Clemens would seem to have believed that the business would resume, and for a time Rogers appears to have comforted him in his hope, but we cannot believe that it long survived. Young Hall, who had made such a struggle for its salvation, was eager to go on, but he must presently have seen the futility of any effort in that direction.

Of course the failure of Mark Twain's firm made a great stir in the country, and it is easy to understand that loyal friends would rally in his behalf.

To Mrs. Clemens, in Paris:

April 22, '94.

Dear old darling, we all think the creditors are going to allow us to resume business; and if they do we shall pull through and pay the debts. I am prodigiously glad we made an assignment. And also glad that we did not make it sooner. Earlier we should have made a poor showing; but now we shall make a good one.

I meet flocks of people, and they all shake me cordially by the hand and say "I was so sorry to hear of the assignment, but so glad you did it. It was around, this long time, that the concern was tottering, and all your friends were afraid you would delay the assignment too long."

John Mackay called yesterday, and said, "Don't let it disturb you, Sam—we all have to do it, at one time or another; it's nothing to be ashamed of."

One stranger out in New York State sent me a dollar bill and thought he would like to get up a dollar-subscription for me. And Poultney Bigelow's note came promptly, with his check for $1,000. I had been meeting him every day at the Club and liking him better and better all the time. I couldn't take his money, of course, but I thanked him cordially for his good will.

Now and then a good and dear Joe Twichell or Susy Warner condoles with me and says "Cheer up—don't be downhearted," and some other friend says, "I am glad and surprised to see how cheerful you are and how bravely you stand it"—and none of them suspect what a burden has been lifted from me and how blithe I am inside. Except when I think of you, dear heart—then I am not blithe; for I seem to see you grieving and ashamed, and dreading to look people in the face. For in the thick of the fight there is cheer, but you are far away and cannot hear the drums nor see the wheeling squadrons. You only seem to see rout, retreat, and dishonored colors dragging in the dirt—whereas none of these things exist. There is temporary defeat, but no dishonor—and we will march again. Charley Warner said to-day, "Sho, Livy isn't worrying. So long as she's got you and the children she doesn't care what happens. She knows it isn't her affair." Which didn't convince me.

Good bye my darling, I love you and all of the kids—and you can tell Clara I am not a spitting gray kitten.

SAML.

Clemens sailed for Europe as soon as his affairs would permit him to go. He must get settled where he could work comfortably. Type-setter prospects seemed promising, but meantime there was need of funds.

He began writing on the ship, as was his habit, and had completed his article on Fenimore Cooper by the time he reached London. In August we find him writing to Mr. Rogers from Etretat, a little Norman watering-place.

To H. H. Rogers, in New York:

ETRETAT, (NORMANDIE)

CHALET DES ABRIS

Aug. 25, '94.

DEAR MR. ROGERS,—I find the Madam ever so much better in health and strength. The air is superb and soothing and wholesome, and the Chalet is remote from noise and people, and just the place to write in. I shall begin work this afternoon.

Mrs. Clemens is in great spirits on, account of the benefit which she has received from the electrical treatment in Paris and is bound to take it up again and continue it all the winter, and of course I am perfectly willing. She requires me to drop the lecture platform out of my mind and go straight ahead with Joan until the book is finished. If I should have to go home for even a week she means to go with me—won't consent to be separated again—but she hopes I won't need to go.

I tell her all right, "I won't go unless you send, and then I must."

She keeps the accounts; and as she ciphers it we can't get crowded for money for eight months yet. I didn't know that. But I don't know much anyway.

Sincerely yours,

S. L. CLEMENS.

The reader may remember that Clemens had written the first half of his Joan of Arc book at the Villa Viviani, in Florence, nearly two years before. He had closed the manuscript then with the taking of Orleans, and was by no means sure that he would continue the story beyond that point. Now, however, he was determined to reach the tale's tragic conclusion.

To H. H. Rogers, in New York:

ETRETAT,

Sunday, Sept. 9, '94.

DEAR MR. ROGERS, I drove the quill too hard, and I broke down—in my head. It has now been three days since I laid up. When I wrote you a week ago I had added 10,000 words or thereabout to Joan. Next day I added 1,500 which was a proper enough day's work though not a full one; but during Tuesday and Wednesday I stacked up an aggregate of 6,000 words—and that was a very large mistake. My head hasn't been worth a cent since.

However, there's a compensation; for in those two days I reached and passed—successfully—a point which I was solicitous about before I ever began the book: viz., the battle of Patay. Because that would naturally be the next to the last chapter of a work consisting of either two books or one. In the one case one goes right along from that point (as I shall do now); in the other he would add a wind-up chapter and make the book consist of Joan's childhood and military career alone.

I shall resume work to-day; and hereafter I will not go at such an intemperate' rate. My head is pretty cobwebby yet.

I am hoping that along about this time I shall hear that the machine is beginning its test in the Herald office. I shall be very glad indeed to know the result of it. I wish I could be there.

Sincerely yours

S. L. CLEMENS.

Rouen, where Joan met her martyrdom, was only a short distance away, and they halted there en route to Paris, where they had arranged to spend the winter. The health of Susy Clemens was not good, and they lingered in Rouen while Clemens explored the old city and incidentally did some writing of another sort. In a note to Mr. Rogers he said: "To put in my odd time I am writing some articles about Paul Bourget and his Outre-Mer chapters—laughing at them and at some of our oracular owls who find them important. What the hell makes them important, I should like to know!"

He was still at Rouen two weeks later and had received encouraging news from Rogers concerning the type-setter, which had been placed for trial in the office of the Chicago Herald. Clemens wrote: "I can hardly keep from sending a hurrah by cable. I would certainly do it if I wasn't superstitious." His restraint, though wise, was wasted the end was near.

To H. H. Rogers, in New York:

169 RUE DE L'UNIVERSITE,

PARIS, Dec. 22; '94.

DEAR MR. ROGERS,—I seemed to be entirely expecting your letter, and also prepared and resigned; but Lord, it shows how little we know ourselves and how easily we can deceive ourselves. It hit me like a thunder-clap. It knocked every rag of sense out of my head, and I went flying here and there and yonder, not knowing what I was doing, and only one clearly defined thought standing up visible and substantial out of the crazy storm-drift that my dream of ten years was in desperate peril, and out of the 60,000 or 90,000 projects for its rescue that came floating through my skull, not one would hold still long enough for me to examine it and size it up. Have you ever been like that? Not so much so, I reckon.

There was another clearly defined idea—I must be there and see it die. That is, if it must die; and maybe if I were there we might hatch up some next-to-impossible way to make it take up its bed and take a walk.

So, at the end of four hours I started, still whirling and walked over to the rue Scribe—4 P. M.—and asked a question or two and was told I should be running a big risk if I took the 9 P. M. train for London and Southampton; "better come right along at 6.52 per Havre special and step aboard the New York all easy and comfortable." Very! and I about two miles from home, with no packing done.

Then it occurred to me that none of these salvation-notions that were whirl-winding through my head could be examined or made available unless at least a month's time could be secured. So I cabled you, and said to myself that I would take the French steamer tomorrow (which will be Sunday).

By bedtime Mrs. Clemens had reasoned me into a fairly rational and contented state of mind; but of course it didn't last long. So I went on thinking—mixing it with a smoke in the dressing room once an hour—until dawn this morning. Result—a sane resolution; no matter what your answer to my cable might be, I would hold still and not sail until I should get an answer to this present letter which I am now writing, or a cable answer from you saying "Come" or "Remain."

I have slept 6 hours, my pond has clarified, and I find the sediment of my 70,000 projects to be of this character:

[Several pages of suggestions for reconstructing the machine follow.]

Don't say I'm wild. For really I'm sane again this morning.

....

I am going right along with Joan, now, and wait untroubled till I hear from you. If you think I can be of the least use, cable me "Come." I can write Joan on board ship and lose no time. Also I could discuss my plan with the publisher for a deluxe Joan, time being an object, for some of the pictures could be made over here cheaply and quickly, but would cost much time and money in America.

....

If the meeting should decide to quit business Jan. 4, I'd like to have Stoker stopped from paying in any more money, if Miss Harrison doesn't mind that disagreeable job. And I'll have to write them, too, of course.

With love,

S. L. CLEMENS.

The "Stoker" of this letter was Bram Stoker, long associated with Sir Henry Irving. Irving himself had also taken stock in the machine. The address, 169 Rue de l'Universite, whence these letters are written, was the beautiful studio home of the artist Pomroy which they had taken for the winter.

To H. H. Rogers, in New York:

169 RUE DE L'UNIVERSITE,

PARIS, Dec. 27, '94.

DEAR MR. ROGERS,—Notwithstanding your heart is "old and hard," you make a body choke up. I know you "mean every word you say" and I do take it "in the same spirit in which you tender it." I shall keep your regard while we two live—that I know; for I shall always remember what you have done for me, and that will insure me against ever doing anything that could forfeit it or impair it. I am 59 years old; yet I never had a friend before who put out a hand and tried to pull me ashore when he found me in deep waters.

It is six days or seven days ago that I lived through that despairing day, and then through a night without sleep; then settled down next day into my right mind (or thereabouts,) and wrote you. I put in the rest of that day till 7 P. M. plenty comfortably enough writing a long chapter of my book; then went to a masked ball blacked up as Uncle Remus, taking Clara along; and we had a good time. I have lost no day since and suffered no discomfort to speak of, but drove my troubles out of my mind and had good success in keeping them out—through watchfulness. I have done a good week's work and put the book a good way ahead in the Great Trial, which is the difficult part which requires the most thought and carefulness. I cannot see the end of the Trial yet, but I am on the road. I am creeping surely toward it.

"Why not leave them all to me." My business bothers? I take you by the hand! I jump at the chance!

I ought to be ashamed and I am trying my best to be ashamed—and yet I do jump at the chance in spite of it. I don't want to write Irving and I don't want to write Stoker. It doesn't seem as if I could. But I can suggest something for you to write them; and then if you see that I am unwise, you can write them something quite different. Now this is my idea:

1. *To return Stoker's $100 to him and keep his stock.*
2. *And tell Irving that when luck turns with me I will make good to him what the salvage from the dead Co. fails to pay him of his $500.*

P. S. Madam says No, I must face the music. So I enclose my effort to be used if you approve, but not otherwise.

There! Now if you will alter it to suit your judgment and bang away, I shall be eternally obliged.

We shall try to find a tenant for our Hartford house; not an easy matter, for it costs heavily to live in. We can never live in it again; though it would break the family's hearts if they could believe it.

Nothing daunts Mrs. Clemens or makes the world look black to her—which is the reason I haven't drowned myself.

We all send our deepest and warmest greetings to you and all of yours and a Happy New Year!

S. L. CLEMENS.

Enclosure:

MY DEAR STOKER,—I am not dating this because it is not to be mailed at present.

When it reaches you it will mean that there is a hitch in my machine-enterprise—a hitch so serious as to make it take to itself the aspect of a dissolved dream. This letter, then, will contain cheque for the $100 which you have paid. And will you tell Irving for me—I can't get up courage enough to talk about this misfortune myself, except to you, whom by good luck I haven't damaged yet that when the wreckage presently floats ashore he will get a good deal of his $500 back; and a dab at a time I will make up to him the rest.

I'm not feeling as fine as I was when I saw you there in your home. Please remember me kindly to Mrs. Stoker. I gave up that London lecture-project entirely. Had to—there's never been a chance since to find the time.

Sincerely yours,

S. L. CLEMENS.

XXXV. LETTERS, 1895-96, TO H. H. ROGERS AND OTHERS. FINISHING "JOAN OF ARC." THE TRIP AROUND THE WORLD. DEATH OF SUSY CLEMENS.

To H. H. Rogers, in New York City:

[No date.]

DEAR MR. ROGERS,—Yours of Dec. 21 has arrived, containing the circular to stockholders and I guess the Co. will really quit—there doesn't seem to be any other wise course.

There's one thing which makes it difficult for me to soberly realize that my ten year dream is actually dissolved; and that is, that it reveries my horoscope. The proverb says, "Born lucky, always lucky," and I am very superstitious. As a small boy I was notoriously lucky. It was usual for one or two of our lads (per annum) to get drowned in the Mississippi or in Bear Creek, but I was pulled out in a 2/3 drowned condition 9 times before I learned to swim, and was considered to be a cat in disguise. When the "Pennsylvania" blew up and the telegraph reported my brother as fatally injured (with 60 others) but made no mention of me, my uncle said to my mother "It means that Sam was somewhere else, after being on that boat a year and a half—he was born lucky." Yes, I was somewhere else. I am so superstitious that I have always been afraid to have business dealings with certain relatives and friends of mine because they were unlucky people. All my life I have stumbled upon lucky chances of large size, and whenever they were wasted it was because of my own stupidity and carelessness. And so I have felt entirely certain that that machine would turn up trumps eventually. It disappointed me lots of times, but I couldn't shake off the confidence of a life-time in my luck.

Well, whatever I get out of the wreckage will be due to good luck—the good luck of getting you into the scheme—for, but for that, there wouldn't be any wreckage; it would be total loss.

I wish you had been in at the beginning. Then we should have had the good luck to step promptly ashore.

Miss Harrison has had a dream which promises me a large bank account, and I want her to go ahead and dream it twice more, so as to make the prediction sure to be fulfilled.

I've got a first rate subject for a book. It kept me awake all night, and I began it and completed it in my mind. The minute I finish Joan I will take it up.

Love and Happy New Year to you all.

Sincerely yours,

S. L. CLEMENS.

This was about the end of the machine interests so far as Clemens was concerned. Paige succeeded in getting some new people interested, but nothing important happened, or that in any way affected Mark Twain. Characteristically he put the whole matter behind him and plunged into his work, facing comparative poverty and a burden of debts with a stout heart. The beginning of the new year found him really poorer in purse than he had ever been in his life, but certainly not crushed, or even discouraged—at least, not permanently—and never more industrious or capable.

To H. H. Rogers, in New York City:

169 RUE DE L'UNIVERSITE,

PARIS, Jan. 23, '95.

DEAR MR. ROGERS,—After I wrote you, two or three days ago I thought I would make a holiday of the rest of the day—the second deliberate holiday since I had the gout. On the first holiday I wrote a tale of about

6,000 words, which was 3 days' work in one; and this time I did 8,000 before midnight. I got nothing out of that first holiday but the recreation of it, for I condemned the work after careful reading and some revision; but this time I fared better—I finished the Huck Finn tale that lies in your safe, and am satisfied with it.

The Bacheller syndicate (117 Tribune Building) want a story of 5,000 words (lowest limit of their London agent) for $1,000 and offer to plank the check on delivery, and it was partly to meet that demand that I took that other holiday. So as I have no short story that suits me (and can't and shan't make promises), the best I can do is to offer the longer one which I finished on my second holiday—"Tom Sawyer, Detective."

It makes 27 or 28,000 words, and is really written for grown folks, though I expect young folk to read it, too. It transfers to the banks of the Mississippi the incidents of a strange murder which was committed in Sweden in old times.

I'll refer applicants for a sight of the story to you or Miss Harrison.—[Secretary to Mr. Rogers.]

Yours sincerely,

S. L. CLEMENS.

To H. H. Rogers, in New York City:

169 RUE DE L'UNIVERSITE,

Apr. 29, '95.

DEAR MR. ROGERS,—Your felicitous delightful letter of the 15th arrived three days ago, and brought great pleasure into the house.

There is one thing that weighs heavily on Mrs. Clemens and me. That is Brusnahan's money. If he is satisfied to have it invested in the Chicago enterprise, well and good; if not, we would like to have the money paid back to him. I will give him as many months to decide in as he pleases—let him name 6 or 10 or 12—and we will let the money stay where it is in your hands till the time is up. Will Miss Harrison tell him so? I mean if you approve. I would like him to have a good investment, but would meantime prefer to protect him against loss.

At 6 minutes past 7, yesterday evening, Joan of Arc was burned at the stake.

With the long strain gone, I am in a sort of physical collapse today, but it will be gone tomorrow. I judged that this end of the book would be hard work, and it turned out so. I have never done any work before that cost so much thinking and weighing and measuring and planning and cramming, or so much cautious and painstaking execution. For I wanted the whole Rouen trial in, if it could be got in in such a way that the reader's interest would not flag—in fact I wanted the reader's interest to increase; and so I stuck to it with that determination in view—with the result that I have left nothing out but unimportant repetitions. Although it is mere history—history pure and simple—history stripped naked of flowers, embroideries, colorings, exaggerations, invention—the family agree that I have succeeded. It was a perilous thing to try in a tale, but I never believed it a doubtful one—provided I stuck strictly to business and didn't weaken and give up: or didn't get lazy and skimp the work. The first two-thirds of the book were easy; for I only needed to keep my historical road straight; therefore I used for reference only one French history and one English one—and shoveled in as much fancy work and invention on both sides of the historical road as I pleased. But on this last third I have constantly used five French sources and five English ones and I think no telling historical nugget in any of them has escaped me.

Possibly the book may not sell, but that is nothing—it was written for love.

There—I'm called to see company. The family seldom require this of me, but they know I am not working today.

Yours sincerely,

S. L. CLEMENS.

"Brusnahan," of the foregoing letter, was an employee of the New York Herald, superintendent of the press-room—who had invested some of his savings in the type-setter.

In February Clemens returned to New York to look after matters connected with his failure and to close arrangements for a reading-tour around the world. He was nearly sixty years old, and time had not lessened his loathing for the platform. More than once, however, in earlier years, he had turned to it as a debt-payer, and never yet had his burden been so great as now. He concluded arrangements with Major Pond to take him as far as the Pacific Coast, and with R. S. Smythe, of Australia, for the rest of the tour. In April we find him once more back in Paris preparing to bring the family to America, He had returned by way of London, where he had visited Stanley the explorer—an old friend.

To H. H. Rogers, in New York City:

169 RUE DE L'UNIVERSITE,

Sunday, Apr. 7, '95.

DEAR MR. ROGERS,—..... Stanley is magnificently housed in London, in a grand mansion in the midst of the official world, right off Downing Street and Whitehall. He had an extraordinary assemblage of brains and fame there to meet me—thirty or forty (both sexes) at dinner, and more than a hundred came in, after dinner. Kept it up till after midnight. There were cabinet ministers, ambassadors, admirals, generals, canons, Oxford professors, novelists, playwrights, poets, and a number of people equipped with rank and brains. I told some yarns and made some speeches. I promised to call on all those people next time I come to London, and show them the wife and the daughters. If I were younger and very strong I would dearly love to spend a season in London—provided I had no work on hand, or no work more exacting than lecturing. I think I will lecture there a month or two when I return from Australia.

There were many delightful ladies in that company. One was the wife of His Excellency Admiral Bridge, Commander-in Chief of the Australian Station, and she said her husband was able to throw wide all doors to me in that part of the world and would be glad to do it, and would yacht me and my party around, and excursion us in his flag-ship and make us have a great time; and she said she would write him we were coming, and we would find him ready. I have a letter from her this morning enclosing a letter of introduction to the Admiral. I already know the Admiral commanding in the China Seas and have promised to look in on him out there. He sleeps with my books under his pillow. P'raps it is the only way he can sleep.

According to Mrs. Clemens's present plans—subject to modification, of course—we sail in May; stay one day, or two days in New York, spend June, July and August in Elmira and prepare my lectures; then lecture in San Francisco and thereabouts during September and sail for Australia before the middle of October and open the show there about the middle of November. We don't take the girls along; it would be too expensive and they are quite willing to remain behind anyway.

Mrs. C. is feeling so well that she is not going to try the New York doctor till we have gone around the world and robbed it and made the finances a little easier.

With a power of love to you all,

S. L. CLEMENS.

There would come moments of depression, of course, and a week later he wrote: "I am tired to death all the time:" To a man of less vitality, less vigor of mind and body, it is easy to believe that under such circumstances this condition would have remained permanent. But perhaps, after all, it was his comic outlook on things in general that was his chief life-saver.

To H. H. Rogers, in New York City:

169 RUE DE L'UNIVERSITE, Apr. 29, '95.

DEAR MR. ROGERS,—I have been hidden an hour or two, reading proof of Joan and now I think I am a lost child. I can't find anybody on the place. The baggage has all disappeared, including the family. I reckon that in the hurry and bustle of moving to the hotel they forgot me. But it is no matter. It is peacefuller now than I have known it for days and days and days.

In these Joan proofs which I have been reading for the September Harper I find a couple of tip-top platform readings—and I mean to read them on our trip. If the authorship is known by then; and if it isn't, I will reveal it. The fact is, there is more good platform-stuff in Joan than in any previous book of mine, by a long sight.

Yes, every danged member of the tribe has gone to the hotel and left me lost. I wonder how they can be so careless with property. I have got to try to get there by myself now.

All the trunks are going over as luggage; then I've got to find somebody on the dock who will agree to ship 6 of them to the Hartford Customhouse. If it is difficult I will dump them into the river. It is very careless of Mrs. Clemens to trust trunks and things to me.

Sincerely yours,

S. L. CLEMENS.

By the latter part of May they were at Quarry Farm, and Clemens, laid up there with a carbuncle, was preparing for his long tour.

The outlook was not a pleasant one. To Mr. Rogers he wrote: "I sha'n't be able to stand on the platform before we start west. I sha'n't get a single chance to practice my reading; but will have to appear in Cleveland without the essential preparation. Nothing in this world can save it from being a shabby, poor disgusting performance. I've got to stand; I can't do it and talk to a house, and how in the nation am I going to sit? Land of Goshen, it's this night week! Pray for me."

The opening at Cleveland July 15th appears not to have been much of a success, though from another reason, one that doubtless seemed amusing to him later.

To H. H. Rogers, in New York City:

(Forenoon)

CLEVELAND, July 16, '95.

DEAR MR. ROGERS,—Had a roaring success at the Elmira reformatory Sunday night. But here, last night, I suffered defeat—There were a couple of hundred little boys behind me on the stage, on a lofty tier of benches which made them the most conspicuous objects in the house. And there was nobody to watch them or keep them quiet. Why, with their scufflings and horse-play and noise, it was just a menagerie. Besides, a concert of amateurs had been smuggled into the program (to precede me,) and their families and friends (say ten per cent of the audience) kept encoring them and they always responded. So it was 20 minutes to 9 before I got the platform in front of those 2,600 people who had paid a dollar apiece for a chance to go to hell in this fashion.

I got started magnificently, but inside of half an hour the scuffling boys had the audience's maddened attention and I saw it was a gone case; so I skipped a third of my program and quit. The newspapers are kind, but between you and me it was a defeat. There ain't going to be any more concerts at my lectures. I care nothing for this defeat, because it was not my fault. My first half hour showed that I had the house, and I could have kept it if I hadn't been so handicapped.

Yours sincerely,

S. L. CLEMENS.

P. S. Had a satisfactory time at Petoskey. Crammed the house and turned away a crowd. We had $548 in the house, which was $300 more than it had ever had in it before. I believe I don't care to have a talk go off better than that one did.

Mark Twain, on this long tour, was accompanied by his wife and his daughter Clara—Susy and Jean Clemens remaining with their aunt at Quarry Farm. The tour was a financial success from the start. By the time they were ready to sail from Vancouver five thousand dollars had been remitted to Mr. Rogers against that day of settlement when the debts of Webster & Co. were to be paid. Perhaps it should be stated here that a legal settlement had been arranged on a basis of fifty cents on the dollar, but neither Clemens nor his wife consented to this as final. They would pay in full.

They sailed from Vancouver August 23, 1895. About the only letter of this time is an amusing note to Rudyard Kipling, written at the moment of departure.

To Rudyard Kipling, in England:

August, 1895.

DEAR KIPLING,—It is reported that you are about to visit India. This has moved me to journey to that far country in order that I may unload from my conscience a debt long due to you. Years ago you came from India to Elmira to visit me, as you said at the time. It has always been my purpose to return that visit and that great compliment some day. I shall arrive next January and you must be ready. I shall come riding my ayah with his tusks adorned with silver bells and ribbons and escorted by a troop of native howdahs richly clad and mounted upon a herd of wild bungalows; and you must be on hand with a few bottles of ghee, for I shall be thirsty.

Affectionately,

S. L. CLEMENS.

Clemens, platforming in Australia, was too busy to write letters. Everywhere he was welcomed by great audiences, and everywhere lavishly entertained. He was beset by other carbuncles, but would seem not to have been seriously delayed by them. A letter to his old friend Twichell carries the story.

To Rev. Jos. H. Twichell, in Hartford:

FRANK MOELLER'S MASONIC HOTEL,

NAPIER, NEW ZEALAND,

November 29, '95.

DEAR JOE,—Your welcome letter of two months and five days ago has just arrived, and finds me in bed with another carbuncle. It is No. 3. Not a serious one this time. I lectured last night without inconvenience, but the doctors thought best to forbid to-night's lecture. My second one kept me in bed a week in Melbourne.

... We are all glad it is you who is to write the article, it delights us all through.

I think it was a good stroke of luck that knocked me on my back here at Napier, instead of some hotel in the centre of a noisy city. Here we have the smooth and placidly-complaining sea at our door, with nothing between us and it but 20 yards of shingle—and hardly a suggestion of life in that space to mar it or make a noise. Away down here fifty-five degrees south of the Equator this sea seems to murmur in an unfamiliar tongue—a foreign tongue—tongue bred among the ice-fields of the Antarctic—a murmur with a note of melancholy in it proper to the vast unvisited solitudes it has come from. It was very delicious and solacing to wake in the night and find it still pulsing there. I wish you were here—land, but it would be fine!

Livy and Clara enjoy this nomadic life pretty well; certainly better than one could have expected they would. They have tough experiences, in the way of food and beds and frantic little ships, but they put up with the worst that befalls with heroic endurance that resembles contentment.

No doubt I shall be on the platform next Monday. A week later we shall reach Wellington; talk there 3 nights, then sail back to Australia. We sailed for New Zealand October 30.

Day before yesterday was Livy's birthday (under world time), and tomorrow will be mine. I shall be 60—no thanks for it.

I and the others send worlds and worlds of love to all you dear ones.

MARK.

The article mentioned in the foregoing letter was one which Twichell had been engaged by Harper's Magazine to write concerning the home life and characteristics of Mark Twain. By the time the Clemens party had completed their tour of India—a splendid, triumphant tour, too full of work and recreation for letter-writing—and had reached South Africa, the article had appeared, a satisfactory one, if we may judge by Mark Twain's next.

This letter, however, has a special interest in the account it gives of Mark Twain's visit to the Jameson raiders, then imprisoned at Pretoria.

To Rev. Jos. H. Twichell, in Hartford:

PRETORIA, SOUTH AFRICAN REPUBLIC,

The Queen's Birthday, '96.

(May 24)

DEAR OLD JOE,—Harper for May was given to me yesterday in Johannesburg by an American lady who lives there, and I read your article on me while coming up in the train with her and an old friend and fellow-Missourian of mine, Mrs. John Hays Hammond, the handsome and spirited wife of the chief of the 4 Reformers, who lies in prison here under a 15-year sentence, along with 50 minor Reformers who are in for 1 and 5-year terms. Thank you a thousand times Joe, you have praised me away above my deserts, but I am not the man to quarrel with you for that; and as for Livy, she will take your very hardiest statements at par, and be grateful to you to the bottom of her heart. Between you and Punch and Brander Matthews, I am like to have my opinion of myself raised sufficiently high; and I guess the children will be after you, for it is the study of their lives to keep my self-appreciation down somewhere within bounds.

I had a note from Mrs. Rev. Gray (nee Tyler) yesterday, and called on her to-day. She is well.

Yesterday I was allowed to enter the prison with Mrs. Hammond. A Boer guard was at my elbow all the time, but was courteous and polite, only he barred the way in the compound (quadrangle or big open court) and wouldn't let me cross a white mark that was on the ground—the "death-line" one of the prisoners called it. Not in earnest, though, I think. I found that I had met Hammond once when he was a Yale senior and a guest of Gen. Franklin's. I also found that I had known Capt. Mein intimately 32 years ago. One of the English prisoners had heard me lecture in London 23 years ago. After being introduced in turn to all the prisoners, I was allowed to see some of the cells and examine their food, beds, etc. I was told in Johannesburg that Hammond's salary of $150,000 a year is not stopped, and that the salaries of some of the others are still continued. Hammond was looking very well indeed, and I can say the same of all the others. When the trouble first fell upon them it hit some of them very hard; several fell sick (Hammond among them), two or three had to be removed to the hospital, and one of the favorites lost his mind and killed himself, poor fellow, last week. His funeral, with a sorrowing following of 10,000, took the place of the public demonstration the Americans were getting up for me.

These prisoners are strong men, prominent men, and I believe they are all educated men. They are well off; some of them are wealthy. They have a lot of books to read, they play games and smoke, and for awhile they will be able to bear up in their captivity; but not for long, not for very long, I take it. I am told they have times of deadly brooding and depression. I made them a speech—sitting down. It just happened so. I don't prefer that attitude. Still, it has one advantage—it is only a talk, it doesn't take the form of a speech. I have tried it once before on this trip. However, if a body wants to make sure of having "liberty," and feeling at home, he had better stand up, of course. I advised them at considerable length to stay where they were—they would get used to it and like it presently; if they got out they would only get in again somewhere else, by the look of their countenances; and I promised to go and see the President and do what I could to get him to double their jail-terms.

We had a very good sociable time till the permitted time was up and a little over, and we outsiders had to go. I went again to-day, but the Rev. Mr. Gray had just arrived, and the warden, a genial, elderly Boer named Du Plessis—explained that his orders wouldn't allow him to admit saint and sinner at the same time, particularly on a Sunday. Du Plessis—descended from the Huguenot fugitives, you see, of 200 years ago—but he hasn't any French left in him now—all Dutch.

It gravels me to think what a goose I was to make Livy and Clara remain in Durban; but I wanted to save them the 30-hour railway trip to Johannesburg. And Durban and its climate and opulent foliage were so lovely, and the friends there were so choice and so hearty that I sacrificed myself in their interests, as I thought. It is just the beginning of winter, and although the days are hot, the nights are cool. But it's lovely weather in these regions, too; and the friends are as lovely as the weather, and Johannesburg and Pretoria are brimming with interest. I talk here twice more, then return to Johannesburg next Wednesday for a fifth talk there; then to the Orange Free State capital, then to some town on the way to Port Elizabeth, where the two will join us by sea from Durban; then the gang will go to Kimberley and presently to the Cape—and so, in the course of time, we shall get through and sail for England; and then we will hunt up a quiet village and I will write and Livy edit, for a few months, while Clara and Susy and Jean study music and things in London.

We have had noble good times everywhere and every day, from Cleveland, July 15, to Pretoria, May 24, and never a dull day either on sea or land, notwithstanding the carbuncles and things. Even when I was laid up 10 days at Jeypore in India we had the charmingest times with English friends. All over India the English well, you will never know how good and fine they are till you see them.

Midnight and after! and I must do many things to-day, and lecture tonight.

A world of thanks to you, Joe dear, and a world of love to all of you.

MARK.

Perhaps for readers of a later day a word as to what constituted the Jameson raid would not be out of place here. Dr. Leander Starr

Jameson was an English physician, located at Kimberley. President Kruger (Oom Paul), head of the South African Republic, was one of his patients; also, Lobengula, the Matabele chief. From Lobengula concessions were obtained which led to the formation of the South African Company. Jameson gave up his profession and went in for conquest, associating himself with the projects of Cecil Rhodes. In time he became administrator of Rhodesia. By the end of 1894. he was in high feather, and during a visit to England was feted as a sort of romantic conqueror of the olden time. Perhaps this turned his head; at all events at the end of 1895 came the startling news that "Dr. Jim," as he was called, at the head of six hundred men, had ridden into the Transvaal in support of a Rhodes scheme for an uprising at Johannesburg. The raid was a failure. Jameson, and those other knights of adventure, were captured by the forces of "Oom Paul," and some of them barely escaped execution. The Boer president handed them over to the English Government for punishment, and they received varying sentences, but all were eventually released. Jameson, later, became again prominent in South-African politics, but there is no record of any further raids.

....

The Clemens party sailed from South Africa the middle of July, 1896, and on the last day of the month reached England. They had not planned to return to America, but to spend the winter in or near London in some quiet place where Clemens could write the book of his travels.

The two daughters in America, Susy and Jean, were expected to arrive August 12th, but on that day there came, instead, a letter saying that Susy Clemens was not well enough to sail. A cable inquiry was immediately sent, but the reply when it came was not satisfactory, and Mrs. Clemens and Clara sailed for America without further delay. This was on August 15th. Three days later, in the old home at Hartford, Susy Clemens died of cerebral fever. She had been visiting Mrs. Charles Dudley Warner, but by the physician's advice had been removed to the comfort and quiet of her own home, only a few steps away.

Mark Twain, returning from his triumphant tour of the world in the hope that soon, now, he might be free from debt, with his family happily gathered about him, had to face alone this cruel blow. There was no purpose in his going to America; Susy would be buried long before his arrival. He awaited in England the return of his broken family. They lived that winter in a quiet corner of Chelsea, No. 23 Tedworth Square.

To Rev. Joseph H. Twichell, in Hartford, Conn.:

Permanent address:

% CHATTO & WINDUS

111 T. MARTIN'S LANE, LONDON,

Sept. 27, '96.

Through Livy and Katy I have learned, dear old Joe, how loyally you stood poor Susy's friend, and mine, and Livy's: how you came all the way down, twice, from your summer refuge on your merciful errands to bring the peace and comfort of your beloved presence, first to that poor child, and again to the broken heart of her poor desolate mother. It was like you; like your good great heart, like your matchless and unmatchable self. It was no surprise to me to learn that you stayed by Susy long hours, careless of fatigue and heat, it was no surprise to me to learn that you could still the storms that swept her spirit when no other could; for she loved you, revered you, trusted you, and "Uncle Joe" was no empty phrase upon her lips! I am grateful to you, Joe, grateful to the bottom of my heart, which has always been filled with love for you, and respect and admiration; and I would have chosen you out of all the world to take my place at Susy's side and Livy's in those black hours.

Susy was a rare creature; the rarest that has been reared in Hartford in this generation. And Livy knew it, and you knew it, and Charley Warner and George, and Harmony, and the Hillyers and the Dunhams and the Cheneys, and Susy and Lilly, and the Bunces, and Henry Robinson and Dick Burton, and perhaps others. And I also was of the number, but not in the same degree—for she was above my duller comprehension. I merely knew that she was my superior in fineness of mind, in the delicacy and subtlety of her intellect, but to fully measure her I was not competent. I know her better now; for I have read her private writings and sounded the deeps of her mind; and I know better, now, the treasure that was mine than I knew it when I had it. But I have this consolation: that dull as I was, I always knew enough to be proud when she commended me or my work—as proud as if Livy had done it herself—and I took it as the accolade from the hand of genius. I see now—as Livy always saw—that she had greatness in her; and that she herself was dimly conscious of it.

And now she is dead—and I can never tell her.

God bless you Joe—and all of your house.

S. L. C.

To Mr. Henry C. Robinson, Hartford, Conn.:

LONDON, Sept. 28, '96.

It is as you say, dear old friend, "the pathos of it" yes, it was a piteous thing—as piteous a tragedy as any the year can furnish. When we started westward upon our long trip at half past ten at night, July 14, 1895, at Elmira, Susy stood on the platform in the blaze of the electric light waving her good-byes to us as the train glided away, her mother throwing back kisses and watching her through her tears. One year, one month, and one week later, Clara and her mother having exactly completed the circuit of the globe, drew up at that platform at the same hour of the night, in the same train and the same car—and again Susy had come a journey and was near at hand to meet them. She was waiting in the house she was born in, in her coffin.

All the circumstances of this death were pathetic—my brain is worn to rags rehearsing them. The mere death would have been cruelty enough, without overloading it and emphasizing it with that score of harsh and wanton details. The child was taken away when her mother was within three days of her, and would have given three decades for sight of her.

In my despair and unassuageable misery I upbraid myself for ever parting with her. But there is no use in that. Since it was to happen it would have happened.

With love

S. L. C.

The life at Tedworth Square that winter was one of almost complete privacy. Of the hundreds of friends which Mark Twain had in London scarcely half a dozen knew his address. He worked steadily on his book of travels, 'Following the Equator', and wrote few letters beyond business communications to Mr. Rogers. In one of these he said, "I am appalled! Here I am trying to load you up with work again after you have been dray-horsing over the same tiresome ground for a year. It's too bad, and I am ashamed of it."

But late in November he sent a letter of a different sort—one that was to have an important bearing on the life of a girl today of unique and world-wide distinction.

To Mrs. H. H. Rogers, in New York City:

For and in behalf of Helen Keller, stone blind and deaf, and formerly dumb.

DEAR MRS. ROGERS,—Experience has convinced me that when one wishes to set a hard-worked man at something which he mightn't prefer to be bothered with, it is best to move upon him behind his wife. If she can't convince him it isn't worth while for other people to try.

Mr. Rogers will remember our visit with that astonishing girl at Lawrence Hutton's house when she was fourteen years old. Last July, in Boston, when she was 16 she underwent the Harvard examination for admission to Radcliffe College. She passed without a single condition. She was allowed the same amount of time that is granted to other applicants, and this was shortened in her case by the fact that the question papers had to be read to her. Yet she scored an average of 90 as against an average of 78 on the part of the other applicants.

It won't do for America to allow this marvelous child to retire from her studies because of poverty. If she can go on with them she will make a fame that will endure in history for centuries. Along her special lines she is the most extraordinary product of all the ages.

There is danger that she must retire from the struggle for a College degree for lack of support for herself and for Miss Sullivan, (the teacher who has been with her from the start—Mr. Rogers will remember her.) Mrs. Hutton writes to ask me to interest rich Englishmen in her case, and I would gladly try, but my secluded life will not permit it. I see nobody. Nobody knows my address. Nothing but the strictest hiding can enable me to write my long book in time.

So I thought of this scheme: Beg you to lay siege to your husband and get him to interest himself and Mess. John D. and William Rockefeller and the other Standard Oil chiefs in Helen's case; get them to subscribe an annual aggregate of six or seven hundred or a thousand dollars—and agree to continue this for three or four years, until she has completed her college course. I'm not trying to limit their generosity—indeed no, they may pile that Standard Oil, Helen Keller College Fund as high as they please, they have my consent.

Mrs. Hutton's idea is to raise a permanent fund the interest upon which shall support Helen and her teacher and put them out of the fear of want. I shan't say a word against it, but she will find it a difficult and disheartening job, and meanwhile what is to become of that miraculous girl?

No, for immediate and sound effectiveness, the thing is for you to plead with Mr. Rogers for this hampered wonder of your sex, and send him clothed with plenary powers to plead with the other chiefs—they have spent mountains of money upon the worthiest benevolences, and I think that the same spirit which moved them to put their hands down through their hearts into their pockets in those cases will answer "Here!" when its name is called in this one. 638

There—I don't need to apologize to you or to H. H. for this appeal that I am making; I know you too well for that.

Good-bye with love to all of you

S. L. CLEMENS.

Laurence Hutton is on the staff of Harper's Monthly—close by, and handy when wanted.

The plea was not made in vain. Mr. and Mrs. Rogers interested themselves most liberally in Helen Keller's fortune, and certainly no one can say that any of those who contributed to her success ever had reason for disappointment.

In his letter of grateful acknowledgment, which follows, Clemens also takes occasion to thank Mr. Rogers for his further efforts in the matter of his own difficulties. This particular reference concerns the publishing, complications which by this time had arisen between the American Publishing Company, of Hartford, and the house in Franklin Square.

LONDON, Dec. 22, '96.

DEAR MRS. ROGERS,—It is superb! And I am beyond measure grateful to you both. I knew you would be interested in that wonderful girl, and that Mr. Rogers was already interested in her and touched by her; and I was sure that if nobody else helped her you two would; but you have gone far and away beyond the sum I expected—may your lines fall in pleasant places here and Hereafter for it!

The Huttons are as glad and grateful as they can be, and I am glad for their sakes as well as for Helen's.

I want to thank Mr. Rogers for crucifying himself again on the same old cross between Bliss and Harper; and goodness knows I hope he will come to enjoy it above all other dissipations yet, seeing that it has about it the elements of stability and permanency. However, at any time that he says sign, we're going to do it.

Ever sincerely Yours

S. L. CLEMENS.

XXXVI. LETTERS 1897. LONDON, SWITZERLAND, VIENNA

Mark Twain worked steadily on his book that sad winter and managed to keep the gloom out of his chapters, though it is noticeable that 'Following the Equator' is more serious than his other books of travel. He wrote few letters, and these only to his three closest friends, Howells, Twichell, and Rogers. In the letter to Twichell, which follows, there is mention of two unfinished manuscripts which he expects to resume. One of these was a dream story, enthusiastically begun, but perhaps with insufficient plot to carry it through, for it never reached conclusion. He had already tried it in one or two forms and would begin it again presently. The identity of the other tale is uncertain.

To Rev. J. H. Twichell, in Hartford:

LONDON, Jan. 19, '97.

DEAR JOE,—Do I want you to write to me? Indeed I do. I do not want most people to write, but I do want you to do it. The others break my heart, but you will not. You have a something divine in you that is not in other men. You have the touch that heals, not lacerates. And you know the secret places of our hearts. You know our life—the outside of it—as the others do—and the inside of it—which they do not. You have seen our whole voyage. You have seen us go to sea, a cloud of sail—and the flag at the peak; and you see us now, chartless, adrift—derelicts; battered, water-logged, our sails a ruck of rags, our pride gone. For it is gone. And there is nothing in its place. The vanity of life was all we had, and there is no more vanity left in us. We are even ashamed of that we had; ashamed that we trusted the promises of life and builded high—to come to this!

I did know that Susy was part of us; I did not know that she could go away; I did not know that she could go away, and take our lives with her, yet leave our dull bodies behind. And I did not know what she was. To me she was but treasure in the bank; the amount known, the need to look at it daily, handle it, weigh it, count it, realize it, not necessary; and now that I would do it, it is too late; they tell me it is not there, has vanished away in a night, the bank is broken, my fortune is gone, I am a pauper. How am I to comprehend this? How am I to have it? Why am I robbed, and who is benefited?

Ah, well, Susy died at home. She had that privilege. Her dying eyes rested upon nothing that was strange to them, but only upon things which they had known and loved always and which had made her young years glad; and she had you, and Sue, and Katy, and John, and Ellen. This was happy fortune—I am thankful that it was vouchsafed to her. If she had died in another house-well, I think I could not have borne that. To us, our house was not unsentient matter—it had a heart, and a soul, and eyes to see us with; and approvals, and solicitudes, and deep sympathies; it was of us, and we were in its confidence, and lived in its grace and in the peace of its benediction. We never came home from an absence that its face did not light up and speak out its eloquent welcome—and we could not enter it unmoved. And could we now, oh, now, in spirit we should enter it unshod.

I am trying to add to the "assets" which you estimate so generously. No, I am not. The thought is not in my mind. My purpose is other. I am working, but it is for the sake of the work—the "surcease of sorrow" that is found there. I work all the days, and trouble vanishes away when I use that magic. This book will not long stand between it and me, now; but that is no matter, I have many unwritten books to fly to for my preservation; the interval between the finishing of this one and the beginning of the next will not be more than an hour, at most. Continuances, I mean; for two of them are already well along—in fact have reached exactly the same stage in their journey: 19,000 words each. The present one will contain 180,000 words—130,000 are done. I am well protected; but Livy! She has nothing in the world to turn to; nothing but housekeeping, and doing things for the children and me. She does not see people, and cannot; books have lost their interest for her. She sits solitary; and all the day, and all the days, wonders how it all happened, and why. We others were always busy with our affairs, but Susy was her comrade—had to be driven from her loving persecutions—sometimes at 1 in the morning. To Livy the persecutions were welcome. It was heaven to her to be plagued like that. But it is ended now. Livy stands so in need of help; and none among us all could help her like you.

Some day you and I will walk again, Joe, and talk. I hope so. We could have such talks! We are all grateful to you and Harmony—how grateful it is not given to us to say in words. We pay as we can, in love; and in this coin practicing no economy.

Good bye, dear old Joe!

MARK.

The letters to Mr. Rogers were, for the most part, on matters of business, but in one of them he said: "I am going to write with all my might on this book, and follow it up with others as fast as I can in the hope that within three years I can clear out the stuff that is in me waiting to be written, and that I shall then die in the promptest kind of a way and no fooling around." And in one he wrote: "You are the best friend ever a man had, and the surest."

To W. D. Howells, in New York

LONDON, Feb. 23, '97.

DEAR HOWELLS,—I find your generous article in the Weekly, and I want to thank you for its splendid praises, so daringly uttered and so warmly. The words stir the dead heart of me, and throw a glow of color into a life which sometimes seems to have grown wholly wan. I don't mean that I am miserable; no—worse than that—indifferent. Indifferent to nearly everything but work. I like that; I enjoy it, and stick to it. I do it without purpose and without ambition; merely for the love of it.

This mood will pass, some day—there is history for it. But it cannot pass until my wife comes up out of the submergence. She was always so quick to recover herself before, but now there is no rebound, and we are dead people who go through the motions of life. Indeed I am a mud image, and it will puzzle me to know what it is in me that writes, and has comedy-fancies and finds pleasure in phrasing them. It is a law of our nature, of course, or it wouldn't happen; the thing in me forgets the presence of the mud image and goes its own way, wholly unconscious of it and apparently of no kinship with it. I have finished my book, but I go on as if the end were indefinitely away—as indeed it is. There is no hurry—at any rate there is no limit.

Jean's spirits are good; Clara's are rising. They have youth—the only thing that was worth giving to the race.

These are sardonic times. Look at Greece, and that whole shabby muddle. But I am not sorry to be alive and privileged to look on. If I were not a hermit I would go to the House every day and see those people scuffle over it and blether about the brotherhood of the human race. This has been a bitter year for English pride, and I don't like to see England humbled—that is, not too much. We are sprung from her loins, and it hurts me. I am for republics, and she is the only comrade we've got, in that. We can't count France, and there is hardly enough of Switzerland to count. Beneath the governing crust England is sound-hearted—and sincere, too, and nearly straight. But I am appalled to notice that the wide extension of the surface has damaged her manners, and made her rather Americanly uncourteous on the lower levels.

Won't you give our love to the Howellses all and particular?

Sincerely yours

S. L. CLEMENS.

The travel-book did not finish easily, and more than once when he thought it completed he found it necessary to cut and add and change. The final chapters were not sent to the printer until the middle of May, and in a letter to Mr. Rogers he commented: "A successful book is not made of what is in it, but what is left out of it." Clemens was at the time contemplating a uniform edition of his books, and in one of his letters to Mr. Rogers on the matter he wrote, whimsically, "Now I was proposing to make a thousand sets at a hundred dollars a set, and do the whole canvassing myself..... I would load up every important jail and saloon in America with de luxe editions of my books. But Mrs. Clemens and the children object to this, I do not know why." And, in a moment of depression: "You see the lightning refuses to strike me—there is where the defect is. We have to do our own striking as Barney Barnato did. But nobody ever gets the courage until he goes crazy."

They went to Switzerland for the summer to the village of Weggis, on Lake Lucerne—"The charmingest place we ever lived in," he declared, "for repose, and restfulness, and superb scenery." It was here that he began work on a new story of Tom and Huck, and at least upon one other manuscript. From a brief note to Mr. Rogers we learn something of his employments and economies.

To Henry H. Rogers, in New York:

LUCERNE, August the something or other, 1897.

DEAR MR. ROGERS,—I am writing a novel, and am getting along very well with it.

I believe that this place (Weggis, half an hour from Lucerne,) is the loveliest in the world, and the most satisfactory. We have a small house on the hillside all to ourselves, and our meals are served in it from the inn below on the lake shore. Six francs a day per head, house and food included. The scenery is beyond comparison beautiful. We have a row boat and some bicycles, and good roads, and no visitors. Nobody knows we are here. And Sunday in heaven is noisy compared to this quietness.

Sincerely yours

S. L. C.

To Rev. J. H. Twichell, in Hartford:

LUCERNE, Aug. 22, '97.

DEAR JOE,—Livy made a noble find on the Lucerne boat the other day on one of her shopping trips—George Williamson Smith—did I tell you about it? We had a lovely time with him, and such intellectual refreshment as we had not tasted in many a month.

And the other night we had a detachment of the jubilee Singers—6. I had known one of them in London 24 years ago. Three of the 6 were born in slavery, the others were children of slaves. How charming they were—in spirit, manner, language, pronunciation, enunciation, grammar, phrasing, matter, carriage, clothes—in every detail that goes to make the real lady and gentleman, and welcome guest. We went down to the village hotel and bought our tickets and entered the beer-hall, where a crowd of German and Swiss men and women sat grouped at round tables with their beer mugs in front of them—self-contained and unimpressionable looking people, an indifferent and unposted and disheartened audience—and up at the far end of the room sat the Jubilees in a row. The Singers got up and stood—the talking and glass jingling went on. Then rose and swelled out above those common earthly sounds one of those rich chords the secret of whose make only the Jubilees possess, and a spell fell upon that house. It was fine to see the faces light up with the pleased wonder and surprise of it. No one was indifferent any more; and when the singers finished, the camp was theirs. It was a triumph. It reminded me of Launcelot riding in Sir Kay's armor and astonishing complacent Knights who thought they had struck a soft thing. The Jubilees sang a lot of pieces. Arduous and painstaking cultivation has not diminished or artificialized their music, but on the contrary—to my surprise—has mightily reinforced its eloquence and beauty. Away back in the beginning—to my mind—their music made all other vocal music cheap; and that early notion is emphasized now. It is utterly beautiful, to me; and it moves me infinitely more than any other music can. I think that in the Jubilees and their songs America has produced the perfectest flower of the ages; and I wish it were a foreign product, so that she would worship it and lavish money on it and go properly crazy over it.

Now, these countries are different: they would do all that, if it were native. It is true they praise God, but that is merely a formality, and nothing in it; they open out their whole hearts to no foreigner.

The musical critics of the German press praise the Jubilees with great enthusiasm—acquired technique etc, included.

One of the jubilee men is a son of General Joe Johnson, and was educated by him after the war. The party came up to the house and we had a pleasant time.

This is paradise, here—but of course we have got to leave it by and by. The 18th of August—[Anniversary of Susy Clemens's death.]—has come and gone, Joe—and we still seem to live.

With love from us all.

MARK.

Clemens declared he would as soon spend his life in Weggis "as anywhere else in the geography," but October found them in Vienna for the winter, at the Hotel Metropole. The Austrian capital was just then in a political turmoil, the character of which is hinted in the following:

To Rev. J. H. Twichell, in Hartford:

HOTEL METROPOLE,

VIENNA, Oct. 23, '97.

DEAR JOE,—We are gradually getting settled down and wonted. Vienna is not a cheap place to live in, but I have made one small arrangement which: has a distinctly economical aspect. The Vice Consul made the contract for me yesterday-to-wit: a barber is to come every morning 8.30 and shave me and keep my hair trimmed for $2.50 a month. I used to pay $1.50 per shave in our house in Hartford.

Does it suggest to you reflections when you reflect that this is the most important event which has happened to me in ten days—unless I count—in my handing a cabman over to the police day before yesterday, with the proper formalities, and promised to appear in court when his case comes up.

If I had time to run around and talk, I would do it; for there is much politics agoing, and it would be interesting if a body could get the hang of it. It is Christian and Jew by the horns—the advantage with the superior man, as usual—the superior man being the Jew every time and in all countries. Land, Joe, what chance would the Christian have in a country where there were 3 Jews to 10 Christians! Oh, not the shade of a shadow of a chance. The difference between the brain of the average Christian and that of the average Jew—certainly in Europe—is about the difference between a tadpole's and an Archbishop's. It's a marvelous, race—by long odds the most marvelous that the world has produced, I suppose.

And there's more politics—the clash between Czech and Austrian. I wish I could understand these quarrels, but of course I can't.

With the abounding love of us all

MARK.

In Following the Equator there was used an amusing picture showing Mark Twain on his trip around the world. It was a trick photograph made from a picture of Mark Twain taken in a steamer-chair, cut out and combined with a dilapidated negro-cart drawn by a horse and an ox. In it Clemens appears to be sitting luxuriously in the end of the disreputable cart. His companions are two negroes. To the creator of this ingenious effect Mark Twain sent a characteristic acknowledgment.

To T. S. Frisbie

VIENNA, Oct. 25, '97.

MR. T. S. FRISBIE,—Dear Sir: The picture has reached me, and has moved me deeply. That was a steady, sympathetic and honorable team, and although it was not swift, and not showy, it pulled me around the globe successfully, and always attracted its proper share of attention, even in the midst of the most costly and fashionable turnouts. Princes and dukes and other experts were always enthused by the harness and could hardly keep from trying to buy it. The barouche does not look as fine, now, as it did earlier-but that was before the earthquake.

The portraits of myself and uncle and nephew are very good indeed, and your impressionist reproduction of the palace of the Governor General of India is accurate and full of tender feeling.

I consider that this picture is much more than a work of art. How much more, one cannot say with exactness, but I should think two-thirds more.

Very truly yours

MARK TWAIN.

Following the Equator was issued by subscription through Mark Twain's old publishers, the Blisses, of Hartford. The sale of it was large, not only on account of the value of the book itself, but also because of the sympathy of the American people with Mark Twain's brave struggle to pay his debts. When the newspapers began to print exaggerated stories of the vast profits that were piling up, Bliss became worried, for he thought it would modify the sympathy. He cabled Clemens for a denial, with the following result:

To Frank E. Bliss, in Hartford:

VIENNA, Nov. 4, 1897.

DEAR BLISS,—Your cablegram informing me that a report is in circulation which purports to come from me and which says I have recently made $82,000 and paid all my debts has just reached me, and I have cabled back my regret to you that it is not true. I wrote a letter—a private letter—a short time ago, in which I expressed the belief that I should be out of debt within the next twelvemonth. If you make as much as usual for me out of the book, that belief will crystallize into a fact, and I shall be wholly out of debt. I am encoring you now.

It is out of that moderate letter that the Eighty-Two Thousand-Dollar mare's nest has developed. But why do you worry about the various reports? They do not worry me. They are not unfriendly, and I don't see how they can do any harm. Be patient; you have but a little while to wait; the possible reports are nearly all in. It has been reported that I was seriously ill—it was another man; dying—it was another man; dead—the other man again. It has been reported that I have received a legacy it was another man; that I am out of debt—it was another man; and now comes this $82,000—still another man. It has been reported that I am writing books—for publication; I am not doing anything of the kind. It would surprise (and gratify) me if I should be able to get another book ready for the press within the next three years. You can see, yourself, that there isn't anything more to be reported—invention is exhausted. Therefore, don't worry, Bliss—the long night is breaking. As far as I can see, nothing remains to be reported, except that I have become a foreigner. When you hear it, don't you believe it. And don't take the trouble to deny it. Merely just raise the American flag on our house in Hartford, and let it talk.

Truly yours,

MARK TWAIN.

P. S. This is not a private letter. I am getting tired of private letters.

To Rev. J. H. Twichell, in Hartford:

VIENNA

HOTEL METROPOLE, NOV. 19, '97.

DEAR JOE,—Above is our private (and permanent) address for the winter. You needn't send letters by London.

I am very much obliged for Forrest's Austro-Hungarian articles. I have just finished reading the first one: and in it I find that his opinion and Vienna's are the same, upon a point which was puzzling me—the paucity (no, the absence) of Austrian Celebrities. He and Vienna both say the country cannot afford to allow great names to grow up; that the whole safety and prosperity of the Empire depends upon keeping things quiet; can't afford to have geniuses springing up and developing ideas and stirring the public soul. I am assured that every time a man finds himself blooming into fame, they just softly snake him down and relegate him to a wholesome obscurity. It is curious and interesting.

Three days ago the New York World sent and asked a friend of mine (correspondent of a London daily) to get some Christmas greetings from the celebrities of the Empire. She spoke of this. Two or three bright Austrians were present. They said "There are none who are known all over the world! none who have achieved fame; none who can point to their work and say it is known far and wide in the earth: there are no names; Kossuth (known because he had a father) and Lecher, who made the 12 hour speech; two names-nothing more. Every other country in the world, perhaps, has a giant or two whose heads are away up and can be seen, but ours. We've got the material—have always had it—but we have to suppress it; we can't afford to let it develop; our political salvation depends upon tranquillity—always has."

Poor Livy! She is laid up with rheumatism; but she is getting along now. We have a good doctor, and he says she will be out of bed in a couple of days, but must stay in the house a week or ten.

Clara is working faithfully at her music, Jean at her usual studies, and we all send love.

MARK.

Mention has already been made of the political excitement in Vienna. The trouble between the Hungarian and German legislative bodies presently became violent. Clemens found himself intensely interested, and was present in one of the galleries when it was cleared by the police. All sorts of stories were circulated as to what happened to him, one of which was cabled to America. A letter to Twichell sets forth what really happened.

To Rev. J. H. Twichell, in Hartford:

HOTEL METROPOLE,

VIENNA, Dec. 10, '97.

DEAR JOE,—Pond sends me a Cleveland paper with a cablegram from here in it which says that when the police invaded the parliament and expelled the 11 members I waved my handkerchief and shouted 'Hoch die Deutschen!' and got hustled out. Oh dear, what a pity it is that one's adventures never happen! When the Ordner (sergeant-at-arms) came up to our gallery and was hurrying the people out, a friend tried to get leave for me to stay, by saying, "But this gentleman is a foreigner—you don't need to turn him out—he won't do any harm."

"Oh, I know him very well—I recognize him by his pictures; and I should be very glad to let him stay, but I haven't any choice, because of the strictness of the orders."

And so we all went out, and no one was hustled. Below, I ran across the London Times correspondent, and he showed me the way into the first gallery and I lost none of the show. The first gallery had not misbehaved, and was not disturbed.

... We cannot persuade Livy to go out in society yet, but all the lovely people come to see her; and Clara and I go to dinner parties, and around here and there, and we all have a most hospitable good time. Jean's woodcarving flourishes, and her other studies.

Good-bye Joe—and we all love all of you.

MARK.

Clemens made an article of the Austrian troubles, one of the best things he ever wrote, and certainly one of the clearest elucidations of the Austro-Hungarian confusions. It was published in Harper's Magazine, and is now included in his complete works.

Thus far none of the Webster Company debts had been paid—at least, none of importance. The money had been accumulating in Mr. Rogers's hands, but Clemens was beginning to be depressed by the heavy burden. He wrote asking for relief.

Fragment of a letter to H. H. Rogers, in New York:

DEAR MR. ROGERS,—I throw up the sponge. I pull down the flag. Let us begin on the debts. I cannot bear the weight any longer. It totally unfits me for work. I have lost three entire months now. In that time I have begun twenty magazine articles and books—and flung every one of them aside in turn. The debts interfered every time, and took the spirit out of any work. And yet I have worked like a bond slave and wasted no time and spared no effort——

Rogers wrote, proposing a plan for beginning immediately upon the debts. Clemens replied enthusiastically, and during the next few weeks wrote every few days, expressing his delight in liquidation.

Extracts from letters to H. H. Rogers, in New York:

... We all delighted with your plan. Only don't leave B—out. Apparently that claim has been inherited by some women—daughters, no doubt. We don't want to see them lose any thing. B——- is an ass, and disgruntled, but I don't care for that. I am responsible for the money and must do the best I can to pay it..... I am writing hard—writing for the creditors.

Dec. 29.

Land we are glad to see those debts diminishing. For the first time in my life I am getting more pleasure out of paying money out than pulling it in.

Jan. 2.

Since we have begun to pay off the debts I have abundant peace of mind again—no sense of burden. Work is become a pleasure again—it is not labor any longer.

March 7.

Mrs. Clemens has been reading the creditors' letters over and over again and thanks you deeply for sending them, and says it is the only really happy day she has had since Susy died.

XXXVII. LETTERS, 1898, TO HOWELLS AND TWICHELL. LIFE IN VIENNA. PAYMENT OF THE DEBTS. ASSASSINATION OF THE EMPRESS.

The end of January saw the payment of the last of Mark Twain's debts. Once more he stood free before the world—a world that sounded his praises. The latter fact rather amused him. "Honest men must be pretty scarce," he said, "when they make so much fuss over even a defective specimen." When the end was in sight Clemens wrote the news to Howells in a letter as full of sadness as of triumph.

To W. D. Howells, in New York:

HOTEL METROPOLE,

VIENNA, Jan. 22, '98.

DEAR HOWELLS,—Look at those ghastly figures. I used to write it "Hartford, 1871." There was no Susy then—there is no Susy now. And how much lies between—one long lovely stretch of scented fields, and meadows, and shady woodlands, and suddenly Sahara! You speak of the glorious days of that old time—and they were. It is my quarrel—that traps like that are set. Susy and Winnie given us, in miserable sport, and then taken away.

About the last time I saw you I described to you the culminating disaster in a book I was going to write (and will yet, when the stroke is further away)—a man's dead daughter brought to him when he had been through all other possible misfortunes—and I said it couldn't be done as it ought to be done except by a man who had lived it—it must be written with the blood out of a man's heart. I couldn't know, then, how soon I was to be made competent. I have thought of it many a time since. If you were here I think we could cry down each other's necks, as in your dream. For we are a pair of old derelicts drifting around, now, with some of our passengers gone and the sunniness of the others in eclipse.

I couldn't get along without work now. I bury myself in it up to the ears. Long hours—8 and 9 on a stretch, sometimes. And all the days, Sundays included. It isn't all for print, by any means, for much of it fails to suit me; 50,000 words of it in the past year. It was because of the deadness which invaded me when Susy died. But I have made a change lately—into dramatic work—and I find it absorbingly entertaining. I don't know that I can write a play that will play: but no matter, I'll write half a dozen that won't, anyway. Dear me, I didn't know there was such fun in it. I'll write twenty that won't play. I get into immense spirits as soon as my day is fairly started. Of course a good deal of this friskiness comes of my being in sight of land—on the Webster & Co. debts, I mean. (Private.) We've lived close to the bone and saved every cent we could, and there's no undisputed claim, now, that we can't cash. I have marked this "private" because it is for the friends who are attending to the matter for us in New York to reveal it when they want to and if they want to. There are only two claims which I dispute and which I mean to look into personally before I pay them. But they are small. Both together they amount to only $12,500. I hope you will never get the like of the load saddled onto you that was saddled onto me 3 years ago. And yet there is such a solid pleasure in paying the things that I reckon maybe it is worth while to get into that kind of a hobble, after all. Mrs. Clemens gets millions of delight out of it; and the children have never uttered one complaint about the scrimping, from the beginning.

We all send you and all of you our love.

MARK.

Howells wrote: "I wish you could understand how unshaken you are, you old tower, in every way; your foundations are struck so deep that you will catch the sunshine of immortal years, and bask in the same light as Cervantes and Shakespeare."

The Clemens apartments at the Metropole became a sort of social clearing-house of the Viennese art and literary life, much more like an embassy than the home of a mere literary man. Celebrities in every walk of life, persons of social and official rank, writers for the press, assembled there on terms hardly possible in any other home in Vienna. Wherever Mark Twain appeared in public he was a central figure. Now and then he read or spoke to aid some benefit, and these were great gatherings attended by members of the royal family. It was following one such event that the next letter was written.

(Private)

To Rev. J. H. Twichell, in Hartford:

HOTEL METROPOLE,

VIENNA, Feb. 3, '98.

DEAR JOE, There's that letter that I began so long ago—you see how it is: can't get time to finish anything. I pile up lots of work, nevertheless. There may be idle people in the world, but I'm not one of them. I say "Private" up there because I've got an adventure to tell, and you mustn't let a breath of it get out. First I thought I would lay it up along with a thousand others that I've laid up for the same purpose—to talk to you about, but—those others have vanished out of my memory; and that must not happen with this.

The other night I lectured for a Vienna charity; and at the end of it Livy and I were introduced to a princess who is aunt to the heir apparent of the imperial throne—a beautiful lady, with a beautiful spirit, and very cordial in her praises of my books and thanks to me for writing them; and glad to meet me face to face and shake me by the hand—just the kind of princess that adorns a fairy tale and makes it the prettiest tale there is.

Very well, we long ago found that when you are noticed by supremacies, the correct etiquette is to go, within a couple of days, and pay your respects in the quite simple form of writing your name in the Visitors' Book kept in the office of the establishment. That is the end of it, and everything is squared up and ship-shape.

So at noon today Livy and I drove to the Archducal palace, and got by the sentries all right, and asked the grandly-uniformed porter for the book and said we wished to write our names in it. And he called a servant in livery and was sending us up stairs; and said her Royal Highness was out but would soon be in. Of course Livy said "No—no—we only want the book;" but he was firm, and said, "You are Americans?"

"Yes."

"Then you are expected, please go up stairs."

"But indeed we are not expected—please let us have the book and—"

"Her Royal Highness will be back in a very little while—she commanded me to tell you so—and you must wait."

Well, the soldiers were there close by—there was no use trying to resist—so we followed the servant up; but when he tried to beguile us into a drawing-room, Livy drew the line; she wouldn't go in. And she wouldn't stay up there, either. She said the princess might come in at any moment and catch us, and it would be too infernally ridiculous for anything. So we went down stairs again—to my unspeakable regret. For it was too darling a comedy to spoil. I was hoping and praying the princess would come, and catch us up there, and that those other Americans who were expected would arrive, and be taken for impostors by the portier, and shot by the sentinels—and then it would all go into the papers, and be cabled all over the world, and make an immense stir and be perfectly lovely. And by that time the princess would discover that we were not the right ones, and the Minister of War would be ordered out, and the garrison, and they would come for us, and there would be another prodigious time, and that would get cabled too, and—well, Joe, I was in a state of perfect bliss. But happily, oh, so happily, that big portier wouldn't let us out—he was sorry, but he must obey orders—we must go back up stairs and wait. Poor Livy—I couldn't help but enjoy her distress. She said we were in a fix, and how were we going to explain, if the princess should arrive before the rightful Americans came? We went up stairs again—laid off our wraps, and were conducted through one drawing room and into another, and left alone there and the door closed upon us.

Livy was in a state of mind! She said it was too theatrically ridiculous; and that I would never be able to keep my mouth shut; that I would be sure to let it out and it would get into the papers—and she tried to make me promise—"Promise what?" I said—"to be quiet about this? Indeed I won't—it's the best thing that ever happened; I'll tell it, and add to it; and I wish Joe and Howells were here to make it perfect; I can't make all the rightful blunders myself—it takes all three of us to do justice to an opportunity like this. I would just like to see Howells get down to his work and explain, and lie, and work his futile and inventionless subterfuges when that princess comes raging in here and wanting to know." But Livy could not hear fun—it was not a time to be trying to be funny—we were in a most miserable and shameful situation, and if—

Just then the door spread wide and our princess and 4 more, and 3 little princes flowed in! Our princess, and her sister the Archduchess Marie Therese (mother to the imperial Heir and to the young girl Archduchesses present, and aunt to the 3 little princes)—and we shook hands all around and sat down and had a most sociable good time for half an hour—and by and by it turned out that we were the right ones, and had been sent for by a messenger who started too late to catch us at the hotel. We were invited for 2 o'clock, but we beat that arrangement by an hour and a half.

Wasn't it a rattling good comedy situation? Seems a kind of pity we were the right ones. It would have been such nuts to see the right ones come, and get fired out, and we chatting along comfortably and nobody suspecting us for impostors.

We send lots and lots of love.

MARK.

The reader who has followed these pages has seen how prone Mark Twain was to fall a victim to the lure of a patent-right—how he wasted several small fortunes on profitless contrivances, and one large one on that insatiable demon of intricacy and despair, the Paige type-setter. It seems incredible that, after that experience and its attending disaster, he should have been tempted again. But scarcely was the ink dry on the receipts from his creditors when he was once more borne into the clouds on the prospect of millions, perhaps even billions, to be made from a marvelous carpet-pattern machine, the invention of Sczezepanik, an Austrian genius. That Clemens appreciated his own tendencies is shown by the parenthetic line with which he opens his letter on the subject to Mr. Rogers. Certainly no man was ever a more perfect prototype of Colonel Sellers than the creator of that lovely, irrepressible visionary.

To Mr. Rogers, in New York:

March 24, '98.

DEAR MR. ROGERS,—(I feel like Col. Sellers).

Mr. Kleinberg [agent for Sczezepanik] came according to appointment, at 8.30 last night, and brought his English-speaking Secretary. I asked questions about the auxiliary invention (which I call "No. 2 ") and got as good an idea of it as I could. It is a machine. It automatically punches the holes in the jacquard cards, and does it with mathematical accuracy. It will do for $1 what now costs $3. So it has value, but "No. 2" is the great thing (the designing invention.) It saves $9 out of $10 and the jacquard looms must have it.

Then I arrived at my new project, and said to him in substance, this:

"You are on the point of selling the No. 2 patents to Belgium, Italy, etc. I suggest that you stop those negotiations and put those people off two or three months. They are anxious now, they will not be less anxious then—just the reverse; people always want a thing that is denied them.

"So far as I know, no great world-patent has ever yet been placed in the grip of a single corporation. This is a good time to begin.

"We have to do a good deal of guess-work here, because we cannot get hold of just the statistics we want. Still, we have some good statistics—and I will use those for a test.

"You say that of the 1500 Austrian textile factories, 800 use the jacquard. Then we will guess that of the 4,000 American factories 2,000 use the jacquard and must have our No. 2.

"You say that a middle-sized Austrian factory employs from 20 to 30 designers and pays them from 800 to 3,000 odd florins a year—(a florin is 2 francs). Let us call the average wage 1500 florins ($600).

"Let us apply these figures (the low wages too) to the 2,000 American factories—with this difference, to guard against over-guessing; that instead of allowing for 20 to 30 designers to a middle-sized factory, we allow only an average of 10 to each of the 2,000 factories—a total of 20,000 designers. Wages at $600, a total of $12,000,000. Let us consider that No. 2 will reduce this expense to $2,000,000 a year. The saving is $5,000,000 per each of the $200,000,000 of capital employed in the jacquard business over there.

"Let us consider that in the countries covered by this patent, an aggregate of $1,500,000,000 of capital is employed in factories requiring No. 2.

"The saving (as above) is $75,000,000 a year. The Company holding in its grip all these patents would collar $50,000,000 of that, as its share. Possibly more.

"Competition would be at an end in the Jacquard business, on this planet. Price-cutting would end. Fluctuations in values would cease. The business would be the safest and surest in the world; commercial panics could not seriously affect it; its stock would be as choice an investment as Government bonds. When the patents died the Company would be so powerful that it could still keep the whole business in its hands. Would you like to grant me the privilege of placing the whole jacquard business of the world in the grip of a single Company? And don't you think that the business would grow-grow like a weed?"

"Ach, America—it is the country of the big! Let me get my breath—then we will talk."

So then we talked—talked till pretty late. Would Germany and England join the combination? I said the Company would know how to persuade them.

Then I asked for a Supplementary Option, to cover the world, and we parted.

I am taking all precautions to keep my name out of print in connection with this matter. And we will now keep the invention itself out of print as well as we can. Descriptions of it have been granted to the "Dry Goods Economist" (New York) and to a syndicate of American papers. I have asked Mr. Kleinberg to suppress these, and he feels pretty sure he can do it.

With love,

S. L. C.

If this splendid enthusiasm had not cooled by the time a reply came from Mr. Rogers, it must have received a sudden chill from the letter which he inclosed—the brief and concise report from a carpet-machine expert, who said: "I do not feel that it would be of any value to us in our mills, and the number of jacquard looms in America is so limited that I am of the opinion that there is no field for a company to develop the invention here. A cursory examination of the pamphlet leads me to place no very high value upon the invention, from a practical standpoint."

With the receipt of this letter carpet-pattern projects would seem to have suddenly ceased to be a factor in Mark Twain's calculations. Such a letter in the early days of the type-machine would have saved him a great sum in money and years of disappointment. But perhaps he would not have heeded it then.

The year 1898 brought the Spanish-American War. Clemens was constitutionally against all wars, but writing to Twichell, whose son had enlisted, we gather that this one was an exception.

To Rev. J. H. Twichell, in Hartford:

KALTENLEUTGEBEN, NEAR VIENNA,

June 17, '98.

DEAR JOE,—You are living your war-days over again in Dave, and it must be a strong pleasure, mixed with a sauce of apprehension—enough to make it just schmeck, as the Germans say. Dave will come out with two or three stars on his shoulder-straps if the war holds, and then we shall all be glad it happened.

We started with Bull Run, before. Dewey and Hobson have introduced an improvement on the game this time.

I have never enjoyed a war-even in written history—as I am enjoying this one. For this is the worthiest one that was ever fought, so far as my knowledge goes. It is a worthy thing to fight for one's freedom; it is another sight finer to fight for another man's. And I think this is the first time it has been done.

Oh, never mind Charley Warner, he would interrupt the raising of

Lazarus. He would say, the will has been probated, the property distributed, it will be a world of trouble to settle the rows—better leave well enough alone; don't ever disturb anything, where it's going to break the soft smooth flow of things and wobble our tranquillity.

Company! (Sh! it happens every day—and we came out here to be quiet.)

Love to you all.

MARK.

They were spending the summer at Kaltenleutgeben, a pleasant village near Vienna, but apparently not entirely quiet. Many friends came out from Vienna, including a number of visiting Americans. Clemens, however, appears to have had considerable time for writing, as we gather from the next to Howells.

To W. D. Howells, in America:

KALTENLEUTGEBEN, BEI WIEN,

Aug. 16, '98.

DEAR HOWELLS,—Your letter came yesterday. It then occurred to me that I might have known (per mental telegraph) that it was due; for a couple of weeks ago when the Weekly came containing that handsome reference to me I was powerfully moved to write you; and my letter went on writing itself while I was at work at my other literature during the day. But next day my other literature was still urgent—and so on and so on; so my letter didn't get put into ink at all. But I see now, that you were writing, about that time, therefore a part of my stir could have come across the Atlantic per mental telegraph. In 1876 or '75 I wrote 40,000 words of a story called "Simon Wheeler" wherein the nub was the preventing of an execution through testimony furnished by mental telegraph from the other side of the globe. I had a lot of people scattered about the globe who carried in their pockets something like the old mesmerizer-button, made of different metals, and when they wanted to call up each other and have a talk, they "pressed the button" or did something, I don't remember what, and communication was at once opened. I didn't finish the story, though I re-began it in several new ways, and spent altogether 70,000 words on it, then gave it up and threw it aside.

This much as preliminary to this remark: some day people will be able to call each other up from any part of the world and talk by mental telegraph—and not merely by impression, the impression will be articulated into words. It could be a terrible thing, but it won't be, because in the upper civilizations everything like sentimentality (I was going to say sentiment) will presently get materialized out of people along with the already fading spiritualities; and so when a man is called who doesn't wish to talk he will be like those visitors you mention: "not chosen"—and will be frankly damned and shut off.

Speaking of the ill luck of starting a piece of literary work wrong-and again and again; always aware that there is a way, if you could only think it out, which would make the thing slide effortless from the pen—the one right way, the sole form for you, the other forms being for men whose line those forms are, or who are capabler than yourself: I've had no end of experience in that (and maybe I am the only one—let us hope so.) Last summer I started 16 things wrong—3 books and 13 mag. articles—and could only make 2 little wee things, 1500 words altogether, succeed:—only that out of piles and stacks of diligently-wrought MS., the labor of 6 weeks' unremitting effort. I could make all of those things go if I would take the trouble to re-begin each one half a dozen times on a new plan. But none of them was important enough except one: the story I (in the wrong form) mapped out in Paris three or four years ago and told you about in New York under seal of confidence—no other person knows of it but Mrs. Clemens—the story to be called "Which was the Dream?"

A week ago I examined the MS—10,000 words—and saw that the plan was a totally impossible one-for me; but a new plan suggested itself, and straightway the tale began to slide from the pen with ease and confidence. I think I've struck the right one this time. I have already put 12,000 words of it on paper and Mrs. Clemens is pretty outspokenly satisfied with it-a hard critic to content. I feel sure that all of the first half of the story—and I hope three-fourths—will be comedy; but by the former plan the whole of it (except the first 3 chapters) would have been tragedy and unendurable, almost. I think I can carry the reader a long way before he suspects that I am laying a tragedy-trap. In the present form I could spin 16 books out of it with comfort and joy; but I shall deny myself and restrict it to one. (If you should see a little short story in a magazine in the autumn called "My Platonic Sweetheart" written 3 weeks ago) that is not this one. It may have been a suggester, though.

I expect all these singular privacies to interest you, and you are not to let on that they don't.

We are leaving, this afternoon, for Ischl, to use that as a base for the baggage, and then gad around ten days among the lakes and mountains to rest-up Mrs. Clemens, who is jaded with housekeeping. I hope I can get a chance to work a little in spots—I can't tell. But you do it—therefore why should you think I can't?

[Remainder missing.]

The dream story was never completed. It was the same that he had worked on in London, and perhaps again in Switzerland. It would be tried at other times and in other forms, but it never seemed to accommodate itself to a central idea, so that the good writing in it eventually went to waste. The short story mentioned, "My Platonic Sweetheart," a charming, idyllic tale, was not published during Mark Twain's lifetime. Two years after his death it appeared in Harper's Magazine.

The assassination of the Empress of Austria at Geneva was the startling event of that summer. In a letter to Twichell Clemens presents the tragedy in a few vivid paragraphs. Later he treated it at some length in a magazine article which, very likely because of personal relations with members of the Austrian court, he withheld from print. It has since been included in a volume of essays, What Is Man, etc.

To Rev. J. H. Twichell, in Hartford:

KALTENLEUTGEBEN, Sep. 13, '98.

DEAR JOE,—You are mistaken; people don't send us the magazines. No—Harper, Century and McClure do; an example I should like to recommend to other publishers. And so I thank you very much for sending me Brander's article. When you say "I like Brander Matthews; he impresses me as a man of parts and power," I back you, right up to the hub—I feel the same way—. And when you say he has earned your gratitude for cuffing me for my crimes against the Leather stockings and the Vicar, I ain't making any objection. Dern your gratitude!

His article is as sound as a nut. Brander knows literature, and loves it; he can talk about it and keep his temper; he can state his case so lucidly and so fairly and so forcibly that you have to agree with him, even when you don't agree with him; and he can discover and praise such merits as a book has, even when they are half a dozen diamonds scattered through an acre of mud. And so he has a right to be a critic.

To detail just the opposite of the above invoice is to describe me. I haven't any right to criticise books, and I don't do it except when I hate them. I often want to criticise Jane Austen, but her books madden me so that I can't conceal my frenzy from the reader; and therefore I have to stop every time I begin.

That good and unoffending lady the Empress is killed by a mad-man, and I am living in the midst of world-history again. The Queen's jubilee last year, the invasion of the Reichsrath by the police, and now this murder, which will still be talked of and described and painted a thousand years from now.

To have a personal friend of the wearer of the crown burst in at the gate in the deep dusk of the evening and say in a voice broken with tears, "My God the Empress is murdered," and fly toward her home before we can utter a question-why, it brings the giant event home to you, makes you a part of it and personally interested; it is as if your neighbor Antony should come flying and say "Caesar is butchered—the head of the world is fallen!"

Of course there is no talk but of this. The mourning is universal and genuine, the consternation is stupefying. The Austrian Empire is being draped with black. Vienna will be a spectacle to see, by next Saturday, when the funeral cortege marches. We are invited to occupy a room in the sumptuous new hotel (the "Krantz" where we are to live during the Fall and Winter) and view it, and we shall go.

Speaking of Mrs. Leiter, there is a noble dame in Vienna, about whom they retail similar slanders. She said in French—she is weak in French—that she had been spending a Sunday afternoon in a gathering of the "demimonde." Meaning the unknown land, that mercantile land, that mysterious half-world which underlies the aristocracy. But these Malaproperies are always inventions—they don't happen.

Yes, I wish we could have some talks; I'm full to the eye-lids. Had a noble good one with Parker and Dunham—land, but we were grateful for that visit!

Yours with all our loves.

MARK.

[Inclosed with the foregoing.]

Among the inadequate attempts to account for the assassination we must concede high rank to the German Emperor's. He justly describes it as a "deed unparalleled for ruthlessness," and then adds that it was "ordained from above."

I think this verdict will not be popular "above." A man is either a free agent or he isn't. If a man is a free agent, this prisoner is responsible for what he has done; but if a man is not a free agent, if the deed was ordained from above, there is no rational way of making this prisoner even partially responsible for it, and the German court cannot condemn him without manifestly committing a crime. Logic is logic; and by disregarding its laws even Emperors as capable and acute as William II can be beguiled into making charges which should not be ventured upon except in the shelter of plenty of lightning-rods.

MARK.

The end of the year 1898 found Mark Twain once more in easy, even luxurious, circumstances. The hard work and good fortune which had enabled him to pay his debts had, in the course of another year, provided what was comparative affluence: His report to Howells is characteristic and interesting.

To W. D. Howells, in New York:

HOTEL KRANTZ, WIEN, L. NEVER MARKT 6

Dec. 30, '98.

DEAR HOWELLS,—I begin with a date—including all the details—though I shall be interrupted presently by a South-African acquaintance who is passing through, and it may be many days before I catch another leisure moment. Note how suddenly a thing can become habit, and how indestructible the habit is, afterward! In your house in Cambridge a hundred years ago, Mrs. Howells said to me, "Here is a bunch of your letters, and the dates are of no value, because you don't put any in—the years, anyway." That remark diseased me with a habit which has cost me worlds of time and torture and ink, and millions of vain efforts and buckets of tears to break it, and here it is yet—I could easier get rid of a virtue.....

I hope it will interest you (for I have no one else who would much care to know it) that here lately the dread of leaving the children in difficult circumstances has died down and disappeared and I am now having peace from that long, long nightmare, and can sleep as well as anyone. Every little while, for these three years, now, Mrs. Clemens has come with pencil and paper and figured up the condition of things (she keeps the accounts and the bank-book) and has proven to me that the clouds were lifting, and so has hoisted my spirits temporarily and kept me going till another figuring-up was necessary. Last night she figured up for her own satisfaction, not mine, and found that we own a house and furniture in Hartford; that my English and American copyrights pay an income which represents a value of $200,000; and that we have $107,000 cash in the bank. I have been out and bought a box of 6-cent cigars; I was smoking 4 1/2 centers before.

At the house of an English friend, on Christmas Eve, we saw the Mouse-Trap played and well played. I thought the house would kill itself with laughter. By George they played with life! and it was most devastatingly funny. And it was well they did, for they put us Clemenses in the front seat, and if they played it poorly I would have assaulted them. The head young man and girl were Americans, the other parts were taken by English, Irish and Scotch girls. Then there was a nigger-minstrel show, of the genuine old sort, and I enjoyed that, too, for the nigger-show was always a passion of mine. This one was created and managed by a Quaker doctor from Philada., (23 years old) and he was the middle man. There were 9 others—5 Americans from 5 States and a Scotchman, 2 Englishmen and an Irishman—all post-graduate-medical young fellows, of course—or, it could be music; but it would be bound to be one or the other.

It's quite true—I don't read you "as much as I ought," nor anywhere near half as much as I want to; still I read you all I get a chance to. I saved up your last story to read when the numbers should be complete, but before that time arrived some other admirer of yours carried off the papers. I will watch admirers of yours when the Silver Wedding journey begins, and that will not happen again. The last chance at a bound book of yours was in London nearly two years ago—the last volume of your short things, by the Harpers. I read the whole book twice through and some of the chapters several times, and the reason that that was as far as I got with it was that I lent it to another admirer of yours and he is admiring it yet. Your admirers have ways of their own; I don't know where they get them.

Yes, our project is to go home next autumn if we find we can afford to live in New York. We've asked a friend to inquire about flats and expenses. But perhaps nothing will come of it. We do afford to live in the finest hotel in Vienna, and have 4 bedrooms, a dining-room, a drawing-room, 3 bath-rooms and 3 Vorzimmers, (and food) but we couldn't get the half of it in New York for the same money ($600 a month).

Susy hovers about us this holiday week, and the shadows fall all about us of

"The days when we went gipsying

A long time ago."

Death is so kind, so benignant, to whom he loves; but he goes by us others and will not look our way. We saw the "Master of Palmyra" last night. How Death, with the gentleness and majesty, made the human grand-folk around him seem little and trivial and silly!

With love from all of us to all of you.

MARK.

XXXVIII. LETTERS, 1899, TO HOWELLS AND OTHERS. VIENNA. LONDON. A SUMMER IN SWEDEN.

The beginning of 1899 found the Clemens family still in Vienna, occupying handsome apartments at the Hotel Krantz. Their rooms, so often thronged with gay and distinguished people, were sometimes called the "Second Embassy." Clemens himself was the central figure of these assemblies. Of all the foreign visitors in the Austrian capital he was the most notable. Everywhere he was surrounded by a crowd of listeners—his sayings and opinions were widely quoted.

A project for world disarmament promulgated by the Czar of Russia would naturally interest Mark Twain, and when William T. Stead, of the Review of Reviews, cabled him for an opinion on the matter, he sent at first a brief word and on the same day followed it with more extended comment. The great war which has since devastated the world gives to this incident an added interest.

To Wm. T. Stead, in London:

No. 1.

VIENNA, Jan. 9.

DEAR MR. STEAD,—The Czar is ready to disarm: I am ready to disarm. Collect the others, it should not be much of a task now.

MARK TWAIN.

To Wm. T. Stead, in London:

No. 2.

DEAR MR. STEAD,—Peace by compulsion. That seems a better idea than the other. Peace by persuasion has a pleasant sound, but I think we should not be able to work it. We should have to tame the human race first, and history seems to show that that cannot be done. Can't we reduce the armaments little by little—on a pro rata basis—by concert of the powers? Can't we get four great powers to agree to reduce their strength 10 per cent a year and thrash the others into doing likewise? For, of course, we cannot expect all of the powers to be in their right minds at one time. It has been tried. We are not going to try to get all of them to go into the scheme peaceably, are we? In that case I must withdraw my influence; because, for business reasons, I must preserve the outward signs of sanity. Four is enough if they can be securely harnessed together. They can compel peace, and peace without compulsion would be against nature and not operative. A sliding scale of reduction of 10 per cent a year has a sort of plausible look, and I am willing to try that if three other powers will join. I feel sure that the armaments are now many times greater than necessary for the requirements of either peace or war. Take wartime for instance. Suppose circumstances made it necessary for us to fight another Waterloo, and that it would do what it did before—settle a large question and bring peace. I will guess that 400,000 men were on hand at Waterloo (I have forgotten the figures). In five hours they disabled 50,000 men. It took them that tedious, long time because the firearms delivered only two or three shots a minute. But we would do the work now as it was done at Omdurman, with shower guns, raining 600 balls a minute. Four men to a gun—is that the number? A hundred and fifty shots a minute per man. Thus a modern soldier is 149 Waterloo soldiers in one. Thus, also, we can now retain one man out of each 150 in service, disband the others, and fight our Waterloos just as effectively as we did eighty-five years ago. We should do the same beneficent job with 2,800 men now that we did with 400,000 then. The allies could take 1,400 of the men, and give Napoleon 1,400 and then whip him.

But instead what do we see? In war-time in Germany, Russia and France, taken together we find about 8 million men equipped for the field. Each man represents 149 Waterloo men, in usefulness and killing capacity. Altogether they constitute about 350 million Waterloo men, and there are not quite that many grown males of the human race now on this planet. Thus we have this insane fact—that whereas those three countries could arm 18,000 men with modern weapons and make them the equals of 3 million men of Napoleon's day, and accomplish with them all necessary war work, they waste their money and their prosperity creating forces of their populations in piling together 349,982,000 extra Waterloo equivalents which they would have no sort of use for if they would only stop drinking and sit down and cipher a little.

Perpetual peace we cannot have on any terms, I suppose; but I hope we can gradually reduce the war strength of Europe till we get it down to where it ought to be—20,000 men, properly armed. Then we can have all the peace that is worth while, and when we want a war anybody can afford it.

VIENNA, January 9.

P. S.—In the article I sent the figures are wrong—"350 million" ought to be 450 million; "349,982,000" ought to be 449,982,000, and the remark about the sum being a little more than the present number of males on the planet—that is wrong, of course; it represents really one and a half the existing males.

Now and then one of Mark Twain's old comrades still reached out to him across the years. He always welcomed such letters—they came as from a lost land of romance, recalled always with tenderness. He sent light, chaffing replies, but they were never without an undercurrent of affection.

To Major "Jack" Downing, in Middleport, Ohio:

HOTEL KRANTZ, WEIN, I, NEUER MART 6,

Feb. 26, 1899.

DEAR MAJOR,—No: it was to Bixby that I was apprenticed. He was to teach me the river for a certain specified sum. I have forgotten what it was, but I paid it. I steered a trip for Bart Bowen, of Keokuk, on the A. T. Lacy, and I was partner with Will Bowen on the A. B. Chambers (one trip), and with Sam Bowen a whole summer on a small Memphis packet.

The newspaper report you sent me is incorrect. Bixby is not 67: he is 97. I am 63 myself, and I couldn't talk plain and had just begun to walk when I apprenticed myself to Bixby who was then passing himself off for 57 and successfully too, for he always looked 60 or 70 years younger than he really was. At that time he was piloting the Mississippi on a Potomac commission granted him by George Washington who was a personal friend of his before the Revolution. He has piloted every important river in America, on that commission, he has also used it as a passport in Russia. I have never revealed these facts before. I notice, too, that you are deceiving the people concerning your age. The printed portrait which you have enclosed is not a portrait of you, but a portrait of me when I was 19. I remember very well when it was common for people to mistake Bixby for your grandson. Is it spreading, I wonder—this disposition of pilots to renew their youth by doubtful methods? Beck Jolly and Joe Bryan—they probably go to Sunday school now—but it will not deceive.

Yes, it is as you say. All of the procession but a fraction has passed. It is time for us all to fall in.

Sincerely yours,

S. L. CLEMENS.

To W. D. Howells, in New York:

HOTEL KRANTZ, WIEN I. NEUER MARKT 6

April 2, '99.

DEAR HOWELLS,—I am waiting for the April Harper, which is about due now; waiting, and strongly interested. You are old enough to be a weary man, with paling interests, but you do not show it. You do your work in the same old delicate and delicious and forceful and searching and perfect way. I don't know how you can—but I suspect. I suspect that to you there is still dignity in human life, and that Man is not a joke—a poor joke—the poorest that was ever contrived. Since I wrote my Bible, (last year)—["What Is Man."]—which Mrs. Clemens loathes, and shudders over, and will not listen to the last half nor allow me to print any part of it, Man is not to me the respect-worthy person he was before; and so I have lost my pride in him, and can't write gaily nor praisefully about him any more. And I don't intend to try. I mean to go on writing, for that is my best amusement, but I shan't print much (for I don't wish to be scalped, any more than another.)

April 5. The Harper has come. I have been in Leipzig with your party, and then went on to Karlsbad and saw Mrs. Marsh's encounter with the swine with the toothpick and the other manners—["Their Silver Wedding Journey."]—At this point Jean carried the magazine away.

Is it imagination, or—Anyway I seem to get furtive and fleeting glimpses which I take to be the weariness and condolence of age; indifference to sights and things once brisk with interest; tasteless stale stuff which used to be champagne; the boredom of travel: the secret sigh behind the public smile, the private What-in-hell-did-I-come-for!

But maybe that is your art. Maybe that is what you intend the reader to detect and think he has made a Columbus-discovery. Then it is well done, perfectly done. I wrote my last travel book—[Following the Equator.]—in hell; but I let on, the best I could, that it was an excursion through heaven. Some day I will read it, and if its lying cheerfulness fools me, then I shall believe it fooled the reader. How I did loathe that journey around the world!—except the sea-part and India.

Evening. My tail hangs low. I thought I was a financier—and I bragged to you. I am not bragging, now. The stock which I sold at such a fine profit early in January, has never ceased to advance, and is now worth $60,000 more than I sold it for. I feel just as if I had been spending $20,000 a month, and I feel reproached for this showy and unbecoming extravagance.

Last week I was going down with the family to Budapest to lecture, and to make a speech at a banquet. Just as I was leaving here I got a telegram from London asking for the speech for a New York paper. I (this is strictly private) sent it. And then I didn't make that speech, but another of a quite different character—a speech born of something which the introducer said. If that said speech got cabled and printed, you needn't let on that it was never uttered.

That was a darling night, and those Hungarians were lively people. We were there a week and had a great time. At the banquet I heard their chief orator make a most graceful and easy and beautiful and delicious speech—I never heard one that enchanted me more—although I did not understand a word of it, since it was in Hungarian. But the art of it!—it was superlative.

They are wonderful English scholars, these people; my lecture audience—all Hungarians—understood me perfectly—to judge by the effects. The English clergyman told me that in his congregation are 150 young English women who earn their living teaching their language; and that there are others besides these.

For 60 cents a week the telephone reads the morning news to you at home; gives you the stocks and markets at noon; gives you lessons in 3 foreign languages during 3 hours; gives you the afternoon telegrams; and at night the concerts and operas. Of course even the clerks and seamstresses and bootblacks and everybody else are subscribers.

(Correction. Mrs. Clemens says it is 60 cents a month.)

I am renewing my youth. I made 4 speeches at one banquet here last Saturday night. And I've been to a lot of football matches.

Jean has been in here examining the poll for the Immortals ("Literature," March 24,) in the hope, I think, that at last she should find me at the top and you in second place; and if that is her ambition she has suffered disappointment for the third time—and will never fare any better, I hope, for you are where you belong, by every right. She wanted to know who it is that does the voting, but I was not able to tell her. Nor when the election will be completed and decided.

Next Morning. I have been reading the morning paper. I do it every morning—well knowing that I shall find in it the usual depravities and basenesses and hypocrisies and cruelties that make up civilization, and cause me to put in the rest of the day pleading for the damnation of the human race. I cannot seem to get my prayers answered, yet I do not despair.

(Escaped from) 5 o'clock tea ('sh!) Oh, the American girl in Europe!

Often she is creditable, but sometimes she is just shocking. This one, a minute ago—19, fat-face, raspy voice, pert ways, the self-complacency of God; and with it all a silly laugh (embarrassed) which kept breaking out through her chatter all along, whereas there was no call for it, for she said nothing that was funny. "Spose so many 've told y' how they 'njoyed y'r chapt'r on the Germ' tongue it's bringin' coals to Newcastle Kehe! say anything 'bout it Ke-hehe! Spent m' vacation 'n Russia, 'n saw Tolstoi; he said—" It made me shudder.

April 12. Jean has been in here with a copy of Literature, complaining that I am again behind you in the election of the 10 consecrated members; and seems troubled about it and not quite able to understand it. But I have explained to her that you are right there on the ground, inside the pool-booth, keeping game—and that that makes a large difference in these things.

13th. I have been to the Knustausstellung with Mrs. Clemens. The office of art seems to be to grovel in the dirt before Emperors and this and that and the other damned breed of priests.

Yrs ever

MARK.

Howells and Clemens were corresponding regularly again, though not with the frequency of former years. Perhaps neither of them was bubbling over with things to say; perhaps it was becoming yearly less attractive to pick up a pen and write, and then, of course, there was always the discouragement of distance. Once Howells wrote: "I know this will find you in Austria before I can well turn round, but I must make believe you are in Kennebunkport before I can begin it." And in another letter: "It ought to be as pleasant to sit down and write to you as to sit down and talk to you, but it isn't..... The only reason why I write is that I want another letter from you, and because I have a whole afternoon for the job. I have the whole of every afternoon, for I cannot work later than lunch. I am fagged by that time, and Sunday is the only day that brings unbearable leisure. I hope you will be in New York another winter; then I shall know what to do with these foretastes of eternity."

Clemens usually wrote at considerable length, for he had a good deal to report of his life in the Austrian capital, now drawing to a close.

To W. D. Howells, in New York:

May 12, 1899.

DEAR HOWELLS,—7.15 p. m. Tea (for Mr. and Mrs. Tower, who are leaving for Russia) just over; nice people and rather creditable to the human race: Mr. and Mrs. Tower; the new Minister and his wife; the Secretary of Legation; the Naval (and Military) Attach; several English ladies; an Irish lady; a Scotch lady; a particularly nice young Austrian baron who wasn't invited but came and went supposing it was the usual thing and wondered at the unusually large gathering; two other Austrians and several Americans who were also in his fix; the old Baronin Langeman, the only Austrian invited; the rest were Americans. It made just a comfortable crowd in our parlor, with an overflow into Clara's through the folding doors. I don't enjoy teas, and am daily spared them by Mrs. Clemens, but this was a pleasant one. I had only one accident. The old Baronin Langeman is a person I have a strong fondness for, for we violently disagree on some subjects and as violently agree on others—for instance, she is temperance and I am not: she has religious beliefs and feelings and I have none; (she's a Methodist!) she is a democrat and so am I; she is woman's rights and so am I; she is laborers' rights and approves trades unions and strikes, and that is me. And so on. After she was gone an English lady whom I greatly like, began to talk sharply against her for contributing money, time, labor, and public expression of favor to a strike that is on (for an 11-hour day) in the silk factories of Bohemia—and she caught me unprepared and betrayed me into over-warm argument. I am sorry: for she didn't know anything about the subject, and I did; and one should be gentle with the ignorant, for they are the chosen of God.

(The new Minister is a good man, but out of place. The Sec. of Legation is a good man, but out of place. The Attache is a good man, but out of place. Our government for displacement beats the new White Star ship; and her possible is 17,200 tons.)

May 13, 4 p. m. A beautiful English girl and her handsome English husband came up and spent the evening, and she certainly is a bird. English parents—she was born and reared in Roumania and couldn't talk English till she was 8 or 10. She came up clothed like the sunset, and was a delight to look at. (Roumanian costume.).....

Twenty-four young people have gone out to the Semmering to-day (and to-morrow) and Mrs. Clemens and an English lady and old Leschetitzky and his wife have gone to chaperon them. They gave me a chance to go, but there are no snow mountains that I want to look at. Three hours out, three hours back, and sit up all night watching the young people dance; yelling conversationally and being yelled at, conversationally, by new acquaintances, through the deafening music, about how I like Vienna, and if it's my first visit, and how long we expect to stay, and did I see the foot-washing, and am I writing a book about Vienna, and so on. The terms seemed too severe. Snow mountains are too dear at the price....

For several years I have been intending to stop writing for print as soon as I could afford it. At last I can afford it, and have put the pot-boiler pen away. What I have been wanting is a chance to write a book without reserves—a book which should take account of no one's feelings, and no one's prejudices, opinions, beliefs, hopes, illusions, delusions; a book which should say my say, right out of my heart, in the plainest language and without a limitation of any sort. I judged that that would be an unimaginable luxury, heaven on earth.

It is under way, now, and it is a luxury! an intellectual drunk: Twice I didn't start it right; and got pretty far in, both times, before I found it out. But I am sure it is started right this time. It is in tale-form. I believe I can make it tell what I think of Man, and how he is constructed, and what a shabby poor ridiculous thing he is, and how mistaken he is in his estimate of his character and powers and qualities and his place among the animals.

So far, I think I am succeeding. I let the madam into the secret day before yesterday, and locked the doors and read to her the opening chapters. She said—

"It is perfectly horrible—and perfectly beautiful!"

"Within the due limits of modesty, that is what I think."

I hope it will take me a year or two to write it, and that it will turn out to be the right vessel to contain all the abuse I am planning to dump into it.

Yours ever

MARK.

The story mentioned in the foregoing, in which Mark Twain was to give his opinion of man, was The Mysterious Stranger. It was not finished at the time, and its closing chapter was not found until after his death. Six years later (1916) it was published serially in Harper's Magazine, and in book form.

The end of May found the Clemens party in London, where they were received and entertained with all the hospitality they had known in earlier years. Clemens was too busy for letter-writing, but in the midst of things he took time to report to Howells an amusing incident of one of their entertainments.

To W. D. Howells, in America:

LONDON, July 3, '99

DEAR HOWELLS,—..... I've a lot of things to write you, but it's no use—I can't get time for anything these days. I must break off and write a postscript to Canon Wilberforce before I go to bed. This afternoon he left a luncheon-party half an hour ahead of the rest, and carried off my hat (which has Mark Twain in a big hand written in it.) When the rest of us came out there was but one hat that would go on my head—it fitted exactly, too. So wore it away. It had no name in it, but the Canon was the only man who was absent. I wrote him a note at 8 p.m.; saying that for four hours I had not been able to take anything that did not belong to me, nor stretch a fact beyond the frontiers of truth, and my family were getting alarmed. Could he explain my trouble? And now at 8.30 p.m. comes a note from him to say that all the afternoon he has been exhibiting a wonder-compelling mental vivacity and grace of expression, etc., etc., and have I missed a hat? Our letters have crossed.

Yours ever

MARK.

News came of the death of Robert Ingersoll. Clemens had been always one of his most ardent admirers, and a warm personal friend. To Ingersoll's niece he sent a word of heartfelt sympathy.

To Miss Eva Farrell, in New York:

30 WELLINGTON COURT, ALBERT GATE.

DEAR MISS FARRELL,—Except my daughter's, I have not grieved for any death as I have grieved for his. His was a great and beautiful spirit, he was a man—all man from his crown to his foot soles. My reverence for him was deep and genuine; I prized his affection for me and returned it with usury.

Sincerely Yours,

S. L. CLEMENS.

Clemens and family decided to spend the summer in Sweden, at Sauna, in order to avail themselves of osteopathic treatment as practised by Heinrick Kellgren. Kellgren's method, known as the "Swedish movements," seemed to Mark Twain a wonderful cure for all ailments, and he heralded the discovery far and wide. He wrote to friends far and near advising them to try Kellgren for anything they might happen to have. Whatever its beginning, any letter was likely to close with some mention of the new panacea.

To Rev. J. H. Twichell, traveling in Europe:

SANNA, Sept. 6, '99.

DEAR JOE,—I've no business in here—I ought to be outside. I shall never see another sunset to begin with it this side of heaven. Venice? land, what a poor interest that is! This is the place to be. I have seen about 60 sunsets here; and a good 40 of them were clear and away beyond anything I had ever imagined before for dainty and exquisite and marvellous beauty and infinite change and variety. America? Italy? The tropics? They have no notion of what a sunset ought to be. And this one—this unspeakable wonder! It discounts all the rest. It brings the tears, it is so unutterably beautiful.

If I had time, I would say a word about this curative system here. The people actually do several of the great things the Christian Scientists pretend to do. You wish to advise with a physician about it? Certainly. There is no objection. He knows next to something about his own trade, but that will not embarrass him in framing a verdict about this one. I respect your superstitions—we all have them. It would be quite natural for the cautious

Chinaman to ask his native priest to instruct him as to the value of the new religious specialty which the Western missionary is trying to put on the market, before investing in it. (He would get a verdict.)

Love to you all!

Always Yours

MARK.

Howells wrote that he was going on a reading-tour-dreading it, of course-and asking for any advice that Clemens felt qualified to give. Naturally, Clemens gave him the latest he had in stock, without realizing, perhaps, that he was recommending an individual practice which few would be likely to imitate. Nevertheless, what he says is interesting.

To W. D. Howells, in America:

SANNA, SWEDEN, Sept. 26, '99.

DEAR HOWELLS,—Get your lecture by heart—it will pay you. I learned a trick in Vienna—by accident—which I wish I had learned years ago. I meant to read from a Tauchnitz, because I knew I hadn't well memorized the pieces; and I came on with the book and read a few sentences, then remembered that the sketch needed a few words of explanatory introduction; and so, lowering the book and now and then unconsciously using it to gesture with, I talked the introduction, and it happened to carry me into the sketch itself, and then I went on, pretending that I was merely talking extraneous matter and would come to the sketch presently. It was a beautiful success. I knew the substance of the sketch and the telling phrases of it; and so, the throwing of the rest of it into informal talk as I went along limbered it up and gave it the snap and go and freshness of an impromptu. I was to read several pieces, and I played the same game with all of them, and always the audience thought I was being reminded of outside things and throwing them in, and was going to hold up the book and begin on the sketch presently—and so I always got through the sketch before they were entirely sure that it had begun. I did the same thing in Budapest and had the same good time over again. It's a new dodge, and the best one that was ever invented. Try it. You'll never lose your audience—not even for a moment. Their attention is fixed, and never wavers. And that is not the case where one reads from book or MS., or where he stands up without a note and frankly exposes the fact, by his confident manner and smooth phrasing, that he is not improvising, but reciting from memory. And in the heat of telling a thing that is memorised in substance only, one flashes out the happiest suddenly-begotten phrases every now and then! Try it. Such a phrase has a life and sparkle about it that twice as good a one could not exhibit if prepared beforehand, and it "fetches" an audience in such an enthusing and inspiring and uplifting way that that lucky phrase breeds another one, sure.

Your September instalment—["Their Silver Wedding journey."]—was delicious—every word of it. You haven't lost any of your splendid art. Callers have arrived.

With love

MARK.

"Yes," wrote Howells, "if I were a great histrionic artist like you I would get my poor essays by heart, and recite them, but being what I am I should do the thing so lifelessly that I had better recognise their deadness frankly and read them."

From Vienna Clemens had contributed to the Cosmopolitan, then owned by John Brisben Walker, his first article on Christian Science. It was a delicious bit of humor and found such enthusiastic appreciation that Walker was moved to send an additional $200 check in payment for it. This brought prompt acknowledgment.

To John Brisben Walker, in Irvington, N. Y.:

LONDON, Oct. 19, '99

DEAR MR. WALKER,—By gracious but you have a talent for making a man feel proud and good! To say a compliment well is a high art—and few possess it. You know how to do it, and when you confirm its sincerity with a handsome cheque the limit is reached and compliment can no higher go. I like to work for you: when you don't approve an article you say so, recognizing that I am not a child and can stand it; and when you approve an article I don't have to dicker with you as if I raised peanuts and you kept a stand; I know I shall get every penny the article is worth.

You have given me very great pleasure, and I thank you for it.

Sincerely Yours

S. L. CLEMENS.

On the same day he sent word to Howells of the good luck which now seemed to be coming his way. The Joan of Arc introduction was the same that today appears in his collected works under the title of Saint Joan of Arc.

To W. D. Howells, in New York:

LONDON, Oct. 19, '99.

DEAR HOWELLS,—My, it's a lucky day!—of the sort when it never rains but it pours. I was to write an introduction to a nobler book—the English translation of the Official Record (unabridged) of the Trials and Rehabilitation of Joan of Arc, and make a lot of footnotes. I wrote the introduction in Sweden, and here a few days ago I tore loose from a tale I am writing, and took the MS book and went at the grind of note-making—a fearful job for a man not used to it. This morning brought a note from my excellent friend Murray, a rich Englishman who edits the translation, saying,

"Never mind the notes—we'll make the translators do them." That was comfort and joy.

The same mail brought a note from Canon Wilberforce, asking me to talk Joan of Arc in his drawing-room to the Dukes and Earls and M. P.'s—(which would fetch me out of my seclusion and into print, and I couldn't have that,) and so of course I must run down to the Abbey and explain—and lose an hour. Just then came Murray and said "Leave that to me—I'll go and do the explaining and put the thing off 3 months; you write a note and tell him I am coming."

(Which I did, later.) Wilberforce carried off my hat from a lunch party last summer, and in to-day's note he said he wouldn't steal my new hat this time. In my note I said I couldn't make the drawing-room talk, now—Murray would explain; and added a P. S.: "You mustn't think it is because I am afraid to trust my hat in your reach again, for I assure you upon honor it isn't. I should bring my old one."

I had suggested to Murray a fortnight ago, that he get some big guns to write introductory monographs for the book.

Miss X, Joan's Voices and Prophecies.

The Lord Chief Justice of England, the legal prodigies which she performed before her judges.

Lord Roberts, her military genius.

Kipling, her patriotism.

And so on. When he came this morning he said he had captured Miss X; that Lord Roberts and Kipling were going to take hold and see if they could do monographs worthy of the book. He hadn't run the others to cover yet, but was on their track. Very good news. It is a grand book, and is entitled to the best efforts of the best people. As for me, I took pains with my Introduction, and I admit that it is no slouch of a performance.

Then I came down to Chatto's, and found your all too beautiful letter, and was lifted higher than ever. Next came letters from America properly glorifying my Christian Science article in the Cosmopolitan (and one roundly abusing it,) and a letter from John Brisben Walker enclosing $200 additional pay for the article (he had already paid enough, but I didn't mention that—which wasn't right of me, for this is the second time he has done such a thing, whereas Gilder has done it only once and no one else ever.) I make no prices with Walker and Gilder—I can trust them.

And last of all came a letter from M-. Hcw I do wish that man was in hell. Even-the briefest line from that idiot puts me in a rage.

But on the whole it has been a delightful day, and with M——in hell it would have been perfect. But that will happen, and I can wait.

Ah, if I could look into the inside of pecple as you do, and put it on paper, and invent things for them to do and say, and tell how they said it, I could writs a fine and readable book now, for I've got a prime subject. I've written 30,000 words of it and satisfied myself that the stuff is there; so I am going to discard that MS and begin all over again and have a good time with it.

Oh, I know how you feel! I've been in hell myself. You are there tonight. By difference in time you are at luncheon, now—and not eating it. Nothing is so lonesome as gadding around platforming. I have declined 45 lectures to-day-England and Scotland. I wanted the money, but not the torture: Good luck to you!—and repentance.

With love to all of you

MARK.

XXXIX. LETTERS OF 1900, MAINLY TO TWICHELL. THE BOER WAR. BOXER TROUBLES. THE RETURN TO AMERICA.

The New Year found Clemens still in London, chiefly interested in osteopathy and characteristically glorifying the practice at the expense of other healing methods.

To Rev. J. H. Twichell, in Hartford:

LONDON, Jan. 8, 1900.

DEAR JOE,—Mental Telepathy has scored another. Mental Telegraphy will be greatly respected a century hence.

By the accident of writing my sister and describing to her the remarkable cures made by Kellgren with his hands and without drugs, I brought upon myself a quite stunning surprise; for she wrote to me that she had been taking this very treatment in Buffalo—and that it was an American invention.

Well, it does really turn out that Dr. Still, in the middle of Kansas, in a village, began to experiment in 1874, only five years after Kellgren began the same work obscurely in the village of Gotha, in Germany. Dr. Still seems to be an honest man; therefore I am persuaded that Kellgren moved him to his experiments by Mental Telegraphy across six hours of longitude, without need of a wire. By the time Still began to experiment, Kellgren had completed his development of the principles of his system and established himself in a good practice in London—1874—and was in good shape to convey his discovery to Kansas, Mental Telegraphically.

Yes, I was greatly surprised to find that my mare's nest was much in arrears: that this new science was well known in America under the name of Osteopathy. Since then, I find that in the past 3 years it has got itself legalized in 14 States in spite of the opposition of the physicians; that it has established 20 Osteopathic schools and colleges; that among its students are 75 allopathic physicians; that there is a school in Boston and another in Philadelphia, that there are about 100 students in the parent college (Dr. Still's at Kirksville, Missouri,) and that there are about 2,000 graduates practicing in America. Dear me, there are not 30 in Europe. Europe is so sunk in superstitions and prejudices that it is an almost impossible thing to get her to do anything but scoff at a new thing—unless it come from abroad; as witness the telegraph, dentistry, &c.

Presently the Osteopath will come over here from America and will soon make himself a power that must be recognized and reckoned with; and then, 25 years from now, England will begin to claim the invention and tell all about its origin, in the Cyclopedia B——-as in the case of the telegraph, applied anaesthetics and the other benefactions which she heaped her abuse upon when her inventors first offered them to her.

I cannot help feeling rather inordinately proud of America for the gay and hearty way in which she takes hold of any new thing that comes along and gives it a first rate trial. Many an ass in America, is getting a deal of benefit out of X-Science's new exploitation of an age-old healing principle—faith, combined with the patient's imagination—let it boom along! I have no objection. Let them call it by what name they choose, so long as it does helpful work among the class which is numerically vastly the largest bulk of the human race, i.e. the fools, the idiots, the pudd'nheads.

We do not guess, we know that 9 in 10 of the species are pudd'nheads. We know it by various evidences; and one of them is, that for ages the race has respected (and almost venerated) the physician's grotesque system—the emptying of miscellaneous and harmful drugs into a person's stomach to remove ailments which in many cases the drugs could not reach at all; in many cases could reach and help, but only at cost of damage to some other part of the man; and in the remainder of the cases the drug either retarded the cure, or the disease was cured by nature in spite of the nostrums. The doctor's insane system has not only been permitted to continue its follies for ages, but has been protected by the State and made a close monopoly—an infamous thing, a crime against a free-man's proper right to choose his own assassin or his own method of defending his body against disease and death.

And yet at the same time, with curious and senile inconsistency, the State has allowed the man to choose his own assassin—in one detail—the patent-medicine detail—making itself the protector of that perilous business, collecting money out of it, and appointing no committee of experts to examine the medicines and forbid them when extra dangerous. Really, when a man can prove that he is not a jackass, I think he is in the way to prove that he is no legitimate member of the race.

I have by me a list of 52 human ailments—common ones—and in this list I count 19 which the physician's art cannot cure. But there isn't one which Osteopathy or Kellgren cannot cure, if the patient comes early.

Fifteen years ago I had a deep reverence for the physician and the surgeon. But 6 months of closely watching the Kellgren business has revolutionized all that, and now I have neither reverence nor respect for the physician's trade, and scarcely any for the surgeon's,—I am convinced that of all quackeries, the physician's is the grotesquest and the silliest. And they know they are shams and humbugs. They have taken the place of those augurs who couldn't look each other in the face without laughing.

See what a powerful hold our ancient superstitions have upon us: two weeks ago, when Livy committed an incredible imprudence and by consequence was promptly stricken down with a heavy triple attack—influenza, bronchitis, and a lung affected—she recognized the gravity of the situation, and her old superstitions rose: she thought she ought to send for a doctor—Think of it—the last man in the world I should want around at such a time. Of course I did not say no—not that I was indisposed to take the responsibility, for I was not, my notion of a dangerous responsibility being quite the other way—but because it is unsafe to distress a sick person; I only said we knew no good doctor, and it could not be good policy to choose at hazard; so she allowed me to send for Kellgren. To-day she is up and around—cured. It is safe to say that persons hit in the same way at the same time are in bed yet, and booked to stay there a good while, and to be in a shackly condition and afraid of their shadows for a couple of years or more to come.

It will be seen by the foregoing that Mark Twain's interest in the

Kellgren system was still an ardent one. Indeed, for a time he gave most of his thought to it, and wrote several long appreciations, perhaps with little idea of publication, but merely to get his enthusiasm physically expressed. War, however, presently supplanted medicine—the Boer troubles in South Africa and the Boxer insurrection in China. It was a disturbing, exciting year.

To W. D. Howells, in Boston:

WELLINGTON COURT, KNIGHTSBRIDGE,

Jan. 25, 1900.

DEAR HOWELLS,—If you got half as much as Pond prophesied, be content and praise God—it has not happened to another. But I am sorry he didn't go with you; for it is marvelous to hear him yarn. He is good company, cheery and hearty, and his mill is never idle. Your doing a lecture tour was heroic. It was the highest order of grit, and you have a right to be proud of yourself. No mount of applause or money or both could save it from being a hell to a man constituted as you are. It is that even to me, who am made of coarser stuff.

I knew the audiences would come forward and shake hands with you—that one infallible sign of sincere approval. In all my life, wherever it failed me I left the hall sick and ashamed, knowing what it meant.

Privately speaking, this is a sordid and criminal war, and in every way shameful and excuseless. Every day I write (in my head) bitter magazine articles about it, but I have to stop with that. For England must not fall; it would mean an inundation of Russian and German political degradations which would envelop the globe and steep it in a sort of Middle-Age night and slavery which would last till Christ comes again. Even wrong—and she is wrong—England must be upheld. He is an enemy of the human race who shall speak against her now. Why was the human race created? Or at least why wasn't something creditable created in place of it. God had his opportunity. He could have made a reputation. But no, He must commit this grotesque folly—a lark which must have cost him a regret or two when He came to think it over and observe effects. For a giddy and unbecoming caprice there has been nothing like it till this war. I talk the war with both sides—always waiting until the other man introduces the topic. Then I say "My head is with the Briton, but my heart and such rags of morals as I have are with the Boer—now we will talk, unembarrassed and without prejudice." And so we discuss, and have no trouble.

Jan. 26.

It was my intention to make some disparaging remarks about the human race; and so I kept this letter open for that purpose, and for the purpose of telling my dream, wherein the Trinity were trying to guess a conundrum, but I can do better—for I can snip out of the "Times" various samples and side-lights which bring the race down to date, and expose it as of yesterday. If you will notice, there is seldom a telegram in a paper which fails to show up one or more members and beneficiaries of our Civilization as promenading in his shirt-tail, with the rest of his regalia in the wash.

I love to see the holy ones air their smug pieties and admire them and smirk over them, and at the same moment frankly and publicly show their contempt for the pieties of the Boer—confidently expecting the approval of the country and the pulpit, and getting it.

I notice that God is on both sides in this war; thus history repeats itself. But I am the only person who has noticed this; everybody here thinks He is playing the game for this side, and for this side only.

With great love to you all

MARK.

One cannot help wondering what Mark Twain would have thought of human nature had he lived to see the great World War, fought mainly by the Christian nations who for nearly two thousand years had been preaching peace on earth and goodwill toward men. But his opinion of the race could hardly have been worse than it was. And nothing that human beings could do would have surprised him.

To Rev. J. H. Twichell, in Hartford:

LONDON, Jan. 27, 1900.

DEAR JOE,—Apparently we are not proposing to set the Filipinos free and give their islands to them; and apparently we are not proposing to hang the priests and confiscate their property. If these things are so, the war out there has no interest for me.

I have just been examining chapter LXX of "Following the Equator," to see if the Boer's old military effectiveness is holding out. It reads curiously as if it had been written about the present war.

I believe that in the next chapter my notion of the Boer was rightly conceived. He is popularly called uncivilized, I do not know why. Happiness, food, shelter, clothing, wholesale labor, modest and rational ambitions, honesty, kindliness, hospitality, love of freedom and limitless courage to fight for it, composure and fortitude in time of disaster, patience in time of hardship and privation, absence of noise and brag in time of victory, contentment with a humble and peaceful life void of insane excitements—if there is a higher and better form of civilization than this, I am not aware of it and do not know where to look for it. I suppose we have the habit of imagining that a lot of artistic, intellectual and other artificialities must be added, or it isn't complete. We and the English have these latter; but as we lack the great bulk of these others, I think the Boer civilization is the best of the two. My idea of our civilization is that it is a shabby poor thing and full of cruelties, vanities, arrogancies, meannesses, and hypocrisies. As for the word, I hate the sound of it, for it conveys a lie; and as for the thing itself, I wish it was in hell, where it belongs.

Provided we could get something better in the place of it. But that is not possible, perhaps. Poor as it is, it is better than real savagery, therefore we must stand by it, extend it, and (in public) praise it. And so we must not utter any hateful word about England in these days, nor fail to hope that she will win in this war, for her defeat and fall would be an irremediable disaster for the mangy human race.... Naturally, then, I am for England; but she is profoundly in the wrong, Joe, and no (instructed) Englishman doubts it. At least that is my belief.

Maybe I managed to make myself misunderstood, as to the Osteopathists. I wanted to know how the men impress you. As to their Art, I know fairly well about that, and should not value Hartford's opinion of it; nor a physician's; nor that of another who proposed to enlighten me out of his ignorance. Opinions based upon theory, superstition and ignorance are not very precious.

Livy and the others are off for the country for a day or two.

Love to you all

MARK.

The next letter affords a pleasant variation. Without doubt it was written on realizing that good nature and enthusiasm had led him into indiscretion. This was always happening to him, and letters like this are not infrequent, though generally less entertaining.

To Mr. Ann, in London:

WELLINGTON COURT, Feb. 23, '00.

DEAR MR. ANN,—Upon sober second thought, it won't do!—I withdraw that letter. Not because I said anything in it which is not true, for I didn't; but because when I allow my name to be used in forwarding a stock-scheme I am assuming a certain degree of responsibility as toward the investor, and I am not willing to do that. I have another objection, a purely selfish one: trading upon my name, whether the enterprise scored a success or a failure would damage me. I can't afford that; even the Archbishop of Canterbury couldn't afford it, and he has more character to spare than I have. (Ah, a happy thought! If he would sign the letter with me that would change the whole complexion of the thing, of course. I do not know him, yet I would sign any commercial scheme that he would sign. As he does not know me, it follows that he would sign anything that I would sign. This is unassailable logic—but really that is all that can be said for it.)

No, I withdraw the letter. This virgin is pure up to date, and is going to remain so.

Ys sincerely,

S. L. C.

To Rev. J. H. Twichell, in Hartford:

WELLINGTON COURT,

KNIGHTSBRIDGE, Mch. 4, '00.

DEAR JOE,—Henry Robinson's death is a sharp wound to me, and it goes very deep. I had a strong affection for him, and I think he had for me. Every Friday, three-fourths of the year for 16 years he was of the billiard-party in our house. When we come home, how shall we have billiard-nights again—with no Ned Bunce and no Henry Robinson? I believe I could not endure that. We must find another use for that room. Susy is gone, George is gone, Libby Hamersley, Ned Bunce, Henry Robinson. The friends are passing, one by one; our house, where such warm blood and such dear blood flowed so freely, is become a cemetery. But not in any repellent sense. Our dead are welcome there; their life made it beautiful, their death has hallowed it, we shall have them with us always, and there will be no parting.

It was a moving address you made over Ward Cheney—that fortunate, youth! Like Susy, he got out of life all that was worth the living, and got his great reward before he had crossed the tropic frontier of dreams and entered the Sahara of fact. The deep consciousness of Susy's good fortune is a constant comfort to me.

London is happy-hearted at last. The British victories have swept the clouds away and there are no uncheerful faces. For three months the private dinner parties (we go to no public ones) have been Lodges of Sorrow, and just a little depressing sometimes; but now they are smiley and animated again. Joe, do you know the Irish gentleman and the Irish lady, the Scotch gentleman and the Scotch lady? These are darlings, every one. Night before last it was all Irish—24. One would have to travel far to match their ease and sociability and animation and sparkle and absence of shyness and self-consciousness.

It was American in these fine qualities. This was at Mr. Lecky's. He is Irish, you know. Last night it was Irish again, at Lady Gregory's. Lord Roberts is Irish; and Sir William Butler; and Kitchener, I think; and a disproportion of the other prominent Generals are of Irish and Scotch breed-keeping up the traditions of Wellington, and Sir Colin Campbell of the Mutiny. You will have noticed that in S. A. as in the Mutiny, it is usually the Irish and the Scotch that are placed in the fore-front of the battle. An Irish friend of mine says this is because the Kelts are idealists, and enthusiasts, with age-old heroisms to emulate and keep bright before the world; but that the low-class Englishman is dull and without ideals, fighting bull-doggishly while he has a leader, but losing his head and going to pieces when his leader falls—not so with the Kelt. Sir Wm. Butler said, "the Kelt is the spear-head of the British lance."

Love to you all.

MARK.

The Henry Robinson mentioned in the foregoing letter was Henry C. Robinson, one-time Governor of Connecticut, long a dear and intimate friend of the Clemens household. "Lecky" was W. E. H. Lecky, the Irish historian whose History of European Morals had been, for many years, one of Mark Twain's favorite books:

In July the Clemenses left the small apartment at 30 Wellington Court and established a summer household a little way out of London, at Dollis Hill. To-day the place has been given to the public under the name of Gladstone Park, so called for the reason that in an earlier time Gladstone had frequently visited there. It was a beautiful spot, a place of green grass and spreading oaks. In a letter in which Mrs. Clemens wrote to her sister she said: "It is simply divinely beautiful and peaceful; the great, old trees are beyond everything. I believe nowhere in the world do you find such trees as in England." Clemens wrote to Twichell: "From the house you can see little but spacious stretches of hay-fields and green turf..... Yet the massed, brick blocks of London are reachable in three minutes on a horse. By rail we can be in the heart of London, in Baker Street, in seventeen minutes—by a smart train in five."

Mail, however, would seem to have been less prompt.

To the Editor of the Times, in London:

SIR,—It has often been claimed that the London postal service was swifter than that of New York, and I have always believed that the claim was justified. But a doubt has lately sprung up in my mind. I live eight miles from Printing House Square; the Times leaves that point at 4 o'clock in the morning, by mail, and reaches me at 5 in the afternoon, thus making the trip in thirteen hours.

It is my conviction that in New York we should do it in eleven.

C.

DOLLIS HILL, N. W.

To Rev. J. H. Twichell, in Hartford:

DOLLIS HILL HOUSE, KILBURN, N. W.

LONDON, Aug. 12, '00.

DEAR JOE,—The Sages Prof. Fiske and Brander Matthews were out here to tea a week ago and it was a breath of American air to see them. We furnished them a bright day and comfortable weather—and they used it all up, in their extravagant American way. Since then we have sat by coal fires, evenings.

We shall sail for home sometime in October, but shall winter in New York where we can have an osteopath of good repute to continue the work of putting this family in proper condition.

Livy and I dined with the Chief Justice a month ago and he was as well-conditioned as an athlete.

It is all China, now, and my sympathies are with the Chinese. They have been villainously dealt with by the sceptred thieves of Europe, and I hope they will drive all the foreigners out and keep them out for good. I only wish it; of course I don't really expect it.

Why, hang it, it occurs to me that by the time we reach New York you Twichells will be invading Europe and once more we shall miss the connection. This is thoroughly exasperating. Aren't we ever going to meet again?

With no end of love from all of us,

MARK.

P. S. Aug. 18.

DEAR JOE,—It is 7.30 a. m. I have been waking very early, lately. If it occurs once more, it will be habit; then I will submit and adopt it.

This is our day of mourning. It is four years since Susy died; it is five years and a month that I saw her alive for the last time-throwing kisses at us from the railway platform when we started West around the world.

Sometimes it is a century; sometimes it was yesterday.

With love

MARK.

We discover in the foregoing letter that the long European residence was drawing to an end. More than nine years had passed since the closing of the Hartford house—eventful years that had seen failure, bereavement, battle with debt, and rehabilitated fortunes. All the family were anxious to get home—Mark Twain most anxious of all.

They closed Dollis Hill House near the end of September, and put up for a brief period at a family hotel, an amusing picture of which follows.

To J. Y. M. MacAlister, in London:

Sep. 1900.

MY DEAR MACALISTER,—We do really start next Saturday. I meant to sail earlier, but waited to finish some studies of what are called Family Hotels. They are a London specialty, God has not permitted them to exist elsewhere; they are ramshackle clubs which were dwellings at the time of the Heptarchy. Dover and Albemarle Streets are filled with them. The once spacious rooms are split up into coops which afford as much discomfort as can be had anywhere out of jail for any money. All the modern inconveniences are furnished, and some that have been obsolete for a century. The prices are astonishingly high for what you get. The bedrooms are hospitals for incurable furniture. I find it so in this one. They exist upon a tradition; they represent the vanishing home-like inn of fifty years ago, and are mistaken by foreigners for it. Some quite respectable Englishmen still frequent them through inherited habit and arrested development; many Americans also, through ignorance and superstition. The rooms are as interesting as the Tower of London, but older I think. Older and dearer. The lift was a gift of William the Conqueror, some of the beds are prehistoric. They represent geological periods. Mine is the oldest. It is formed in strata of Old Red Sandstone, volcanic tufa, ignis fatuus, and bicarbonate of hornblende, superimposed upon argillaceous shale, and contains the prints of prehistoric man. It is in No. 149. Thousands of scientists come to see it. They consider it holy. They want to blast out the prints but cannot. Dynamite rebounds from it.

Finished studies and sail Saturday in Minnehaha.

Yours ever affectionately,

MARK TWAIN.

They sailed for New York October 6th, and something more than a week later America gave them a royal welcome. The press, far and wide, sounded Mark Twain's praises once more; dinners and receptions were offered on every hand; editors and lecture agents clamored for him.

The family settled in the Earlington Hotel during a period of house-hunting. They hoped eventually to return to Hartford, but after a brief visit paid by Clemens alone to the old place he wrote:

To Sylvester Baxter, in Boston:

NEW YORK, Oct. 26, 1900.

DEAR MR. BAXTER,—It was a great pleasure to me to renew the other days with you, and there was a pathetic pleasure in seeing Hartford and the house again; but I realize that if we ever enter the house again to live, our hearts will break. I am not sure that we shall ever be strong enough to endure that strain.

Sincerely yours,

S. L. CLEMENS.

Mr. and Mrs. Rogers wished to have them in their neighborhood, but the houses there were not suitable, or were too expensive. Through Mr. Frank Doubleday they eventually found, at 14 West Tenth Street, a large residence handsomely furnished, and this they engaged for the winter. "We were lucky to get this big house furnished," he wrote MacAlister in London. "There was not another one in town procurable that would answer us, but this one is all right—space enough in it for several families, the rooms all old-fashioned, great size."

The little note that follows shows that Mark Twain had not entirely forgotten the days of Tom Sawyer and Huck Finn.

To a Neighbor on West Tenth Street, New York:

Nov. 30.

DEAR MADAM,—I know I ought to respect my duty and perform it, but I am weak and faithless where boys are concerned, and I can't help secretly approving pretty bad and noisy ones, though I do object to the kind that ring door-bells. My family try to get me to stop the boys from holding conventions on the front steps, but I basely shirk out of it, because I think the boys enjoy it.

My wife has been complaining to me this evening about the boys on the front steps and under compulsion I have made some promises. But I am very forgetful, now that I am old, and my sense of duty is getting spongy.

Very truly yours,

S. L. CLEMENS.

MARK TWAIN'S LETTERS—1853-1866

VOLUME 5

XL. LETTERS OF 1901, CHIEFLY TO TWICHELL. MARK TWAIN AS A REFORMER. SUMMER AT SARANAC. ASSASSINATION OF PRESIDENT McKINLEY.

An editorial in the Louisville Courier-Journal, early in 1901, said: "A remarkable transformation, or rather a development, has taken place in Mark Twain. The genial humorist of the earlier day is now a reformer of the vigorous kind, a sort of knight errant who does not hesitate to break a lance with either Church or State if he thinks them interposing on that broad highway over which he believes not a part but the whole of mankind has the privilege of passing in the onward march of the ages."

Mark Twain had begun "breaking the lance" very soon after his return from Europe. He did not believe that he could reform the world, but at least he need not withhold his protest against those things which stirred his wrath. He began by causing the arrest of a cabman who had not only overcharged but insulted him; he continued by writing openly against the American policy in the Philippines, the missionary propaganda which had resulted in the Chinese uprising and massacre, and against Tammany politics. Not all of his efforts were in the line of reform; he had become a sort of general spokesman which the public flocked to hear, whatever the subject. On the occasion of a Lincoln Birthday service at Carnegie Hall he was chosen to preside, and he was obliged to attend more dinners than were good for his health. His letters of this period were mainly written to his old friend Twichell, in Hartford. Howells, who lived in New York, he saw with considerable frequency.

In the letter which follows the medicine which Twichell was to take was Plasmon, an English proprietary remedy in which Mark Twain had invested—a panacea for all human ills which osteopathy could not reach.

To Rev. Joseph Twichell, in Hartford:

14 W. 10TH ST. Jan. 23, '01.

DEAR JOE,—Certainly. I used to take it in my coffee, but it settled to the bottom in the form of mud, and I had to eat it with a spoon; so I dropped the custom and took my 2 teaspoonfuls in cold milk after breakfast. If we were out of milk I shoveled the dry powder into my mouth and washed it down with water. The only essential is to get it down, the method is not important.

No, blame it, I can't go to the Alumni dinner, Joe. It takes two days, and I can't spare the time. Moreover I preside at the Lincoln birthday celebration in Carnegie Hall Feb. 11, and I must not make two speeches so close together. Think of it—two old rebels functioning there—I as President, and Watterson as Orator of the Day! Things have changed somewhat in these 40 years, thank God.

Look here—when you come down you must be our guest—we've got a roomy room for you, and Livy will make trouble if you go elsewhere. Come straight to 14 West 10th.

Jan. 24. Livy says Amen to that; also, can you give us a day or two's notice, so the room will be sure to be vacant?

I'm going to stick close to my desk for a month, now, hoping to write a small book.

Ys Ever

MARK

The letter which follows is a fair sample of Mark Twain's private violence on a subject which, in public print, he could only treat effectively by preserving his good humor. When he found it necessary to boil over, as he did, now and then, for relief, he always found a willing audience in Twichell. The mention of his "Private Philosophy" refers to 'What Is Man?', privately published in 1906; reissued by his publishers in 1916.

To Rev. J. H. Twichell, in Hartford:

14 W. 10th Jan. 29, '01.

DEAR JOE,—I'm not expecting anything but kicks for scoffing, and am expecting a diminution of my bread and butter by it, but if Livy will let me I will have my say. This nation is like all the others that have been spewed upon the earth—ready to shout for any cause that will tickle its vanity or fill its pocket. What a hell of a heaven it will be, when they get all these hypocrites assembled there!

I can't understand it! You are a public guide and teacher, Joe, and are under a heavy responsibility to men, young and old; if you teach your people—as you teach me—to hide their opinions when they believe the flag is being abused and dishonored, lest the utterance do them and a publisher a damage, how do you answer for it to your conscience? You are sorry for me; in the fair way of give and take, I am willing to be a little sorry for you.

However, I seem to be going counter to my own Private Philosophy—which Livy won't allow me to publish—because it would destroy me. But I hope to see it in print before I die. I planned it 15 years ago, and wrote it in '98. I've often tried to read it to Livy, but she won't have it; it makes her melancholy. The truth always has that effect on people. Would have, anyway, if they ever got hold of a rag of it—Which they don't.

You are supposing that I am supposing that I am moved by a Large Patriotism, and that I am distressed because our President has blundered up to his neck in the Philippine mess; and that I am grieved because this great big ignorant nation, which doesn't know even the A B C facts of the Philippine episode, is in disgrace before the sarcastic world—drop that idea! I care nothing for the rest—I am only distressed and troubled because I am befouled by these things. That is all. When I search myself away down deep, I find this out. Whatever a man feels or thinks or does, there is never any but one reason for it—and that is a selfish one.

At great inconvenience, and expense of precious time I went to the chief synagogue the other night and talked in the interest of a charity school of poor Jew girls. I know—to the finest, shades—the selfish ends that moved me; but no one else suspects. I could give you the details if I had time. You would perceive how true they are.

I've written another article; you better hurry down and help Livy squelch it.

She's out pottering around somewhere, poor housekeeping slave; and Clara is in the hands of the osteopath, getting the bronchitis pulled and hauled out of her. It was a bad attack, and a little disquieting. It came day before yesterday, and she hasn't sat up till this afternoon. She is getting along satisfactorily, now.

Lots of love to you all.

MARK

Mark Twain's religion had to do chiefly with humanity in its present incarnation, and concerned itself very little with any possible measure of reward or punishment in some supposed court of the hereafter. Nevertheless, psychic investigation always interested him, and he was good-naturedly willing to explore, even hoping, perhaps, to be convinced that individuality continues beyond death. The letter which follows indicates his customary attitude in relation to spiritualistic research. The experiments here mentioned, however, were not satisfactory.

To Mrs. Charles McQuiston:

DOBBS FERRY, N. Y.

March 26, 1901.

DEAR MRS. McQUISTON,—I have never had an experience which moved me to believe the living can communicate with the dead, but my wife and I have experimented in the matter when opportunity offered and shall continue to do so.

I enclose a letter which came this morning—the second from the same source. Mrs. K——is a Missourian, and lately she discovered, by accident, that she was a remarkable hypnotiser. Her best subject is a Missouri girl, Miss White, who is to come here soon and sustain strictly scientific tests before professors at Columbia University. Mrs. Clemens and I intend to be present. And we shall ask the pair to come to our house to do whatever things they can do. Meantime, if you thought well of it, you might write her and arrange a meeting, telling her it is by my suggestion and that I gave you her address.

Someone has told me that Mrs. Piper is discredited. I cannot be sure, but I think it was Mr. Myers, President of the London Psychical Research Society—we heard of his death yesterday. He was a spiritualist. I am afraid he was a very easily convinced man. We visited two mediums whom he and Andrew Lang considered quite wonderful, but they were quite transparent frauds.

Mrs. Clemens corrects me: One of those women was a fraud, the other not a fraud, but only an innocent, well-meaning, driveling vacancy.

Sincerely yours,

S. L. CLEMENS.

In Mark Twain's Bermuda chapters entitled Idle Notes of an Idle Excursion he tells of an old sea captain, one Hurricane Jones, who explained biblical miracles in a practical, even if somewhat startling, fashion. In his story of the prophets of Baal, for instance, the old captain declared that the burning water was nothing more nor less than petroleum. Upon reading the "notes," Professor Phelps of Yale wrote that the same method of explaining miracles had been offered by Sir Thomas Browne.

Perhaps it may be added that Captain Hurricane Jones also appears in Roughing It, as Captain Ned Blakely.

To Professor William Lyon Phelps;

YALE UNIVERSITY,

NEW YORK, April 24, 1901.

MY DEAR SIR,—I was not aware that old Sir Thomas had anticipated that story, and I am much obliged to you for furnishing me the paragraph.

It is curious that the same idea should leave entered two heads so unlike as the head of that wise old philosopher and that of Captain Ned Wakeman, a splendidly uncultured old sailor, but in his own opinion a thinker by divine right. He was an old friend of mine of many years' standing; I made two or three voyages with him, and found him a darling in many ways. The petroleum story was not told to me; he told it to Joe Twichell, who ran across him by accident on a sea voyage where I think the two were the only passengers. A delicious pair, and admirably mated, they took to each other at once and became as thick as thieves. Joe was passing under a fictitious name, and old Wakeman didn't suspect that he was a parson; so he gave his profanity full swing, and he was a master of that great art. You probably know Twichell, and will know that that is a kind of refreshment which he is very capable of enjoying.

Sincerely yours,

S. L. CLEMENS.

For the summer Clemens and his family found a comfortable lodge in the Adirondacks—a log cabin called "The Lair"—on Saranac Lake. Soon after his arrival there he received an invitation to attend the celebration of Missouri's eightieth anniversary. He sent the following letter:

To Edward L. Dimmitt, in St. Louis:

AMONG THE ADIRONDACK LAKES, July 19, 1901.

DEAR MR. DIMMITT,—By an error in the plans, things go wrong end first in this world, and much precious time is lost and matters of urgent importance are fatally retarded. Invitations which a brisk young fellow should get, and which would transport him with joy, are delayed and impeded and obstructed until they are fifty years overdue when they reach him.

It has happened again in this case.

When I was a boy in Missouri I was always on the lookout for invitations but they always miscarried and went wandering through the aisles of time; and now they are arriving when I am old and rheumatic and can't travel and must lose my chance.

I have lost a world of delight through this matter of delaying invitations. Fifty years ago I would have gone eagerly across the world to help celebrate anything that might turn up. IT would have made no difference to me what it was, so that I was there and allowed a chance to make a noise.

The whole scheme of things is turned wrong end to. Life should begin with age and its privileges and accumulations, and end with youth and its capacity to splendidly enjoy such advantages. As things are now, when in youth a dollar would bring a hundred pleasures, you can't have it. When you are old, you get it and there is nothing worth buying with it then.

It's an epitome of life. The first half of it consists of the capacity to enjoy without the chance; the last half consists of the chance without the capacity.

I am admonished in many ways that time is pushing me inexorably along. I am approaching the threshold of age; in 1977 I shall be 142. This is no time to be flitting about the earth. I must cease from the activities proper to youth and begin to take on the dignities and gravities and inertia proper to that season of honorable senility which is on its way and imminent as indicated above.

Yours is a great and memorable occasion, and as a son of Missouri I should hold it a high privilege to be there and share your just pride in the state's achievements; but I must deny myself the indulgence, while thanking you earnestly for the prized honor you have done me in asking me to be present.

Very truly yours,

S. L. CLEMENS.

In the foregoing Mark Twain touches upon one of his favorite fancies: that life should begin with old age and approach strong manhood, golden youth, to end at last with pampered and beloved babyhood. Possibly he contemplated writing a story with this idea as the theme, but He seems never to have done so.

The reader who has followed these letters may remember Yung Wing, who had charge of the Chinese educational mission in Hartford, and how Mark Twain, with Twichell, called on General Grant in behalf of the mission. Yung Wing, now returned to China, had conceived the idea of making an appeal to the Government of the United States for relief of his starving countrymen.

To J. H. Twichell, in Hartford:

AMPERSAND, N. Y., July 28, '01.

DEAR JOE,—As you say, it is impracticable—in my case, certainly. For me to assist in an appeal to that Congress of land-thieves and liars would be to bring derision upon it; and for me to assist in an appeal for cash to pass through the hands of those missionaries out there, of any denomination, Catholic or Protestant, wouldn't do at all. They wouldn't handle money which I had soiled, and I wouldn't trust them with it anyway. They would devote it to the relief of suffering—I know that—but the sufferers selected would be converts. The missionary-utterances exhibit no humane feeling toward the others, but in place of it a spirit of hate and hostility. And it is natural; the Bible forbids their presence there, their trade is unlawful, why shouldn't their characters be of necessity in harmony with—but never mind, let it go, it irritates me.

Later.... I have been reading Yung Wing's letter again. It may be that he is over-wrought by his sympathies, but it may not be so. There may be other reasons why the missionaries are silent about the Shensi-2-year famine and cannibalism. It may be that there are so few Protestant converts there that the missionaries are able to take care of them. That they are not likely to largely concern themselves about Catholic converts and the others, is quite natural, I think.

That crude way of appealing to this Government for help in a cause which has no money in it, and no politics, rises before me again in all its admirable innocence! Doesn't Yung Wing know us yet? However, he has been absent since '96 or '97. We have gone to hell since then. Kossuth couldn't raise 30 cents in Congress, now, if he were back with his moving Magyar-Tale.

I am on the front porch (lower one—main deck) of our little bijou of a dwelling-house. The lake-edge (Lower Saranac) is so nearly under me that I can't see the shore, but only the water, small-pored with rain-splashes—for there is a heavy down-pour. It is charmingly like sitting snuggled up on a ship's deck with the stretching sea all around—but very much more satisfactory, for at sea a rain-storm is depressing, while here of course the effect engendered is just a deep sense of comfort and contentment. The heavy forest shuts us solidly in on three sides there are no neighbors. There are beautiful little tan-colored impudent squirrels about. They take tea, 5 p. m., (not invited) at the table in the woods where Jean does my typewriting, and one of them has been brave enough to sit upon Jean's knee with his tail curved over his back and munch his food. They come to dinner, 7 p. m., on the front porch (not invited). They all have the one name—Blennerhasset, from Burr's friend—and none of them answers to it except when hungry.

We have been here since June 21st. For a little while we had some warm days—according to the family's estimate; I was hardly discommoded myself. Otherwise the weather has been of the sort you are familiar with in these regions: cool days and cool nights. We have heard of the hot wave every Wednesday, per the weekly paper—we allow no dailies to intrude. Last week through visitors also—the only ones we have had—Dr. Root and John Howells.

We have the daily lake-swim; and all the tribe, servants included (but not I) do a good deal of boating; sometimes with the guide, sometimes without him—Jean and Clara are competent with the oars. If we live another year, I hope we shall spend its summer in this house.

We have taken the Appleton country seat, overlooking the Hudson, at Riverdale, 25 minutes from the Grand Central Station, for a year, beginning Oct. 1, with option for another year. We are obliged to be close to New York for a year or two.

Aug. 3rd. I go yachting a fortnight up north in a 20-knot boat 225 feet long, with the owner, (Mr. Rogers), Tom Reid, Dr. Rice, Col. A. G. Paine and one or two others. Judge Howland would go, but can't get away from engagements; Professor Sloane would go, but is in the grip of an illness. Come—will you go? If you can manage it, drop a post-card to me c/o H.H. Rogers, 26 Broadway. I shall be in New York a couple of days before we sail—July 31 or Aug. 1, perhaps the latter,—and I think I shall stop at the Hotel Grosvenor, cor. 10th St and 5th ave.

We all send you and the Harmonies lots and gobs of love.

MARK

To Rev. J. H. Twichell, in Hartford:

AMPERSAND, N. Y., Aug. 28.

DEAR JOE,—Just a word, to scoff at you, with your extravagant suggestion that I read the biography of Phillips Brooks—the very dullest book that has been printed for a century. Joe, ten pages of Mrs. Cheney's masterly biography of her fathers—no, five pages of it—contain more meat, more sense, more literature, more brilliancy, than that whole basketful of drowsy rubbish put together. Why, in that dead atmosphere even Brooks himself is dull—he wearied me; oh how he wearied me!

We had a noble good time in the Yacht, and caught a Chinese missionary and drowned him.

Love from us all to you all.

MARK.

The assassination of President McKinley occurred September 6, 1901.

Such an event would naturally stir Mark Twain to comment on human nature in general. His letter to Twichell is as individual as it is sound in philosophy. At what period of his own life, or under what circumstances, he made the long journey with tragic intent there is no means of knowing now. There is no other mention of it elsewhere in the records that survive him.

To Rev. J. H. Twichell, in Hartford:

AMPERSAND, Tuesday, (Sept. 10, 1901)

DEAR JOE,—It is another off day, but tomorrow I shall resume work to a certainty, and bid a long farewell to letter-scribbling.

The news of the President looks decidedly hopeful, and we are all glad, and the household faces are much improved, as to cheerfulness. Oh, the talk in the newspapers! Evidently the Human Race is the same old Human Race. And how unjust, and unreflectingly discriminating, the talkers are. Under the unsettling effects of powerful emotion the talkers are saying wild things, crazy things—they are out of themselves, and do not know it; they are temporarily insane, yet with one voice they declare the assassin sane—a man who has been entertaining fiery and reason—debauching maggots in his head for weeks and months. Why, no one is sane, straight along, year in and year out, and we all know it. Our insanities are of varying sorts, and express themselves in varying forms—fortunately harmless forms as a rule—but in whatever form they occur an immense upheaval of feeling can at any time topple us distinctly over the sanity-line for a little while; and then if our form happens to be of the murderous kind we must look out—and so must the spectator.

This ass with the unpronounceable name was probably more insane than usual this week or two back, and may get back upon his bearings by and by, but he was over the sanity-border when he shot the President. It is possible that it has taken him the whole interval since the murder of the King of Italy to get insane enough to attempt the President's life. Without a doubt some thousands of men have been meditating the same act in the same interval, but new and strong interests have intervened and diverted their over-excited minds long enough to give them a chance to settle, and tranquilize, and get back upon a healthy level again. Every extraordinary occurrence unsettles the heads of hundreds of thousands of men for a few moments or hours or days. If there had been ten kings around when Humbert fell they would have been in great peril for a day or more—and from men in whose presence they would have been quite safe after the excess of their excitement had had an interval in which to cool down. I bought a revolver once and travelled twelve hundred miles to kill a man. He was away. He was gone a day. With nothing else to do, I had to stop and think—and did. Within an hour—within half of it—I was ashamed of myself—and felt unspeakably ridiculous. I do not know what to call it if I was not insane. During a whole week my head was in a turmoil night and day fierce enough and exhausting enough to upset a stronger reason than mine.

All over the world, every day, there are some millions of men in that condition temporarily. And in that time there is always a moment—perhaps only a single one when they would do murder if their man was at hand. If the opportunity comes a shade too late, the chances are that it has come permanently too late. Opportunity seldom comes exactly at the supreme moment. This saves a million lives a day in the world—for sure.

No Ruler is ever slain but the tremendous details of it are ravenously devoured by a hundred thousand men whose minds dwell, unaware, near the temporary-insanity frontier—and over they go, now! There is a day—two days—three—during which no Ruler would be safe from perhaps the half of them; and there is a single moment wherein he would not be safe from any of them, no doubt.

It may take this present shooting-case six months to breed another ruler-tragedy, but it will breed it. There is at least one mind somewhere which will brood, and wear, and decay itself to the killing-point and produce that tragedy.

Every negro burned at the stake unsettles the excitable brain of another one—I mean the inflaming details of his crime, and the lurid theatricality of his exit do it—and the duplicate crime follows; and that begets a repetition, and that one another one and so on. Every lynching-account unsettles the brains of another set of excitable white men, and lights another pyre—115 lynchings last year, 102 inside of 8 months this year; in ten years this will be habit, on these terms.

Yes, the wild talk you see in the papers! And from men who are sane when not upset by overwhelming excitement. A U. S. Senator-Cullom—wants this Buffalo criminal lynched! It would breed other lynchings—of men who are not dreaming of committing murders, now, and will commit none if Cullom will keep quiet and not provide the exciting cause.

And a District Attorney wants a law which shall punish with death attempts upon a President's life—this, mind you, as a deterrent. It would have no effect—or the opposite one. The lunatic's mind-space is all occupied—as mine was—with the matter in hand; there is no room in it for reflections upon what may happen to him. That comes after the crime.

It is the noise the attempt would make in the world that would breed the subsequent attempts, by unsettling the rickety minds of men who envy the criminal his vast notoriety—his obscure name tongued by stupendous Kings and Emperors—his picture printed everywhere, the trivialest details of his movements, what he eats, what he drinks; how he sleeps, what he says, cabled abroad over the whole globe at cost of fifty thousand dollars a day—and he only a lowly shoemaker yesterday!—like the assassin of the President of France—in debt three francs to his landlady, and insulted by her—and to-day she is proud to be able to say she knew him "as familiarly as you know your own brother," and glad to stand till she drops and pour out columns and pages of her grandeur and her happiness upon the eager interviewer.

Nothing will check the lynchings and ruler-murder but absolute silence—the absence of pow-pow about them. How are you going to manage that? By gagging every witness and jamming him into a dungeon for life; by abolishing all newspapers; by exterminating all newspaper men; and by extinguishing God's most elegant invention, the Human Race. It is quite simple, quite easy, and I hope you will take a day off and attend to it, Joe. I blow a kiss to you, and am

Lovingly Yours,

MARK.

When the Adirondack summer ended Clemens settled for the winter in the beautiful Appleton home at Riverdale-on-the-Hudson. It was a place of wide-spreading grass and shade-a house of ample room. They were established in it in time for Mark Twain to take an active interest in the New York elections and assist a ticket for good government to defeat Tammany Hall.

XLI. LETTERS OF 1902. RIVERDALE. YORK HARBOR. ILLNESS OF MRS. CLEMENS

The year 1902 was an eventful one for Mark Twain. In April he received a degree of LL.D. from the University of Missouri and returned to his native State to accept it. This was his last journey to the Mississippi River. During the summer Mrs. Clemens's health broke down and illnesses of one sort or another visited other members of the family. Amid so much stress and anxiety Clemens had little time or inclination for work. He wrote not many letters and mainly somber ones. Once, by way of diversion, he worked out the idea of a curious club—which he formed—its members to be young girls—girls for the most part whom he had never seen. They were elected without their consent from among those who wrote to him without his consent, and it is not likely that any one so chosen declined membership. One selection from his letters to the French member, Miss Helene Picard, of St.-Die, France, will explain the club and present a side of Mask Twain somewhat different from that found in most of his correspondence.

To Miss Picard, in St.-Die, France:

RIVERDALE-ON-THE-HUDSON, February 22, 1902.

DEAR MISS HELENE,—If you will let me call you so, considering that my head is white and that I have grownup daughters. Your beautiful letter has given me such deep pleasure! I will make bold to claim you for a friend and lock you up with the rest of my riches; for I am a miser who counts his spoil every day and hoards it secretly and adds to it when he can, and is grateful to see it grow.

Some of that gold comes, like yourself, in a sealed package, and I can't see it and may never have the happiness; but I know its value without that, and by what sum it increases my wealth.

I have a Club, a private Club, which is all my own. I appoint the

Members myself, and they can't help themselves, because I don't allow them to vote on their own appointment and I don't allow them to resign! They are all friends whom I have never seen (save one), but who have written friendly letters to me.

By the laws of my Club there can be only one Member in each country, and there can be no male Member but myself. Some day I may admit males, but I don't know—they are capricious and inharmonious, and their ways provoke me a good deal. It is a matter which the Club shall decide.

I have made four appointments in the past three or four months: You as Member for France, a young Highland girl as Member for Scotland, a Mohammedan girl as Member for Bengal, and a dear and bright young niece of mine as Member for the United States—for I do not represent a country myself, but am merely Member at Large for the Human Race.

You must not try to resign, for the laws of the Club do not allow that. You must console yourself by remembering that you are in the best of company; that nobody knows of your membership except myself—that no Member knows another's name, but only her country; that no taxes are levied and no meetings held (but how dearly I should like to attend one!).

One of my Members is a Princess of a royal house, another is the daughter of a village book-seller on the continent of Europe. For the only qualification for Membership is intellect and the spirit of good will; other distinctions, hereditary or acquired, do not count.

May I send you the Constitution and Laws of the Club? I shall be so pleased if I may. It is a document which one of my daughters typewrites for me when I need one for a new Member, and she would give her eyebrows to know what it is all about, but I strangle her curiosity by saying: "There are much cheaper typewriters than you are, my dear, and if you try to pry into the sacred mysteries of this Club one of your prosperities will perish sure."

My favorite? It is "Joan of Arc." My next is "Huckleberry Finn," but the family's next is "The Prince and the Pauper." (Yes, you are right—I am a moralist in disguise; it gets me into heaps of trouble when I go thrashing around in political questions.)

I wish you every good fortune and happiness and I thank you so much for your letter.

Sincerely yours,

S. L. CLEMENS.

Early in the year Clemens paid a visit to Twichell in Hartford, and after one of their regular arguments on theology and the moral accountability of the human race, arguments that had been going on between them for more than thirty years—Twichell lent his visitor Freedom of the Will, by Jonathan Edwards, to read on the way home. The next letter was the result.

To Rev. J. H. Twichell, in Hartford:

RIVERDALE-ON-THE-HUDSON.

Feb. '02.

DEAR JOE,—"After compliments."—[Meaning "What a good time you gave me; what a happiness it was to be under your roof again; etc., etc." See opening sentence of all translations of letters passing between Lord Roberts and Indian princes and rulers.]—From Bridgeport to New York; thence to home; and continuously until near midnight I wallowed and reeked with Jonathan in his insane debauch; rose immediately refreshed and fine at 10 this morning, but with a strange and haunting sense of having been on a three days' tear with a drunken lunatic. It is years since I have known these sensations. All through the book is the glaze of a resplendent intellect gone mad—a marvelous spectacle. No, not all through the book—the drunk does not come on till the last third, where what I take to be Calvinism and its God begins to show up and shine red and hideous in the glow from the fires of hell, their only right and proper adornment. By God I was ashamed to be in such company.

Jonathan seems to hold (as against the Arminian position) that the Man (or his Soul or his Will) never creates an impulse itself, but is moved to action by an impulse back of it. That's sound!

Also, that of two or more things offered it, it infallibly chooses the one which for the moment is most pleasing to ITSELF. Perfectly correct! An immense admission for a man not otherwise sane.

Up to that point he could have written chapters III and IV of my suppressed "Gospel." But there we seem to separate. He seems to concede the indisputable and unshakable dominion of Motive and Necessity (call them what he may, these are exterior forces and not under the man's authority, guidance or even suggestion)—then he suddenly flies the logic track and (to all seeming) makes the man and not these exterior forces responsible to God for the man's thoughts, words and acts. It is frank insanity.

I think that when he concedes the autocratic dominion of Motive and Necessity he grants, a third position of mine—that a man's mind is a mere machine—an automatic machine—which is handled entirely from the outside, the man himself furnishing it absolutely nothing: not an ounce of its fuel, and not so much as a bare suggestion to that exterior engineer as to what the machine shall do, nor how it shall do it nor when.

After that concession, it was time for him to get alarmed and shirk—for he was pointing straight for the only rational and possible next-station on that piece of road the irresponsibility of man to God.

And so he shirked. Shirked, and arrived at this handsome result:

Man is commanded to do so-and-so. It has been ordained from the beginning of time that some men shan't and others can't.

These are to be blamed: let them be damned.

I enjoy the Colonel very much, and shall enjoy the rest of him with an obscene delight.

Joe, the whole tribe shout love to you and yours!

MARK.

We have not heard of Joe Goodman since the trying days of '90 and '91, when he was seeking to promote the fortunes of the type-setting machine. Goodman, meantime, who had in turn been miner, printer, publisher, and farmer; had been devoting his energies and genius to something entirely new: he had been translating the prehistoric Mayan inscriptions of Yucatan, and with such success that his work was elaborately published by an association of British scientists. In due time a copy of this publication came to Clemens, who was full of admiration of the great achievement.

To J. T. Goodman, in California:

RIVERDALE-ON-THE-HUDSON,

June 13, '02.

DEAR JOE,—I am lost in reverence and admiration! It is now twenty-four hours that I have been trying to cool down and contemplate with quiet blood this extraordinary spectacle of energy, industry, perseverance, pluck, analytical genius, penetration, this irruption of thunders and fiery splendors from a fair and flowery mountain that nobody had supposed was a sleeping volcano, but I seem to be as excited as ever. Yesterday I read as much as half of the book, not understanding a word but enchanted nevertheless—partly by the wonder of it all, the study, the erudition, the incredible labor, the modesty, the dignity, the majestic exclusiveness of the field and its lofty remoteness from things and contacts sordid and mean and earthy, and partly by the grace and beauty and limpidity of the book's unsurpassable English. Science, always great and worshipful, goes often in hodden grey, but you have clothed her in garments meet for her high degree.

You think you get "poor pay" for your twenty years? No, oh no. You have lived in a paradise of the intellect whose lightest joys were beyond the reach of the longest purse in Christendom, you have had daily and nightly emancipation from the world's slaveries and gross interests, you have received a bigger wage than any man in the land, you have dreamed a splendid dream and had it come true, and to-day you could not afford to trade fortunes with anybody—not even with another scientist, for he must divide his spoil with his guild, whereas essentially the world you have discovered is your own and must remain so.

It is all just magnificent, Joe! And no one is prouder or gladder than

Yours always

MARK.

At York Harbor, Maine, where they had taken a cottage for the summer—a pretty place, with Howells not far distant, at Kittery Point—Mrs. Clemens's health gave way. This was at a period when telegraphic communication was far from reliable. The old-time Western Union had fallen from grace; its "system" no longer justified the best significance of that word. The new day of reorganization was coming, and it was time for it. Mark Twain's letter concerning the service at York Harbor would hardly be warranted today, but those who remember conditions of that earlier time will agree that it was justified then, and will appreciate its satire.

To the President of The Western Union, in New York:

"THE PINES"

YORK HARBOR, MAINE.

DEAR SIR,—I desire to make a complaint, and I bring it to you, the head of the company, because by experience I know better than to carry it to a subordinate.

I have been here a month and a half, and by testimony of friends, reinforced by personal experience I now feel qualified to claim as an established fact that the telegraphic service here is the worst in the world except that Boston.

These services are actually slower than was the New York and Hartford service in the days when I last complained to you—which was fifteen or eighteen years ago, when telegraphic time and train time between the mentioned points was exactly the same, to-wit, three hours and a half. Six days ago—it was that raw day which provoked so much comment—my daughter was on her way up from New York, and at noon she telegraphed me from New Haven asking that I meet her with a cloak at Portsmouth. Her telegram reached me four hours and a quarter later—just 15 minutes too late for me to catch my train and meet her.

I judge that the telegram traveled about 200 miles. It is the best telegraphic work I have seen since I have been here, and I am mentioning it in this place not as a complaint but as a compliment. I think a compliment ought always to precede a complaint, where one is possible, because it softens resentment and insures for the complaint a courteous and gentle reception.

Still, there is a detail or two connected with this matter which ought perhaps to be mentioned. And now, having smoothed the way with the compliment, I will venture them. The head corpse in the York Harbor office sent me that telegram altho (1) he knew it would reach me too late to be of any value; (2) also, that he was going to send it to me by his boy; (3) that the boy would not take the trolley and come the 2 miles in 12 minutes, but would walk; (4) that he would be two hours and a quarter on the road; (5) and that he would collect 25 cents for transportation, for a telegram which the he knew to be worthless before he started it. From these data I infer that the Western Union owes me 75 cents; that is to say, the amount paid for combined wire and land transportation—a recoup provided for in the printed paragraph which heads the telegraph-blank.

By these humane and Christian stages we now arrive at the complaint proper. We have had a grave case of illness in the family, and a relative was coming some six hundred miles to help in the sick-room during the convalescing period. It was an anxious time, of course, and I wrote and asked to be notified as to the hour of the expected arrival of this relative in Boston or in York Harbor. Being afraid of the telegraph—which I think ought not to be used in times of hurry and emergency—I asked that the desired message be brought to me by some swift method of transportation. By the milkman, if he was coming this way. But there are always people who think they know more than you do, especially young people; so of course the young fellow in charge of this lady used the telegraph. And at Boston, of all places! Except York Harbor.

The result was as usual; let me employ a statelier and exacter term, and say, historical.

The dispatch was handed to the h. c. of the Boston office at 9 this morning. It said, "Shall bring A. S. to you eleven forty-five this morning." The distance traveled by the dispatch is forty or fifty miles, I suppose, as the train-time is five minutes short of two hours, and the trains are so slow that they can't give a W. U. telegram two hours and twenty minutes start and overtake it.

As I have said, the dispatch was handed in at Boston at 9. The expected visitors left Boston at 9.40, and reached my house at 12 noon, beating the telegram 2 solid hours, and 5 minutes over.

The boy brought the telegram. It was bald-headed with age, but still legible. The boy was prostrate with travel and exposure, but still alive, and I went out to condole with him and get his last wishes and send for the ambulance. He was waiting to collect transportation before turning his passing spirit to less serious affairs. I found him strangely intelligent, considering his condition and where he is getting his training. I asked him at what hour the telegram was handed to the h. c. in Boston. He answered brightly, that he didn't know.

I examined the blank, and sure enough the wary Boston h. c. had thoughtfully concealed that statistic. I asked him at what hour it had started from Boston. He answered up as brightly as ever, and said he didn't know.

I examined the blank, and sure enough the Boston h. c. had left that statistic out in the cold, too. In fact it turned out to be an official concealment—no blank was provided for its exposure. And none required by the law, I suppose. "It is a good one-sided idea," I remarked; "They can take your money and ship your telegram next year if they want to—you've no redress. The law ought to extend the privilege to all of us."

The boy looked upon me coldly.

I asked him when the telegram reached York Harbor. He pointed to some figures following the signature at the bottom of the blank—"12.14." I said it was now 1.45 and asked—

"Do you mean that it reached your morgue an hour and a half ago?"

He nodded assent.

"It was at that time half an hour too late to be of any use to me, if I wanted to go and meet my people—which was the case—for by the wording of the message you can see that they were to arrive at the station at 11.45. Why did, your h. c. send me this useless message? Can't he read? Is he dead?"

"It's the rules."

"No, that does not account for it. Would he have sent it if it had been three years old, I in the meantime deceased, and he aware of it?"

The boy didn't know.

"Because, you know, a rule which required him to forward to the cemetery to-day a dispatch due three years ago, would be as good a rule as one which should require him to forward a telegram to me to-day which he knew had lost all its value an hour or two before he started it. The construction of such a rule would discredit an idiot; in fact an idiot—I mean a common ordinary Christian idiot, you understand—would be ashamed of it, and for the sake of his reputation wouldn't make it. What do you think?"

He replied with much natural brilliancy that he wasn't paid for thinking.

This gave me a better opinion of the commercial intelligence pervading his morgue than I had had before; it also softened my feelings toward him, and also my tone, which had hitherto been tinged with bitterness.

"Let bygones be bygones," I said, gently, "we are all erring creatures, and mainly idiots, but God made us so and it is dangerous to criticise."

Sincerely

S. L. CLEMENS.

One day there arrived from Europe a caller with a letter of introduction from Elizabeth, Queen of Rumania, better known as Carmen Sylva. The visitor was Madam Hartwig, formerly an American girl, returning now, because of reduced fortunes, to find profitable employment in her own land. Her husband, a man of high principle, had declined to take part in an "affair of honor," as recognized by the Continental code; hence his ruin. Elizabeth of Rumania was one of the most loved and respected of European queens and an author of distinction. Mark Twain had known her in Vienna. Her letter to him and his own letter to the public (perhaps a second one, for its date is two years later) follow herewith.

From Carmen Sylva to Mark Twain:

BUCAREST, May 9, 1902.

HONORED MASTER,—If I venture to address you on behalf of a poor lady, who is stranded in Bucarest I hope not to be too disagreeable.

Mrs. Hartwig left America at the age of fourteen in order to learn to sing which she has done thoroughly. Her husband had quite a brilliant situation here till he refused to partake 'dans une afaire onereuse', so it seems. They haven't a penny and each of them must try to find a living. She is very nice and pleasant and her school is so good that she most certainly can give excellent singing lessons.

I beg your pardon for being a bore to one I so deeply love and admire, to whom I owe days and days of forgetfulness of self and troubles and the intensest of all joys: Hero-worship! People don't always realize what a happiness that is! God bless you for every beautiful thought you poured into my tired heart and for every smile on a weary way!

CARMEN SYLVA.

From Mark Twain to the Public:

Nov. 16, '04.

TO WHOM IT MAY CONCERN,—I desire to recommend Madame Hartwig to my friends and the public as a teacher of singing and as a concert-vocalist. She has lived for fifteen years at the court of Roumania, and she brought with her to America an autograph letter in which her Majesty the Queen of Roumania cordially certified her to me as being an accomplished and gifted singer and teacher of singing, and expressed a warm hope that her professional venture among us would meet with success; through absence in Europe I have had no opportunity to test the validity of the Queen's judgment in the matter, but that judgment is the utterance of an entirely competent authority—the best that occupies a throne, and as good as any that sits elsewhere, as the musical world well knows—and therefore back it without hesitation, and endorse it with confidence.

I will explain that the reason her Majesty tried to do her friend a friendly office through me instead of through someone else was, not that I was particularly the right or best person for the office, but because I was not a stranger. It is true that I am a stranger to some of the monarchs—mainly through their neglect of their opportunities—but such is not the case in the present instance. The latter fact is a high compliment to me, and perhaps I ought to conceal it. Some people would.

MARK TWAIN.

Mrs. Clemens's improvement was scarcely perceptible. It was not until October that they were able to remove her to Riverdale, and then only in a specially arranged invalid-car. At the end of the long journey she was carried to her room and did not leave it again for many months.

To Rev. J. H. Twichell, in Hartford:

RIVERDALE, N. Y., Oct. 31, '02.

DEAR JOE,—It is ten days since Susy [Twichell] wrote that you were laid up with a sprained shoulder, since which time we have had no news about it. I hope that no news is good news, according to the proverb; still, authoritative confirmation of it will be gladly received in this family, if some of you will furnish it. Moreover, I should like to know how and where it happened. In the pulpit, as like as not, otherwise you would not be taking so much pains to conceal it. This is not a malicious suggestion, and not a personally-invented one: you told me yourself, once, that you threw artificial power and impressiveness into places in your sermons where needed, by "banging the bible"—(your own words.) You have reached a time of life when it is not wise to take these risks. You would better jump around. We all have to change our methods as the infirmities of age creep upon us. Jumping around will be impressive now, whereas before you were gray it would have excited remark.

Poor Livy drags along drearily. It must be hard times for that turbulent spirit. It will be a long time before she is on her feet again. It is a most pathetic case. I wish I could transfer it to myself. Between ripping and raging and smoking and reading, I could get a good deal of a holiday out of it.

Clara runs the house smoothly and capably. She is discharging a trial-cook today and hiring another.

A power of love to you all!

MARK.

Such was the state of Mrs. Clemens's health that visitors were excluded from the sick room, and even Clemens himself was allowed to see her no more than a few moments at a time. These brief, precious visits were the chief interests of his long days. Occasionally he was allowed to send her a few lines, reporting his occupations, and these she was sometimes permitted to answer. Only one of his notes has been preserved, written after a day, now rare, of literary effort. Its signature, the letter Y, stands for "Youth," always her name for him.

To Mrs. Clemens:

DEAR HEART,—I've done another full day's work, and finished before 4. I have been reading and dozing since and would have had a real sleep a few minutes ago but for an incursion to bring me a couple of unimportant letters. I've stuck to the bed all day and am getting back my lost ground. Next time I will be strictly careful and make my visit very short—just a kiss and a rush. Thank you for your dear, dear note; you who are my own and only sweetheart.

Sleep well!

Y.

XLII. LETTERS OF 1903. TO VARIOUS PERSONS. HARD DAYS AT RIVERDALE. LAST SUMMER AT ELMIRA. THE RETURN TO ITALY.

The reader may perhaps recall that H. H. Rogers, some five or six years earlier, had taken charge of the fortunes of Helen Keller, making it possible for her to complete her education. Helen had now written her first book—a wonderful book—'The Story of My Life', and it had been successfully published. For a later generation it may be proper to explain that the Miss Sullivan, later Mrs. Macy, mentioned in the letter which follows, was the noble woman who had devoted her life to the enlightenment of this blind, dumb girl—had made it possible for her to speak and understand, and, indeed, to see with the eyes of luminous imagination.

The case of plagiarism mentioned in this letter is not now remembered, and does not matter, but it furnished a text for Mark Twain, whose remarks on the subject in general are eminently worth while.

To Helen Keller, in Wrentham, Mass.:

RIVERDALE-ON-THE-HUDSON,

ST. PATRICK'S DAY, '03.

DEAR HELEN,—I must steal half a moment from my work to say how glad I am to have your book, and how highly I value it, both for its own sake and as a remembrances of an affectionate friendship which has subsisted between us for nine years without a break, and without a single act of violence that I can call to mind. I suppose there is nothing like it in heaven; and not likely to be, until we get there and show off. I often think of it with longing, and how they'll say, "There they come—sit down in front!" I am practicing with a tin halo. You do the same. I was at Henry Rogers's last night, and of course we talked of you. He is not at all well; you will not like to hear that; but like you and me, he is just as lovely as ever.

I am charmed with your book-enchanted. You are a wonderful creature, the most wonderful in the world—you and your other half together—Miss Sullivan, I mean, for it took the pair of you to make a complete and perfect whole. How she stands out in her letters! her brilliancy, penetration, originality, wisdom, character, and the fine literary competencies of her pen—they are all there.

Oh, dear me, how unspeakably funny and owlishly idiotic and grotesque was that "plagiarism" farce! As if there was much of anything in any human utterance, oral or written, except plagiarism! The kernel, the soul—let us go further and say the substance, the bulk, the actual and valuable material of all human utterances—is plagiarism. For substantially all ideas are second-hand, consciously and unconsciously drawn from a million outside sources, and daily used by the garnerer with a pride and satisfaction born of the superstition that he originated them; whereas there is not a rag of originality about them anywhere except the little discoloration they get from his mental and moral calibre and his temperament, and which is revealed in characteristics of phrasing. When a great orator makes a great speech you are listening to ten centuries and ten thousand men—but we call it his speech, and really some exceedingly small portion of it is his. But not enough to signify. It is merely a Waterloo. It is Wellington's battle, in some degree, and we call it his; but there are others that contributed. It takes a thousand men to invent a telegraph, or a steam engine, or a phonograph, or a photograph, or a telephone or any other important thing—and the last man gets the credit and we forget the others. He added his little mite—that is all he did. These object lessons should teach us that ninety-nine parts of all things that proceed from the intellect are plagiarisms, pure and simple; and the lesson ought to make us modest. But nothing can do that.

Then why don't we unwittingly reproduce the phrasing of a story, as well as the story itself? It can hardly happen—to the extent of fifty words except in the case of a child: its memory-tablet is not lumbered with impressions, and the actual language can have graving-room there, and preserve the language a year or two, but a grown person's memory-tablet is a palimpsest, with hardly a bare space upon which to engrave a phrase. It must be a very rare thing that a whole page gets so sharply printed upon a man's mind, by a single reading, that it will stay long enough to turn up some time or other and be mistaken by him for his own. No doubt we are constantly littering our literature with disconnected sentences borrowed from books at some unremembered time and now imagined to be our own, but that is about the most we can do. In 1866 I read Dr. Holmes's poems, in the Sandwich Islands. A year and a half later I stole his dictation, without knowing it, and used it to dedicate my "Innocents Abroad" with. Then years afterwards I was talking with Dr. Holmes about it. He was not an ignorant ass—no, not he: he was not a collection of decayed human turnips, like your "Plagiarism Court;" and so when I said, "I know now where I stole it, but whom did you steal it from," he said, "I don't remember; I only know I stole it from somebody, because I have never originated anything altogether myself, nor met anybody who had."

To think of those solemn donkeys breaking a little child's heart with their ignorant rubbish about plagiarism! I couldn't sleep for blaspheming about it last night. Why, their whole lives, their whole histories, all their learning, all their thoughts, all their opinions were one solid ruck of plagiarism, and they didn't know it and never suspected it. A gang of dull and hoary pirates piously setting themselves the task of disciplining and purifying a kitten that they think they've caught filching a chop! Oh, dam—

But you finish it, dear, I am running short of vocabulary today. Ever lovingly your friend,

MARK.

(Edited and modified by Clara Clemens, deputy to her mother, who for more than 7 months has been ill in bed and unable to exercise her official function.)

The burden of the Clemens household had fallen almost entirely upon Clara Clemens. In addition to supervising its customary affairs, she also shouldered the responsibility of an unusual combination of misfortunes, for besides the critical condition of her mother, her sister, Jean Clemens, was down with pneumonia, no word of which must come to Mrs. Clemens. Certainly it was a difficult position. In some account of it, which he set down later, Clemens wrote: "It was fortunate for us all that Clara's reputation for truthfulness was so well established in her mother's mind. It was our daily protection from disaster. The mother never doubted Clara's word. Clara could tell her large improbabilities without exciting any suspicion, whereas if I tried to market even a small and simple one the case would have been different. I was never able to get a reputation like Clara's."

The accumulation of physical ailments in the Clemens home had somewhat modified Mark Twain's notion of medical practice. He was no longer radical; he had become eclectic. It is a good deal of a concession that he makes to Twichell, after those earlier letters from Sweden, in which osteopathy had been heralded as the anodyne for all human ills.

To Rev. J. H. Twichell, in Hartford:

DEAR JOE,—Livy does really make a little progress these past 3 or 4 days, progress which is visible to even the untrained eye. The physicians are doing good work with her, but my notion is, that no art of healing is the best for all ills. I should distribute the ailments around: surgery cases to the surgeons; lupus to the actinic-ray specialist; nervous prostration to the Christian Scientist; most ills to the allopath and the homeopath; (in my own particular case) rheumatism, gout and bronchial attacks to the osteopathist.

Mr. Rogers was to sail southward this morning—and here is this weather! I am sorry. I think it's a question if he gets away tomorrow.

Ys Ever

MARK.

It was through J. Y. M. MacAlister, to whom the next letter is written, that Mark Twain had become associated with the Plasmon Company, which explains the reference to "shares." He had seen much of MacAlister during the winter at Tedworth Square, and had grown fond of him. It is a characteristic letter, and one of interesting fact.

To J. Y. M. MacAlister, in London:

RIVERDALE, NEW YORK.

April, 7, '03.

DEAR MACALISTER,—Yours arrived last night, and God knows I was glad to get it, for I was afraid I had blundered into an offence in some way and forfeited your friendship—a kind of blunder I have made so many times in my life that I am always standing in a waiting and morbid dread of its occurrence.

Three days ago I was in condition—during one horribly long night—to sympathetically roast with you in your "hell of troubles." During that night I was back again where I was in the black days when I was buried under a mountain of debt. I called the daughters to me in private council and paralysed them with the announcement, "Our outgo has increased in the past 8 months until our expenses are now 125 per cent. greater than our income."

It was a mistake. When I came down in the morning a gray and aged wreck, and went over the figures again, I found that in some unaccountable way (unaccountable to a business man but not to me) I had multiplied the totals by 2. By God I dropped 75 years on the floor where I stood.

Do you know it affected me as one is affected when he wakes out of a hideous dream and finds that it was only a dream. It was a great comfort and satisfaction to me to call the daughters to a private meeting of the Board again and say, "You need not worry any more; our outgo is only a third more than our income; in a few months your mother will be out of her bed and on her feet again—then we shall drop back to normal and be all right."

Certainly there is a blistering and awful reality about a well-arranged unreality. It is quite within the possibilities that two or three nights like that night of mine could drive a man to suicide. He would refuse to examine the figures; they would revolt him so, and he could go to his death unaware that there was nothing serious about them. I cannot get that night out of my head, it was so vivid, so real, so ghastly. In any other year of these 33 the relief would have been simple: go where you can cut your cloth to fit your income. You can't do that when your wife can't be moved, even from one room to the next.

Clam spells the trained nurse afternoons; I am allowed to see Mrs. Clemens 20 minutes twice a day and write her two letters a day provided I put no news in them. No other person ever sees her except the physician and now and then a nerve-specialist from New York. She saw there was something the matter that morning, but she got no facts out of me. But that is nothing—she hasn't had anything but lies for 8 months. A fact would give her a relapse.

The doctor and a specialist met in conspiracy five days ago, and in their belief she will by and by come out of this as good as new, substantially. They ordered her to Italy for next winter—which seems to indicate that by autumn she will be able to undertake the voyage. So Clara is writing a Florence friend to take a look round among the villas for us in the regions near that city. It seems early to do this, but Joan Bergheim thought it would be wise.

He and his wife lunched with us here yesterday. They have been abroad in Havana 4 months, and they sailed for England this morning.

I am enclosing an order for half of my (your) Founders shares. You are not to refuse them this time, though you have done it twice before. They are yours, not mine, and for your family's sake if not your own you cannot in these cloudy days renounce this property which is so clearly yours and theirs. You have been generous long enough; be just, now to yourself. Mr. Rogers is off yachting for 5 or 6 weeks—I'll get them when he returns. The head of the house joins me in warmest greetings and remembrances to you and Mrs. MacAlister.

Ever yours,

Mark.

May 8. Great Scott! I never mailed this letter! I addressed it, put "Registered" on it—then left it lying unsealed on the arm of my chair, and rushed up to my bed quaking with a chill. I've never been out of the bed since—oh, bronchitis, rheumatism, two sets of teeth aching, land, I've had a dandy time for 4 weeks. And to-day—great guns, one of the very worst!...

I'm devilish sorry, and I do apologise—for although I am not as slow as you are about answering letters, as a rule, I see where I'm standing this time.

Two weeks ago Jean was taken down again—this time with measles, and I haven't been able to go to her and she hasn't been able to come to me.

But Mrs. Clemens is making nice progress, and can stand alone a moment or two at a time.

Now I'll post this.

MARK

The two letters that follow, though written only a few days apart, were separated in their arrival by a period of seven years. The second letter was, in some way, mislaid and not mailed; and it was not until after the writer of it was dead that it was found and forwarded.

Mark Twain could never get up much enthusiasm for the writings of Scott. His praise of Quentin Durward is about the only approval he ever accorded to the works of the great romanticist.

To Brander Matthews, in New York:

NEW YORK CITY, May 4, '03.

DEAR BRANDER,—I haven't been out of my bed for four weeks, but—well, I have been reading, a good deal, and it occurs to me to ask you to sit down, some time or other when you have 8 or 9 months to spare, and jot me down a certain few literary particulars for my help and elevation. Your time need not be thrown away, for at your further leisure you can make Colombian lectures out of the results and do your students a good turn.

1. Are there in Sir Walter's novels passages done in good English—English which is neither slovenly or involved?

2. Are there passages whose English is not poor and thin and commonplace, but is of a quality above that?

3. Are there passages which burn with real fire—not punk, fox-fire, make believe?

4. Has he heroes and heroines who are not cads and cadesses?

5. Has he personages whose acts and talk correspond with their characters as described by him?

6. Has he heroes and heroines whom the reader admires, admires, and knows why?

7. Has he funny characters that are funny, and humorous passages that are humorous?

8. Does he ever chain the reader's interest, and make him reluctant to lay the book down?

9. Are there pages where he ceases from posing, ceases from admiring the placid flood and flow of his own dilutions, ceases from being artificial, and is for a time, long or short, recognizably sincere and in earnest?

10. Did he know how to write English, and didn't do it because he didn't want to?

11. Did he use the right word only when he couldn't think of another one, or did he run so much to wrong because he didn't know the right one when he saw it?

13. Can you read him? and keep your respect for him? Of course a person could in his day—an era of sentimentality and sloppy romantics—but land! can a body do it today?

Brander, I lie here dying, slowly dying, under the blight of Sir Walter. I have read the first volume of Rob Roy, and as far as chapter XIX of Guy Mannering, and I can no longer hold my head up nor take my nourishment. Lord, it's all so juvenile! so artificial, so shoddy; and such wax figures and skeletons and spectres. Interest? Why, it is impossible to feel an interest in these bloodless shams, these milk-and-water humbugs. And oh, the poverty of the invention! Not poverty in inventing situations, but poverty in furnishing reasons for them. Sir Walter usually gives himself away when he arranges for a situation—elaborates, and elaborates, and elaborates, till if you live to get to it you don't believe in it when it happens.

I can't find the rest of Rob Roy, I can't stand any more Mannering—I do not know just what to do, but I will reflect, and not quit this great study rashly. He was great, in his day, and to his proper audience; and so was God in

Jewish times, for that matter, but why should either of them rank high now? And do they?—honest, now, do they? Dam'd if I believe it.

My, I wish I could see you and Leigh Hunt!

Sincerely Yours

S. L. CLEMENS.

To Brander Matthews, in New York:

RIVERDALE, May 8, '03 (Mailed June, 1910).

DEAR BRANDER,—I'm still in bed, but the days have lost their dulness since I broke into Sir Walter and lost my temper. I finished Guy Mannering—that curious, curious book, with its mob of squalid shadows jabbering around a single flesh-and-blood being—Dinmont; a book crazily put together out of the very refuse of the romance-artist's stage properties—finished it and took up Quentin Durward, and finished that.

It was like leaving the dead to mingle with the living: it was like withdrawing from the infant class in the College of journalism to sit under the lectures in English literature in Columbia University.

I wonder who wrote Quentin Durward?

Yrs ever

MARK.

In 1903, preparations were going on for a great world's fair, to be held in St. Louis, and among other features proposed was a World's Literary Convention, with a week to be set apart in honor of Mark Twain, and a special Mark Twain Day in it, on which the National Association would hold grand services in honor of the distinguished Missourian. A letter asking his consent to the plan brought the following reply.

To T. F. Gatts, of Missouri:

NEW YORK, May 30, 1903.

DEAR MR. GATTS,—It is indeed a high compliment which you offer me in naming an association after me and in proposing the setting apart of a Mark Twain day at the great St. Louis fair, but such compliments are not proper for the living; they are proper and safe for the dead only. I value the impulse which moves you to tender me these honors. I value it as highly as any one can, and am grateful for it, but I should stand in a sort of terror of the honors themselves. So long as we remain alive we are not safe from doing things which, however righteously and honorably intended, can wreck our repute and extinguish our friendships.

I hope that no society will be named for me while I am still alive, for I might at some time or other do something which would cause its members to regret having done me that honor. After I shall have joined the dead I shall follow the customs of those people and be guilty of no conduct that can wound any friend; but until that time shall come I shall be a doubtful quantity like the rest of our race.

Very truly yours,

S. L. CLEMENS.

The National Mark Twain Association did not surrender easily. Mr. Gatts wrote a second letter full of urgent appeal. If Mark Twain was tempted, we get no hint of it in his answer.

To T. F. Gatts, of Missouri:

NEW YORK, June 8, 1903.

DEAR MR. GATTS,—While I am deeply touched by the desire of my friends of Hannibal to confer these great honors upon me, I must still forbear to accept them. Spontaneous and unpremeditated honors, like those which came to me at Hannibal, Columbia, St. Louis and at the village stations all down the line, are beyond all price and are a treasure for life in the memory, for they are a free gift out of the heart and they come without solicitations; but I am a Missourian and so I shrink from distinctions which have to be arranged beforehand and with my privity, for I then became a party to my own exalting. I am humanly fond of honors that happen but chary of those that come by canvass and intention. With sincere thanks to you and your associates for this high compliment which you have been minded to offer me, I am,

Very truly yours,

S. L. CLEMENS.

We have seen in the letter to MacAlister that Mark Twain's wife had been ordered to Italy and plans were in progress for an establishment there. By the end of June Mrs. Clemens was able to leave Riverdale, and she made the journey to Quarry Farm, Elmira, where they would remain until October, the month planned for their sailing. The house in Hartford had been sold; and a house which, prior to Mrs. Clemens's breakdown they had bought near Tarrytown (expecting to settle permanently on the Hudson) had been let. They were going to Europe for another indefinite period.

At Quarry Farm Mrs. Clemens continued to improve, and Clemens, once more able to work, occupied the study which Mrs. Crane had built for him thirty years before, and where Tom Sawyer and Huck Finn and the Wandering Prince had been called into being.

To Rev. J. H. Twichell, in Hartford, Conn.:

QUARRY FARM, ELMIRA, N. Y.,

July 21, '03.

DEAR JOE,—That love-letter delighted Livy beyond any like utterance received by her these thirty years and more. I was going to answer it for her right away, and said so; but she reserved the privilege to herself. I judge she is accumulating Hot Stuff—as George Ade would say....

Livy is coming along: eats well, sleeps some, is mostly very gay, not very often depressed; spends all day on the porch, sleeps there a part of the night, makes excursions in carriage and in wheel-chair; and, in the matter of superintending everything and everybody, has resumed business at the old stand.

Did you ever go house-hunting 3,000 miles away? It costs three months of writing and telegraphing to pull off a success. We finished 3 or 4 days ago, and took the Villa Papiniano (dam the name, I have to look at it a minutes after writing it, and then am always in doubt) for a year by cable. Three miles outside of Florence, under Fiesole—a darling location, and apparently a choice house, near Fiske.

There's 7 in our gang. All women but me. It means trunks and things. But thanks be! To-day (this is private) comes a most handsome voluntary document with seals and escutcheons on it from the Italian Ambassador (who is a stranger to me) commanding the Customs people to keep their hands off the Clemens's things. Now wasn't it lovely of him? And wasn't it lovely of me to let Livy take a pencil and edit my answer and knock a good third of it out?

And that's a nice ship—the Irene! new—swift—13,000 tons—rooms up in the sky, open to sun and air—and all that. I was desperately troubled for Livy—about the down-cellar cells in the ancient "Latin."

The cubs are in Riverdale, yet; they come to us the first week in August.

With lots and lots of love to you all,

MARK.

The arrangement for the Villa Papiniano was not completed, after all, and through a good friend, George Gregory Smith, a resident of Florence, the Villa Quarto, an ancient home of royalty, on the hills west of Florence, was engaged. Smith wrote that it was a very beautiful place with a south-eastern exposure, looking out toward Valombrosa and the Chianti Hills. It had extensive grounds and stables, and the annual rental for it all was two thousand dollars a year. It seemed an ideal place, in prospect, and there was great hope that Mrs. Clemens would find her health once more in the Italian climate which she loved.

Perhaps at this point, when Mark Twain is once more leaving America, we may offer two letters from strangers to him—letters of appreciation—such as he was constantly receiving from those among the thousands to whom he had given happiness. The first is from Samuel Merwin, one day to become a popular novelist, then in the hour of his beginnings.

To Mark Twain, from Samuel Merwin:

PLAINFIELD, N. J.

August 4, 1903.

DEAR MR. CLEMENS,—For a good many years I have been struggling with the temptation to write you and thank you for the work you have done; and to-day I seem to be yielding.

During the past two years I have been reading through a group of writers who seem to me to represent about the best we have—Sir Thomas Malory, Spenser, Shakespeare, Boswell, Carlyle, Le Sage. In thinking over one and then another, and then all of them together, it was plain to see why they were great men and writers: each brought to his time some new blood, new ideas,—turned a new current into the stream. I suppose there have always been the careful, painstaking writers, the men who are always taken so seriously by their fellow craftsmen. It seems to be the unconventional man who is so rare—I mean the honestly unconventional man, who has to express himself in his own big way because the conventional way isn't big enough, because ne needs room and freedom.

We have a group of the more or less conventional men now—men of dignity and literary position. But in spite of their influence and of all the work they have done, there isn't one of them to whom one can give one's self up without reservation, not one whose ideas seem based on the deep foundation of all true philosophy,—except Mark Twain.

I hope this letter is not an impertinence. I have just been turning about, with my head full of Spenser and Shakespeare and "Gil Blas," looking for something in our own present day literature to which I could surrender myself as to those five gripping old writings. And nothing could I find until I took up "Life on the Mississippi," and "Huckleberry Finn," and, just now, the "Connecticut Yankee." It isn't the first time I have read any of these three, and it's because I know it won't be the last, because these books are the only ones written in my lifetime that claim my unreserved interest and admiration and, above all, my feelings, that I've felt I had to write this letter.

I like to think that "Tom Sawyer" and "Huckleberry Finn" will be looked upon, fifty or a hundred years from now, as the picture of buoyant, dramatic, human American life. I feel, deep in my own heart, pretty sure that they will be. They won't be looked on then as the work of a "humorist" any more than we think of Shakespeare as a humorist now. I don't mean by this to set up a comparison between Mark Twain and Shakespeare: I don't feel competent to do it; and I'm not at all sure that it could be done until Mark Twain's work shall have its fair share of historical perspective. But Shakespeare was a humorist and so, thank Heaven! is Mark Twain. And Shakespeare plunged deep into the deep, sad things of life; and so, in a different way (but in a way that has more than once brought tears to my eyes) has Mark Twain. But after all, it isn't because of any resemblance for anything that was ever before written that Mark Twain's books strike in so deep: it's rather because they've brought something really new into our literature—new, yet old as Adam and Eve and the Apple. And this achievement, the achievement of putting something into literature that was not there before, is, I should think, the most that any writer can ever hope to do. It is the one mark of distinction between the "lonesome" little group of big men and the vast herd of medium and small ones. Anyhow, this much I am sure of—to the young man who hopes, however feebly, to accomplish a little something, someday, as a writer, the one inspiring example of our time is Mark Twain. Very truly yours, SAMUEL MERWIN.

Mark Twain once said he could live a month on a good compliment, and from his reply, we may believe this one to belong in, that class.

To Samuel Merwin, in Plainfield, N. J.:

Aug. 16, '03.

DEAR MR. MERWIN,—What you have said has given me deep pleasure—indeed I think no words could be said that could give me more.

Very sincerely yours,

S. L. CLEMENS.

The next "compliment" is from one who remains unknown, for she failed to sign her name in full. But it is a lovely letter, and loses nothing by the fact that the writer of it was willing to remain in obscurity.

To Mark Twain, from Margaret M——:

PORTLAND, OREGON

Aug. 18, 1903.

MY DEAR, DEAR MARK TWAIN,—May a little girl write and tell you how dearly she loves and admires your writings? Well, I do and I want to tell you your ownself. Don't think me too impertinent for indeed I don't mean to be that! I have read everything of yours that I could get and parts that touch me I have read over and over again. They seem such dear friends to me, so like real live human beings talking and laughing, working and suffering too! One cannot but feel that it is your own life and experience that you have painted. So do not wonder that you seem a dear friend to me who has never even seen you. I often think of you as such in my own thoughts. I wonder if you will laugh when I tell you I have made a hero of you? For when people seem very sordid and mean and stupid (and it seems as if everybody was) then the thought will come like a little crumb of comfort "well, Mark Twain isn't anyway." And it does really brighten me up.

You see I have gotten an idea that you are a great, bright spirit of kindness and tenderness. One who can twist everybody's-even your own-faults and absurdities into hearty laughs. Even the person mocked must laugh! Oh, Dear! How often you have made me laugh! And yet as often you have struck something infinite away down deep in my heart so that I want to cry while half laughing!

So this all means that I want to thank you and to tell you. "God always love Mark Twain!" is often my wish. I dearly love to read books, and I never tire of reading yours; they always have a charm for me. Good-bye, I am afraid I have not expressed what I feel. But at least I have tried.

Sincerely yours.

MARGARET M.——

Clemens and family left Elmira October the 5th for New York City.

They remained at the Hotel Grosvenor until their sailing date,

October 24th. A few days earlier, Mr. Frank Doubleday sent a volume of Kipling's poems and de Blowitz's Memoirs for entertainment on the ship. Mark Twain's acknowledgment follows.

To F. N. Doubleday, in New York:

THE GROSVENOR,

October 12, '03.

DEAR DOUBLEDAY,—The books came—ever so many thanks. I have been reading "The Bell Buoy" and "The Old Men" over and over again—my custom with Kipling's work-and saving up the rest for other leisurely and luxurious meals. A bell-buoy is a deeply impressive fellow-being. In these many recent trips up and down the Sound in the Kanawha—[Mr. Rogers's yacht.]—he has talked to me nightly, sometimes in his pathetic and melancholy way, sometimes with his strenuous and urgent note, and I got his meaning—now I have his words! No one but Kipling could do this strong and vivid thing. Some day I hope to hear the poem chanted or sung—with the bell-buoy breaking in, out of the distance.

"The Old Men," delicious, isn't it? And so comically true. I haven't arrived there yet, but I suppose I am on the way....

Yours ever,

MARK.

P. S. Your letter has arrived. It makes me proud and glad—what Kipling says. I hope Fate will fetch him to Florence while we are there. I would rather see him than any other man.

We've let the Tarrytown house for a year. Man, you would never have believed a person could let a house in these times. That one's for sale, the Hartford one is sold. When we buy again may we—may I—be damned....

I've dipped into Blowitz and find him quaintly and curiously interesting. I think he tells the straight truth, too. I knew him a little, 23 years ago.

The appreciative word which Kipling had sent Doubleday was: "I love to think of the great and God-like Clemens. He is the biggest man you have on your side of the water by a damn sight, and don't you forget it. Cervantes was a relation of his."

XLIII. LETTERS OF 1904. TO VARIOUS PERSONS. LIFE IN VILLA QUARTO. DEATH OF MRS. CLEMENS. THE RETURN TO AMERICA.

Mrs. Clemens stood the voyage to Italy very well and, in due time, the family were installed in the Villa Reale di Quarto, the picturesque old Palace of Cosimo, a spacious, luxurious place, even if not entirely cheerful or always comfortable during the changeable Tuscan winter. Congratulated in a letter from MacAlister in being in the midst of Florentine sunshine, he answered: "Florentine sunshine? Bless you, there isn't any. We have heavy fogs every morning, and rain all day. This house is not merely large, it is vast—therefore I think it must always lack the home feeling."

Neither was their landlady, the American wife of an Italian count, all that could be desired. From a letter to Twichell, however, we learn that Mark Twain's work was progressing well.

To Rev. J. H. Twichell, in Hartford:

VILLA DI QUARTO,

FLORENCE, Jan. 7, '04.

DEAR JOE,—... I have had a handsome success, in one way, here. I left

New York under a sort of half promise to furnish to the Harper magazines 30,000 words this year. Magazining is difficult work because every third page represents 2 pages that you have put in the fire; (because you are nearly sure to start wrong twice) and so when you have finished an article and are willing to let it go to print it represents only 10 cents a word instead of 30.

But this time I had the curious (and unprecedented) luck to start right in each case. I turned out 37,000 words in 25 working days; and the reason I think I started right every time is, that not only have I approved and accepted the several articles, but the court of last resort (Livy) has done the same.

On many of the between-days I did some work, but only of an idle and not necessarily necessary sort, since it will not see print until I am dead. I shall continue this (an hour per day) but the rest of the year I expect to put in on a couple of long books (half-completed ones.) No more magazine-work hanging over my head.

This secluded and silent solitude this clean, soft air and this enchanting view of Florence, the great valley and the snow-mountains that frame it are the right conditions for work. They are a persistent inspiration. To-day is very lovely; when the afternoon arrives there will be a new picture every hour till dark, and each of them divine—or progressing from divine to diviner and divinest. On this (second) floor Clara's room commands the finest; she keeps a window ten feet high wide open all the time and frames it in. I go in from time to time, every day and trade sass for a look. The central detail is a distant and stately snow-hump that rises above and behind blackforested hills, and its sloping vast buttresses, velvety and sun-polished with purple shadows between, make the sort of picture we knew that time we walked in Switzerland in the days of our youth.

I wish I could show your letter to Livy—but she must wait a week or so for it. I think I told you she had a prostrating week of tonsillitis a month ago; she has remained very feeble ever since, and confined to the bed of course, but we allow ourselves to believe she will regain the lost ground in another month. Her physician is Professor Grocco—she could not have a better. And she has a very good trained nurse.

Love to all of you from all of us. And to all of our dear Hartford friends.

MARK

P. S. 3 days later.

Livy is as remarkable as ever. The day I wrote you—that night, I mean—she had a bitter attack of gout or rheumatism occupying the whole left arm from shoulder to fingers, accompanied by fever. The pains racked her 50 or 60 hours; they have departed, now—and already she is planning a trip to Egypt next fall, and a winter's sojourn there! This is life in her yet.

You will be surprised that I was willing to do so much magazine-writing—a thing I have always been chary about—but I had good reasons. Our expenses have been so prodigious for a year and a half, and are still so prodigious, that Livy was worrying altogether too much about them, and doing a very dangerous amount of lying awake on their account. It was necessary to stop that, and it is now stopped.

Yes, she is remarkable, Joe. Her rheumatic attack set me to cursing and swearing, without limit as to time or energy, but it merely concentrated her patience and her unconquerable fortitude. It is the difference between us. I can't count the different kinds of ailments which have assaulted her in this fiendish year and a half—and I forgive none of them—but here she comes up again as bright and fresh and enterprising as ever, and goes to planning about Egypt, with a hope and a confidence which are to me amazing.

Clara is calling for me—we have to go into town and pay calls.

MARK.

In Florence, that winter, Clemens began dictating to his secretary some autobiographical chapters. This was the work which was "not to see print until I am dead." He found it a pleasant, lazy occupation and wrote his delight in it to Howells in a letter which seems not to have survived. In his reply, Howells wrote: "You do stir me mightily with the hope of dictating and I will try it when I get the chance. But there is the tempermental difference. You are dramatic and unconscious; you count the thing more than yourself; I am cursed with consciousness to the core, and can't say myself out; I am always saying myself in, and setting myself above all that I say, as of more worth. Lately I have felt as if I were rotting with egotism. I don't admire myself; I am sick of myself; but I can't think of anything else. Here I am at it now, when I ought to be rejoicing with you at the blessing you have found.... I'd like, immensely, to read your autobiography. You always rather bewildered me by your veracity, and I fancy you may tell the truth about yourself. But all of it? The black truth which we all know of ourselves in our hearts, or only the whity-brown truth of the pericardium, or the nice, whitened truth of the shirtfront? Even you won't tell the black heart's—truth. The man who could do it would be famed to the last day the sun shone upon."

We gather from Mark Twain's answer that he was not deceiving himself in the matter of his confessions.

To W. D. Howells, in New York:

VILLA DI QUARTO, FLORENCE,

March 14, '04.

DEAR HOWELLS,—Yes, I set up the safeguards, in the first day's dictating; taking this position: that an autobiography is the truest of all books; for while it inevitably consists mainly of extinctions of the truth, shirkings of the truth, partial revealments of the truth, with hardly an instance of plain straight truth, the remorseless truth is there, between the lines, where the author is raking dust upon it, the result being that the reader knows the author in spite of his wily diligences.

The summer in England! you can't ask better luck than that. Then you will run over to Florence; we shall all be hungry to see you-all. We are hunting for another villa, (this one is plenty large enough but has no room in it) but even if we find it I am afraid it will be months before we can move Mrs. Clemens. Of course it will. But it comforts us to let on that we think otherwise, and these pretensions help to keep hope alive in her.

Good-bye, with love, Amen.

Yours ever

MARK.

News came of the death of Henry M. Stanley, one of Mark Twain's oldest friends. Clemens once said that he had met Stanley in St. Louis where he (Clemens) had delivered a lecture which Stanley had reported. In the following letter he fixes the date of their meeting as early in 1867, which would be immediately after Mark Twain's return from California, and just prior to the Quaker City excursion—a fact which is interesting only because it places the two men together when each was at the very beginning of a great career.

To Lady Stanley, in England:

VILLA DI QUARTO, FIRENZE, May 11, '04.

DEAR LADY STANLEY,—I have lost a dear and honored friend—how fast they fall about me now, in my age! The world has lost a tried and proved hero. And you—what have you lost? It is beyond estimate—we who know you, and what he was to you, know that. How far he stretches across my life! I knew him when his work was all before him five years before the great day that he wrote his name far-away up on the blue of the sky for the world to see and applaud and remember; I have known him as friend and intimate ever since. It is 37 years. I have known no other friend and intimate so long, except John Hay—a friendship which dates from the same year and the same half of it, the first half of 1867. I grieve with you and with your family, dear Lady Stanley, it is all I can do; but that I do out of my heart. It would be we, instead of I, if Mrs. Clemens knew, but in all these 20 months that she has lain a prisoner in her bed we have hidden from her all things that could sadden her. Many a friend is gone whom she still asks about and still thinks is living.

In deepest sympathy I beg the privilege of signing myself

Your friend,

S. L. CLEMENS.

To Rev. J. H. Twichell, in Hartford:

VILLA DI QUARTO, May 11, '04

DEAR JOE,—Yours has this moment arrived—just as I was finishing a note to poor Lady Stanley. I believe the last country-house visit we paid in England was to Stanley's. Lord, how my friends and acquaintances fall about me now, in my gray-headed days! Vereschagin, Mommsen, Dvorak, Lenbach, Jokai—all so recently, and now Stanley. I had known Stanley 37 years. Goodness, who is it I haven't known! As a rule the necrologies find me personally interested—when they treat of old stagers. Generally when a man dies who is worth cabling, it happens that I have run across him somewhere, some time or other.

Oh, say! Down by the Laurentian Library there's a marble image that has been sitting on its pedestal some 450 Years, if my dates are right—Cosimo I.

I've seen the back of it many a time, but not the front; but yesterday I twisted my head around after we had driven by, and the profane exclamation burst from my mouth before I could think: "there's Chauncey Depew!"

I mean to get a photo of it—and use it if it confirms yesterday's conviction. That's a very nice word from the Catholic Magazine and I am glad you sent it. I mean to show it to my priest—we are very fond of him. He is a stealing man, and is also learnedly scientific. He invented the thing which records the seismatic disturbances, for the peoples of the earth. And he's an astronomer and has an observatory of his own.

Ah, many's the cry I have, over reflecting that maybe we could have had Young Harmony for Livy, and didn't have wit enough to think of it.

Speaking of Livy reminds me that your inquiry arrives at a good time (unberufen) It has been weeks (I don't know how many!) since we could have said a hopeful word, but this morning Katy came the minute the day-nurse came on watch and said words of a strange and long-forgotten sound: "Mr. Clemens, Mrs. Clemens is really and truly better!—anybody can see it; she sees it herself; and last night at 9 o'clock she said it."

There—it is heart-warming, it is splendid, it is sublime; let us enjoy it, let us make the most of it today—and bet not a farthing on tomorrow. The tomorrows have nothing for us. Too many times they have breathed the word of promise to our ear and broken it to our hope. We take no tomorrow's word any more.

You've done a wonder, Joe: you've written a letter that can be sent in to Livy—that doesn't often happen, when either a friend or a stranger writes. You did whirl in a P. S. that wouldn't do, but you wrote it on a margin of a page in such a way that I was able to clip off the margin clear across both pages, and now Livy won't perceive that the sheet isn't the same size it used to was. It was about Aldrich's son, and I came near forgetting to remove it. It should have been written on a loose strip and enclosed. That son died on the 5th of March and Aldrich wrote me on the night before that his minutes were numbered. On the 18th Livy asked after that patient, and I was prepared, and able to give her a grateful surprise by telling her "the Aldriches are no longer uneasy about him."

I do wish I could have been present and heard Charley Clark. When he can't light up a dark place nobody can.

With lots of love to you all.

MARK.

Mrs. Clemens had her bad days and her good days-days when there seemed no ray of light, and others that seemed almost to promise recovery. The foregoing letter to Twichell, and the one which follows, to Richard Watson Gilder, reflect the hope and fear that daily and hourly alternated at Villa Quarto

To Richard Watson Gilder, in New York:

VILLA DI QUARTO, FLORENCE,

May 12, '04.

DEAR GILDER,—A friend of ours (the Baroness de Nolda) was here this afternoon and wanted a note of introduction to the Century, for she has something to sell to you in case you'll want to make her an offer after seeing a sample of the goods. I said "With pleasure: get the goods ready, send the same to me, I will have Jean type-write them, then I will mail them to the Century and tonight I will write the note to Mr. Gilder and start it along. Also write me a letter embodying what you have been saying to me about the goods and your proposed plan of arranging and explaining them, and I will forward that to Gilder too."

As to the Baroness. She is a German; 30 years old; was married at 17; is very pretty-indeed I might say very pretty; has a lot of sons (5) running up from seven to 12 years old. Her husband is a Russian. They live half the time in Russia and the other half in Florence, and supply population alternately to the one country and then to the other. Of course it is a family that speaks languages. This occurs at their table—I know it by experience: It is Babel come again. The other day, when no guests were present to keep order, the tribes were all talking at once, and 6 languages were being traded in; at last the littlest boy lost his temper and screamed out at the top of his voice, with angry sobs: "Mais, vraiment, io non capisco gar nichts."

The Baroness is a little afraid of her English, therefore she will write her remarks in French—I said there's a plenty of translators in New York. Examine her samples and drop her a line.

For two entire days, now, we have not been anxious about Mrs. Clemens (unberufen). After 20 months of bed-ridden solitude and bodily misery she all of a sudden ceases to be a pallid shrunken shadow, and looks bright and young and pretty. She remains what she always was, the most wonderful creature of fortitude, patience, endurance and recuperative power that ever was. But ah, dear, it won't last; this fiendish malady will play new treacheries upon her, and I shall go back to my prayers again—unutterable from any pulpit!

With love to you and yours,

S. L. C.

May 13 10 A.M. I have just paid one of my pair of permitted 2 minutes visits per day to the sick room. And found what I have learned to expect—retrogression, and that pathetic something in the eye which betrays the secret of a waning hope.

The year of the World's Fair had come, and an invitation from Gov. Francis, of Missouri, came to Mark Twain in Florence, personally inviting him to attend the great celebration and carry off first prize. We may believe that Clemens felt little in the spirit of humor, but to such an invitation he must send a cheerful, even if disappointing, answer.

To Gov. Francis, of Missouri:

VILLA DI QUARTO, FIRENZE,

May 26, 1904.

DEAR GOVERNOR FRANCIS,—It has been a dear wish of mine to exhibit myself at the Great Fair and get a prize, but circumstances beyond my control have interfered, and I must remain in Florence. Although I have never taken prizes anywhere else I used to take them at school in Missouri half a century ago, and I ought to be able to repeat, now, if I could have a chance. I used to get the medal for good spelling, every week, and I could have had the medal for good conduct if there hadn't been so much corruption in Missouri in those days; still, I got it several times by trading medals and giving boot. I am willing to give boot now, if—however, those days are forever gone by in Missouri, and perhaps it is better so. Nothing ever stops the way it was in this changeable world. Although I cannot be at the Fair, I am going to be represented there anyway, by a portrait, by Professor Gelli. You will find it excellent. Good judges here say it is better than the original. They say it has all the merits of the original and keeps still, besides. It sounds like flattery, but it is just true.

I suppose you will get a prize, because you have created the most prodigious and in all ways most wonderful Fair the planet has ever seen. Very well, you have indeed earned it: and with it the gratitude of the State and the nation.

Sincerely yours,

MARK TWAIN

It was only a few days after the foregoing was written that death entered Villa Quarto—unexpectedly at last—for with the first June days Mrs. Clemens had seemed really to improve. It was on Sunday, June 5th, that the end came. Clemens, with his daughter Jean, had returned from a long drive, during which they had visited a Villa with the thought of purchase. On their return they were told that their patient had been better that afternoon than for three months. Yet it was only a few hours later that she left them, so suddenly and quietly that even those near her did not at first realize that she was gone.

To W. D. Howells, in New York.

VILLA DI QUARTO, FLORENCE,

June 6, '94.

DEAR HOWELLS,—Last night at 9.20 I entered Mrs. Clemens's room to say the usual goodnight—and she was dead—tho' no one knew it. She had been cheerfully talking, a moment before. She was sitting up in bed—she had not lain down for months—and Katie and the nurse were supporting her. They supposed she had fainted, and they were holding the oxygen pipe to her mouth, expecting to revive her. I bent over her and looked in her face, and I think I spoke—I was surprised and troubled that she did not notice me. Then we understood, and our hearts broke. How poor we are today!

But how thankful I am that her persecutions are ended. I would not call her back if I could.

Today, treasured in her worn old Testament, I found a dear and gentle letter from you, dated Far Rockaway, Sept. 13, 1896, about our poor Susy's death. I am tired and old; I wish I were with Livy.

I send my love-and hers-to you all.

S. L. C.

In a letter to Twichell he wrote: "How sweet she was in death; how young, how beautiful, how like her dear, girlish self cf thirty years ago; not a gray hair showing."

The family was now without plans for the future until they remembered the summer home of R. W. Gilder, at Tyringham, Massachusetts, and the possibility of finding lodgment for themselves in that secluded corner of New England. Clemens wrote without delay, as follows:

To R. W. Gilder, in New York:

VILLA DI QUARTO, FLORENCE,

June 7, '04.

DEAR GILDER FAMILY,—I have been worrying and worrying to know what to do: at last I went to the girls with an idea: to ask the Gilders to get us shelter near their summer home. It was the first time they have not shaken their heads. So to-morrow I will cable to you and shall hope to be in time.

An hour ago the best heart that ever beat for me and mine went silent out of this house, and I am as one who wanders and has lost his way. She who is gone was our head, she was our hands. We are now trying to make plans—we: we who have never made a plan before, nor ever needed to. If she could speak to us she would make it all simple and easy with a word, and our perplexities would vanish away. If she had known she was near to death she would have told us where to go and what to do: but she was not suspecting, neither were we. (She had been chatting cheerfully a moment before, and in an instant she was gone from us and we did not know it. We were not alarmed, we did not know anything had happened. It was a blessed death—she passed away without knowing it.) She was all our riches and she is gone: she was our breath, she was our life and now we are nothing.

We send you our love—and with it the love of you that was in her heart when she died.

S. L. CLEMENS.

Howells wrote his words of sympathy, adding: "The character which now remains a memory was one of the most perfect ever formed on the earth," and again, after having received Clemens's letter: "I cannot speak of your wife's having kept that letter of mine where she did. You know how it must humiliate a man in his unworthiness to have anything of his so consecrated. She hallowed what she touched, far beyond priests."

To W. D. Howells, in New York:

VILLA DI QUARTO, '04.

June 12, 6 p. m.

DEAR HOWELLS,—We have to sit and hold our hands and wait—in the silence and solitude of this prodigious house; wait until June 25, then we go to Naples and sail in the Prince Oscar the 26th. There is a ship 12 days earlier (but we came in that one.) I see Clara twice a day—morning and evening—greeting—nothing more is allowed. She keeps her bed, and says nothing. She has not cried yet. I wish she could cry. It would break Livy's heart to see Clara. We excuse ourselves from all the friends that call—though of course only intimates come. Intimates—but they are not the old old friends, the friends of the old, old times when we laughed.

Shall we ever laugh again? If I could only see a dog that I knew in the old times! and could put my arms around his neck and tell him all, everything, and ease my heart.

Think—in 3 hours it will be a week!—and soon a month; and by and by a year. How fast our dead fly from us.

She loved you so, and was always as pleased as a child with any notice you took of her.

Soon your wife will be with you, oh fortunate man! And John, whom mine was so fond of. The sight of him was such a delight to her. Lord, the old friends, how dear they are.

S. L. C.

To Rev. J. R. Twichell, in Hartford:

VILLA DI QUARTO, FLORENCE,

June 18, '04.

DEAR JOE,—It is 13 days. I am bewildered and must remain so for a time longer. It was so sudden, so unexpected. Imagine a man worth a hundred millions who finds himself suddenly penniless and fifty million in debt in his old age.

I was richer than any other person in the world, and now I am that pauper without peer. Some day I will tell you about it, not now.

MARK.

A tide of condolence flowed in from all parts of the world. It was impossible to answer all. Only a few who had been their closest friends received a written line, but the little printed acknowledgment which was returned was no mere formality. It was a heartfelt, personal word.

They arrived in America in July, and were accompanied by Twichell to Elmira, and on the 14th Mrs. Clemens was laid to rest by the side of Susy and little Langdon. R. W. Gilder had arranged for them to occupy, for the summer, a cottage on his place at Tyringham, in the Berkshire Hills. By November they were at the Grosvenor, in New York, preparing to establish themselves in a house which they had taken on the corner of Ninth Street and Fifth Avenue—Number 21.

To F. N. Doubleday, in New York:

DEAR DOUBLEDAY,—I did not know you were going to England: I would have freighted you with such messages of homage and affection to Kipling. And I would have pressed his hand, through you, for his sympathy with me in my crushing loss, as expressed by him in his letter to Gilder. You know my feeling for Kipling and that it antedates that expression.

I was glad that the boys came here to invite me to the house-warming and I think they understood why a man in the shadow of a calamity like mine could not go.

It has taken three months to repair and renovate our house—corner of 9th and 5th Avenue, but I shall be in it in io or 15 days hence. Much of the furniture went into it today (from Hartford). We have not seen it for 13 years. Katy Leary, our old housekeeper, who has been in our service more than 24 years, cried when she told me about it to-day. She said "I had forgotten it was so beautiful, and it brought Mrs. Clemens right back to me—in that old time when she was so young and lovely."

Jean and my secretary and the servants whom we brought from Italy because Mrs. Clemens liked them so well, are still keeping house in the Berkshire hills—and waiting. Clara (nervously wrecked by her mother's death) is in the hands of a specialist in 69th St., and I shall not be allowed to have any communication with her—even telephone—for a year. I am in this comfortable little hotel, and still in bed—for I dasn't budge till I'm safe from my pet devil, bronchitis.

Isn't it pathetic? One hour and ten minutes before Mrs. Clemens died I was saying to her "To-day, after five months search, I've found the villa that will content you: to-morrow you will examine the plans and give it your consent and I will buy it." Her eyes danced with pleasure, for she longed for a home of her own. And there, on that morrow, she lay white and cold. And unresponsive to my reverent caresses—a new thing to me and a new thing to her; that had not happened before in five and thirty years.

I am coming to see you and Mrs. Doubleday by and bye. She loved and honored Mrs. Doubleday and her work.

Always yours,

MARK.

It was a presidential year and the air was thick with politics. Mark Twain was no longer actively interested in the political situation; he was only disheartened by the hollowness and pretense of office-seeking, and the methods of office-seekers in general. Grieved that Twichell should still pin his faith to any party when all parties were so obviously venal and time-serving, he wrote in outspoken and rather somber protest.

To Rev. J. H. Twichell, in Hartford:

THE GROSVENOR, Nov. 4, '04.

Oh, dear! get out of that sewer—party politics—dear Joe. At least with your mouth. We hail only two men who could make speeches for their parties and preserve their honor and their dignity. One of them is dead. Possibly there were four. I am sorry for John Hay; sorry and ashamed. And yet I know he couldn't help it. He wears the collar, and he had to pay the penalty. Certainly he had no more desire to stand up before a mob of confiding human incapables and debauch them than you had. Certainly he took no more real pleasure in distorting history, concealing facts, propagating immoralities, and appealing to the sordid side of human nature than did you; but he was his party's property, and he had to climb away down and do it.

It is interesting, wonderfully interesting—the miracles which party-politics can do with a man's mental and moral make-up. Look at McKinley, Roosevelt, and yourself: in private life spotless in character; honorable, honest, just, humane, generous; scorning trickeries, treacheries, suppressions of the truth, mistranslations of the meanings of facts, the filching of credit earned by another, the condoning of crime, the glorifying of base acts: in public political life the reverse of all this.

McKinley was a silverite—you concealed it. Roosevelt was a silverite—you concealed it. Parker was a silverite—you publish it. Along with a shudder and a warning: "He was unsafe then. Is he any safer now?"

Joe, even I could be guilty of such a thing as that—if I were in party-politics; I really believe it.

Mr. Cleveland gave the country the gold standard; by implication you credit the matter to the Republican party.

By implication you prove the whole annual pension-scoop, concealing the fact that the bulk of the money goes to people who in no way deserve it. You imply that all the batteners upon this bribery-fund are Republicans. An indiscreet confession, since about half of them must have been Democrats before they were bought.

You as good as praise Order 78. It is true you do not shout, and you do not linger, you only whisper and skip—still, what little you do in the matter is complimentary to the crime.

It means, if it means anything, that our outlying properties will all be given up by the Democrats, and our flag hauled down. All of them? Not only the properties stolen by Mr. McKinley and Mr. Roosevelt, but the properties honestly acquired? Joe, did you believe that hardy statement when you made it? Yet you made it, and there it stands in permanent print. Now what moral law would suffer if we should give up the stolen ones? But—

"You know our standard-bearer. He will maintain all that we have gained"—by whatever process. Land, I believe you!

By George, Joe, you are as handy at the game as if you had been in training for it all your life. Your campaign Address is built from the ground up upon the oldest and best models. There isn't a paragraph in it whose facts or morals will wash—not even a sentence, I believe.

But you will soon be out of this. You didn't want to do it—that is sufficiently apparent, thanks be!—but you couldn't well get out of it. In a few days you will be out of it, and then you can fumigate yourself and take up your legitimate work again and resume your clean and wholesome private character once more and be happy—and useful.

I know I ought to hand you some guff, now, as propitiation and apology for these reproaches, but on the whole I believe I won't.

I have inquired, and find that Mitsikuri does not arrive here until to-morrow night. I shall watch out, and telephone again, for I greatly want to see him.

Always Yours,

MARK.

P. S.—Nov, 4. I wish I could learn to remember that it is unjust and dishonorable to put blame upon the human race for any of its acts. For it did not make itself, it did not make its nature, it is merely a machine, it is moved wholly by outside influences, it has no hand in creating the outside influences nor in choosing which of them it will welcome or reject, its performance is wholly automatic, it has no more mastership nor authority over its mind than it has over its stomach, which receives material from the outside and does as it pleases with it, indifferent to it's proprietor's suggestions, even, let alone his commands; wherefore, whatever the machine does—so called crimes and infamies included—is the personal act of its Maker, and He, solely, is responsible. I wish I could learn to pity the human race instead of censuring it and laughing at it; and I could, if the outside influences of old habit were not so strong upon my machine. It vexes me to catch myself praising the clean private citizen Roosevelt, and blaming the soiled President Roosevelt, when I know that neither praise nor blame is due to him for any thought or word or deed of his, he being merely a helpless and irresponsible coffee-mill ground by the hand of God.

Through a misunderstanding, Clemens, something more than a year earlier, had severed his connection with the Players' Club, of which he had been one of the charter members. Now, upon his return to New York, a number of his friends joined in an invitation to him to return. It was not exactly a letter they sent, but a bit of an old Scotch song—

"To Mark Twain
from
The Clansmen.

Will ye no come back again,
Will ye no come back again?
Better lo'ed ye canna be.
Will ye no come back again?"

Those who signed it were David Monroe, of the North American Review; Robert Reid, the painter, and about thirty others of the Round Table Group, so called because its members were accustomed to lunching at a large round table in a bay window of the Player dining-room. Mark Twain's reply was prompt and heartfelt. He wrote:

To Robt. Reid and the Others:

WELL-BELOVED,—Surely those lovely verses went to Prince Charley's heart, if he had one, and certainly they have gone to mine. I shall be glad and proud to come back again after such a moving and beautiful compliment as this from comrades whom I have loved so long. I hope you can poll the necessary vote; I know you will try, at any rate. It will be many months before I can foregather with you, for this black border is not perfunctory, not a convention; it symbolizes the loss of one whose memory is the only thing I worship.

It is not necessary for me to thank you—and words could not deliver what I feel, anyway. I will put the contents of your envelope in the small casket where I keep the things which have become sacred to me.

S. L. C.

A year later, Mark Twain did "come back again," as an honorary life member, and was given a dinner of welcome by those who had signed the lines urging his return.

XLIV. LETTERS OF 1905. TO TWICHELL, MR. DUNEKA AND OTHERS. POLITICS AND HUMANITY. A SUMMER AT DUBLIN. MARK TWAIN AT 70.

In 1884 Mark Twain had abandoned the Republican Party to vote for Cleveland. He believed the party had become corrupt, and to his last day it was hard for him to see anything good in Republican policies or performance. He was a personal friend of Theodore Roosevelt's but, as we have seen in a former letter, Roosevelt the politician rarely found favor in his eyes. With or without justification, most of the President's political acts invited his caustic sarcasm and unsparing condemnation. Another letter to Twichell of this time affords a fair example.

To Rev. J. H. Twichell, in Hartford:

Feb. 16, '05.

DEAR JOE,—I knew I had in me somewhere a definite feeling about the President if I could only find the words to define it with. Here they are, to a hair—from Leonard Jerome: "For twenty years I have loved Roosevelt the man and hated Roosevelt the statesman and politician."

It's mighty good. Every time, in 25 years, that I have met Roosevelt the man, a wave of welcome has streaked through me with the hand-grip; but whenever (as a rule) I meet Roosevelt the statesman and politician, I find him destitute of morals and not respectworthy. It is plain that where his political self and his party self are concerned he has nothing resembling a conscience; that under those inspirations he is naively indifferent to the restraints of duty and even unaware of them; ready to kick the Constitution into the back yard whenever it gets in the way; and whenever he smells a vote, not only willing but eager to buy it, give extravagant rates for it and pay the bill not out of his own pocket or the party's, but out of the nation's, by cold pillage. As per Order 78 and the appropriation of the Indian trust funds.

But Roosevelt is excusable—I recognize it and (ought to) concede it. We are all insane, each in his own way, and with insanity goes irresponsibility. Theodore the man is sane; in fairness we ought to keep in mind that Theodore, as statesman and politician, is insane and irresponsible.

Do not throw these enlightenments aside, but study them, let them raise you to higher planes and make you better. You taught me in my callow days, let me pay back the debt now in my old age out of a thesaurus with wisdom smelted from the golden ores of experience.

Ever yours for sweetness and light

MARK.

The next letter to Twichell takes up politics and humanity in general, in a manner complimentary to neither. Mark Twain was never really a pessimist, but he had pessimistic intervals, such as come to most of us in life's later years, and at such times he let himself go without stint concerning "the damned human race," as he called it, usually with a manifest sense of indignation that he should be a member of it. In much of his later writing —A Mysterious Stranger for example—he said his say with but small restraint, and certainly in his purely intellectual moments he was likely to be a pessimist of the most extreme type, capably damning the race and the inventor of it. Yet, at heart, no man loved his kind more genuinely, or with deeper compassion, than Mark Twain, perhaps for its very weaknesses. It was only that he had intervals—frequent intervals, and rather long ones—when he did not admire it, and was still more doubtful as to the ways of providence.

To Rev. J. H. Twichell, in Hartford:

March 14, '05.

DEAR JOE,—I have a Puddn'head maxim:

"When a man is a pessimist before 48 he knows too much; if he is an optimist after it, he knows too little."

It is with contentment, therefore, that I reflect that I am better and wiser than you. Joe, you seem to be dealing in "bulks," now; the "bulk" of the farmers and U. S. Senators are "honest." As regards purchase and sale with money? Who doubts it? Is that the only measure of honesty? Aren't there a dozen kinds of honesty which can't be measured by the money-standard? Treason is treason—and there's more than one form of it; the money-form is but one of them. When a person is disloyal to any confessed duty, he is plainly and simply dishonest, and knows it; knows it, and is privately troubled about it and not proud of himself. Judged by this standard—and who will challenge the validity of it?—there isn't an honest man in Connecticut, nor in the Senate, nor anywhere else. I do not even except myself, this time.

Am I finding fault with you and the rest of the populace? No—I assure you I am not. For I know the human race's limitations, and this makes it my duty—my pleasant duty—to be fair to it. Each person in it is honest in one or several ways, but no member of it is honest in all the ways required by—by what? By his own standard. Outside of that, as I look at it, there is no obligation upon him.

Am I honest? I give you my word of honor (private) I am not. For seven years I have suppressed a book which my conscience tells me I ought to publish. I hold it a duty to publish it. There are other difficult duties which I am equal to, but I am not equal to that one. Yes, even I am dishonest. Not in many ways, but in some. Forty-one, I think it is. We are certainly all honest in one or several ways—every man in the world—though I have reason to think I am the only one whose black-list runs so light. Sometimes I feel lonely enough in this lofty solitude.

Yes, oh, yes, I am not overlooking the "steady progress from age to age of the coming of the kingdom of God and righteousness." "From age to age"—yes, it describes that giddy gait. I (and the rocks) will not live to see it arrive, but that is all right—it will arrive, it surely will. But you ought not to be always ironically apologizing for the Deity. If that thing is going to arrive, it is inferable that He wants it to arrive; and so it is not quite kind of you, and it hurts me, to see you flinging sarcasms at the gait of it. And yet it would not be fair in me not to admit that the sarcasms are deserved. When the Deity wants a thing, and after working at it for "ages and ages" can't show even a shade of progress toward its accomplishment, we—well, we don't laugh, but it is only because we dasn't. The source of "righteousness"—is in the heart? Yes. And engineered and directed by the brain? Yes. Well, history and tradition testify that the heart is just about what it was in the beginning; it has undergone no shade of change. Its good and evil impulses and their consequences are the same today that they were in Old Bible times, in Egyptian times, in Greek times, in Middle Age times, in Twentieth Century times. There has been no change.

Meantime, the brain has undergone no change. It is what it always was. There are a few good brains and a multitude of poor ones. It was so in Old Bible times and in all other times—Greek, Roman, Middle Ages and Twentieth Century. Among the savages—all the savages—the average brain is as competent as the average brain here or elsewhere. I will prove it to you, some time, if you like. And there are great brains among them, too. I will prove that also, if you like.

Well, the 19th century made progress—the first progress after "ages and ages"—colossal progress. In what? Materialities. Prodigious acquisitions were made in things which add to the comfort of many and make life harder for as many more. But the addition to righteousness? Is that discoverable? I think not. The materialities were not invented in the interest of righteousness; that there is more righteousness in the world because of them than there, was before, is hardly demonstrable, I think. In Europe and America, there is a vast change (due to them) in ideals—do you admire it? All Europe and all America, are feverishly scrambling for money. Money is the supreme ideal—all others take tenth place with the great bulk of the nations named. Money-lust has always existed, but not in the history of the world was it ever a craze, a madness, until your time and mine. This lust has rotted these nations; it has made them hard, sordid, ungentle, dishonest, oppressive.

Did England rise against the infamy of the Boer war? No—rose in favor of it. Did America rise against the infamy of the Phillipine war? No—rose in favor of it. Did Russia rise against the infamy of the present war? No—sat still and said nothing. Has the Kingdom of God advanced in Russia since the beginning of time?

Or in Europe and America, considering the vast backward step of the money-lust? Or anywhere else? If there has been any progress toward righteousness since the early days of Creation—which, in my ineradicable honesty, I am obliged to doubt—I think we must confine it to ten per cent of the populations of Christendom, (but leaving, Russia, Spain and South America entirely out.) This gives us 320,000,000 to draw the ten per cent from. That is to say, 32,000,000 have advanced toward righteousness and the Kingdom of God since the "ages and ages" have been flying along, the Deity sitting up there admiring. Well, you see it leaves 1,200,000,000 out of the race. They stand just where they have always stood; there has been no change.

N. B. No charge for these informations. Do come down soon, Joe.

With love,

MARK.

St. Clair McKelway, of The Brooklyn Eagle, narrowly escaped injuries in a railway accident, and received the following. Clemens and McKelway were old friends.

To St. Clair McKelway, in Brooklyn:

21 FIFTH AVE. Sunday Morning.

April 30, 1905.

DEAR McKELWAY, Your innumerable friends are grateful, most grateful.

As I understand the telegrams, the engineer of your train had never seen a locomotive before. Very well, then, I am once more glad that there is an Ever-watchful Providence to foresee possible results and send Ogdens and McIntyres along to save our friends.

The Government's Official report, showing that our railways killed twelve hundred persons last year and injured sixty thousand convinces me that under present conditions one Providence is not enough to properly and efficiently take care of our railroad business. But it is characteristically American—always trying to get along short-handed and save wages.

I am helping your family congratulate themselves, and am your friend as always.

S. L. CLEMENS.

Clemens did not spend any more summers at Quarry Farm. All its associations were beautiful and tender, but they could only sadden him. The life there had been as of another world, sunlit, idyllic, now forever vanished. For the summer of 1905 he leased the Copley Green house at Dublin, New Hampshire, where there was a Boston colony of writing and artistic folk, including many of his long-time friends. Among them was Colonel Thomas Wentworth Higginson, who wrote a hearty letter of welcome when he heard the news. Clemens replied in kind.

To Col. Thomas Wentworth Higginson, in Boston:

21 FIFTH AVE. Sunday, March 26, 1905.

DEAR COL. HIGGINSON,—I early learned that you would be my neighbor in the Summer and I rejoiced, recognizing in you and your family a large asset. I hope for frequent intercourse between the two households. I shall have my youngest daughter with me. The other one will go from the rest-cure in this city to the rest-cure in Norfolk Conn and we shall not see her before autumn. We have not seen her since the middle of October.

Jean (the youngest daughter) went to Dublin and saw the house and came back charmed with it. I know the Thayers of old—manifestly there is no lack of attractions up there. Mrs. Thayer and I were shipmates in a wild excursion perilously near 40 years ago.

You say you "send with this" the story. Then it should be here but it isn't, when I send a thing with another thing, the other thing goes but the thing doesn't, I find it later—still on the premises. Will you look it up now and send it?

Aldrich was here half an hour ago, like a breeze from over the fields, with the fragrance still upon his spirit. I am tired of waiting for that man to get old.

Sincerely yours,

S. L. C.

Mark Twain was in his seventieth year, old neither in mind nor body, but willing to take life more quietly, to refrain from travel and gay events. A sort of pioneers' reunion was to be held on the Pacific Coast, and a letter from Robert Fulton, of Reno, Nevada, invited Clemens to attend. He did not go, but he sent a letter that we may believe was the next best thing to those who heard it read.

To Robert Fulton, in Reno, Nevada:

IN THE MOUNTAINS,

May 24, 1905.

DEAR MR. FULTON,—I remember, as if it were yesterday, that when I disembarked from the overland stage in front of the Ormsby in Carson City in August, 1861, I was not expecting to be asked to come again. I was tired, discouraged, white with alkali dust, and did not know anybody; and if you had said then, "Cheer up, desolate stranger, don't be down-hearted—pass on, and come again in 1905," you cannot think how grateful I would have been and how gladly I would have closed the contract. Although I was not expecting to be invited, I was watching out for it, and was hurt and disappointed when you started to ask me and changed it to, "How soon are you going away?"

But you have made it all right, now, the wound is closed. And so I thank you sincerely for the invitation; and with you, all Reno, and if I were a few years younger I would accept it, and promptly. I would go. I would let somebody else do the oration, but, as for me, I would talk—just talk. I would renew my youth; and talk—and talk—and talk—and have the time of my life! I would march the unforgotten and unforgettable antiques by, and name their names, and give them reverent Hailand-farewell as they passed: Goodman, McCarthy, Gillis, Curry, Baldwin, Winters, Howard, Nye, Stewart; Neely Johnson, Hal Clayton, North, Root,—and my brother, upon whom be peace!—and then the desperadoes, who made life a joy and the "Slaughter-house" a precious possession: Sam Brown, Farmer Pete, Bill Mayfield, Six-fingered Jake, Jack Williams and the rest of the crimson discipleship—and so on and so on. Believe me, I would start a resurrection it would do you more good to look at than the next one will, if you go on the way you are doing now.

Those were the days! those old ones. They will come no more. Youth will come no more. They were so full to the brim with the wine of life; there have been no others like them. It chokes me up to think of them. Would you like me to come out there and cry? It would not beseem my white head.

Good-bye. I drink to you all. Have a good time—and take an old man's blessing.

MARK TWAIN.

A few days later he was writing to H. H. Bancroft, of San Francisco, who had invited him for a visit in event of his coming to the Coast. Henry James had just been there for a week and it was hoped that Howells would soon follow.

To H. H. Bancroft, in San Francisco:

UP IN NEW HAMPSHIRE,

May 27, 1905.

DEAR MR. BANCROFT,—I thank you sincerely for the tempting hospitalities which you offer me, but I have to deny myself, for my wandering days are over, and it is my desire and purpose to sit by the fire the rest of my remnant of life and indulge myself with the pleasure and repose of work—work uninterrupted and unmarred by duties or excursions.

A man who like me, is going to strike 70 on the 30th of next November has no business to be flitting around the way Howells does—that shameless old fictitious butter fly. (But if he comes, don't tell him I said it, for it would hurt him and I wouldn't brush a flake of powder from his wing for anything. I only say it in envy of his indestructible youth, anyway. Howells will be 88 in October.) With thanks again,

Sincerely yours,

S. L. C.

Clemens found that the air of the New Hampshire hills agreed with him and stimulated him to work. He began an entirely new version of

The Mysterious Stranger, of which he already had a bulky and nearly finished manuscript, written in Vienna. He wrote several hundred pages of an extravaganza entitled, Three Thousand Years Among the Microbes, and then, having got his superabundant vitality reduced (it was likely to expend itself in these weird mental exploits), he settled down one day and wrote that really tender and beautiful idyl, Eve's Diary, which he had begun, or at least planned, the previous summer at Tyringham. In a letter to Mr. Frederick A. Duneka, general manager of Harper & Brothers, he tells something of the manner of the story; also his revised opinion of Adam's Diary, written in '93, and originally published as a souvenir of Niagara Falls.

To Frederick A. Duneka, in New York:

DUBLIN, July 16, '05.

DEAR MR. DUNEKA,—I wrote Eve's Diary, she using Adam's Diary as her (unwitting and unconscious) text, of course, since to use any other text would have been an imbecility—then I took Adam's Diary and read it. It turned my stomach. It was not literature; yet it had been literature once—before I sold it to be degraded to an advertisement of the Buffalo Fair. I was going to write and ask you to melt the plates and put it out of print.

But this morning I examined it without temper, and saw that if I abolished the advertisement it would be literature again.

So I have done it. I have struck out 700 words and inserted 5 MS pages of new matter (650 words), and now Adam's Diary is dam good—sixty times as good as it ever was before.

I believe it is as good as Eve's Diary now—no, it's not quite that good, I guess, but it is good enough to go in the same cover with Eve's. I'm sure of that.

I hate to have the old Adam go out any more—don't put it on the presses again, let's put the new one in place of it; and next Xmas, let us bind Adam and Eve in one cover. They score points against each other—so, if not bound together, some of the points would not be perceived.....

P. S. Please send another Adam's Diary, so that I can make 2 revised copies. Eve's Diary is Eve's love-Story, but we will not name it that.

Yrs ever,

MARK.

The peace-making at Portsmouth between Japan and Russia was not satisfactory to Mark Twain, who had fondly hoped there would be no peace until, as he said, "Russian liberty was safe. One more battle would have abolished the waiting chains of millions upon millions of unborn Russians and I wish it could have been fought." He set down an expression of his feelings for the Associated Press, and it invited many letters. Charles Francis Adams wrote, "It attracted my attention because it so exactly expresses the views I have myself all along entertained."

Clemens was invited by Colonel George Harvey to dine with the Russian emissaries, Baron Rosen and Sergius Witte. He declined, but his telegram so pleased Witte that he asked permission to publish it, and announced that he would show it to the Czar.

Telegram. To Col. George Harvey, in New York:

TO COLONEL HARVEY,—I am still a cripple, otherwise I should be more than glad of this opportunity to meet the illustrious magicians who came here equipped with nothing but a pen, and with it have divided the honors of the war with the sword. It is fair to presume that in thirty centuries history will not get done admiring these men who attempted what the world regarded as impossible and achieved it.

Witte would not have cared to show the Czar the telegram in its original form, which follows.

Telegram (unsent). To Col. George Harvey, in New York:

TO COLONEL HARVEY,—I am still a cripple, otherwise I should be more than glad of this opportunity to meet those illustrious magicians who with the pen have annulled, obliterated, and abolished every high achievement of the Japanese sword and turned the tragedy of a tremendous war into a gay and blithesome comedy. If I may, let me in all respect and honor salute them as my fellow-humorists, I taking third place, as becomes one who was not born to modesty, but by diligence and hard work is acquiring it. MARK.

Nor still another unsent form, perhaps more characteristic than either of the foregoing.

Telegram (unsent). To Col. George Harvey, in New York:

DEAR COLONEL,—No, this is a love-feast; when you call a lodge of sorrow send for me.

MARK.

To Mrs. Crane, Quarry Farm:

DUBLIN, Sept. 24, '05.

Susy dear, I have had a lovely dream. Livy, dressed in black, was sitting up in my bed (here) at my right and looking as young and sweet as she used to do when she was in health. She said: "what is the name of your sweet sister?" I said, "Pamela." "Oh, yes, that is it, I thought it was—" (naming a name which has escaped me) "Won't you write it down for me?" I reached eagerly for a pen and pad—laid my hands upon both—then said to myself, "It is only a dream," and turned back sorrowfully and there she was, still. The conviction flamed through me that our lamented disaster was a dream, and this a reality. I said, "How blessed it is, how blessed it is, it was all a dream, only a dream!" She only smiled and did not ask what dream I meant, which surprised me. She leaned her head against mine and I kept saying, "I was perfectly sure it was a dream, I never would have believed it wasn't."

I think she said several things, but if so they are gone from my memory. I woke and did not know I had been dreaming. She was gone. I wondered how she could go without my knowing it, but I did not spend any thought upon that, I was too busy thinking of how vivid and real was the dream that we had lost her and how unspeakably blessed it was to find that it was not true and that she was still ours and with us.

S. L. C.

One day that summer Mark Twain received a letter from the actress, Minnie Maddern Fiske, asking him to write something that would aid her in her crusade against bull-fighting. The idea appealed to him; he replied at once.

To Mrs. Fiske:

DEAR MRS. FISKE,—I shall certainly write the story. But I may not get it to suit me, in which case it will go in the fire. Later I will try again—and yet again—and again. I am used to this. It has taken me twelve years to write a short story—the shortest one I ever wrote, I think.—[Probably "The Death Disk."]—So do not be discouraged; I will stick to this one in the same way. Sincerely yours,

S. L. CLEMENS.

He did not delay in his beginning, and a few weeks later was sending word to his publisher about it.

To Frederick A. Duneka, in New York:

Oct. 2, '05.

DEAR MR. DUNEKA,—I have just finished a short story which I "greatly admire," and so will you—"A Horse's Tale"—about 15,000 words, at a rough guess. It has good fun in it, and several characters, and is lively. I shall finish revising it in a few days or more, then Jean will type it.

Don't you think you can get it into the Jan. and Feb. numbers and issue it as a dollar booklet just after the middle of Jan. when you issue the Feb. number?

It ought to be ably illustrated.

Why not sell simultaneous rights, for this once, to the Ladies' Home Journal or Collier's, or both, and recoup yourself?—for I would like to get it to classes that can't afford Harper's. Although it doesn't preach, there's a sermon concealed in it.

Yr sincerely,

MARK.

Five days later he added some rather interesting facts concerning the new story.

To F. A. Duneka, in New York:

Oct. 7, 1906. ['05]

DEAR MR. DUNEKA,—... I've made a poor guess as to number of words. I think there must be 20,000. My usual page of MS. contains about 130 words; but when I am deeply interested in my work and dead to everything else, my hand-writing shrinks and shrinks until there's a great deal more than 130 on a page—oh, yes, a deal more. Well, I discover, this morning, that this tale is written in that small hand.

This strong interest is natural, for the heroine is my daughter, Susy, whom we lost. It was not intentional—it was a good while before I found it out.

So I am sending you her picture to use—and to reproduce with photographic exactness the unsurpassable expression and all. May you find an artist who has lost an idol!

Take as good care of the picture as you can and restore it to me when I come.

I hope you will illustrate this tale considerably. Not humorous pictures. No. When they are good (or bad) one's humor gets no chance to play surprises on the reader. A humorous subject illustrated seriously is all right, but a humorous artist is no fit person for such work. You see, the humorous writer pretends to absolute seriousness (when he knows his trade) then for an artist—to step in and give his calculated gravity all away with a funny picture—oh, my land! It gives me the dry gripes just to think of it. It would be just about up to the average comic artist's intellectual level to make a funny picture of the horse kicking the lungs out of a trader. Hang it, the remark is funny—because the horse is not aware of it but the fact is not humorous, it is tragic and it is no subject for a humorous picture.

Could I be allowed to sit in judgment upon the pictures before they are accepted—at least those in which Cathy may figure?

This is not essential. It is but a suggestion, and it is hereby withdrawn, if it would be troublesome or cause delay.

I hope you will reproduce the cat-pile, full page. And save the photo for me in as good condition as possible. When Susy and Clara were little tots those cats had their profoundest worship, and there is no duplicate of this picture. These cats all had thundering names, or inappropriate ones—

furnished by the children with my help. One was named Buffalo Bill.

Are you interested in coincidences?

After discovering, about the middle of the book, that Cathy was Susy Clemens, I put her picture with my MS., to be reproduced. After the book was finished it was discovered that Susy had a dim model of Soldier Boy in her arms; I had forgotten all about that toy.

Then I examined the cat-picture and laid it with the MS. for introduction; but it was not until yesterday that I remembered that one of the cats was named Buffalo Bill.

Sincerely yours,

MARK.

The reference in this letter to shrinkage of his hand-writing with the increasing intensity of his interest, and the consequent addition of the number of words to the page, recalls another fact, noted by Mr. Duneka, viz.: that because of his terse Anglo-Saxon diction, Mark Twain could put more words on a magazine page than any other writer. It is hardly necessary to add that he got more force into what he put on the page for the same reason.

There was always a run of reporters at Mark Twain's New York home. His opinion was sought for on every matter of public interest, and whatever happened to him in particular was considered good for at least half a column of copy, with his name as a catch-line at the top. When it was learned that he was to spend the summer in New Hampshire, the reporters had all wanted to find out about it. Now that the summer was ending, they began to want to know how he had liked it, what work he had done and what were his plans for another year. As they frequently applied to his publishers for these details it was finally suggested to him that he write a letter furnishing the required information. His reply, handed to Mr. Duneka, who was visiting him at the moment, is full of interest.

Mem. for Mr. Duneka:

DUBLIN, Oct. 9, 1905.

... As to the other matters, here are the details.

Yes, I have tried a number of summer homes, here and in Europe together.

Each of these homes had charms of its own; charms and delights of its own, and some of them—even in Europe had comforts. Several of them had conveniences, too. They all had a "view."

It is my conviction that there should always be some water in a view—a lake or a river, but not the ocean, if you are down on its level. I think that when you are down on its level it seldom inflames you with an ecstasy which you could not get out of a sand-flat. It is like being on board ship, over again; indeed it is worse than that, for there's three months of it. On board ship one tires of the aspects in a couple of days, and quits looking. The same vast circle of heaving humps is spread around you all the time, with you in the centre of it and never gaining an inch on the horizon, so far as you can see; for variety, a flight of flying-fish, mornings; a flock of porpoises throwing summersaults afternoons; a remote whale spouting, Sundays; occasional phosphorescent effects, nights; every other day a streak of black smoke trailing along under the horizon; on the one single red letter day, the illustrious iceberg. I have seen that iceberg thirty-four times in thirty-seven voyages; it is always the same shape, it is always the same size, it always throws up the same old flash when the sun strikes it; you may set it on any New York door-step of a June morning and light it up with a mirror-flash; and I will engage to recognize it. It is artificial, and it is provided and anchored out by the steamer companies. I used to like the sea, but I was young then, and could easily get excited over any kind of monotony, and keep it up till the monotonies ran out, if it was a fortnight.

Last January, when we were beginning to inquire about a home for this summer, I remembered that Abbott Thayer had said, three years before, that the New Hampshire highlands was a good place. He was right—it was a good place. Any place that is good for an artist in paint is good for an artist in morals and ink. Brush is here, too; so is Col. T. W. Higginson; so is Raphael Pumpelly; so is Mr. Secretary Hitchcock; so is Henderson; so is Learned; so is Summer; so is Franklin MacVeigh; so is Joseph L. Smith; so is Henry Copley Greene, when I am not occupying his house, which I am doing this season. Paint, literature, science, statesmanship, history, professorship, law, morals,—these are all represented here, yet crime is substantially unknown.

The summer homes of these refugees are sprinkled, a mile apart, among the forest-clad hills, with access to each other by firm smooth country roads which are so embowered in dense foliage that it is always twilight in there, and comfortable. The forests are spider-webbed with these good roads, they go everywhere; but for the help of the guide-boards, the stranger would not arrive anywhere.

The village—Dublin—is bunched together in its own place, but a good telephone service makes its markets handy to all those outliars. I have spelt it that way to be witty. The village executes orders on, the Boston plan—promptness and courtesy.

The summer homes are high-perched, as a rule, and have contenting outlooks. The house we occupy has one. Monadnock, a soaring double hump, rises into the sky at its left elbow—that is to say, it is close at hand. From the base of the long slant of the mountain the valley spreads away to the circling frame of the hills, and beyond the frame the billowy sweep of remote great ranges rises to view and flows, fold upon fold, wave upon wave, soft and blue and unwordly, to the horizon fifty miles away. In these October days

Monadnock and the valley and its framing hills make an inspiring picture to look at, for they are sumptuously splashed and mottled and be-torched from sky-line to sky-line with the richest dyes the autumn can furnish; and when they lie flaming in the full drench of the mid-afternoon sun, the sight affects the spectator physically, it stirs his blood like military music.

These summer homes are commodious, well built, and well furnished—facts which sufficiently indicate that the owners built them to live in themselves. They have furnaces and wood fireplaces, and the rest of the comforts and conveniences of a city home, and can be comfortably occupied all the year round.

We cannot have this house next season, but I have secured Mrs. Upton's house which is over in the law and science quarter, two or three miles from here, and about the same distance from the art, literary, and scholastic groups. The science and law quarter has needed improving, this good while.

The nearest railway-station is distant something like an hour's drive; it is three hours from there to Boston, over a branch line. You can go to New York in six hours per branch lines if you change cars every time you think of it, but it is better to go to Boston and stop over and take the trunk line next day, then you do not get lost.

It is claimed that the atmosphere of the New Hampshire highlands is exceptionally bracing and stimulating, and a fine aid to hard and continuous work. It is a just claim, I think. I came in May, and wrought 35 successive days without a break. It is possible that I could not have done it elsewhere. I do not know; I have not had any disposition to try it, before. I think I got the disposition out of the atmosphere, this time. I feel quite sure, in fact, that that is where it came from.

I am ashamed to confess what an intolerable pile of manuscript I ground out in the 35 days, therefore I will keep the number of words to myself. I wrote the first half of a long tale—"The Adventures of a Microbe" and put it away for a finish next summer, and started another long tale—"The Mysterious Stranger;" I wrote the first half of it and put it with the other for a finish next summer. I stopped, then. I was not tired, but I had no books on hand that needed finishing this year except one that was seven years old. After a little I took that one up and finished it. Not for publication, but to have it ready for revision next summer.

Since I stopped work I have had a two months' holiday. The summer has been my working time for 35 years; to have a holiday in it (in America) is new for me. I have not broken it, except to write "Eve's Diary" and "A Horse's Tale"—short things occupying the mill 12 days.

This year our summer is 6 months long and ends with November and the flight home to New York, but next year we hope and expect to stretch it another month and end it the first of December.

[No signature.]

The fact that he was a persistent smoker was widely known, and many friends and admirers of Mark Twain sent him cigars, most of which he could not use, because they were too good. He did not care for Havana cigars, but smoked the fragrant, inexpensive domestic tobacco with plenty of "pep" in it, as we say today. Now and then he had an opportunity to head off some liberal friend, who wrote asking permission to contribute to his cigar collection, as instance the following.

To Rev. L. M. Powers, in Haverhill, Mass.:

Nov. 9, 1905.

DEAR MR. POWERS,—I should accept your hospitable offer at once but for the fact I couldn't do it and remain honest. That is to say if I allowed you to send me what you believe to be good cigars it would distinctly mean that I meant to smoke them, whereas I should do nothing of the kind. I know a good cigar better than you do, for I have had 60 years experience.

No, that is not what I mean; I mean I know a bad cigar better than anybody else; I judge by the price only; if it costs above 5 cents I know it to be either foreign or half-foreign, and unsmokeable. By me I have many boxes of Havana cigars, of all prices from 20 cts apiece up to 1.66 apiece; I bought none of them, they were all presents, they are an accumulation of several years. I have never smoked one of them and never shall, I work them off on the visitor. You shall have a chance when you come.

Pessimists are born not made; optimists are born not made; but no man is born either pessimist wholly or optimist wholly, perhaps; he is pessimistic along certain lines and optimistic along certain others. That is my case.

Sincerely yours,

S. L. CLEMENS.

In spite of all the fine photographs that were made of him, there recurred constantly among those sent him to be autographed a print of one which, years before, Sarony had made and placed on public sale. It was a good photograph, mechanically and even artistically, but it did not please Mark Twain. Whenever he saw it he recalled Sarony with bitterness and severity. Once he received an inquiry concerning it, and thus feelingly expressed himself.

To Mr. Row (no address):

21 FIFTH AVENUE, NEW YORK,

November 14, 1905.

DEAR MR. ROW,—That alleged portrait has a private history. Sarony was as much of an enthusiast about wild animals as he was about photography; and when Du Chaillu brought the first Gorilla to this country in 1819 he came to me in a fever of excitement and asked me if my father was of record and authentic. I said he was; then Sarony, without any abatement of his excitement asked if my grandfather also was of record and authentic. I said he was. Then Sarony, with still rising excitement and with joy added to it, said he had found my great grandfather in the person of the gorilla, and had recognized him at once by his resemblance to me. I was deeply hurt but did not reveal this, because I knew Saxcny meant no offense for the gorilla had not done him any harm, and he was not a man who would say an unkind thing about a gorilla wantonly. I went with him to inspect the ancestor, and examined him from several points of view, without being able to detect anything more than a passing resemblance. "Wait," said Sarony with confidence, "let me show you." He borrowed my overcoat—and put it on the gorilla. The result was surprising. I saw that the gorilla while not looking distinctly like me was exactly what my great grand father would have looked like if I had had one. Sarong photographed the creature in that overcoat, and spread the picture about the world. It has remained spread about the world ever since. It turns up every week in some newspaper somewhere or other. It is not my favorite, but to my exasperation it is everybody else's. Do you think you could get it suppressed for me? I will pay the limit.

Sincerely yours,

S. L. CLEMENS.

The year 1905 closed triumphantly for Mark Twain. The great "Seventieth Birthday" dinner planned by Colonel George Harvey is remembered to-day as the most notable festival occasion in New York literary history. Other dinners and ovations followed. At seventy he had returned to the world, more beloved, more honored than ever before.

XLV. LETTERS, 1906, TO VARIOUS PERSONS. THE FAREWELL LECTURE. A SECOND SUMMER IN DUBLIN. BILLIARDS AND COPYRIGHT.

MARK TWAIN at "Pier Seventy," as he called it, paused to look backward and to record some memoirs of his long, eventful past. The Autobiography dictations begun in Florence were resumed, and daily he traveled back, recalling long-ago scenes and all-but-forgotten places. He was not without reminders. Now and again there came some message that brought back the old days—the Tom Sawyer and Huck Finn days—or the romance of the river that he never recalled other than with tenderness and a tone of regret that it was gone. An invitation to the golden wedding of two ancient friends moved and saddened him, and his answer to it conveys about all the story of life.

To Mr. and Mrs. Gordon:

21 FIFTH AVENUE,

Jan. 24, '06.

DEAR GORDONS,—I have just received your golden-wedding "At Home" and am trying to adjust my focus to it and realize how much it means. It is inconceivable! With a simple sweep it carries me back over a stretch of time measurable only in astronomical terms and geological periods. It brings before me Mrs. Gordon, young, round-limbed, handsome; and with her the Youngbloods and their two babies, and Laura Wright, that unspoiled little maid, that fresh flower of the woods and the prairies. Forty-eight years ago!

Life was a fairy-tale, then, it is a tragedy now. When I was 43 and John Hay 41 he said life was a tragedy after 40, and I disputed it. Three years ago he asked me to testify again: I counted my graves, and there was nothing for me to say.

I am old; I recognize it but I don't realize it. I wonder if a person ever really ceases to feel young—I mean, for a whole day at a time. My love to you both, and to all of us that are left.

MARK.

Though he used very little liquor of any kind, it was Mark Twain's custom to keep a bottle of Scotch whiskey with his collection of pipes and cigars and tobacco on a little table by his bed-side. During restless nights he found a small quantity of it conducive to sleep. Andrew Carnegie, learning of this custom, made it his business to supply Scotch of his own special importation. The first case came, direct from Scotland. When it arrived Clemens sent this characteristic acknowledgment.

To Andrew Carnegie, in Scotland:

21 FIFTH AVE. Feb. 10, '06.

DEAR ST. ANDREW,—The whisky arrived in due course from over the water; last week one bottle of it was extracted from the wood and inserted into me, on the instalment plan, with this result: that I believe it to be the best, smoothest whisky now on the planet. Thanks, oh, thanks: I have discarded Peruna.

Hoping that you three are well and happy and will be coming back before the winter sets in.

I am,

Sincerely yours,

MARK.

It must have been a small bottle to be consumed by him in a week, or perhaps he had able assistance. The next brief line refers to the manuscript of his article, "Saint Joan of Arc," presented to the museum at Rouen.

To Edward E. Clarke:

21 FIFTH AVE., Feb., 1906.

DEAR SIR,—I have found the original manuscript and with great pleasure I transmit it herewith, also a printed copy.

It is a matter of great pride to me to have any word of mine concerning the world's supremest heroine honored by a place in that Museum.

Sincerely yours,

S. L. CLEMENS.

The series of letters which follows was prepared by Mark Twain and General Fred Grant, mainly with a view of advertising the lecture that Clemens had agreed to deliver for the benefit of the Robert Fulton Monument Association. It was, in fact, to be Mark Twain's "farewell lecture," and the association had really proposed to pay him a thousand dollars for it. The exchange of these letters, however, was never made outside of Mark Twain's bed-room. Propped against the pillows, pen in hand, with General Grant beside him, they arranged the series with the idea of publication. Later the plan was discarded, so that this pleasant foolery appears here for the first, time.

PRIVATE AND CONFIDENTIAL

(Correspondence)

Telegram

Army Headquarters (date)

MARK TWAIN, New York,—Would you consider a proposal to talk at Carnegie Hall for the benefit of the Robert Fulton Monument Association, of which you are a Vice President, for a fee of a thousand dollars?

F. D. GRANT,

President,

Fulton Monument Association.

Telegraphic Answer:

MAJOR-GENERAL F. D. GRANT, Army Headquarters,—I shall be glad to do it, but I must stipulate that you keep the thousand dollars and add it to the Monument fund as my contribution.

CLEMENS.

Letters:

DEAR MR. CLEMENS,—You have the thanks of the Association, and the terms shall be as you say. But why give all of it? Why not reserve a portion—why should you do this work wholly without compensation?

Truly yours

FRED. D. GRANT.

MAJOR GENERAL GRANT, Army Headquarters.

DEAR GENERAL,—Because I stopped talking for pay a good many years ago, and I could not resume the habit now without a great deal of personal discomfort. I love to hear myself talk, because I get so much instruction and moral upheaval out of it, but I lose the bulk of this joy when I charge for it. Let the terms stand.

General, if I have your approval, I wish to use this good occasion to retire permanently from the platform.

Truly yours

S. L. CLEMENS.

DEAR MR. CLEMENS,—Certainly. But as an old friend, permit me to say, Don't do that. Why should you?—you are not old yet.

Yours truly,

FRED D. GRANT.

DEAR GENERAL,—I mean the pay-platform; I shan't retire from the gratis-platform until after I am dead and courtesy requires me to keep still and not disturb the others.

What shall I talk about? My idea is this: to instruct the audience about Robert Fulton, and.... Tell me—was that his real name, or was it his nom de plume? However, never mind, it is not important—I can skip it, and the house will think I knew all about it, but forgot. Could you find out for me if he was one of the Signers of the Declaration, and which one? But if it is any trouble, let it alone, I can skip it. Was he out with Paul Jones? Will you ask Horace Porter? And ask him if he brought both of them home. These will be very interesting facts, if they can be established. But never mind, don't trouble Porter, I can establish them anyway. The way I look at it, they are historical gems—gems of the very first water.

Well, that is my idea, as I have said: first, excite the audience with a spoonful of information about Fulton, then quiet down with a barrel of illustration drawn by memory from my books—and if you don't say anything the house will think they never heard of it before, because people don't really read your books, they only say they do, to keep you from feeling bad. Next, excite the house with another spoonful of Fultonian fact, then tranquilize them again with another barrel of illustration. And so on and so on, all through the evening; and if you are discreet and don't tell them the illustrations don't illustrate anything, they won't notice it and I will send them home as well-informed about Robert Fulton as I am myself. Don't be afraid; I know all about audiences, they believe everything you say, except when you are telling the truth.

Truly yours,

S. L. CLEMENS.

P.S. Mark all the advertisements "Private and Confidential," otherwise the people will not read them.

M. T.

DEAR MR. CLEMENS,—How long shall you talk? I ask in order that we may be able to say when carriages may be called.

Very Truly yours,

HUGH GORDON MILLER,

Secretary.

DEAR MR. MILLER,—I cannot say for sure. It is my custom to keep on talking till I get the audience cowed. Sometimes it takes an hour and fifteen minutes, sometimes I can do it in an hour.

Sincerely yours,

S. L. CLEMENS.

Mem. My charge is 2 boxes free. Not the choicest—sell the choicest, and give me any 6-seat boxes you please.

S. L. C.

I want Fred Grant (in uniform) on the stage; also the rest of the officials of the Association; also other distinguished people—all the attractions we can get. Also, a seat for Mr. Albert Bigelow Paine, who may be useful to me if he is near me and on the front.

S. L. C.

The seat chosen for the writer of these notes was to be at the front of the stage in order that the lecturer might lean over now and then and pretend to be asking information concerning Fulton. I was not entirely happy in the thought of this showy honor, and breathed more freely when this plan was abandoned and the part assigned to General Grant.

The lecture was given in Carnegie Hall, which had been gayly decorated for the occasion. The house was more than filled, and a great sum of money was realized for the fund.

It was that spring that Gorky and Tchaikowski, the Russian revolutionists, came to America hoping to arouse interest in their cause. The idea of the overthrow of the Russian dynasty was pleasant to Mark Twain. Few things would have given him greater comfort than to have known that a little more than ten years would see the downfall of Russian imperialism. The letter which follows was a reply to an invitation from Tchaikowski, urging him to speak at one of the meetings.

DEAR MR. TCHAIKOWSKI,—I thank you for the honor of the invitation, but I am not able to accept it, because on Thursday evening I shall be presiding at a meeting whose object is to find remunerative work for certain classes of our blind who would gladly support themselves if they had the opportunity.

My sympathies are with the Russian revolution, of course. It goes without saying. I hope it will succeed, and now that I have talked with you I take heart to believe it will. Government by falsified promises; by lies, by treacheries, and by the butcher-knife for the aggrandizement of a single family of drones and its idle and vicious kin has been borne quite long enough in Russia, I should think, and it is to be hoped that the roused nation, now rising in its strength, will presently put an end to it and set up the republic in its place. Some of us, even of the white headed, may live to see the blessed day when Czars and Grand Dukes will be as scarce there as I trust they are in heaven.

Most sincerely yours,

MARK TWAIN.

There came another summer at Dublin, New Hampshire, this time in the fine Upton residence on the other slope of Monadnock, a place of equally beautiful surroundings, and an even more extended view. Clemens was at this time working steadily on his so-called Autobiography, which was not that, in fact, but a series of remarkable chapters, reminiscent, reflective, commentative, written without any particular sequence as to time or subject-matter. He dictated these chapters to a stenographer, usually in the open air, sitting in a comfortable rocker or pacing up and down the long veranda that faced a vast expanse of wooded slope and lake and distant blue mountains. It became one of the happiest occupations of his later years.

To W. D. Howells, in Maine:

DUBLIN, Sunday, June 17, '06.

DEAR HOWELLS,—..... The dictating goes lazily and pleasantly on. With intervals. I find that I have been at it, off and on, nearly two hours a day for 155 days, since Jan. 9. To be exact I've dictated 75 hours in 80 days and loafed 75 days. I've added 60,000 words in the month that I've been here; which indicates that I've dictated during 20 days of that time—40 hours, at an average of 1,500 words an hour. It's a plenty, and I am satisfied.

There's a good deal of "fat" I've dictated, (from Jan. 9) 210,000 words, and the "fat" adds about 50,000 more.

The "fat" is old pigeon-holed things, of the years gone by, which I or editors didn't das't to print. For instance, I am dumping in the little old book which I read to you in Hartford about 30 years ago and which you said "publish—and ask Dean Stanley to furnish an introduction; he'll do it." ("Captain Stormfield's Visit to Heaven.") It reads quite to suit me, without altering a word, now that it isn't to see print until I am dead.

To-morrow I mean to dictate a chapter which will get my heirs and assigns burnt alive if they venture to print it this side of 2006 A.D.—which I judge they won't. There'll be lots of such chapters if I live 3 or 4 years longer. The edition of A.D. 2006 will make a stir when it comes out. I shall be hovering around taking notice, along with other dead pals. You are invited.

MARK.

His tendency to estimate the measure of the work he was doing, and had completed, must have clung to him from his old printer days.

The chapter which was to get his heirs and assigns burned alive was on the orthodox God, and there was more than one such chapter. In the next letter he refers to two exquisite poems by Howells, and the writer of these notes recalls his wonderful reading of them aloud. 'In Our Town' was a collection of short stories then recently issued by William Allen White. Howells had recommended them.

To W. D. Howells, in Maine:

21 FIFTH AVE., Tuesday Eve.

DEAR HOWELLS,—It is lovely of you to say those beautiful things—I don't know how to thank you enough. But I love you, that I know.

I read "After the Wedding" aloud and we felt all the pain of it and the truth. It was very moving and very beautiful—would have been overcomingly moving, at times, but for the haltings and pauses compelled by the difficulties of MS—these were a protection, in that they furnished me time to brace up my voice, and get a new start. Jean wanted to keep the MS for another reading-aloud, and for "keeps," too, I suspected, but I said it would be safest to write you about it.

I like "In Our Town," particularly that Colonel, of the Lookout Mountain Oration, and very particularly pages 212-16. I wrote and told White so.

After "After the Wedding" I read "The Mother" aloud and sounded its human deeps with your deep-sea lead. I had not read it before, since it was first published.

I have been dictating some fearful things, for 4 successive mornings—for no eye but yours to see until I have been dead a century—if then. But I got them out of my system, where they had been festering for years—and that was the main thing. I feel better, now.

I came down today on business—from house to house in 12 1/2 hours, and expected to arrive dead, but am neither tired nor sleepy.

Yours as always

MARK.

To William Allen White, in Emporia, Kans.:

DUBLIN, NEW HAMPSHIRE,

June 24, 1906.

DEAR MR. WHITE,—Howells told me that "In Our Town" was a charming book, and indeed it is. All of it is delightful when read one's self, parts of it can score finely when subjected to the most exacting of tests—the reading aloud. Pages 197 and 216 are of that grade. I have tried them a couple of times on the family, and pages 212 and 216 are qualified to fetch any house of any country, caste or color, endowed with those riches which are denied to no nation on the planet—humor and feeling.

Talk again—the country is listening.

Sincerely yours,

S. L. CLEMENS.

Witter Bynner, the poet, was one of the editors of McClure's Magazine at this time, but was trying to muster the courage to give up routine work for verse-making and the possibility of poverty. Clemens was fond of Bynner and believed in his work. He did not advise him, however, to break away entirely from a salaried position—at least not immediately; but one day Bynner did so, and reported the step he had taken, with some doubt as to the answer he would receive.

To Witter Bynner, in New York:

DUBLIN, Oct. 5, 1906.

DEAR POET,—You have certainly done right for several good reasons; at least, of them, I can name two:

1. With your reputation you can have your freedom and yet earn your living. 2. if you fall short of succeeding to your wish, your reputation will provide you another job. And so in high approval I suppress the scolding and give you the saintly and fatherly pat instead.

MARK TWAIN.

On another occasion, when Bynner had written a poem to Clara Clemens, her father pretended great indignation that the first poem written by Bynner to any one in his household should not be to him, and threatened revenge. At dinner shortly after he produced from his pocket a slip of paper on which he had set down what he said was "his only poem." He read the lines that follow:

"Of all sad words of tongue or pen,
The saddest are these: It might have been.
Ah, say not so! as life grows longer, leaner, thinner,
We recognize, O God, it might have Bynner!"

He returned to New York in October and soon after was presented by Mrs. H. H. Rogers with a handsome billiard-table.

He had a passion for the game, but had played comparatively little since the old Hartford days of fifteen years before, when a group of his friends used to assemble on Friday nights in the room at the top of the house for long, strenuous games and much hilarity. Now the old fever all came back; the fascinations of the game superseded even his interest in the daily dictations.

To Mrs. H. H. Rogers, in New York:

21 FIFTH AVENUE, Monday, Nov., 1906.

DEAR MRS. ROGERS,—The billiard table is better than the doctors. It is driving out the heartburn in a most promising way. I have a billiardist on the premises, and I walk not less than ten miles every day with the cue in my hand. And the walking is not the whole of the exercise, nor the most health-giving part of it, I think. Through the multitude of the positions and attitudes it brings into play every muscle in the body and exercises them all.

The games begin right after luncheon, daily, and continue until midnight, with 2 hours' intermission for dinner and music. And so it is 9 hours' exercise per day, and 10 or 12 on Sunday. Yesterday and last night it was 12—and I slept until 8 this morning without waking. The billiard table, as a Sabbath breaker can beat any coal-breaker in Pennsylvania, and give it 30 in, the game. If Mr. Rogers will take to daily billiards he can do without doctors and the massageur, I think.

We are really going to build a house on my farm, an hour and a half from New York. It is decided. It is to be built by contract, and is to come within $25,000.

With love and many thanks.

S. L. C.

P.S. Clara is in the sanitarium—till January 28 when her western concert tour will begin. She is getting to be a mighty competent singer. You must know Clara better; she is one of the very finest and completest and most satisfactory characters I have ever met. Others knew it before, but I have always been busy with other matters.

The "billiardist on the premises" was the writer of these notes, who, earlier in the year, had become his biographer, and, in the course of time, his daily companion and friend. The farm mentioned was one which he had bought at Redding, Connecticut, where, later, he built the house known as "Stormfield."

Henry Mills Alden, for nearly forty years editor of Harper's

Magazine, arrived at his seventieth birthday on November 11th that year, and Harper & Brothers had arranged to give him a great dinner in the offices of Franklin Square, where, for half a century, he had been an active force. Mark Twain, threatened with a cold, and knowing the dinner would be strenuous, did not feel able to attend, so wrote a letter which, if found suitable, could be read at the gathering.

To Mr. Henry Alden:

ALDEN,—dear and ancient friend—it is a solemn moment. You have now reached the age of discretion. You have been a long time arriving. Many years ago you docked me on an article because the subject was too old; later, you docked me on an article because the subject was too new; later still, you docked me on an article because the subject was betwixt and between. Once, when I wrote a Letter to Queen Victoria, you did not put it in the respectable part of the Magazine, but interred it in that potter's field, the Editor's Drawer. As a result, she never answered it. How often we recall, with regret, that Napoleon once shot at a magazine editor and missed him and killed a publisher. But we remember, with charity, that his intentions were good.

You will reform, now, Alden. You will cease from these economies, and you will be discharged. But in your retirement you will carry with you the admiration and earnest good wishes of the oppressed and toiling scribes. This will be better than bread. Let this console you when the bread fails.

You will carry with you another thing, too—the affection of the scribes; for they all love you in spite of your crimes. For you bear a kind heart in your breast, and the sweet and winning spirit that charms away all hostilities and animosities, and makes of your enemy your friend and keeps him so. You have reigned over us thirty-six years, and, please God, you shall reign another thirty-six—"and peace to Mahmoud on his golden throne!"

Always yours

MARK

A copyright bill was coming up in Washington and a delegation of authors went down to work for it. Clemens was not the head of the delegation, but he was the most prominent member of it, as well as the most useful. He invited the writer to accompany him, and elsewhere I have told in detail the story of that excursion,—[See Mark Twain; A Biography, chap. ccli,]—which need be but briefly touched upon here.

His work was mainly done aside from that of the delegation. They had him scheduled for a speech, however, which he made without notes and with scarcely any preparation. Meantime he had applied to Speaker Cannon for permission to allow him on the floor of the House, where he could buttonhole the Congressmen. He was not eligible to the floor without having received the thanks of Congress, hence the following letter:

To Hon. Joseph Cannon, House of Representatives:

Dec. 7, 1906.

DEAR UNCLE JOSEPH,—Please get me the thanks of the Congress—not next week but right away. It is very necessary. Do accomplish this for your affectionate old friend right away; by persuasion, if you can, by violence if you must, for it is imperatively necessary that I get on the floor for two or three hours and talk to the members, man by man, in behalf of the support, encouragement and protection of one of the nation's most valuable assets and industries—its literature. I have arguments with me, also a barrel, with liquid in it.

Give me a chance. Get me the thanks of Congress. Don't wait for others; there isn't time. I have stayed away and let Congress alone for seventy-one years and I am entitled to thanks. Congress knows it perfectly well and I have long felt hurt that this quite proper and earned expression of gratitude has been merely felt by the House and never publicly uttered. Send me an order on the Sergeant-at-Arms quick. When shall I come? With love and a benediction.

MARK TWAIN.

This was mainly a joke. Mark Twain did not expect any "thanks," but he did hope for access to the floor, which once, in an earlier day, had been accorded him. We drove to the Capitol and he delivered his letter to "Uncle Joe" by hand. "Uncle Joe" could not give him the privilege of the floor; the rules had become more stringent. He declared they would hang him if he did such a thing. He added that he had a private room down-stairs, where Mark Twain might establish headquarters, and that he would assign his colored servant, Neal, of long acquaintanceship with many of the members, to pass the word that Mark Twain was receiving.

The result was a great success. All that afternoon members of Congress poured into the Speaker's room and, in an atmosphere blue with tobacco smoke, Mark Twain talked the gospel of copyright to his heart's content.

The bill did not come up for passage that session, but Mark Twain lived to see his afternoon's lobbying bring a return. In 1909, Champ Clark, and those others who had gathered around him that afternoon, passed a measure that added fourteen years to the copyright term.

The next letter refers to a proposed lobby of quite a different sort.

To Helen Keller, in Wrentham, Mass.:

21 FIFTH AVENUE,

Dec. 23, '06.

DEAR HELEN KELLER,—... You say, "As a reformer, you know that ideas must be driven home again and again."

Yes, I know it; and by old experience I know that speeches and documents and public meetings are a pretty poor and lame way of accomplishing it. Last year I proposed a sane way—one which I had practiced with success for a quarter of a century—but I wasn't expecting it to get any attention, and it didn't.

Give me a battalion of 200 winsome young girls and matrons, and let me tell them what to do and how to do it, and I will be responsible for shining results. If I could mass them on the stage in front of the audience and instruct them there, I could make a public meeting take hold of itself and do something really valuable for once. Not that the real instruction would be done there, for it wouldn't; it would be previously done privately, and merely repeated there.

But it isn't going to happen—the good old way will be stuck to: there'll be a public meeting: with music, and prayer, and a wearying report, and a verbal description of the marvels the blind can do, and 17 speeches—then the call upon all present who are still alive, to contribute. This hoary program was invented in the idiot asylum, and will never be changed. Its function is to breed hostility to good causes.

Some day somebody will recruit my 200—my dear beguilesome Knights of the Golden Fleece—and you will see them make good their ominous name.

Mind, we must meet! not in the grim and ghastly air of the platform, mayhap, but by the friendly fire—here at 21.

Affectionately your friend,

S. L. CLEMENS.

They did meet somewhat later that winter in the friendly parlors of No. 21, and friends gathered in to meet the marvelous blind girl and to pay tribute to Miss Sullivan (Mrs. Macy) for her almost incredible achievement.

MARK TWAIN'S LETTERS—1853-1866

VOLUME 6

XLVI. LETTERS 1907-08. A DEGREE FROM OXFORD. THE NEW HOME AT REDDING.

The author, J. Howard Moore, sent a copy of his book, The Universal Kinship, with a letter in which he said: "Most humorists have no anxiety except to glorify themselves and add substance to their pocket-books by making their readers laugh. You have shown, on many occasions, that your mission is not simply to antidote the melancholy of a world, but includes a real and intelligent concern for the general welfare of your fellowman."

The Universal Kinship was the kind of a book that Mark Twain appreciated, as his acknowledgment clearly shows.

To Mr. J. Howard Moore:

Feb. 2, '07.

DEAR MR. MOORE, The book has furnished me several days of deep pleasure and satisfaction; it has compelled my gratitude at the same time, since it saves me the labor of stating my own long-cherished opinions and reflections and resentments by doing it lucidly and fervently and irascibly for me.

There is one thing that always puzzles me: as inheritors of the mentality of our reptile ancestors we have improved the inheritance by a thousand grades; but in the matter of the morals which they left us we have gone backward as many grades. That evolution is strange, and to me unaccountable and unnatural. Necessarily we started equipped with their perfect and blemishless morals; now we are wholly destitute; we have no real, morals, but only artificial ones—morals created and preserved by the forced suppression of natural and hellish instincts. Yet we are dull enough to be vain of them. Certainly we are a sufficiently comical invention, we humans.

Sincerely Yours,

S. L. CLEMENS.

Mark Twain's own books were always being excommunicated by some librarian, and the matter never failed to invite the attention and amusement of the press, and the indignation of many correspondents. Usually the books were Tom Sawyer and Huck Finn, the morals of which were not regarded as wholly exemplary. But in 1907 a small library, in a very small town, attained a day's national notoriety by putting the ban on Eve's Diary, not so much on account of its text as for the chaste and exquisite illustrations by Lester Ralph. When the reporters came in a troop to learn about it, the author said: "I believe this time the trouble is mainly with the pictures. I did not draw them. I wish I had—they are so beautiful."

Just at this time, Dr. William Lyon Phelps, of Yale, was giving a literary talk to the Teachers' Club, of Hartford, dwelling on the superlative value of Mark Twain's writings for readers old and young. Mrs. F. G. Whitmore, an old Hartford friend, wrote Clemens of the things that Phelps had said, as consolation for Eve's latest banishment. This gave him a chance to add something to what he had said to the reporters.

To Mrs. Whitmore, in Hartford:

Feb. 7, 1907.

DEAR MRS. WHITMORE,—But the truth is, that when a Library expels a book of mine and leaves an unexpurgated Bible lying around where unprotected youth and age can get hold of it, the deep unconscious irony of it delights me and doesn't anger me. But even if it angered me such words as those of Professor Phelps would take the sting all out. Nobody attaches weight to the freaks of the Charlton Library, but when a man like Phelps speaks, the world gives attention. Some day I hope to meet him and thank him for his courage for saying those things out in public. Custom is, to think a handsome thing in private but tame it down in the utterance.

I hope you are all well and happy; and thereto I add my love.

Sincerely yours,

S. L. CLEMENS.

In May, 1907, Mark Twain was invited to England to receive from Oxford the degree of Literary Doctor. It was an honor that came to him as a sort of laurel crown at the end of a great career, and gratified him exceedingly. To Moberly Bell, of the London Times, he expressed his appreciation. Bell had been over in April and Clemens believed him concerned in the matter.

To Moberly Bell, in London:

21 FIFTH AVENUE, May 3, '07

DEAR MR. BELL,—Your hand is in it! and you have my best thanks. Although I wouldn't cross an ocean again for the price of the ship that carried me, I am glad to do it for an Oxford degree. I shall plan to sail for England a shade before the middle of June, so that I can have a few days in London before the 26th.

Sincerely,

S. L. CLEMENS.

He had taken a house at Tuxedo for the summer, desiring to be near New York City, and in the next letter he writes Mr. Rogers concerning his London plans. We discover, also, in this letter that he has begun work on the Redding home and the cost is to come entirely out of the autobiographical chapters then running in the North American Review. It may be of passing interest to note here that he had the usual house-builder's fortune. He received thirty thousand dollars for the chapters; the house cost him nearly double that amount.

To H. H. Rogers, in New York:

TUXEDO PARK,

May 29, '07.

DEAR ADMIRAL,—Why hang it, I am not going to see you and Mrs. Rogers at all in England! It is a great disappointment. I leave there a month from now—June 29. No, I shall see you; for by your itinerary you are most likely to come to London June 21st or along there. So that is very good and satisfactory. I have declined all engagements but two—Whitelaw Reid (dinner) June 21, and the Pilgrims (lunch), June 25. The Oxford ceremony is June 26. I have paid my return passage in the Minne-something, but it is just possible that I may want to stay in England a week or two longer—I can't tell, yet. I do very much want to meet up with the boys for the last time.

I have signed the contract for the building of the house on my Connecticut farm and specified the cost limit, and work has been begun. The cost has to all come out of a year's instalments of Autobiography in the N. A. Review.

Clara, is winning her way to success and distinction with sure and steady strides. By all accounts she is singing like a bird, and is not afraid on the concert stage any more.

Tuxedo is a charming place; I think it hasn't its equal anywhere.

Very best wishes to you both.

S. L. C.

The story of Mark Twain's extraordinary reception and triumph in England has been told.—[Mark Twain; A Biography, chaps. cclvi-cclix]—It was, in fact, the crowning glory of his career. Perhaps one of the most satisfactory incidents of his sojourn was a dinner given to him by the staff of Punch, in the historic offices at 10 Bouverie Street where no other foreign visitor had been thus honored—a notable distinction. When the dinner ended, little joy Agnew, daughter of the chief editor, entered and presented to the chief guest the original drawing of a cartoon by Bernard Partridge, which had appeared on the front page of Punch. In this picture the presiding genius of the paper is offering to Mark Twain health, long life, and happiness from "The Punch Bowl."

A short time after his return to America he received a pretty childish letter from little Miss Agnew acknowledging a photograph he had sent her, and giving a list of her pets and occupations. Such a letter always delighted Mark Twain, and his pleasure in this one is reflected in his reply.

To Miss Joy Agnew, in London:

TUXEDO PARK, NEW YORK.

Unto you greetings and salutation and worship, you dear, sweet little rightly-named Joy! I can see you now almost as vividly as I saw you that night when you sat flashing and beaming upon those sombre swallow-tails.

"Fair as a star when only one

Is shining in the sky."

Oh, you were indeed the only one—there wasn't even the remotest chance of competition with you, dear! Ah, you are a decoration, you little witch!

The idea of your house going to the wanton expense of a flower garden!—aren't you enough? And what do you want to go and discourage the other flowers for? Is that the right spirit? is it considerate? is it kind? How do you suppose they feel when you come around—looking the way you look? And you so pink and sweet and dainty and lovely and supernatural? Why, it makes them feel embarrassed and artificial, of course; and in my opinion it is just as pathetic as it can be. Now then you want to reform—dear—and do right.

Well certainly you are well off, Joy:

3 bantams;

3 goldfish;

3 doves;

6 canaries;

2 dogs;

1 cat;

All you need, now, to be permanently beyond the reach of want, is one more dog—just one more good, gentle, high principled, affectionate, loyal dog who wouldn't want any nobler service than the golden privilege of lying at your door, nights, and biting everything that came along—and I am that very one, and ready to come at the dropping of a hat.

Do you think you could convey my love and thanks to your "daddy" and Owen Seaman and those other oppressed and down-trodden subjects of yours, you darling small tyrant?

On my knees! These—with the kiss of fealty from your other subject—

MARK TWAIN

Elinor Glyn, author of Three Weeks and other erotic tales, was in America that winter and asked permission to call on Mark Twain. An appointment was made and Clemens discussed with her, for an hour or more, those crucial phases of life which have made living a complex problem since the days of Eve in Eden. Mrs. Glyn had never before heard anything like Mark Twain's wonderful talk, and she was anxious to print their interview. She wrote what she could remember of it and sent it to him for approval. If his conversation had been frank, his refusal was hardly less so.

To Mrs. Elinor Glyn, in New York:

Jan. 22, '08.

DEAR MRS. GLYN, It reads pretty poorly—I get the sense of it, but it is a poor literary job; however, it would have to be that because nobody can be reported even approximately, except by a stenographer. Approximations, synopsized speeches, translated poems, artificial flowers and chromos all have a sort of value, but it is small. If you had put upon paper what I really said it would have wrecked your type-machine. I said some fetid, over-vigorous things, but that was because it was a confidential conversation. I said nothing for print. My own report of the same conversation reads like Satan roasting a Sunday school. It, and certain other readable chapters of my autobiography will not be published until all the Clemens family are dead—dead and correspondingly indifferent. They were written to entertain me, not the rest of the world. I am not here to do good—at least not to do it intentionally. You must pardon me for dictating this letter; I am sick a-bed and not feeling as well as I might.

Sincerely Yours,

S. L. CLEMENS.

Among the cultured men of England Mark Twain had no greater admirer, or warmer friend, than Andrew Lang. They were at one on most literary subjects, and especially so in their admiration of the life and character of Joan of Arc. Both had written of her, and both held her to be something almost more than mortal. When, therefore, Anatole France published his exhaustive biography of the maid of Domremy, a book in which he followed, with exaggerated minuteness and innumerable footnotes, every step of Joan's physical career at the expense of her spiritual life, which he was inclined to cheapen, Lang wrote feelingly, and with some contempt, of the performance, inviting the author of the Personal Recollections to come to the rescue of their heroine. "Compare every one of his statements with the passages he cites from authorities, and make him the laughter of the world" he wrote. "If you are lazy about comparing I can make you a complete set of what the authorities say, and of what this amazing novelist says that they say. When I tell you that he thinks the Epiphany (January 6, Twelfth Night) is December 25th—Christmas Day-you begin to see what an egregious ass he is. Treat him like Dowden, and oblige"—a reference to Mark Twain's defense of Harriet Shelley, in which he had heaped ridicule on Dowden's Life of the Poet—a masterly performance; one of the best that ever came from Mark Twain's pen.

Lang's suggestion would seem to have been a welcome one.

To Andrew Lang, in London:

NEW YORK, April 25, 1908.

DEAR MR. LANG,—I haven't seen the book nor any review of it, but only not very-understandable references to it—of a sort which discomforted me, but of course set my interest on fire. I don't want to have to read it in French—I should lose the nice shades, and should do a lot of gross misinterpreting, too. But there'll be a translation soon, nicht wahr? I will wait for it. I note with joy that you say: "If you are lazy about comparing, (which I most certainly am), I can make you a complete set of what the authorities say, and of what this amazing novelist says that they say."

Ah, do it for me! Then I will attempt the article, and (if I succeed in doing it to my satisfaction,) will publish it. It is long since I touched a pen (3 1/2 years), and I was intending to continue this happy holiday to the gallows, but—there are things that could beguile me to break this blessed Sabbath.

Yours very sincerely,

S. L. CLEMENS.

Certainly it is an interesting fact that an Englishman—one of the race that burned Joan—should feel moved to defend her memory against the top-heavy perversions of a distinguished French author.

But Lang seems never to have sent the notes. The copying would have been a tremendous task, and perhaps he never found the time for it. We may regret to-day that he did not, for Mark Twain's article on the French author's Joan would have been at least unique.

Samuel Clemens could never accustom himself to the loss of his wife. From the time of her death, marriage-which had brought him his greatest joy in life-presented itself to him always with the thought of bereavement, waiting somewhere just behind. The news of an approaching wedding saddened him and there was nearly always a somber tinge in his congratulations, of which the following to a dear friend is an example:

To Father Fitz-Simon, in Washington:

June 5, '08.

DEAR FATHER FITZ-SIMON,—Marriage—yes, it is the supreme felicity of life, I concede it. And it is also the supreme tragedy of life. The deeper the love the surer the tragedy. And the more disconsolating when it comes.

And so I congratulate you. Not perfunctorily, not lukewarmly, but with a fervency and fire that no word in the dictionary is strong enough to convey.

And in the same breath and with the same depth and sincerity, I grieve for you. Not for both of you and not for the one that shall go first, but for the one that is fated to be left behind. For that one there is no recompense.—For that one no recompense is possible.

There are times—thousands of times—when I can expose the half of my mind, and conceal the other half, but in the matter of the tragedy of marriage I feel too deeply for that, and I have to bleed it all out or shut it all in. And so you must consider what I have been through, and am passing through and be charitable with me.

Make the most of the sunshine! and I hope it will last long—ever so long.

I do not really want to be present; yet for friendship's sake and because I honor you so, I would be there if I could.

Most sincerely your friend,

S. L. CLEMENS.

The new home at Redding was completed in the spring of 1908, and on the 18th of June, when it was entirely fitted and furnished, Mark Twain entered it for the first time. He had never even seen the place nor carefully examined plans which John Howells had made for his house. He preferred the surprise of it, and the general avoidance of detail. That he was satisfied with the result will be seen in his letters. He named it at first "Innocence at Home"; later changing this title to "Stormfield."

The letter which follows is an acknowledgment of an interesting souvenir from the battle-field of Tewksbury (1471), and some relics of the Cavalier and Roundhead Regiments encamped at Tewksbury in 1643.

To an English admirer:

INNOCENCE AT HOME, REDDING, CONNECTICUT,

Aug. 15, '08.

DEAR SIR,—I highly prize the pipes, and shall intimate to people that "Raleigh" smoked them, and doubtless he did. After a little practice I shall be able to go further and say he did; they will then be the most interesting features of my library's decorations. The Horse-shoe is attracting a good deal of attention, because I have intimated that the conqueror's horse cast it; it will attract more when I get my hand in and say he cast it, I thank you for the pipes and the shoe; and also for the official guide, which I read through at a single sitting. If a person should say that about a book of mine I should regard it as good evidence of the book's interest.

Very truly yours,

S. L. CLEMENS.

In his philosophy, What Is Man?, and now and again in his other writings, we find Mark Twain giving small credit to the human mind as an originator of ideas. The most original writer of his time, he took no credit for pure invention and allowed none to others. The mind, he declared, adapted, consciously or unconsciously; it did not create. In a letter which follows he elucidates this doctrine. The reference in it to the "captain" and to the kerosene, as the reader may remember, have to do with Captain "Hurricane" Jones and his theory of the miracles of "Isaac and of the prophets of Baal," as expounded in Some Rambling Notes of an Idle Excursion.

By a trick of memory Clemens gives The Little Duke as his suggestion for The Prince and the Pauper; he should have written The Prince and the Page, by the same author.

To Rev. F. Y. Christ, in New York:

REDDING, CONN., Aug., '08.

DEAR SIR,—You say "I often owe my best sermons to a suggestion received in reading or from other exterior sources." Your remark is not quite in accordance with the facts. We must change it to—"I owe all my thoughts, sermons and ideas to suggestions received from sources outside of myself." The simplified English of this proposition is—"No man's brains ever originated an idea." It is an astonishing thing that after all these ages the world goes on thinking the human brain machinery can originate a thought.

It can't. It never has done it. In all cases, little and big, the thought is born of a suggestion; and in all cases the suggestions come to the brain from the outside. The brain never acts except from exterior impulse.

A man can satisfy himself of the truth of this by a single process,—let him examine every idea that occurs to him in an hour; a day; in a week—in a lifetime if he please. He will always find that an outside something suggested the thought, something which he saw with his eyes or heard with his ears or perceived by his touch—not necessarily to-day, nor yesterday, nor last year, nor twenty years ago, but sometime or other. Usually the source of the suggestion is immediately traceable, but sometimes it isn't.

However, if you will examine every thought that occurs to you for the next two days, you will find that in at least nine cases out of ten you can put your finger on the outside suggestion—And that ought to convince you that No. 10 had that source too, although you cannot at present hunt it down and find it.

The idea of writing to me would have had to wait a long time if it waited until your brain originated it. It was born of an outside suggestion—Sir Thomas and my old Captain.

The hypnotist thinks he has invented a new thing—suggestion. This is very sad. I don't know where my captain got his kerosene idea. (It was forty-one years ago, and he is long ago dead.) But I know that it didn't originate in his head, but it was born from a suggestion from the outside.

Yesterday a guest said, "How did you come to think of writing 'The Prince and the Pauper?'" I didn't. The thought came to me from the outside—suggested by that pleasant and picturesque little history-book, Charlotte M. Yonge's "Little Duke," I doubt if Mrs. Burnett knows whence came to her the suggestion to write "Little Lord Fauntleroy," but I know; it came to her from reading "The Prince and the Pauper." In all my life I have never originated an idea, and neither has she, nor anybody else.

Man's mind is a clever machine, and can work up materials into ingenious fancies and ideas, but it can't create the material; none but the gods can do that. In Sweden I saw a vast machine receive a block of wood, and turn it into marketable matches in two minutes. It could do everything but make the wood. That is the kind of machine the human mind is. Maybe this is not a large compliment, but it is all I can afford.....

Your friend and well-wisher

S. L. CLEMENS.

To Mrs. H. H. Rogers, in Fair Hawn, Mass.:

REDDING, CONN, Aug. 12, 1908.

DEAR MRS. ROGERS, I believe I am the wellest man on the planet to-day, and good for a trip to Fair Haven (which I discussed with the Captain of the New Bedford boat, who pleasantly accosted me in the Grand Central August 5) but the doctor came up from New York day before yesterday, and gave positive orders that I must not stir from here before frost. It is because

I was threatened with a swoon, 10 or 12 days ago, and went to New York a day or two later to attend my nephew's funeral and got horribly exhausted by the heat and came back here and had a bilious collapse. In 24 hours I was as sound as a nut again, but nobody believes it but me.

This is a prodigiously satisfactory place, and I am so glad I don't have to go back to the turmoil and rush of New York. The house stands high and the horizons are wide, yet the seclusion is perfect. The nearest public road is half a mile away, so there is nobody to look in, and I don't have to wear clothes if I don't want to. I have been down stairs in night-gown and slippers a couple of hours, and have been photographed in that costume; but I will dress, now, and behave myself.

That doctor had half an idea that there is something the matter with my brain... Doctors do know so little and they do charge so much for it. I wish Henry Rogers would come here, and I wish you would come with him. You can't rest in that crowded place, but you could rest here, for sure! I would learn bridge, and entertain you, and rob you.

With love to you both,

Ever yours,

S. L. C.

In the foregoing letter we get the first intimation of Mark Twain's failing health. The nephew who had died was Samuel E. Moffett, son of Pamela Clemens. Moffett, who was a distinguished journalist—an editorial writer on Collier's Weekly, a man beloved by all who knew him—had been drowned in the surf off the Jersey beach.

To W. D. Howells, Kittery Point, Maine:

Aug. 12, '08.

DEAR HOWELLS,—Won't you and Mrs. Howells and Mildred come

and give us as many days as you can spare, and examine John's triumph? It is the most satisfactory house I am acquainted with, and the most satisfactorily situated.

But it is no place to work in, because one is outside of it all the time, while the sun and the moon are on duty. Outside of it in the loggia, where the breezes blow and the tall arches divide up the scenery and frame it.

It's a ghastly long distance to come, and I wouldn't travel such a distance to see anything short of a memorial museum, but if you can't come now you can at least come later when you return to New York, for the journey will be only an hour and a half per express-train. Things are gradually and steadily taking shape inside the house, and nature is taking care of the outside in her ingenious and wonderful fashion—and she is competent and asks no help and gets none. I have retired from New York for good, I have retired from labor for good, I have dismissed my stenographer and have entered upon a holiday whose other end is in the cemetery.

Yours ever,

MARK.

From a gentleman in Buffalo Clemens one day received a letter inclosing an incompleted list of the world's "One Hundred Greatest Men," men who had exerted "the largest visible influence on the life and activities of the race." The writer asked that Mark Twain examine the list and suggest names, adding "would you include Jesus, as the founder of Christianity, in the list?"

To the list of statesmen Clemens added the name of Thomas Paine; to the list of inventors, Edison and Alexander Graham Bell. The question he answered in detail.

To ———, Buffalo, N. Y.

Private. REDDING, CONN, Aug. 28, '08.

DEAR SIR,—By "private," I mean don't print any remarks of mine.

....

I like your list.

The "largest visible influence."

These terms require you to add Jesus. And they doubly and trebly require you to add Satan. From A.D. 350 to A.D. 1850 these gentlemen exercised a vaster influence over a fifth part of the human race than was exercised over that fraction of the race by all other influences combined. Ninety-nine hundredths of this influence proceeded from Satan, the remaining fraction of it from Jesus. During those 1500 years the fear of Satan and Hell made 99 Christians where love of God and Heaven landed one. During those 1500 years, Satan's influence was worth very nearly a hundred times as much to the business as was the influence of all the rest of the Holy Family put together.

You have asked me a question, and I have answered it seriously and sincerely. You have put in Buddha—a god, with a following, at one time, greater than Jesus ever had: a god with perhaps a little better evidence of his godship than that which is offered for Jesus's. How then, in fairness, can you leave Jesus out? And if you put him in, how can you logically leave Satan out? Thunder is good, thunder is impressive; but it is the lightning that does the work.

Very truly yours,

S. L. CLEMENS.

The "Children's Theatre" of the next letter was an institution of the New York East Side in which Mark Twain was deeply interested. The children were most, if not all, of Hebrew parentage, and the performances they gave, under the direction of Alice M. Herts, were really remarkable. It seemed a pity that lack of funds should have brought this excellent educational venture to an untimely end.

The following letter was in reply to one inclosing a newspaper clipping reporting a performance of The Prince and the Pauper, given by Chicago school children.

To Mrs. Hookway, in Chicago:

Sept., 1908.

DEAR MRS. HOOKWAY,—Although I am full of the spirit of work this morning, a rarity with me lately—I must steal a moment or two for a word in person: for I have been reading the eloquent account in the Record-Herald and am pleasurably stirred, to my deepest deeps. The reading brings vividly back to me my pet and pride. The Children's Theatre of the East side, New York. And it supports and re-affirms what I have so often and strenuously said in public that a children's theatre is easily the most valuable adjunct that any educational institution for the young can have, and that no otherwise good school is complete without it.

It is much the most effective teacher of morals and promoter of good conduct that the ingenuity of man has yet devised, for the reason that its lessons are not taught wearily by book and by dreary homily, but by visible and enthusing action; and they go straight to the heart, which is the rightest of right places for them. Book morals often get no further than the intellect, if they even get that far on their spectral and shadowy pilgrimage: but when they travel from a Children's Theatre they do not stop permanently at that halfway house, but go on home.

The children's theatre is the only teacher of morals and conduct and high ideals that never bores the pupil, but always leaves him sorry when the lesson is over. And as for history, no other teacher is for a moment comparable to it: no other can make the dead heroes of the world rise up and shake the dust of the ages from their bones and live and move and breathe and speak and be real to the looker and listener: no other can make the study of the lives and times of the illustrious dead a delight, a splendid interest, a passion; and no other can paint a history-lesson in colors that will stay, and stay, and never fade.

It is my conviction that the children's theatre is one of the very, very great inventions of the twentieth century; and that its vast educational value—now but dimly perceived and but vaguely understood—will presently come to be recognized. By the article which I have been reading I find the same things happening in the Howland School that we have become familiar with in our Children's Theatre (of which I am President, and sufficiently vain of the distinction.) These things among others;

1. The educating history-study does not stop with the little players, but the whole school catches the infection and revels in it.

2. And it doesn't even stop there; the children carry it home and infect the family with it—even the parents and grandparents; and the whole household fall to studying history, and bygone manners and customs and costumes with eager interest. And this interest is carried along to the studying of costumes in old book-plates; and beyond that to the selecting of fabrics and the making of clothes. Hundreds of our children learn, the plays by listening without book, and by making notes; then the listener goes home and plays the piece—all the parts! to the family. And the family are glad and proud; glad to listen to the explanations and analyses, glad to learn, glad to be lifted to planes above their dreary workaday lives. Our children's theatre is educating 7,000 children—and their families. When we put on a play of Shakespeare they fall to studying it diligently; so that they may be qualified to enjoy it to the limit when the piece is staged.

3. Your Howland School children do the construction-work, stage-decorations, etc. That is our way too. Our young folks do everything that is needed by the theatre, with their own hands; scene-designing, scene-painting, gas-fitting, electric work, costume-designing—costume making, everything

and all things indeed—and their orchestra and its leader are from their own ranks.

The article which I have been reading, says—speaking of the historical play produced by the pupils of the Howland School—

"The question naturally arises, What has this drama done for those who so enthusiastically took part?—The touching story has made a year out of the Past live for the children as could no chronology or bald statement of historical events; it has cultivated the fancy and given to the imagination strength and purity; work in composition has ceased to be drudgery, for when all other themes fall flat a subject dealing with some aspect of the drama presented never fails to arouse interest and a rapid pushing of pens over paper."

That is entirely true. The interest is not confined to the drama's story, it spreads out all around the period of the story, and gives to all the outlying and unrelated happenings of that period a fascinating interest—an interest which does not fade out with the years, but remains always fresh, always inspiring, always welcome. History-facts dug by the job, with sweat and tears out of a dry and spiritless text-book—but never mind, all who have suffered know what that is...

I remain, dear madam,

Sincerely yours,

S. L. CLEMENS.

Mark Twain had a special fondness for cats. As a boy he always owned one and it generally had a seat beside him at the table. There were cats at Quarry Farm and at Hartford, and in the house at Redding there was a gray mother-cat named Tammany, of which he was especially fond. Kittens capering about were his chief delight. In a letter to a Chicago woman he tells how those of Tammany assisted at his favorite game.

To Mrs. Mabel Larkin Patterson, in Chicago:

REDDING, CONNECTICUT,

Oct. 2, '08.

DEAR MRS. PATTERSON,—The contents of your letter are very pleasant and very welcome, and I thank you for them, sincerely. If I can find a photograph of my "Tammany" and her kittens, I will enclose it in this.

One of them likes to be crammed into a corner-pocket of the billiard table—which he fits as snugly as does a finger in a glove and then he watches the game (and obstructs it) by the hour, and spoils many a shot by putting out his paw and changing the direction of a passing ball. Whenever a ball is in his arms, or so close to him that it cannot be played upon without risk of hurting him, the player is privileged to remove it to anyone of the 3 spots that chances to be vacant.

Ah, no, my lecturing days are over for good and all.

Sincerely yours,

S. L. CLEMENS.

The letter to Howells which follows was written a short time before the passage of the copyright extension bill, which rendered Mark Twain's new plan, here mentioned, unneeded—at least for the time.

To W. D. Howells, in New York:

Monday, Oct. 26, '08.

Oh, I say! Where are you hiding, and why are you hiding? You promised to come here and you didn't keep your word. (This sounds like astonishment—but don't be misled by that.)

Come, fire up again on your fiction-mill and give us another good promise. And this time keep it—for it is your turn to be astonished. Come and stay as long as you possibly can. I invented a new copyright extension scheme last Friday, and sat up all night arranging its details. It will interest you. Yesterday I got it down on paper in as compact a form as I could. Harvey and I have examined the scheme, and to-morrow or next day he will send me a couple of copyright-experts to arrange about getting certain statistics for me.

Authors, publishers and the public have always been damaged by the copyright laws. The proposed amendment will advantage all three—the public most of all. I think Congress will pass it and settle the vexed question permanently.

I shall need your assent and the assent of about a dozen other authors. Also the assent of all the large firms of the 300 publishers. These authors and publishers will furnish said assent I am sure. Not even the pirates will be able to furnish a serious objection, I think.

Come along. This place seemed at its best when all around was summer-green; later it seemed at its best when all around was burning with the autumn splendors; and now once more it seems at its best, with the trees naked and the ground a painter's palette.

Yours ever,

MARK.

Clemens was a great admirer of the sea stories of W. W. Jacobs and generally kept one or more of this author's volumes in reach of his bed, where most of his reading was done. The acknowledgment that follows was sent when he had finished Salthaven.

To W. W. Jacobs, in England:

REDDING, CONN,

Oct. 28, '08.

DEAR MR. JACOBS,—It has a delightful look. I will not venture to say how delightful, because the words would sound extravagant, and would thereby lose some of their strength and to that degree misrepresent me. It is my conviction that Dialstone Lane holds the supremacy over all purely humorous books in our language, but I feel about Salthaven as the Cape Cod poet feels about Simon Hanks:

"The Lord knows all things, great and small,

With doubt he's not perplexed:

'Tis Him alone that knows it all

But Simon Hanks comes next."

The poet was moved by envy and malice and jealousy, but I am not: I place Salthaven close up next to Dialstone because I think it has a fair and honest right to that high position. I have kept the other book moving; I shall begin to hand this one around now.

And many thanks to you for remembering me.

This house is out in the solitudes of the woods and the hills, an hour and a half from New York, and I mean to stay in it winter and summer the rest of my days. I beg you to come and help occupy it a few days the next time you visit the U.S.

Sincerely yours,

S. L. CLEMENS.

One of the attractions of Stormfield was a beautiful mantel in the billiard room, presented by the Hawaiian Promotion Committee. It had not arrived when the rest of the house was completed, but came in time to be set in place early in the morning of the owner's seventy-third birthday. It was made of a variety of Hawaiian woods, and was the work of a native carver, F. M. Otremba. Clemens was deeply touched by the offering from those "western isles"—the memory of which was always so sweet to him.

To Mr. Wood, in Hawaii:

Nov. 30, '08.

DEAR MR. WOOD,—The beautiful mantel was put in its place an hour ago, and its friendly "Aloha" was the first uttered greeting my 73rd birthday received. It is rich in color, rich in quality, and rich in decoration, therefore it exactly harmonizes with the taste for such things which was born in me and which I have seldom been able to indulge to my content. It will be a great pleasure to me, daily renewed, to have under my eye this lovely reminder of the loveliest fleet of islands that lies anchored in any ocean, and I beg to thank the Committee for providing me that pleasure.

Sincerely Yours,

S. L. CLEMENS.

XLVII. LETTERS, 1909. TO HOWELLS AND OTHERS. LIFE AT STORMFIELD. COPYRIGHT EXTENSION. DEATH OF JEAN CLEMENS

Clemens remained at Stormfield all that winter. New York was sixty miles away and he did not often care to make the journey. He was constantly invited to this or that public gathering, or private party, but such affairs had lost interest for him. He preferred the quiet of his luxurious home with its beautiful outlook, while for entertainment he found the billiard afternoons sufficient. Guests came from the city, now and again, for week-end visits, and if he ever was restless or lonely he did not show it.

Among the invitations that came was one from General O. O. Howard asking him to preside at a meeting to raise an endowment fund for a Lincoln Memorial University at Cumberland Gap, Tennessee. Closing his letter, General Howard said, "Never mind if you did fight on the other side."

To General O. O. Howard:

STORMFIELD, REDDING, CONNECTICUT,

Jan, 12, '09.

DEAR GENERAL HOWARD,—You pay me a most gratifying compliment in asking me to preside, and it causes me very real regret that I am obliged to decline, for the object of the meeting appeals strongly to me, since that object is to aid in raising the $500,000 Endowment Fund for

Lincoln Memorial University. The Endowment Fund will be the most fitting of all the memorials the country will dedicate to the memory of Lincoln, serving, as it will, to uplift his very own people.

I hope you will meet with complete success, and I am sorry I cannot be there to witness it and help you rejoice. But I am older than people think, and besides I live away out in the country and never stir from home, except at geological intervals, to fill left-over engagements in mesozoic times when I was younger and indiscreeter.

You ought not to say sarcastic things about my "fighting on the other side." General Grant did not act like that. General Grant paid me compliments. He bracketed me with Zenophon—it is there in his Memoirs for anybody to read. He said if all the confederate soldiers had followed my example and adopted my military arts he could never have caught enough of them in a bunch to inconvenience the Rebellion. General Grant was a fair man, and recognized my worth; but you are prejudiced, and you have hurt my feelings.

But I have an affection for you, anyway.

MARK TWAIN.

One of Mark Twain's friends was Henniker-Heaton, the so-called "Father of Penny Postage" between England and America. When, after long years of effort, he succeeded in getting the rate established, he at once bent his energies in the direction of cheap cable service and a letter from him came one day to Stormfield concerning his new plans. This letter happened to be over-weight, which gave Mark Twain a chance for some amusing exaggerations at his expense.

To Henniker-Heaton, in London:

STORMFIELD, REDDING, CONNECTICUT,

Jan. 18, 1909.

DEAR HENNIKER-HEATON,—I do hope you will succeed to your heart's desire in your cheap-cablegram campaign, and I feel sure you will. Indeed your cheap-postage victory, achieved in spite of a quarter-century of determined opposition, is good and rational prophecy that you will. Wireless, not being as yet imprisoned in a Chinese wall of private cash and high-placed and formidable influence, will come to your aid and make your new campaign briefer and easier than the other one was.

Now then, after uttering my serious word, am I privileged to be frivolous for a moment? When you shall have achieved cheap telegraphy, are you going to employ it for just your own selfish profit and other people's pecuniary damage, the way you are doing with your cheap postage? You get letter-postage reduced to 2 cents an ounce, then you mail me a 4-ounce letter with a 2-cent stamp on it, and I have to pay the extra freight at this end of the line. I return your envelope for inspection. Look at it. Stamped in one place is a vast "T," and under it the figures "40," and under those figures appears an "L," a sinister and suspicious and mysterious L. In another place, stamped within a circle, in offensively large capitals, you find the words "DUE 8 CENTS." Finally, in the midst of a desert space up nor-noreastard from that circle you find a figure "3" of quite unnecessarily aggressive and insolent magnitude—and done with a blue pencil, so as to be as conspicuous as possible. I inquired about these strange signs and symbols of the postman. He said they were P. O. Department signals for his instruction.

"Instruction for what?"

"To get extra postage."

"Is it so? Explain. Tell me about the large T and the 40.

"It's short for Take 40—or as we postmen say, grab 40"

"Go on, please, while I think up some words to swear with."

"Due 8 means, grab 8 more."

"Continue."

"The blue-pencil 3 was an afterthought. There aren't any stamps for afterthoughts; the sums vary, according to inspiration, and they whirl in the one that suggests itself at the last moment. Sometimes they go several times higher than this one. This one only means hog 3 cents more. And so if you've got 51 cents about you, or can borrow it—"

"Tell me: who gets this corruption?"

"Half of it goes to the man in England who ships the letter on short postage, and the other half goes to the P.O.D. to protect cheap postage from inaugurating a deficit."

"______________________."

"I can't blame you; I would say it myself in your place, if these ladies were not present. But you see I'm only obeying orders, I can't help myself."

"Oh, I know it; I'm not blaming you. Finally, what does that L stand for?"

"Get the money, or give him L. It's English, you know."

"Take it and go. It's the last cent I've got in the world—."

After seeing the Oxford pageant file by the grand stand, picture after picture, splendor after splendor, three thousand five hundred strong, the most moving and beautiful and impressive and historically-instructive show conceivable, you are not to think I would miss the London pageant of next year, with its shining host of 15,000 historical English men and women dug from the misty books of all the vanished ages and marching in the light of the sun—all alive, and looking just as they were used to look! Mr. Lascelles spent yesterday here on the farm, and told me all about it. I shall be in the middle of my 75th year then, and interested in pageants for personal and prospective reasons.

I beg you to give my best thanks to the Bath Club for the offer of its hospitalities, but I shall not be able to take advantage of it, because I am to be a guest in a private house during my stay in London.

Sincerely yours,

S. L. CLEMENS.

It was in 1907 that Clemens had seen the Oxford Pageant—during the week when he had been awarded his doctor's degree. It gave him the greatest delight, and he fully expected to see the next one, planned for 1910.

In the letter to Howells which follows we get another glimpse of Mark Twain's philosophy of man, the irresponsible machine.

To W. D. Howells, in New York:

STORMFIELD, REDDING, CONN.,

Jan. 18, '09.

DEAR HOWELLS,—I have to write a line, lazy as I am, to say how your Poe article delighted me; and to say that I am in agreement with substantially all you say about his literature. To me his prose is unreadable—like Jane Austin's. No, there is a difference. I could read his prose on salary, but not Jane's. Jane is entirely impossible. It seems a great pity that they allowed her to die a natural death.

Another thing: you grant that God and circumstances sinned against Poe, but you also grant that he sinned against himself—a thing which he couldn't do and didn't do.

It is lively up here now. I wish you could come.

Yrs ever,

MARK

To W. D. Howells, in New York:

STORMFIELD, REDDING, CONNECTICUT,

3 in the morning, Apl. 17, '09.

[Written with pencil].

My pen has gone dry and the ink is out of reach. Howells, Did you write me day-before-day before yesterday, or did I dream it? In my mind's eye I most vividly see your hand-write on a square blue envelop in the mailpile. I have hunted the house over, but there is no such letter. Was it an illusion?

I am reading Lowell's letter, and smoking. I woke an hour ago and am reading to keep from wasting the time. On page 305, vol. I. I have just margined a note:

"Young friend! I like that! You ought to see him now."

It seemed startlingly strange to hear a person call you young. It was a brick out of a blue sky, and knocked me groggy for a moment. Ah me, the pathos of it is, that we were young then. And he—why, so was he, but he didn't know it. He didn't even know it 9 years later, when we saw him approaching and you warned me, saying, "Don't say anything about age—he has just turned fifty, and thinks he is old and broods over it."

[Well, Clara did sing! And you wrote her a dear letter.]

Time to go to sleep.

Yours ever,

MARK.

To Daniel Kiefer:

[No date.]

DANL KIEFER ESQ. DEAR SIR,—I should be far from willing to have a political party named after me.

I would not be willing to belong to a party which allowed its members to have political aspirations or to push friends forward for political preferment.

Yours very truly,

S. L. CLEMENS.

The copyright extension, for which the author had been working so long, was granted by Congress in 1909, largely as the result of that afternoon in Washington when Mark Twain had "received" in "Uncle Joe" Cannon's private room, and preached the gospel of copyright until the daylight faded and the rest of the Capitol grew still. Champ Clark was the last to linger that day and they had talked far into the dusk. Clark was powerful, and had fathered the bill. Now he wrote to know if it was satisfactory.

To Champ Clark, in Washington:

STORMFIELD, REDDING, CONN., June 5, '09.

DEAR CHAMP CLARK—Is the new copyright law acceptable to me? Emphatically, yes! Clark, it is the only sane, and clearly defined, and just and righteous copyright law that has ever existed in the United States. Whosoever will compare it with its predecessors will have no trouble in arriving at that decision.

The bill which was before the committee two years ago when I was down there was the most stupefying jumble of conflicting and apparently irreconcilable interests that was ever seen; and we all said "the case is hopeless, absolutely hopeless—out of this chaos nothing can be built." But we were in error; out of that chaotic mass this excellent bill has been instructed; the warring interests have been reconciled, and the result is as comely and substantial a legislative edifice as lifts its domes and towers and protective lightning rods out of the statute book, I think. When I think of that other bill, which even the Deity couldn't understand, and of this one which even I can understand, I take off my hat to the man or men who devised this one. Was it R. U. Johnson? Was it the Author's League? Was it both together? I don't know, but I take off my hat, anyway. Johnson has written a valuable article about the new law—I enclose it.

At last—at last and for the first time in copyright history we are ahead of England! Ahead of her in two ways: by length of time and by fairness to all interests concerned. Does this sound like shouting? Then I must modify it: all we possessed of copyright-justice before the fourth of last March we owed to England's initiative.

Truly Yours,

S. L. CLEMENS.

Because Mark Twain amused himself with certain aspects of Christian Science, and was critical of Mrs. Eddy, there grew up a wide impression that he jeered at the theory of mental healing; when, as a matter of fact, he was one of its earliest converts, and never lost faith in its power. The letter which follows is an excellent exposition of his attitude toward the institution of Christian Science and the founder of the church in America.

To J. Wylie Smith, Glasgow, Scotland:

"STORMFIELD," August 7, 1909

DEAR SIR,—My view of the matter has not changed. To wit, that Christian Science is valuable; that it has just the same value now that it had when Mrs. Eddy stole it from Quimby; that its healing principle (its most valuable asset) possesses the same force now that it possessed a million years ago before Quimby was born; that Mrs. Eddy... organized that force, and is entitled to high credit for that. Then, with a splendid sagacity she hitched it to... a religion, the surest of all ways to secure friends for it, and support. In a fine and lofty way—figuratively speaking—it was a tramp stealing a ride on the lightning express. Ah, how did that ignorant village-born peasant woman know the human being so well? She has no more intellect than a tadpole—until it comes to business then she is a marvel! Am I sorry I wrote the book? Most certainly not. You say you have 500 (converts) in Glasgow. Fifty years from now, your posterity will not count them by the hundred, but by the thousand. I feel absolutely sure of this.

Very truly yours,

S. L. CLEMENS.

Clemens wrote very little for publication that year, but he enjoyed writing for his own amusement, setting down the things that boiled, or bubbled, within him: mainly chapters on the inconsistencies of human deportment, human superstition and human creeds. The "Letters from the Earth" referred to in the following, were supposed to have been written by an immortal visitant from some far realm to a friend, describing the absurdities of mankind. It is true, as he said, that they would not do for publication, though certainly the manuscript contains some of his most delicious writing. Miss Wallace, to whom the next letter is written, had known Mark Twain in Bermuda, and, after his death, published a dainty volume entitled Mark Twain in the Happy Island.

"STORMFIELD," REDDING, CONNECTICUT,

Nov. 13, '09.

DEAR BETSY,—I've been writing "Letters from the Earth," and if you will come here and see us I will—what? Put the MS in your hands, with the places to skip marked? No. I won't trust you quite that far. I'll read messages to you. This book will never be published—in fact it couldn't be, because it would be felony to soil the mails with it, for it has much Holy Scripture in it of the kind that... can't properly be read aloud, except from the pulpit and in family worship. Paine enjoys it, but Paine is going to be damned one of these days, I suppose.

The autumn splendors passed you by? What a pity. I wish you had been here. It was beyond words! It was heaven and hell and sunset and rainbows and the aurora all fused into one divine harmony, and you couldn't look at it and keep the tears back. All the hosannahing strong gorgeousnesses have gone back to heaven and hell and the pole, now, but no matter; if you could look out of my bedroom window at this moment, you would choke up; and when you got your voice you would say: This is not real, this is a dream. Such a singing together, and such a whispering together, and such a snuggling together of cosy soft colors, and such kissing and caressing, and such pretty blushing when the sun breaks out and catches those dainty weeds at it—you remember that weed-garden of mine?—and then—then the far hills sleeping in a dim blue trance—oh, hearing about it is nothing, you should be here to see it.

Good! I wish I could go on the platform and read. And I could, if it could be kept out of the papers. There's a charity-school of 400 young girls in Boston that I would give my ears to talk to, if I had some more; but—oh, well, I can't go, and it's no use to grieve about it.

This morning Jean went to town; also Paine; also the butler; also Katy; also the laundress. The cook and the maid, and the boy and the roustabout and Jean's coachman are left—just enough to make it lonesome, because they are around yet never visible. However, the Harpers are sending Leigh up to play billiards; therefore I shall survive.

Affectionately,

S. L. CLEMENS.

Early in June that year, Clemens had developed unmistakable symptom of heart trouble of a very serious nature. It was angina pectoris, and while to all appearances he was as well as ever and usually felt so, he was periodically visited by severe attacks of acute "breast pains" which, as the months passed, increased in frequency and severity. He was alarmed and distressed—not on his own account, but because of his daughter Jean—a handsome girl, who had long been subject to epileptic seizures. In case of his death he feared that Jean would be without permanent anchorage, his other daughter, Clara—following her marriage to Ossip Gabrilowitsch in October —having taken up residence abroad.

This anxiety was soon ended. On the morning of December 24th, Jean Clemens was found dead in her apartment. She was not drowned in her bath, as was reported, but died from heart exhaustion, the result of her malady and the shock of cold water.

[Questionable diagnosis! D.W. M.D.]

The blow to her father was terrible, but heavy as it was, one may perhaps understand that her passing in that swift, painless way must have afforded him a measure of relief.

To Mrs. Gabrilowitsch, in Europe:

REDDING, CONN.,

Dec. 29, '09.

O, Clara, Clara dear, I am so glad she is out of it and safe—safe! I am not melancholy; I shall never be melancholy again, I think. You see, I was in such distress when I came to realize that you were gone far away and no one stood between her and danger but me—and I could die at any moment, and then—oh then what would become of her! For she was wilful, you know, and would not have been governable.

You can't imagine what a darling she was, that last two or three days; and how fine, and good, and sweet, and noble-and joyful, thank Heaven!—and how intellectually brilliant. I had never been acquainted with Jean before. I recognized that.

But I mustn't try to write about her—I can't. I have already poured my heart out with the pen, recording that last day or two.

I will send you that—and you must let no one but Ossip read it.

Good-bye.

I love you so!

And Ossip.

FATHER.

The writing mentioned in the last paragraph was his article 'The Death of Jean,' his last serious writing, and one of the world's most beautiful examples of elegiac prose.—[Harper's Magazine, Dec., 1910,] and later in the volume, 'What Is Man and Other Essays.'

XLVIII. LETTERS OF 1910. LAST TRIP TO BERMUDA. LETTERS TO PAINE. THE LAST LETTER.

Mark Twain had returned from a month's trip to Bermuda a few days before Jean died. Now, by his physician's advice, he went back to those balmy islands. He had always loved them, since his first trip there with Twichell thirty-three years earlier, and at "Bay House," the residence of Vice-Consul Allen, where he was always a welcome guest, he could have the attentions and care and comforts of a home. Taking Claude, the butler, as his valet, he sailed January 5th, and presently sent back a letter in which he said, "Again I am leading the ideal life, and am immeasurably content."

By his wish, the present writer and his family were keeping the Stormfield house open for him, in order that he might be able to return to its comforts at any time. He sent frequent letters—one or two by each steamer—but as a rule they did not concern matters of general interest. A little after his arrival, however, he wrote concerning an incident of his former visit—a trivial matter—but one which had annoyed him. I had been with him in Bermuda on the earlier visit, and as I remember it, there had been some slight oversight on his part in the matter of official etiquette—something which doubtless no one had noticed but himself.

To A. B. Paine, in Redding:

BAY HOUSE, Jan. 11, 1910.

DEAR PAINE,—... There was a military lecture last night at the Officer's Mess, prospect, and as the lecturer honored me with a special and urgent invitation and said he wanted to lecture to me particularly, I being "the greatest living master of the platform-art," I naturally packed Helen and her mother into the provided carriage and went.

As soon as we landed at the door with the crowd the Governor came to me at once and was very cordial, and apparently as glad to see me as he said he was. So that incident is closed. And pleasantly and entirely satisfactorily. Everything is all right, now, and I am no longer in a clumsy and awkward situation.

I "met up" with that charming Colonel Chapman, and other officers of the regiment, and had a good time.

Commandant Peters of the "Carnegie" will dine here tonight and arrange a private visit for us to his ship, the crowd to be denied access.

Sincerely Yours,

S. L. C.

"Helen" of this letter was Mr. and Mrs. Allen's young daughter, a favorite companion of his walks and drives. "Loomis" and "Lark," mentioned in the letters which follow, were Edward E. Loomis—his nephew by marriage—named by Mark Twain as one of the trustees of his estate, and Charles T. Lark, Mark Twain's attorney.

To A. B. Paine, in Redding:

HAMILTON, Jan. 21, '10.

DEAR PAINE,—Thanks for your letter, and for its contenting news of the situation in that foreign and far-off and vaguely-remembered country where you and Loomis and Lark and other beloved friends are.

I have a letter from Clara this morning. She is solicitous, and wants me well and watchfully taken care of. My, she ought to see Helen and her parents and Claude administer that trust!

Also she says: "I hope to hear from you or Mr. Paine very soon."

I am writing her, and I know you will respond to your part of her prayer. She is pretty desolate now, after Jean's emancipation—the only kindness God ever did that poor unoffending child in all her hard life.

Ys ever

S. L. C.

Send Clara a copy of Howells's gorgeous letter. I want a copy of my article that he is speaking of.

The "gorgeous letter" was concerning Mark Twain's article, "The Turning-point in My Life" which had just appeared in one of the Harper publications. Howells wrote of it, "While your wonderful words are warm in my mind yet, I want to tell you what you know already: that you never wrote anything greater, finer, than that turning-point paper of yours."

From the early Bermuda letters we may gather that Mark Twain's days were enjoyable enough, and that his malady was not giving him serious trouble, thus far. Near the end of January he wrote: "Life continues here the same as usual. There isn't a flaw in it. Good times, good home, tranquil contentment all day and every day, without a break. I shouldn't know how to go about bettering my situation." He did little in the way of literary work, probably finding neither time nor inclination for it. When he wrote at all it was merely to set down some fanciful drolleries with no thought of publication.

To Prof. William Lyon Phelps, Yale College:

HAMILTON, March 12.

DEAR PROFESSOR PHELPS,—I thank you ever so much for the book—[Professor Phelps's Essays on Modern Novelists.]—which I find charming—so charming indeed, that I read it through in a single night, and did not regret the lost night's sleep. I am glad if I deserve what you have said about me: and even if I don't I am proud and well contented, since you think I deserve it.

Yes, I saw Prof. Lounsbury, and had a most pleasant time with him. He ought to have staid longer in this little paradise—partly for his own sake, but mainly for mine.

I knew my poor Jean had written you. I shall not have so dear and sweet a secretary again.

Good health to you, and all good fortune attend you.

Sincerely yours,

S. L. CLEMENS.

He would appear to have written not many letters besides those to Mrs. Gabrilowitsch and to Stormfield, but when a little girl sent him a report of a dream, inspired by reading The Prince and the

Pauper, he took the time and trouble to acknowledge it, realizing, no doubt, that a line from him would give the child happiness.

To Miss Sulamith, in New York:

"BAY HOUSE," BERMUDA, March 21, 1910.

DEAR MISS SULAMITH,—I think it is a remarkable dream for a girl of 13 to have dreamed, in fact for a person of any age to have dreamed, because it moves by regular grade and sequence from the beginning to the end, which is not the habit of dreams. I think your report of it is a good piece of work, a clear and effective statement of the vision.

I am glad to know you like the "Prince and the Pauper" so well and I believe with you that the dream is good evidence of that liking. I think I may say, with your sister that I like myself best when I am serious.

Sincerely yours,

S. L. CLEMENS.

Through February, and most of March, letters and reports from him were about the same. He had begun to plan for his return, and concerning amusements at Stormfield for the entertainment of the neighbors, and for the benefit of the library which he had founded soon after his arrival in Redding. In these letters he seldom mentioned the angina pains that had tortured him earlier. But once, when he sent a small photograph of himself, it seemed to us that his face had become thin and that he had suffered. Certainly his next letter was not reassuring.

To A. B. Paine, in Redding:

DEAR PAINE,—We must look into the magic-lantern business. Maybe the modern lantern is too elaborate and troublesome for back-settlement use, but we can inquire. We must have some kind of a show at "Stormfield" to entertain the countryside with.

We are booked to sail in the "Bermudian" April 23rd, but don't tell anybody, I don't want it known. I may have to go sooner if the pain in my breast doesn't mend its ways pretty considerably. I don't want to die here for this is an unkind place for a person in that condition. I should have to lie in the undertaker's cellar until the ship would remove me and it is dark down there and unpleasant.

The Colliers will meet me on the pier and I may stay with them a week or two before going home. It all depends on the breast pain—I don't want to die there. I am growing more and more particular about the place.

With love,

S. L. C.

This letter had been written by the hand of his "secretary," Helen Allen: writing had become an effort to him. Yet we did not suspect how rapidly the end was approaching and only grew vaguely alarmed. A week later, however, it became evident that his condition was critical.

DEAR PAINE,—.... I have been having a most uncomfortable time for the past 4 days with that breast-pain, which turns out to be an affection of the heart, just as I originally suspected. The news from New York is to the effect that non-bronchial weather has arrived there at last, therefore if I can get my breast trouble in traveling condition I may sail for home a week or two earlier than has heretofore been proposed:

Yours as ever

S. L. CLEMENS,

(per H. S. A.)

In this letter he seems to have forgotten that his trouble had been pronounced an affection of the heart long before he left America, though at first it had been thought that it might be gastritis. The same mail brought a letter from Mr. Allen explaining fully the seriousness of his condition. I sailed immediately for Bermuda, arriving there on the 4th of April. He was not suffering at the moment, though the pains came now with alarming frequency and violence. He was cheerful and brave. He did not complain. He gave no suggestion of a man whose days were nearly ended.

A part of the Stormfield estate had been a farm, which he had given to Jean Clemens, where she had busied herself raising some live stock and poultry. After her death he had wished the place to be sold and the returns devoted to some memorial purpose. The sale had been made during the winter and the price received had been paid in cash. I found him full of interest in all affairs, and anxious to discuss the memorial plan. A day or two later he dictated the following letter-the last he would ever send.

It seemed fitting that this final word from one who had so long given happiness to the whole world should record a special gift to his neighbors.

To Charles T. Lark, in New York:

HAMILTON, BERMUDA.

April 6, 1910.

DEAR MR. LARK,—I have told Paine that I want the money derived from the sale of the farm, which I had given, but not conveyed, to my daughter Jean, to be used to erect a building for the Mark Twain Library of Redding, the building to be called the Jean L. Clemens Memorial Building.

I wish to place the money $6,000.00 in the hands of three trustees,—Paine and two others: H. A. Lounsbury and William E. Hazen, all of Redding, these trustees to form a building Committee to decide on the size and plan of the building needed and to arrange for and supervise the work in such a manner that the fund shall amply provide for the building complete, with necessary furnishings, leaving, if possible, a balance remaining, sufficient for such repairs and additional furnishings as may be required for two years from the time of completion.

Will you please draw a document covering these requirements and have it ready by the time I reach New York (April 14th).

Very sincerely,

S. L. CLEMENS.

We sailed on the 12th of April, reaching New York on the 14th, as he had planned. A day or two later, Mr. and Mrs. Gabrilowitsch, summoned from Italy by cable, arrived. He suffered very little after reaching Stormfield, and his mind was comparatively clear up to the last day. On the afternoon of April 21st he sank into a state of coma, and just at sunset he died. Three days later, at

Elmira, New York, he was laid beside Mrs. Clemens and those others who had preceded him.

THE LAST DAY AT STORMFIELD

By BLISS CARMAN.

At Redding, Connecticut,
The April sunrise pours
Over the hardwood ridges
Softening and greening now
In the first magic of Spring.

The wild cherry-trees are in bloom,
The bloodroot is white underfoot,
The serene early light flows on,

Touching with glory the world,
And flooding the large upper room
Where a sick man sleeps.
Slowly he opens his eyes,
After long weariness, smiles,
And stretches arms overhead,
While those about him take heart.

With his awakening strength,
(Morning and spring in the air,

The strong clean scents of earth,

The call of the golden shaft,

Ringing across the hills)

He takes up his heartening book,

Opens the volume and reads,

A page of old rugged Carlyle,

The dour philosopher

Who looked askance upon life,

Lurid, ironical, grim,

Yet sound at the core.

But weariness returns;

He lays the book aside

With his glasses upon the bed,

And gladly sleeps. Sleep,

Blessed abundant sleep,

Is all that he needs.

And when the close of day

Reddens upon the hills

And washes the room with rose,

In the twilight hush

The Summoner comes to him

Ever so gently, unseen,

Touches him on the shoulder;

And with the departing sun

Our great funning friend is gone.

How he has made us laugh!

A whole generation of men

Smiled in the joy of his wit.

But who knows whether he was not

Like those deep jesters of old

Who dwelt at the courts of Kings,

Arthur's, Pendragon's, Lear's,

Plying the wise fool's trade,

Making men merry at will,

Hiding their deeper thoughts

Under a motley array,—

Keen-eyed, serious men,

Watching the sorry world,

The gaudy pageant of life,

With pity and wisdom and love?

Fearless, extravagant, wild,

His caustic merciless mirth

Was leveled at pompous shams.

Doubt not behind that mask

There dwelt the soul of a man,
Resolute, sorrowing, sage,
As sure a champion of good
As ever rode forth to fray.

Haply—who knows?—somewhere
In Avalon, Isle of Dreams,
In vast contentment at last,
With every grief done away,
While Chaucer and Shakespeare wait,
And Moliere hangs on his words,
And Cervantes not far off
Listens and smiles apart,
With that incomparable drawl
He is jesting with Dagonet now.

About Author

Samuel Langhorne Clemens (November 30, 1835 – April 21, 1910), known by his pen name Mark Twain, was an American writer, humorist, entrepreneur, publisher, and lecturer. He was lauded as the "greatest humorist this country has produced", and William Faulkner called him "the father of American literature". His novels include The Adventures of Tom Sawyer (1876) and its sequel, the Adventures of Huckleberry Finn (1884), the latter often called "The Great American Novel".

Twain was raised in Hannibal, Missouri, which later provided the setting for Tom Sawyer and Huckleberry Finn. He served an apprenticeship with a printer and then worked as a typesetter, contributing articles to the newspaper of his older brother Orion Clemens. He later became a riverboat pilot on the Mississippi River before heading west to join Orion in Nevada. He referred humorously to his lack of success at mining, turning to journalism for the Virginia City Territorial Enterprise. His humorous story, "The Celebrated Jumping Frog of Calaveras County", was published in 1865, based on a story that he heard at Angels Hotel in Angels Camp, California, where he had spent some time as a miner. The short story brought international attention and was even translated into French. His wit and satire, in prose and in speech, earned praise from critics and peers, and he was a friend to presidents, artists, industrialists, and European royalty.

Twain earned a great deal of money from his writings and lectures, but he invested in ventures that lost most of it—such as the Paige Compositor, a mechanical typesetter that failed because of its complexity and imprecision. He filed for bankruptcy in the wake of these financial setbacks, but he eventually overcame his financial troubles with the help of Henry Huttleston Rogers. He eventually paid all his creditors in full, even though his bankruptcy relieved him of having to do so.

Twain was born shortly after an appearance of Halley's Comet, and he predicted that he would "go out with it" as well; he died the day after the comet returned.

Biography

Early life

Samuel Langhorne Clemens was born on November 30, 1835, in Florida, Missouri, the sixth of seven children born to Jane (née Lampton; 1803–1890), a native of Kentucky, and John Marshall Clemens (1798–1847), a native of Virginia. His parents met when his father moved to Missouri, and they were married in 1823. Twain was of Cornish, English, and Scots-Irish descent. Only three of his siblings survived childhood: Orion (1825–1897), Henry (1838–1858), and Pamela (1827–1904). His sister Margaret (1830–1839) died when Twain was three, and his brother Benjamin (1832–1842) died three years later. His brother Pleasant Hannibal (1828) died at three weeks of age.

When he was four, Twain's family moved to Hannibal, Missouri, a port town on the Mississippi River that inspired the fictional town of St. Petersburg in The Adventures of Tom Sawyer and the Adventures of Huckleberry Finn. Slavery was legal in Missouri at the time, and it became a theme in these writings. His father was an attorney and judge, who died of pneumonia in 1847, when Twain was 11. The next year, Twain left school after the fifth grade to become a printer's apprentice. In 1851, he began working as a typesetter, contributing articles and humorous sketches to the Hannibal Journal, a newspaper that Orion owned. When he was 18, he left Hannibal and worked as a printer in New York City, Philadelphia, St. Louis, and Cincinnati, joining the newly formed International Typographical Union, the printers trade union. He educated himself in public libraries in the evenings, finding wider information than at a conventional school.

Twain describes his boyhood in Life on the Mississippi, stating that "there was but one permanent ambition" among his comrades: to be a steamboatman.

Pilot was the grandest position of all. The pilot, even in those days of trivial wages, had a princely salary – from a hundred and fifty to two hundred and fifty dollars a month, and no board to pay.

As Twain describes it, the pilot's prestige exceeded that of the captain. The pilot had to:

> ...get up a warm personal acquaintanceship with every old snag and one-limbed cottonwood and every obscure wood pile that ornaments the banks of this river for twelve hundred miles; and more than that, must... actually know where these things are in the dark

Steamboat pilot Horace E. Bixby took Twain on as a cub pilot to teach him the river between New Orleans and St. Louis for $500 (equivalent to $14,000 in 2018), payable out of Twain's first wages after graduating. Twain studied the Mississippi, learning its landmarks, how to navigate its currents effectively, and how to read the river and its constantly shifting channels, reefs, submerged snags, and rocks that would "tear the life out of the strongest vessel that ever floated". It was more than two years before he received his pilot's license. Piloting also gave him his pen name from "mark twain", the leadsman's cry for a measured river depth of two fathoms (12 feet), which was safe water for a steamboat.

As a young pilot, Clemens served on the steamer A. B. Chambers with Grant Marsh, who became famous for his exploits as a steamboat captain on the Missouri River. The two liked each other, and admired one another, and maintained a correspondence for many years after Clemens left the river.

While training, Samuel convinced his younger brother Henry to work with him, and even arranged a post of mud clerk for him on the steamboat Pennsylvania. On June 13, 1858, the steamboat's boiler exploded; Henry succumbed to his wounds on June 21. Twain claimed to have foreseen this death in a dream a month earlier, which inspired his interest in parapsychology; he was an early member of the Society for Psychical Research. Twain was guilt-stricken and held himself responsible for the rest of his life. He continued to work on the river and was a river pilot until the Civil War broke out in 1861, when traffic was curtailed along the Mississippi River. At the start of hostilities, he enlisted briefly in a local Confederate unit. He later wrote the sketch "The Private History of a Campaign That Failed", describing how he and his friends had been Confederate volunteers for two weeks before disbanding.

He then left for Nevada to work for his brother Orion, who was Secretary of the Nevada Territory. Twain describes the episode in his book Roughing It.

Travels

Orion became secretary to Nevada Territory governor James W. Nye in 1861, and Twain joined him when he moved west. The brothers traveled more than two weeks on a stagecoach across the Great Plains and the Rocky Mountains, visiting the Mormon community in Salt Lake City.

Twain's journey ended in the silver-mining town of Virginia City, Nevada, where he became a miner on the Comstock Lode. He failed as a miner and went to work at the Virginia City newspaper Territorial Enterprise, working under a friend, the writer Dan DeQuille. He first used his pen name here on February 3, 1863, when he wrote a humorous travel account entitled "Letter From Carson – re: Joe Goodman; party at Gov. Johnson's; music" and signed it "Mark Twain".

His experiences in the American West inspired Roughing It, written during 1870–71 and published in 1872. His experiences in Angels Camp (in Calaveras County, California) provided material for "The Celebrated Jumping Frog of Calaveras County" (1865).

Twain moved to San Francisco in 1864, still as a journalist, and met writers such as Bret Harte and Artemus Ward. He may have been romantically involved with the poet Ina Coolbrith.

His first success as a writer came when his humorous tall tale "The Celebrated Jumping Frog of Calaveras County" was published on November 18, 1865, in the New York weekly The Saturday Press, bringing him national attention. A year later, he traveled to the Sandwich Islands (present-day Hawaii) as a reporter for the Sacramento Union. His letters to the Union were popular and became the basis for his first lectures.

In 1867, a local newspaper funded his trip to the Mediterranean aboard the Quaker City, including a tour of Europe and the Middle East. He wrote a collection of travel letters which were later compiled as The Innocents Abroad (1869). It was on this trip that he met fellow passenger Charles Langdon, who showed him a picture of his sister Olivia. Twain later claimed to have fallen in love at first sight.

Upon returning to the United States, Twain was offered honorary membership in Yale University's secret society Scroll and Key in 1868. Its devotion to "fellowship, moral and literary self-improvement, and charity" suited him well.

Marriage and children

Twain and Olivia Langdon corresponded throughout 1868. She rejected his first marriage proposal, but they were married in Elmira, New York in February 1870, where he courted her and managed to overcome her father's initial reluctance. She came from a "wealthy but liberal family"; through her, he met abolitionists, "socialists, principled atheists and activists for women's rights and social equality", including Harriet Beecher Stowe (his next-door neighbor in Hartford, Connecticut), Frederick Douglass, and writer and utopian socialist William Dean Howells, who became a long-time friend. The couple lived in Buffalo, New York, from 1869 to 1871. He owned a stake in the Buffalo Express newspaper and worked as an editor and writer. While they were living in Buffalo, their son Langdon died of diphtheria at the age of 19 months. They had three daughters: Susy (1872–1896), Clara (1874–1962), and Jean (1880–1909).

Twain moved his family to Hartford, Connecticut, where he arranged the building of a home starting in 1873. In the 1870s and 1880s, the family summered at Quarry Farm in Elmira, the home of Olivia's sister, Susan Crane. In 1874, Susan had a study built apart from the main house so that Twain would have a quiet place in which to write. Also, he smoked cigars constantly, and Susan did not want him to do so in her house.

Twain wrote many of his classic novels during his 17 years in Hartford (1874–1891) and over 20 summers at Quarry Farm. They include The Adventures of Tom Sawyer (1876), The Prince and the Pauper (1881), Life on the Mississippi (1883), Adventures of Huckleberry Finn (1884), and A

Connecticut Yankee in King Arthur's Court (1889).

The couple's marriage lasted 34 years until Olivia's death in 1904. All of the Clemens family are buried in Elmira's Woodlawn Cemetery.

Love of science and technology

Twain was fascinated with science and scientific inquiry. He developed a close and lasting friendship with Nikola Tesla, and the two spent much time together in Tesla's laboratory.

Twain patented three inventions, including an "Improvement in Adjustable and Detachable Straps for Garments" (to replace suspenders) and a history trivia game. Most commercially successful was a self-pasting scrapbook; a dried adhesive on the pages needed only to be moistened before use. Over 25,000 were sold.

Twain was an early proponent of fingerprinting as a forensic technique, featuring it in a tall tale in Life on the Mississippi (1883) and as a central plot element in the novel Pudd'nhead Wilson (1894).

Twain's novel A Connecticut Yankee in King Arthur's Court (1889) features a time traveler from the contemporary U.S., using his knowledge of science to introduce modern technology to Arthurian England. This type of historical manipulation became a trope of speculative fiction as alternate histories.

In 1909, Thomas Edison visited Twain at his home in Redding, Connecticut and filmed him. Part of the footage was used in The Prince and the Pauper (1909), a two-reel short film. It is the only known existing film footage of Twain.

Financial troubles

Twain made a substantial amount of money through his writing, but he lost a great deal through investments. He invested mostly in new inventions and technology, particularly the Paige typesetting machine. It was a beautifully engineered mechanical marvel that amazed viewers when it worked, but it was prone to breakdowns. Twain spent $300,000 (equal to $9,000,000 in inflation-adjusted terms) on it between 1880 and 1894, but before it could be perfected it was rendered obsolete by the Linotype. He lost the bulk of his book profits, as well as a substantial portion of his wife's inheritance.

Twain also lost money through his publishing house, Charles L. Webster and Company, which enjoyed initial success selling the memoirs of Ulysses S. Grant but failed soon afterward, losing money on a biography of Pope Leo XIII. Fewer than 200 copies were sold.

Twain and his family closed down their expensive Hartford home in response to the dwindling income and moved to Europe in June 1891. William M. Laffan of The New York Sun and the McClure Newspaper Syndicate offered him the publication of a series of six European letters. Twain, Olivia, and their daughter Susy were all faced with health problems, and they believed that it would be of benefit to visit European baths. The family stayed mainly in France, Germany, and Italy until May 1895, with longer spells at Berlin (winter 1891/92), Florence (fall and winter 1892/93), and Paris (winters and springs 1893/94 and 1894/95). During that period, Twain returned four times to New York due to his enduring business troubles. He took "a cheap room" in September 1893 at $1.50 per day (equivalent to $42 in 2018) at The Players Club, which he had to keep until March 1894; meanwhile, he became "the Belle of New York," in the words of biographer Albert Bigelow Paine.

Twain's writings and lectures enabled him to recover financially, combined with the help of his friend, Henry Huttleston Rogers. He began a friendship with the financier in 1893, a principal of Standard Oil, that lasted the remainder of his life. Rogers first made him file for bankruptcy in April 1894, then had him transfer the copyrights on his written works to his wife to prevent creditors from gaining possession of them. Finally, Rogers took absolute charge of Twain's money until all his creditors were paid.

Twain accepted an offer from Robert Sparrow Smythe and embarked on a year-long, around the world lecture tour in July 1895 to pay off his creditors in full, although he was no longer under any legal obligation to do so. It was a long, arduous journey and he was sick much of the time, mostly from a cold and a carbuncle. The first part of the itinerary took him across northern America to British Columbia, Canada, until the second half of August. For the second part, he sailed across the Pacific Ocean. His scheduled lecture in Honolulu, Hawaii had to be canceled due to a cholera epidemic. Twain went on to Fiji, Australia, New Zealand, Sri Lanka, India, Mauritius, and South Africa. His three months in India became the centerpiece of his 712-page book Following the Equator. In the second half of July 1896, he sailed back to England, completing his circumnavigation of the world begun 14 months before.

Twain and his family spent four more years in Europe, mainly in England and Austria (October 1897 to May 1899), with longer spells in London and Vienna. Clara had wished to study the piano under Theodor Leschetizky in Vienna. However, Jean's health did not benefit from consulting with specialists in Vienna, the "City of Doctors". The family moved to London in spring 1899, following a lead by Poultney Bigelow who had a good experience being treated by Dr. Jonas Henrik Kellgren, a Swedish osteopathic practitioner in Belgravia. They were persuaded to spend the summer at Kellgren's sanatorium by the lake in the Swedish village of Sanna. Coming back in fall, they continued the treatment in London, until Twain was convinced by lengthy inquiries in America that similar osteopathic expertise was available there.

In mid-1900, he was the guest of newspaper proprietor Hugh Gilzean-Reid at Dollis Hill House, located on the north side of London. Twain wrote that he had "never seen any place that was so satisfactorily situated, with its noble trees and stretch of country, and everything that went to make life delightful, and all within a biscuit's throw of the metropolis of the world." He then returned to America in October 1900, having earned enough to pay off his debts. In winter 1900/01, he became his country's most prominent opponent of imperialism, raising the issue in his speeches, interviews, and writings. In January 1901, he began serving as vice-president of the Anti-Imperialist League of New York.

Speaking engagements

Twain was in great demand as a featured speaker, performing solo humorous talks similar to modern stand-up comedy. He gave paid talks to many men's clubs, including the Authors' Club, Beefsteak Club, Vagabonds, White Friars, and Monday Evening Club of Hartford.

In the late 1890s, he spoke to the Savage Club in London and was elected an honorary member. He was told that only three men had been so honored, including the Prince of Wales, and he replied: "Well, it must make the Prince feel mighty fine." He visited Melbourne and Sydney in 1895 as part of a world lecture tour. In 1897, he spoke to the Concordia Press Club in Vienna as a special guest, following the diplomat Charlemagne Tower, Jr. He delivered the speech "Die Schrecken der Deutschen Sprache" ("The Horrors of the German Language")—in German—to the great amusement of the audience. In 1901, he was invited to speak at Princeton University's Cliosophic Literary Society, where he was made an honorary member.

Canadian visits

In 1881, Twain was honored at a banquet in Montreal, Canada where he made reference to securing a copyright. In 1883, he paid a brief visit to Ottawa, and he visited Toronto twice in 1884 and 1885 on a reading tour with George Washington Cable, known as the "Twins of Genius" tour.

The reason for the Toronto visits was to secure Canadian and British copyrights for his upcoming book Adventures of Huckleberry Finn, to which he had alluded in his Montreal visit. The reason for the Ottawa visit had been to secure Canadian and British copyrights for Life on the Mississippi. Publishers in Toronto had printed unauthorized editions of his books at the time, before an international copyright agreement was established in 1891. These were sold in the United States as well as in Canada, depriving him of royalties. He estimated that Belford Brothers' edition of The Adventures of Tom Sawyer alone had cost him ten thousand dollars (equivalent to $280,000 in 2018). He had unsuccessfully attempted to secure the rights for The Prince and the Pauper in 1881, in conjunction with his Montreal trip. Eventually, he received legal advice to register a copyright in Canada (for both Canada and Britain) prior to publishing in the United States, which would restrain the Canadian publishers from printing a version when the American edition was published. There was a requirement that a copyright be registered to a Canadian resident; he addressed this by his short visits to the country.

Later life and death

... the report is greatly exaggerated.

—Twain's reaction to a report of his death

Twain lived in his later years at 14 West 10th Street in Manhattan. He passed through a period of deep depression which began in 1896 when his daughter Susy died of meningitis. Olivia's death in 1904 and Jean's on December 24, 1909, deepened his gloom. On May 20, 1909, his close friend Henry Rogers died suddenly. In 1906, Twain began his autobiography in the North American Review. In April, he heard that his friend Ina Coolbrith had lost nearly all that she owned in the 1906 San Francisco earthquake, and he volunteered a few autographed portrait photographs to be sold for her benefit. To further aid Coolbrith, George Wharton James visited Twain in New York and arranged for a new portrait session. He was resistant initially, but he eventually admitted that four of the resulting images were the finest ones ever taken of him.

Twain formed a club in 1906 for girls whom he viewed as surrogate granddaughters called the Angel Fish and Aquarium Club. The dozen or so members ranged in age from 10 to 16. He exchanged letters with his "Angel Fish" girls and invited them to concerts and the theatre and to play games. Twain wrote in 1908 that the club was his "life's chief delight". In 1907, he met Dorothy Quick (aged 11) on a transatlantic crossing, beginning "a friendship that was to last until the very day of his death".

Oxford University awarded Twain an honorary doctorate in letters in 1907.

Twain was born two weeks after Halley's Comet's closest approach in 1835; he said in 1909:

I came in with Halley's Comet in 1835. It is coming again next year, and I expect to go out with it. It will be the greatest disappointment of my life if

I don't go out with Halley's Comet. The Almighty has said, no doubt: "Now here are these two unaccountable freaks; they came in together, they must go out together".

Twain's prediction was accurate; he died of a heart attack on April 21, 1910, in Redding, Connecticut, one day after the comet's closest approach to Earth.

Upon hearing of Twain's death, President William Howard Taft said:

Mark Twain gave pleasure – real intellectual enjoyment – to millions, and his works will continue to give such pleasure to millions yet to come ... His humor was American, but he was nearly as much appreciated by Englishmen and people of other countries as by his own countrymen. He has made an enduring part of American literature.

Twain's funeral was at the Brick Presbyterian Church on Fifth Avenue, New York. He is buried in his wife's family plot at Woodlawn Cemetery in Elmira, New York. The Langdon family plot is marked by a 12-foot monument (two fathoms, or "mark twain") placed there by his surviving daughter Clara. There is also a smaller headstone. He expressed a preference for cremation (for example, in Life on the Mississippi), but he acknowledged that his surviving family would have the last word.

Officials in Connecticut and New York estimated the value of Twain's estate at $471,000 ($13,000,000 today).

Writing

Overview

Twain began his career writing light, humorous verse, but he became a chronicler of the vanities, hypocrisies, and murderous acts of mankind. At mid-career, he combined rich humor, sturdy narrative, and social criticism in Huckleberry Finn. He was a master of rendering colloquial speech and helped to create and popularize a distinctive American literature built on American themes and language.

Many of his works have been suppressed at times for various reasons. The

Adventures of Huckleberry Finn has been repeatedly restricted in American high schools, not least for its frequent use of the word "nigger", which was in common usage in the pre-Civil War period in which the novel was set.

A complete bibliography of Twain's works is nearly impossible to compile because of the vast number of pieces he wrote (often in obscure newspapers) and his use of several different pen names. Additionally, a large portion of his speeches and lectures have been lost or were not recorded; thus, the compilation of Twain's works is an ongoing process. Researchers rediscovered published material as recently as 1995 and 2015.

Early journalism and travelogues

Twain was writing for the Virginia City newspaper the Territorial Enterprise in 1863 when he met lawyer Tom Fitch, editor of the competing newspaper Virginia Daily Union and known as the "silver-tongued orator of the Pacific". He credited Fitch with giving him his "first really profitable lesson" in writing. "When I first began to lecture, and in my earlier writings," Twain later commented, "my sole idea was to make comic capital out of everything I saw and heard." In 1866, he presented his lecture on the Sandwich Islands to a crowd in Washoe City, Nevada. Afterwards, Fitch told him:

Clemens, your lecture was magnificent. It was eloquent, moving, sincere. Never in my entire life have I listened to such a magnificent piece of descriptive narration. But you committed one unpardonable sin – the unpardonable sin. It is a sin you must never commit again. You closed a most eloquent description, by which you had keyed your audience up to a pitch of the intensest interest, with a piece of atrocious anti-climax which nullified all the really fine effect you had produced.

It was in these days that Twain became a writer of the Sagebrush School; he was known later as its most famous member. His first important work was "The Celebrated Jumping Frog of Calaveras County," published in the New York Saturday Press on November 18, 1865. After a burst of popularity, the Sacramento Union commissioned him to write letters about his travel experiences. The first journey that he took for this job was to ride the steamer Ajax on its maiden voyage to the Sandwich Islands (Hawaii).

All the while, he was writing letters to the newspaper that were meant for publishing, chronicling his experiences with humor. These letters proved to be the genesis to his work with the San Francisco Alta California newspaper, which designated him a traveling correspondent for a trip from San Francisco to New York City via the Panama isthmus.

On June 8, 1867, he set sail on the pleasure cruiser Quaker City for five months, and this trip resulted in The Innocents Abroad or The New Pilgrims' Progress. In 1872, he published his second piece of travel literature, Roughing It, as an account of his journey from Missouri to Nevada, his subsequent life in the American West, and his visit to Hawaii. The book lampoons American and Western society in the same way that Innocents critiqued the various countries of Europe and the Middle East. His next work was The Gilded Age: A Tale of Today, his first attempt at writing a novel. The book, written with his neighbor Charles Dudley Warner, is also his only collaboration.

Twain's next work drew on his experiences on the Mississippi River. Old Times on the Mississippi was a series of sketches published in the Atlantic Monthly in 1875 featuring his disillusionment with Romanticism. Old Times eventually became the starting point for Life on the Mississippi.

Tom Sawyer and Huckleberry Finn

Twain's next major publication was The Adventures of Tom Sawyer, which draws on his youth in Hannibal. Tom Sawyer was modeled on Twain as a child, with traces of schoolmates John Briggs and Will Bowen. The book also introduces Huckleberry Finn in a supporting role, based on Twain's boyhood friend Tom Blankenship.

The Prince and the Pauper was not as well received, despite a storyline that is common in film and literature today. The book tells the story of two boys born on the same day who are physically identical, acting as a social commentary as the prince and pauper switch places. Twain had started Adventures of Huckleberry Finn (which he consistently had problems completing) and had completed his travel book A Tramp Abroad, which describes his travels through central and southern Europe.

Twain's next major published work was the Adventures of Huckleberry Finn, which confirmed him as a noteworthy American writer. Some have called it the first Great American Novel, and the book has become required reading in many schools throughout the United States. Huckleberry Finn was an offshoot from Tom Sawyer and had a more serious tone than its predecessor. Four hundred manuscript pages were written in mid-1876, right after the publication of Tom Sawyer. The last fifth of Huckleberry Finn is subject to much controversy. Some say that Twain experienced a "failure of nerve," as critic Leo Marx puts it. Ernest Hemingway once said of Huckleberry Finn:

If you read it, you must stop where the Nigger Jim is stolen from the boys. That is the real end. The rest is just cheating.

Hemingway also wrote in the same essay:

All modern American literature comes from one book by Mark Twain called Huckleberry Finn.

Near the completion of Huckleberry Finn, Twain wrote Life on the Mississippi, which is said to have heavily influenced the novel. The travel work recounts Twain's memories and new experiences after a 22-year absence from the Mississippi River. In it, he also explains that "Mark Twain" was the call made when the boat was in safe water, indicating a depth of two fathoms (12 feet or 3.7 metres).

Later writing

Twain produced President Ulysses S. Grant's Memoirs through his fledgling publishing house, Charles L. Webster & Company, which he co-owned with Charles L. Webster, his nephew by marriage.

At this time he also wrote "The Private History of a Campaign That Failed" for The Century Magazine. This piece detailed his two-week stint in a Confederate militia during the Civil War. He next focused on A Connecticut Yankee in King Arthur's Court, written with the same historical fiction style as The Prince and the Pauper. A Connecticut Yankee showed the absurdities of political and social norms by setting them in the court of King Arthur. The book was started in December 1885, then shelved a few months later until the summer of 1887, and eventually finished in the spring of 1889.

His next large-scale work was Pudd'nhead Wilson, which he wrote rapidly, as he was desperately trying to stave off bankruptcy. From November 12 to December 14, 1893, Twain wrote 60,000 words for the novel. Critics[who?] have pointed to this rushed completion as the cause of the novel's rough organization and constant disruption of the plot. This novel also contains the tale of two boys born on the same day who switch positions in life, like The Prince and the Pauper. It was first published serially in Century Magazine and, when it was finally published in book form, Pudd'nhead Wilson appeared as the main title; however, the "subtitles" make the entire title read: The Tragedy of Pudd'nhead Wilson and the Comedy of The Extraordinary Twins.

Twain's next venture was a work of straight fiction that he called Personal Recollections of Joan of Arc and dedicated to his wife. He had long said[where?] that this was the work that he was most proud of, despite the criticism that he received for it. The book had been a dream of his since childhood, and he claimed that he had found a manuscript detailing the life of Joan of Arc when he was an adolescent. This was another piece that he was convinced would save his publishing company. His financial adviser Henry Huttleston Rogers quashed that idea and got Twain out of that business altogether, but the book was published nonetheless.[citation needed]

To pay the bills and keep his business projects afloat, Twain had begun to write articles and commentary furiously, with diminishing returns, but it was not enough. He filed for bankruptcy in 1894. During this time of dire financial straits, he published several literary reviews in newspapers to help make ends meet. He famously derided James Fenimore Cooper in his article detailing Cooper's "Literary Offenses". He became an extremely outspoken critic of other authors and other critics; he suggested that, before praising Cooper's work, Thomas Lounsbury, Brander Matthews, and Wilkie Collins "ought to have read some of it".

George Eliot, Jane Austen, and Robert Louis Stevenson also fell under Twain's attack during this time period, beginning around 1890 and continuing until his death. He outlines what he considers to be "quality writing" in several letters and essays, in addition to providing a source for the "tooth and claw" style of literary criticism. He places emphasis on concision, utility of word choice, and realism; he complains, for example, that Cooper's Deerslayer purports to be realistic but has several shortcomings. Ironically, several of his own works were later criticized for lack of continuity (Adventures of Huckleberry Finn) and organization (Pudd'nhead Wilson).

Twain's wife died in 1904 while the couple were staying at the Villa di Quarto in Florence. After some time had passed he published some works that his wife, his de facto editor and censor throughout her married life, had looked down upon. The Mysterious Stranger is perhaps the best known, depicting various visits of Satan to earth. This particular work was not published in Twain's lifetime. His manuscripts included three versions, written between 1897 and 1905: the so-called Hannibal, Eseldorf, and Print Shop versions. The resulting confusion led to extensive publication of a jumbled version, and only recently have the original versions become available as Twain wrote them.

Twain's last work was his autobiography, which he dictated and thought would be most entertaining if he went off on whims and tangents in non-chronological order. Some archivists and compilers have rearranged the biography into a more conventional form, thereby eliminating some of Twain's humor and the flow of the book. The first volume of the autobiography, over 736 pages, was published by the University of California in November 2010, 100 years after his death, as Twain wished. It soon became an unexpected best-seller, making Twain one of a very few authors publishing new best-selling volumes in the 19th, 20th, and 21st centuries.

Censorship

Twain's works have been subjected to censorship efforts. According to Stuart (2013), "Leading these banning campaigns, generally, were religious organizations or individuals in positions of influence – not so much working librarians, who had been instilled with that American "library spirit" which honored intellectual freedom (within bounds of course)". In 1905, the Brooklyn Public Library banned both The Adventures of Huckleberry Finn and The Adventures of Tom Sawyer from the children's department because of their language.

Views

Twain's views became more radical as he grew older. In a letter to friend and fellow writer William Dean Howells in 1887 he acknowledged that his views had changed and developed over his lifetime, referring to one of his favorite works:

When I finished Carlyle's French Revolution in 1871, I was a Girondin; every time I have read it since, I have read it differently – being influenced and changed, little by little, by life and environment ... and now I lay the book down once more, and recognize that I am a Sansculotte! And not a pale, characterless Sansculotte, but a Marat.

Anti-imperialist

Before 1899, Twain was an ardent imperialist. In the late 1860s and early 1870s, he spoke out strongly in favor of American interests in the Hawaiian Islands. He said the war with Spain in 1898 was "the worthiest" war ever fought. In 1899, however, he reversed course. In the New York Herald, October 16, 1900, Twain describes his transformation and political awakening, in the context of the Philippine–American War, to anti-imperialism:

I wanted the American eagle to go screaming into the Pacific ... Why not spread its wings over the Philippines, I asked myself? ... I said to myself, Here are a people who have suffered for three centuries. We can make them as free as ourselves, give them a government and country of their own, put a miniature of the American Constitution afloat in the Pacific, start a brand new republic to take its place among the free nations of the world. It seemed to me a great task to which we had addressed ourselves.

But I have thought some more, since then, and I have read carefully the treaty of Paris [which ended the Spanish–American War], and I have seen that we do not intend to free, but to subjugate the people of the Philippines. We have gone there to conquer, not to redeem.

It should, it seems to me, be our pleasure and duty to make those people free, and let them deal with their own domestic questions in their own way. And so I am an anti-imperialist. I am opposed to having the eagle put its talons on any other land.

During the Boxer rebellion, Twain said that "the Boxer is a patriot. He loves his country better than he does the countries of other people. I wish him success."

From 1901, soon after his return from Europe, until his death in 1910, Twain was vice-president of the American Anti-Imperialist League, which opposed the annexation of the Philippines by the United States and had "tens of thousands of members". He wrote many political pamphlets for the organization. The Incident in the Philippines, posthumously published in 1924, was in response to the Moro Crater Massacre, in which six hundred Moros were killed. Many of his neglected and previously uncollected writings on anti-imperialism appeared for the first time in book form in 1992.

Twain was critical of imperialism in other countries as well. In Following the Equator, Twain expresses "hatred and condemnation of imperialism of all stripes". He was highly critical of European imperialists, such as Cecil Rhodes, who greatly expanded the British Empire, and Leopold II, King of the Belgians. King Leopold's Soliloquy is a stinging political satire about his private colony, the Congo Free State. Reports of outrageous exploitation and grotesque abuses led to widespread international protest in the early 1900s, arguably the first large-scale human rights movement. In the soliloquy, the King argues that bringing Christianity to the country outweighs a little starvation. Leopold's rubber gatherers were tortured, maimed and slaughtered until the movement forced Brussels to call a halt.

During the Philippine–American War, Twain wrote a short pacifist story titled The War Prayer, which makes the point that humanism and Christianity's preaching of love are incompatible with the conduct of war. It was submitted to Harper's Bazaar for publication, but on March 22, 1905, the magazine rejected the story as "not quite suited to a woman's magazine". Eight days later, Twain wrote to his friend Daniel Carter Beard, to whom he had read the story, "I don't think the prayer will be published in my time. None but the dead are permitted to tell the truth." Because he had an exclusive contract with Harper & Brothers, Twain could not publish The War Prayer elsewhere; it remained unpublished until 1923. It was republished as campaigning material by Vietnam War protesters.

Twain acknowledged that he had originally sympathized with the more moderate Girondins of the French Revolution and then shifted his sympathies to the more radical Sansculottes, indeed identifying himself as "a Marat" and writing that the Reign of Terror paled in comparison to the older terrors that preceded it. Twain supported the revolutionaries in Russia against the reformists, arguing that the Tsar must be got rid of by violent means, because peaceful ones would not work. He summed up his views of revolutions in the following statement:

I am said to be a revolutionist in my sympathies, by birth, by breeding and by principle. I am always on the side of the revolutionists, because there never was a revolution unless there were some oppressive and intolerable conditions against which to revolute.

Civil rights

Twain was an adamant supporter of the abolition of slavery and the emancipation of slaves, even going so far as to say, "Lincoln's Proclamation ... not only set the black slaves free, but set the white man free also". He argued that non-whites did not receive justice in the United States, once saying, "I have seen Chinamen abused and maltreated in all the mean, cowardly ways possible to the invention of a degraded nature ... but I never saw a Chinaman righted in a court of justice for wrongs thus done to him". He paid for at least one black person to attend Yale Law School and for another black person to attend a southern university to become a minister.

Twain's sympathetic views on race were not reflected in his early writings on American Indians. Of them, Twain wrote in 1870:

His heart is a cesspool of falsehood, of treachery, and of low and devilish instincts. With him, gratitude is an unknown emotion; and when one does him a kindness, it is safest to keep the face toward him, lest the reward be an arrow in the back. To accept of a favor from him is to assume a debt which you can never repay to his satisfaction, though you bankrupt yourself trying. The scum of the earth!

As counterpoint, Twain's essay on "The Literary Offenses of Fenimore Cooper" offers a much kinder view of Indians. "No, other Indians would have noticed these things, but Cooper's Indians never notice anything. Cooper thinks they are marvelous creatures for noticing, but he was almost always in error about his Indians. There was seldom a sane one among them." In his later travelogue Following the Equator (1897), Twain observes that in colonized lands all over the world, "savages" have always been wronged by "whites" in the most merciless ways, such as "robbery, humiliation, and slow, slow murder, through poverty and the white man's whiskey"; his conclusion is that "there are many humorous things in this world; among them the white man's notion that he is less savage than the other savages". In an expression that captures his East Indian experiences, he wrote, "So far as I am able to judge nothing has been left undone, either by man or Nature, to make India the most extraordinary country that the sun visits on his rounds. Where every prospect pleases, and only man is vile."

Twain was also a staunch supporter of women's rights and an active campaigner for women's suffrage. His "Votes for Women" speech, in which he pressed for the granting of voting rights to women, is considered one of the most famous in history.

Helen Keller benefited from Twain's support as she pursued her college education and publishing despite her disabilities and financial limitations. The two were friends for roughly 16 years.

Through Twain's efforts, the Connecticut legislature voted a pension for Prudence Crandall, since 1995 Connecticut's official heroine, for her efforts towards the education of African-American young ladies in Connecticut. Twain also offered to purchase for her use her former house in Canterbury, home of the Canterbury Female Boarding School, but she declined.

Labor

Twain wrote glowingly about unions in the river boating industry in Life on the Mississippi, which was read in union halls decades later. He supported the labor movement, especially one of the most important unions, the Knights of Labor. In a speech to them, he said:

Who are the oppressors? The few: the King, the capitalist, and a handful of other overseers and superintendents. Who are the oppressed? The many: the nations of the earth; the valuable personages; the workers; they that make the bread that the soft-handed and idle eat.

Religion

Twain was a Presbyterian. He was critical of organized religion and certain elements of Christianity through his later life. He wrote, for example, "Faith is believing what you know ain't so", and "If Christ were here now there is one thing he would not be – a Christian". With anti-Catholic sentiment rampant in 19th century America, Twain noted he was "educated to enmity toward everything that is Catholic". As an adult, he engaged in religious discussions and attended services, his theology developing as he wrestled with the deaths of loved ones and with his own mortality.

Twain generally avoided publishing his most controversial opinions on religion in his lifetime, and they are known from essays and stories that were published later. In the essay Three Statements of the Eighties in the 1880s, Twain stated that he believed in an almighty God, but not in any messages, revelations, holy scriptures such as the Bible, Providence, or retribution in the afterlife. He did state that "the goodness, the justice, and the mercy of God are manifested in His works", but also that "the universe is governed by strict and immutable laws", which determine "small matters", such as who dies in a pestilence. At other times, he wrote or spoke in ways that contradicted a strict deist view, for example, plainly professing a belief in Providence. In some later writings in the 1890s, he was less optimistic about the goodness of God, observing that "if our Maker is all-powerful for good or evil, He is not in His right mind". At other times, he conjectured sardonically that perhaps God had created the world with all its tortures for some purpose of His own, but was otherwise indifferent to humanity, which was too petty and insignificant to deserve His attention anyway.

In 1901, Twain criticized the actions of the missionary Dr. William Scott Ament (1851–1909) because Ament and other missionaries had collected indemnities from Chinese subjects in the aftermath of the Boxer Uprising of 1900. Twain's response to hearing of Ament's methods was published in the North American Review in February 1901: To the Person Sitting in Darkness, and deals with examples of imperialism in China, South Africa, and with the U.S. occupation of the Philippines. A subsequent article, "To My Missionary Critics" published in The North American Review in April 1901, unapologetically continues his attack, but with the focus shifted from Ament to his missionary superiors, the American Board of Commissioners for Foreign Missions.

After his death, Twain's family suppressed some of his work that was especially irreverent toward conventional religion, including Letters from the Earth, which was not published until his daughter Clara reversed her position in 1962 in response to Soviet propaganda about the withholding. The anti-religious The Mysterious Stranger was published in 1916. Little Bessie, a story ridiculing Christianity, was first published in the 1972 collection Mark Twain's Fables of Man.

He raised money to build a Presbyterian Church in Nevada in 1864.

Twain created a reverent portrayal of Joan of Arc, a subject over which he had obsessed for forty years, studied for a dozen years and spent two years writing about. In 1900 and again in 1908 he stated, "I like Joan of Arc best of all my books, it is the best".

Those who knew Twain well late in life recount that he dwelt on the subject of the afterlife, his daughter Clara saying: "Sometimes he believed death ended everything, but most of the time he felt sure of a life beyond."

Twain's frankest views on religion appeared in his final work Autobiography of Mark Twain, the publication of which started in November 2010, 100 years after his death. In it, he said:

There is one notable thing about our Christianity: bad, bloody, merciless, money-grabbing, and predatory as it is – in our country particularly and in all other Christian countries in a somewhat modified degree – it is still a hundred times better than the Christianity of the Bible, with its prodigious crime – the invention of Hell. Measured by our Christianity of to-day, bad as it is, hypocritical as it is, empty and hollow as it is, neither the Deity nor his Son is a Christian, nor qualified for that moderately high place. Ours is a terrible religion. The fleets of the world could swim in spacious comfort in the innocent blood it has spilled.

Twain was a Freemason. He belonged to Polar Star Lodge No. 79 A.F.&A.M., based in St. Louis. He was initiated an Entered Apprentice on May 22, 1861, passed to the degree of Fellow Craft on June 12, and raised to the degree of Master Mason on July 10.

Twain visited Salt Lake City for two days and met there members of The Church of Jesus Christ of Latter-day Saints. They also gave him a Book of Mormon. He later wrote in Roughing It about that book:

The book seems to be merely a prosy detail of imaginary history, with the Old Testament for a model; followed by a tedious plagiarism of the New Testament.

Vivisection

Twain was opposed to the vivisection practices of his day. His objection was not on a scientific basis but rather an ethical one. He specifically cited the pain caused to the animal as his basis of his opposition:

I am not interested to know whether Vivisection produces results that are profitable to the human race or doesn't. ... The pains which it inflicts upon unconsenting animals is the basis of my enmity towards it, and it is to me sufficient justification of the enmity without looking further.

Pen names

Twain used different pen names before deciding on "Mark Twain". He signed humorous and imaginative sketches as "Josh" until 1863. Additionally, he used the pen name "Thomas Jefferson Snodgrass" for a series of humorous letters.

He maintained that his primary pen name came from his years working on Mississippi riverboats, where two fathoms, a depth indicating water safe for the passage of boat, was a measure on the sounding line. Twain is an archaic term for "two", as in "The veil of the temple was rent in twain." The riverboatman's cry was "mark twain" or, more fully, "by the mark twain", meaning "according to the mark [on the line], [the depth is] two [fathoms]", that is, "The water is 12 feet (3.7 m) deep and it is safe to pass."

Twain said that his famous pen name was not entirely his invention. In Life on the Mississippi, he wrote:

Captain Isaiah Sellers was not of literary turn or capacity, but he used to jot down brief paragraphs of plain practical information about the river, and sign them "MARK TWAIN", and give them to the New Orleans Picayune. They related to the stage and condition of the river, and were accurate and valuable; ... At the time that the telegraph brought the news of his death, I was on the Pacific coast. I was a fresh new journalist, and needed a nom de guerre; so I confiscated the ancient mariner's discarded one, and have done my best to make it remain what it was in his hands – a sign and symbol and warrant that whatever is found in its company may be gambled on as being the petrified truth; how I have succeeded, it would not be modest in me to say.

Twain's story about his pen name has been questioned by some with the suggestion that "mark twain" refers to a running bar tab that Twain would regularly incur while drinking at John Piper's saloon in Virginia City, Nevada. Samuel Clemens himself responded to this suggestion by saying, "Mark Twain was the nom de plume of one Captain Isaiah Sellers, who used to write river news over it for the New Orleans Picayune. He died in 1869 and as he could no longer need that signature, I laid violent hands upon it without asking permission of the proprietor's remains. That is the history of the nom de plume I bear."

In his autobiography, Twain writes further of Captain Sellers' use of "Mark Twain":

I was a cub pilot on the Mississippi River then, and one day I wrote a rude and crude satire which was leveled at Captain Isaiah Sellers, the oldest steamboat pilot on the Mississippi River, and the most respected, esteemed, and revered. For many years he had occasionally written brief paragraphs concerning the river and the changes which it had undergone under his observation during fifty years, and had signed these paragraphs "Mark Twain" and published them in the St. Louis and New Orleans journals. In my satire I made rude game of his reminiscences. It was a shabby poor performance, but I didn't know it, and the pilots didn't know it. The pilots thought it was brilliant. They were jealous of Sellers, because when the gray-heads among them pleased their vanity by detailing in the hearing of the younger craftsmen marvels which they had seen in the long ago on the river, Sellers was always likely to step in at the psychological moment and snuff them out with wonders of his own which made their small marvels look pale and sick. However, I have told all about this in "Old Times on the Mississippi." The pilots handed my extravagant satire to a river reporter, and it was published in the New Orleans True Delta. That poor old Captain Sellers was deeply wounded. He had never been held up to ridicule before; he was sensitive, and he never got over the hurt which I had wantonly and stupidly inflicted upon his dignity. I was proud of my performance for a while, and considered it quite wonderful, but I have changed my opinion of it long ago. Sellers never published another paragraph nor ever used his nom de guerre again.

Legacy and depictions

Trademark white suit

While Twain is often depicted wearing a white suit, modern representations suggesting that he wore them throughout his life are unfounded. Evidence suggests that Twain began wearing white suits on the lecture circuit, after the death of his wife Olivia ("Livy") in 1904. However, there is also evidence showing him wearing a white suit before 1904. In 1882, he sent a photograph of himself in a white suit to 18-year-old Edward W. Bok, later publisher of the Ladies Home Journal, with a handwritten dated note. The white suit did eventually become his trademark, as illustrated in anecdotes about this eccentricity (such as the time he wore a white summer suit to a Congressional hearing during the winter). McMasters' The Mark Twain Encyclopedia states that Twain did not wear a white suit in his last three years, except at one banquet speech.

In his autobiography, Twain writes of his early experiments with wearing white out-of-season:

Next after fine colors, I like plain white. One of my sorrows, when the summer ends, is that I must put off my cheery and comfortable white clothes and enter for the winter into the depressing captivity of the shapeless and degrading black ones. It is mid-October now, and the weather is growing cold up here in the New Hampshire hills, but it will not succeed in freezing me out of these white garments, for here the neighbors are few, and it is only of crowds that I am afraid. (Source: Wikipedia)

Lightning Source UK Ltd.
Milton Keynes UK
UKHW011836200520
363522UK00001B/93

9 789353 855505